# VATERUNSER-BIBLIOGRAPHIE

---

# THE LORD'S PRAYER
# A BIBLIOGRAPHY

# THE LORD'S PRAYER

## A BIBLIOGRAPHY

Edited
by
Monica Dorneich

ANNIVERSARY PUBLICATION
OF THE
ORATIO DOMINICA
FOUNDATION
FREIBURG IM BREISGAU
WEST GERMANY 1982

# INHALT

ZUM ANDENKEN AN
FRAU ELISABETH HERDER-DORNEICH
† 21. MAI 1980

Diese Bibliographie erscheint im 20. Jahr des Bestehens der
STIFTUNG ORATIO DOMINICA,
die am 3. November 1962 in Freiburg im Breisgau
gegründet wurde

# VORWORT

„Oratio Dominica", Gebet des Herrn, ist zugleich der Name einer Stiftung, die im November 1962 in Freiburg im Breisgau begründet wurde. Ihre tragende Mitte ist das „Vaterunser", wie dies in den Statuten seinen Ausdruck findet: „Die Stiftung hat den Zweck, die Gedanken des Vaterunsers in der christlichen Verkündigung als das einigende Band der Christenheit zu stärken und der Einigung dienlich zu sein."

Aus Anlaß des 20jährigen Bestehens legt die *Stiftung Oratio Dominica (SOD)* eine internationale Bibliographie vor zum Thema „Vaterunser". Der Wunsch eines solchen „bibliographischen Instrumentariums" liegt Jahre zurück und hat seinen Ursprung beim Begründer und Initiator der Stiftung, dessen Vaterunser-Bibliothek den Grundstock dieser Bibliographie bildet. Darauf aufbauend, wurden die nationalen und internationalen Bibliographien von Frau Eva Thieme (Rom) nach weiteren Titeln durchgesehen und Monographien, Beiträge zu Sammelwerken und Zeitschriftenaufsätze aufgenommen. Für den Zeitraum 1945–1975 ist möglichste Vollständigkeit angestrebt worden; die Titel der Jahre 1976–1981 sind, soweit feststellbar, ebenfalls aufgenommen. Das vorhandene Material reicht jedoch bis zur Jahrhundertwende und teilweise noch weiter zurück. Auch diese Titel sind übernommen worden, um eine umfassendere Dokumentation der Vaterunser-Literatur vorzustellen. Alle Beiträge wurden in ein Autorenalphabet eingearbeitet und die bibliographische Beschreibung auf Verlagsnamen und Untertitel ausgeweitet, da diese für die Erläuterung des Titels oftmals hilfreich sind. Im Bereich der Zeitschriftenbeiträge gibt es eine Anzahl Aufsätze, deren bibliographische Beschreibung leider nur bruchstückhaft sind. Diese Beiträge sind gesondert als Anhang dem alphabetischen Ablauf beigefügt.

Msgr. Leon von Kukowski (gest. 17. 9. 1978), langjähriger Schriftleiter des Münchner „Klerusblattes", hat seine durch Jahrzehnte geführte Sammlung zum Thema des Vaterunser als Vermächtnis der *Stiftung Oratio Dominica* überlassen. Sie hat die hier vorgelegte Vaterunser-Bibliographie sehr bereichert.

Eingeleitet wird die Bibliographie durch den Forschungsbericht von Frau Eleonore Jahnke: „Die mehrstimmige Vertonung des lateinischen Vaterunser in der Zeit von 1500–1700." Die bibliographischen Angaben zu diesem musikalischen Teil wurden von Frau Jahnke bearbeitet und sind ihrer Arbeit im Anhang beigegeben. Der musikalische (2.) Teil der Vaterunser-Bibliographie ist eine eigene Arbeit von Frau Eleonore Jahnke, die sie wie auch den vorliegenden Forschungsbericht in eigener Verantwortung verfaßt hat, der diese Vaterunser-Bibliographie einleitet. Wir danken ihr sehr für die Beiträge.

Beschlossen wird unsere Bibliographie mit dem Arbeitsbericht der Stiftung „Oratio Dominica". Ihr Verfasser, Professor Dr. Walter Strolz, ist Leiter des Religionskundlichen Instituts der Stiftung. Mit den Ausblicken auf künftige Arbeit und Religionsgespräche reicht der Bericht bis ins Jahr 1984.

Allen, die am Zustandekommen der vorliegenden Bibliographie beteiligt waren und in Freiburg das Manuskript für den Druck fertiggestellt haben, möchte ich an dieser Stelle recht herzlich danken: Frau Helene Amann, Frau Hedwig Bauer, Frau Eva Thieme und vor allem Herrn Lukas Lumpp.

Aachen, 21. Mai 1982         Monica Dorneich
                                         Dipl. Bibliothekarin
                                         TH-Bibliothek Aachen

*Eleonore Jahnke*

# Die mehrstimmige Vertonung des lateinischen Vaterunser in der Zeit von 1500–1700

## Überlegungen zum liturgischen Ort des Gebetes und der Vertonung

Im Rahmen der *Stiftung Oratio Dominica* soll dieser musik- und liturgiewissenschaftliche Bericht über das Thema *Die mehrstimmige Vertonung des lateinischen Vaterunser in der Zeit von 1500–1700* informieren; er soll über den bisherigen Stand der Forschung im allgemeinen und über den liturgischen Ort des *Paternoster* (im folgenden PN) im besonderen in Kenntnis setzen, denn sämtliche einschlägigen Fachlexika ignorieren die Thematik der mehrstimmigen Vertonung des Vaterunsers. Es finden sich unter dem Stichwort PN stets nur Abhandlungen über gregorianische Melodien; Hinweise auf polyphone Werke und deren liturgische Funktion hingegen fehlen. Da es bisher an einer umfassenden quellenkundlichen und analytischen Untersuchung mehrstimmiger Vertonungen des lateinischen Vaterunsers mangelt, wurde mit dieser Arbeit erstmals der Versuch unternommen, die Geschichte des mehrstimmigen PN, – diese bis jetzt kaum beachtete Gattung polyphoner geistlicher Vokalmusik –, über einen größeren Zeitraum hinweg zu erfassen. Zudem drängte sich die Frage nach der praktischen Verwendung des mehrstimmigen PN innerhalb der Liturgie auf.

Vor der Erörterung des zuletzt genannten Aspektes folgt noch eine kurze Übersicht über die bisher geleistete Arbeit: zunächst ergab eine gründliche Durchsuchung des Musikwissenschaftlichen Seminars Freiburg eine beachtliche Zahl von bereits edierten Kompositionen (ohne Berücksichtigung ihrer Entstehungszeit). Die Durchforstung weiterer Bibliotheksbestände in vielen europäischen Ländern erbrachte eine unerwartet reiche Ausbeute. Die Funde in den italienischen Archiven (vor allem in denjenigen von Milano und Bologna) ließen schließlich die Zahl der Kompositionen derart in die Höhe schnellen, daß eine zeitliche Abgrenzung des Themas notwendig wurde. Interessant schien mir die Beschränkung auf die Frühgeschichte des mehrstimmigen PN, denn mit den ersten mehrstimmigen Vertonungen setzt auch die Frage nach deren ursprünglicher Funktion in der Liturgie ein. Ein weiterer Grund zur zeitlichen Einschränkung des Themas lag in der Sache selbst: die Kompositionen dieser Zeit liegen handschriftlich bzw. gedruckt in sogenannten Stimmbüchern vor, die zumeist in Quadratnotation überliefert

9

sind; denn damals kannte man noch keine Partitur. Diese Stimmbücher mußten also in die moderne Notenschrift und zur besseren
Übersicht in Partituren übertragen werden, eine langwierige, aber
unentbehrliche Arbeit für weiteres musikwissenschaftliches For-
schen. Eine erste Auswertung der Quellen konnte manch anonymes PN seinem Komponisten zuweisen und Irrtümer aufklären
(z. B. kamen mitunter Doppelzuschreibungen vor, d. h. eine Komposition wurde versehentlich zwei verschiedenen Autoren zugeord-
net). Viele Komponisten waren gebürtige Niederländer[1], den Haupt-
anteil machten die Italiener im Umkreis von Milano[2] aus, weitere
stammten aus verschiedenen europäischen Ländern. Die Kompositionen sind meist 5-, 4-, 6-, 8-, seltener 3-, 9-, 10-, 7- und 2-stimmig
angelegt (analog dieser hier aufgeführten Reihenfolge beläuft sich
die Häufigkeit ihres Auftretens). Insgesamt kam aus der Zeit um
1500–1700 die stattliche Zahl von ca. 130 Kompositionen zustande.

Nach diesem Überblick rückt folgende Frage in den Vordergrund:
zu welchen Anlässen wurden die vielen Kompositionen geschaffen
und aufgeführt? Zunächst einmal spricht nichts gegen die Annahme, daß die Vaterunserverstonungen für den gleichen liturgischen Zweck bestimmt waren wie das Vaterunser als Gebet. Es
empfiehlt sich daher, zunächst den liturgischen Stellenwert des Vaterunsers als Gebet zu untersuchen.

## 1. Der liturgische Ort des Gebetes

Dazu findet sich im Handbuch der Liturgiewissenschaft von *A. G.
Martimort*[3] folgender Hinweis:

> Das Paternoster wurde als Vorbereitungsgebet für die Kommunion und
> mit Vorliebe als Abschluß der Horen des Stundengebets verwendet. In den
> orientalischen Riten wurde es vom Volk gesungen. Volksgesang war das
> Paternoster auch in der gallischen Liturgie. Die anderen lateinischen Riten
> haben das Paternoster dem Priester vorbehalten und dem Volk entweder
> nur die Schlußbitte *Sed libera nos a malo* oder jede Bitte bekräftigendes *Amen*
> überlassen.

Warum eigentlich, so fragt man sich beim Lesen dieser Zeilen,
durfte in der *römischen Liturgie* nur der Priester allein das PN beten?

In einem Brief *Gregors des Großen* ist überliefert, daß das PN in

---

[1] Vertreter der Komponistenschule, die um 1430–1560 die europäische Mu-
sikgeschichte bestimmte; vornehmlich aus dem Gebiet beiderseits der heutigen französisch-belgischen Grenze (Hennegau).

[2] Siehe Anhang, alphabetisches Verzeichnis der Komponisten.

[3] A. G. Martimort, *Handbuch der Liturgiewissenschaft*, Freiburg 1963, Bd. 1,
S. 146.

Rom im Gegensatz zu den Griechen *a solo sacerdote* gesprochen wurde[4]; hieraus folgert die theologische Fachwelt, daß dies überall in der *römischen Liturgie* und zu allen Zeiten (seit *Gregor*) so gehandhabt wurde. Erst die *Instructio vom 3. 9. 58*[5] gestattete es den Gläubigen, bei den gelesenen Messen das PN mit dem Priester gemeinsam zu rezitieren.

Zahlreiche weitere Hinweise zum liturgischen Ort des Gebetes liefert *J. A. Jungmann* in seinem zweibändigen Werk *Missarum Sollemnia*, so daß nahezu jeder Abschnitt des Gottesdienstes mit dem PN belegt werden kann.

Das PN wurde somit an folgenden Stellen der *Messe* gebetet:

1. Vormesse und Eröffnung
   1.1. Praeparatio ad missam[6, 7]
   1.2. Stufengebet[8]
   1.3. Introitus[9]
2. Lesegottesdienst
   2.1. Vor der Predigt[10]
   2.2. Nach der Predigt[11, 12, 13]
3. Opfermesse
   3.1. Offertorium[14]
   3.2. Eucharistiegebet[15]
4. Kommunionkreis
   4.1. Vorbereitungsgebet zur Kommunion[16]
   4.2. Kommuniongesang[17]

---

[4] Gregor der Große, *Ep. IX*, 12 (Pl 77, 957).
[5] *Instr. 1958*, 32 beläßt dem PN bei dem Hochamt den Charakter eines Priestergebetes, während es bei der gesprochenen Messe wie im Orient von allen gesprochen werden kann.
[6] J. A. Jungmann, *Missarum Sollemnia*, Freiburg 1962, Bd. 2, S. 102[33] und Bd. 1, S. 385/386.
[7] A. Beck, *Kirchliche Studien und Quellen*, Amberg 1903, S. 257 ff.
[8] Jungmann, *Miss. Sollemn.*, Bd. 1, S. 397[63].
[9] Jungmann, *Miss. Sollemn.*, Bd. 1, S. 428[59], Berthold von Chiemsee.
[10] Jungmann, *Miss. Sollemn.*, Bd. 1, S. 590[41].
[11] Jungmann, *Miss. Sollemn.*, Bd. 1, S. 626[52] und 626 ff.
[12] P. Göbl, *Geschichte der Katechese im Abendlande*, Kempten 1880, S. 94, Synode von Passau 1470.
[13] vgl. K. Halaski, „Offene Schuld" in *RGG*, S. 1611 (im protestantischen Gottesdienst ebenfalls nach der Predigt oder zu Beginn des Gottesdienstes) und H. B. Meyer, *Luther und die Messe*, Paderborn 1965, S. 121 ff.
[14] Jungmann, *Miss. Sollemn.*, Bd. 2, S. 87[152] und 101 ff.
[15] Jungmann, *Miss. Sollemn.*, Bd. 2, S. 263[58].   [16] A.a.O. S. 3.
[17] Jungmann, *Miss. Sollemn.*, Bd. 2, S. 486 ff. und 502[33]. Weitere Beispiele bei P. Lebrun, *Explication littérale, historique et dogmatique des prières et des cérémonies de la Messe*, Lyon 1860, Bd. 1, 545 Anm.

## 5. Schluß
### 5.1. Vor dem Segen[18]
### 5.2 Abschied vom Altar[19]

Im *Offizium* kamen ebenfalls mehrere Möglichkeiten in Betracht:
1. Zur Vorbereitung vor jeder Hore[20]
2. Preces (Laudes und Vesper)[21]
3. Matutin[22]
4. Schluß jeder Hore[23]

Außerdem blieb das mit *Kyrie eleison* eingeleitete PN in gewissen *Riten* erhalten, so z. B. im *Begräbnisritus*.

Auch an diesen Stellen ist immer nur vom Priester die Rede, der das PN betet oder singt.[24] Hiermit kann die oben zitierte Aussage über die Zuweisung des PN an den Priester[25] auf alle Stellen des Gottesdienstes erweitert werden.

Nach liturgiewissenschaftlichen Erkenntnissen ist das PN folglich in allen Bereichen der *römischen Liturgie* seit *Gregor dem Großen* bis zur *Instructio vom 3. 9. 58* ein reines Priestergebet und deshalb *a solo sacerdote* vorzutragen.

## 2. Das Prinzip a solo sacerdote und die Herausforderung der Mehrstimmigkeit

Da das Prinzip *a solo sacerdote* offensichtlich unvereinbar ist mit der Tatsache der Mehrstimmigkeit, müssen hypothesenartige Erklärungen gefunden werden, die diesen Widerspruch auflösen. Dafür in Betracht kommen:

1. die PN-Vertonungen wurden
   a) gar nicht aufgeführt,
   b) außerhalb des Gottesdienstes, also konzertant oder

---

[18] Beck, *Kirchliche Studien und Quellen*, S. 272 und Jungmann, *Miss. Sollemn.*, Bd. 2, S. 554[60].

[19] Jungmann, *Miss. Sollemn.*, Bd. 2, S. 542[2] und 567[9].

[20] S. Bäumer, *Geschichte des Breviers*, Freiburg 1895, S. 444/445 und *Wetzer und Welte's Kirchenlexikon*, Freiburg 1901, Bd. 12, S. 598 ff.

[21] Bäumer, *Geschichte des Breviers*, S. 443.

[22] Jungmann, „Vaterunser, das ‚Gebet des Herrn'", in: *LThK 10* (1965), S. 627 ff. und *Brevierstudien*, Trier 1958, S. 37.

[23] Jungmann, „Das Gebet des Herrn im Brevier", in: *Liturgisches Erbe und pastorale Gegenwart*, Innsbruck 1960, S. 208–264; vgl. auch a. a. O. S. 3 Anm. 3.

[24] Jungmann, „Vaterunser, das ‚Gebet des Herrn'", in: *LThK 10* (1965), S. 627 ff. und *Wetzer und Welte's Kirchenlexikon*, Bd. 12, S. 600.

[25] A. a. O. S. 3 Anm. 3.

c) in einem weniger verbindlichen liturgischen Rahmen, etwa in einer *Privat-Andacht*

zu Gehör gebracht.

2. Die Liturgievorschriften und -gewohnheiten wurden so modifiziert, daß die neuen Kompositionen ohne Verletzung verbindlicher Regeln in den Gottesdienst eingeführt werden konnten.

3. Obiges Prinzip *a solo sacerdote* wurde für polyphone Kompositionen mißachtet oder aufgehoben.

Die ersten drei Denkmöglichkeiten unter Punkt 1 sind unwahrscheinlich.

zu a): Es ist kaum vorstellbar, daß die zahlreichen PN-Kompositionen, die schon beinahe eine eigene Gattung der damaligen Zeit darstellten, ein papierenes Schattendasein fristeten, ohne an die Öffentlichkeit zu gelangen.[26]

zu b): Zur damaligen Zeit war es nicht üblich, Kompositionen mit liturgischem Text gewissermaßen ästhetisch selbstzweckhaft außerhalb des Gottesdienstes zu handhaben.

zu c): In der Regel sammelten sich mehrstimmige Vertonungen für private Andachten erst im Laufe des 17. und 18. Jahrhunderts an.

zu 2: Man kann annehmen, daß das PN nach dem Vortrag des Gebetes durch den Priester von einem Figuralchor gesungen wurde, gleichsam zur Bekräftigung des Gebetes und zur Erhöhung der Feierlichkeit. Dies entsprach dem Zeitgeist, wo der Mensch der Renaissance neue sinnliche Dimensionen wie Weiträumigkeit und Vielschichtigkeit für sich entdeckte und nutzte.[27]

zu 3: Schließlich ist die Hypothese sinnvoll, daß zumindest in einigen Fällen das Priestergebet durch den Chorgesang ersetzt wurde. Bei einem PN ist dies sicher nachweisbar. Es handelt sich um eine dreistimmige anonyme Komposition aus der *Sammlung Rhau*, RISM 1542[8], XLIII, das *Benedicite:*

Benedicite, Deus, gustate et videte, quoniam suavis est Dominus. Beatus vir, qui sperat in eo. Gloria patri et filio et spiritui sancto, sicut erat in principio er nunc et in saecula saeculorum, Amen. Kyrie eleison. Kyrie eleison. Kyrie eleison. Pater noster ... Et ne nos inducas in tentationem, sed libera nos a malo, oremus. Benedic nos, Domine, et haec dona quae de tua largitate sumus sumpturi. Per Christum Dominum nostrum, Amen.

---

[26] Im übrigen sprechen überlieferte Chorbücher mit liturgisch geordnetem Inhalt für den tatsächlichen Gebrauch der mehrstimmigen PN; vgl. dazu u., S. 13.

[27] G. Fellerer, „Musikalische Gottesdienstgestaltung", in: *Geschichte der katholischen Kirchenmusik*, Kassel 1976, Bd. 2, S. 129 ff. und H. C. Wolff, *Die Musik der alten Niederländer*, Leipzig 1956, S. 20 ff.

Hier steht das PN[28] sozusagen als Bindeglied zwischen *Communio* und *Postcommunio*. Die durchgehende Dreistimmigkeit, die jedes einzelne Wort, auch das dem Priester zustehende *Oremus* erfaßt, zwingt zu der Schlußfolgerung, daß die normalerweise dem *Celebrans* vorbehaltene *Oration* an einen Figuralchor delegiert werden konnte.

Ein ähnlicher Fall liegt vor bei der Motette *Sancti Dei Omnes* von *Jehan Mouton*, bei welcher ebenfalls die priesterliche Aufforderung *Oremus* mehrstimmig auskomponiert ist. *N. Boeker-Heil* ist ebenfalls der Ansicht, daß gelegentlich ein Figuralchor die Funktion des Priesters übernehmen durfte, denn aus oben genanntem Grund und aus der Tatsache der „erdrückenden Zahl von Orationsmotetten aus dem 16. Jahrhundert" muß man seiner Meinung nach zu einer solchen Auffassung gelangen.[29]

## 3. Der liturgische Ort des mehrstimmig gesungenen PN im Lichte quellenkundlicher Aussagen

Im folgenden werden exemplarisch einige Werke im Hinblick auf ihre mögliche liturgische Zuordnung erörtert.

Da zeitgenössische, protokollartige Berichte über den Gottesdienstablauf bisher nicht bekannt sind, muß freilich offen bleiben, ob vertonte Vaterunser-Fassungen zur Vertiefung und Bestärkung des Priestergebetes oder aber an dessen Stelle gesungen wurden.

Dafür läßt sich an Hand von Handschriften und Drucken recht gut belegen, an welchen Stellen des Gottesdienstes das PN erklang.

### 1. Zusammenhänge zwischen Quellenvermerken und deren liturgischer Zuordnung

Bei der Untersuchung des Quellenmaterials stellte sich heraus, daß einige Stimmbücher mit PN-Vertonungen z. B. folgende Hinweise trugen: *De Dominicis Diebus*[30]

Ob damit die *Messe* oder das *Stundengebet* gemeint ist, bleibt unklar. Es geht jedoch aus diesem Vermerk hervor, daß die mehrstimmige *Oratio Dominica* für Sonntage bestimmt war, wohl deshalb, weil man an Sonntagen am ehesten einen Figuralchor zur Verfügung hatte, mit dessen Hilfe die Gottesdienste feierlicher gestaltet werden konnten.[31]

---

[28] Noch nach Art der *Arkandisziplin*.
[29] N. Boeker-Heil, *Die Motetten von Philippe Verdelot*, Frankfurt 1967, S. 87.
[30] U. a. *Wilhelm Formellis*, RISM 1568³ München und *Josquin Desprez*, F Mus. Ms. 1536 München.
[31] A. a. O. S. 7 Anm. 27.

14

Genaueres sagt die Bezeichnung über einem PN von *Michael Prae-torius* aus:

*vocem iucunditatis*[32]

Hiermit ist ein ganz bestimmter Sonntag gemeint, der nach seinem Introitus *Rogate* benannte 5. Sonntag nach Ostern, also der Sonntag, welcher die *Rogations- oder Bittwoche* eröffnet.[33] Dieser eine Sonntag ist als Aufführungstag für die gesungene Version des Vaterunsers vermerkt.

Rätselhafter ist die Überschrift über der Tenorstimme im sechsstimmigen PN von *Leonardus Barré:*

*Ut dictantur septem peccata mortalia*
*Dic septies pater noster et ave maria*[34]

Die erste Tenorstimme, *Tenor primus*, bringt die gregorianische PN-Melodie als *Cantus firmus*[35] durchgehend und vollständig zu Gehör. Gleichzeitig verlaufen die beiden Stimmen, *Tenor secundus* und *Altus secundus*, im Kanon (in der Quinte); sie tragen den Anfang des PN sieben Mal vor (jeweils bis zur ersten Vaterunserbitte).

Möglicherweise diente dieses Werk als Schlußgesang einer *Katechese* oder *Predigt,* oder aber als Tilgungsgesang der *Offenen Schuld.*[36]

## 2. Rückschlüsse von der Mehrtextigkeit auf die liturgische Verwendung

Unter den PN-Vertonungen gibt es eine Gruppe sog. mehrtextiger Kompositionen, d. h. während der Text des PN von einer oder mehreren Stimmen gesungen wird, erklingen zu gleicher Zeit noch ein oder mehrere weitere Gebetstexte in den übrigen Stimmen.

Als Beispiel sei hier die vierstimmige Motette *O bone et dulcis Domine Jesu* von *Josquin Desprez*[37] angeführt. Die drei gleichzeitig vertonten Texte sind folgendermaßen auf die vier Stimmen verteilt:

| | |
|---|---|
| *Superius:* | *O bone et dulcis Domine Jesu*[38] |
| *Altus:* | |
| *Tenor:* | PN |
| *Bassus:* | *Ave Maria* |

---

[32] siehe F. Blume, Vorwort zu: *Musarum Sioniarum Motectae et Psalmi Latini 1607,* Wolfenbüttel – Berlin 1931, Bd. 10.
[33] *Wetzer und Welte's Kirchenlexikon,* Freiburg 1895, Bd. 9, S. 727.
[34] *Leonardus Barré,* 123 (Mus. Ms. 274ᵃ) XVI J Nr. 5 München.
[35] *cantus firmus* = die einem mehrstimmigen Satz vorgegebene Melodie, meist dem Choral entnommen.
[36] A. a. O. S. 4 Anm. 12 und 13.
[37] In: *Werken van Josquin Desprez,* Motetten, Bundel 18, S. 85–87, hrsg. von A. Smijers, Amsterdam 1954.
[38] „O bone et dulcis Domine Jesu, credo firmiter et indubitanter, quidquid

Wäre die liturgische Zugehörigkeit des Gebetstextes *O bone et dulcis Domine Jesu* bekannt (vermutlich diente er als Kommuniongesang), könnte die gesamte Komposition und mit ihr das PN liturgisch bestimmt werden.

Konkreteres hinsichtlich des liturgischen Gebrauchs läßt sich über das sechsstimmige PN von *Jacobus de Kerle*[39] sagen, wo in der Tenorstimme folgender Ruf ständig wiederkehrt:

*Pater de coelis Deus, miserere nobis*

Dieser Text stammt aus dem Beginn der *Allerheiligenlitanei.* Naheliegend ist die Annahme, daß dieses Werk am Ende der *Allerheiligenlitanei* aufgeführt wurde. Der Vers der Litanei dient in dem sie beschließenden PN gleichsam als Nachruf.[40] Anscheinend wurde dieses PN überall da gesungen, wo die Litanei gebetet wurde, z.B. in den *Preces* des *Offiziums (Laudes* und *Vesper).*[41]

Eindeutig ist das PN in der fünfstimmigen *Missa super Pater noster* von *Ludwig Daser*[42] festgelegt. Die beiden Ordinarienteile, *Credo* und *Agnus* sind wie folgt mehrtextig angelegt:

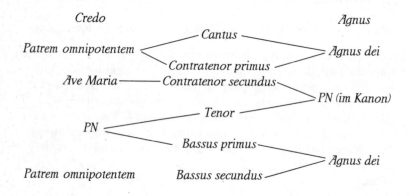

---

sacrosancta credit ecclesia, deprecor tuam pietatem et clementiam: fac me vivere et mori in tua fide. Confiteor enim coram maiestate tua et sanctis angelis tuis, quod servus tuus sum, et quidquid mihi accidat tuus sum fidelis."
[39] *Jacobus de Kerle,* Nr. 105 Selectae quaedam Cantiones, Nürnberg, Theodor Gerlach, 1571, Uppsala.
[40] Vgl. H. Reiffenberg, *Stundengebet und Breviere im Bistum Mainz seit der Romanischen Epoche,* Münster 1964, S. 84 ff.
[41] Vgl. a.a.O. S. 5 Anm. 21.
[42] *Ludwig Daser,* 16 (Mus. Ms. 45) XVI J. 272 Nr. 2 München.

## 3. Liturgischer Zusammenhang zwischen dem PN und ihm voran- bzw. nachstehender Kompositionen

In der bereits oben erwähnten Handschrift, *Sammlung Rhau*, RISM 1542[8], XLIII, steht das anonyme PN in unmittelbarem Bezug zur vorangehenden und nachfolgenden Komposition.[43] Das zum PN überleitende *Benedicite* ist ein bereits in der Urkirche verwendeter *Kommuniongesang*[44], nämlich Vers 9 aus Psalm 34. Dieser und auch die sich dem PN anschließende *Postcommunio* bestätigen den liturgischen Gebrauch des PN an diesem Ort.

Hier sei noch *Jacquelyn A. Mattfeld* erwähnt, die ebenfalls von der Hypothese ausgeht, daß Gebetstexte gelegentlich an Priesters Statt von einem Figuralchor gesungen wurden. Sie schließt deshalb nicht aus, daß das von *Josquin Desprez* sechsstimmig vertonte PN[45] und das gelegentlich mit diesem zusammen überlieferte *Ave Maria*[46] zum Gottesdienstbeginn gesungen wurden.[47] Als Bekräftigung für ihre Vermutung führt sie die Motette *O domine Jesu Christe* von *Josquin Desprez* an. In diesem Werk erklingen gleichzeitig fünf verschiedene Gebete, die – zu Beginn der Messe gebetet – den Gläubigen Ablaß gewähren sollten. Laut Rubrik sollte nach jedem einzelnen der fünf Gebete je ein PN und *Ave Maria* folgen.[48] Diese beiden Gebete sind allerdings nicht in der Vertonung der fünf Texte mit inbegriffen, vielleicht deshalb nicht, so *Mattfeld*, weil man offen lassen wollte, ob sie gebetet oder gesungen werden sollten oder ob man sie eventuell auch zu anderen Anlässen frei verfügbar haben wollte.

## 4. Die Mailänder Quellen

Abschließend sei noch ein bedeutender Fund aus Italien erwähnt, nämlich zwei Chorbücher im Groß-Folioformat, Librone 25 und 26, die im *Archivio della Cappella del Duomo* von Milano aufbewahrt sind

---

[43] Vgl. S. 7.   [44] Vgl. S. 5 Anm. 17.
[45] In: *Werken van Josquin Desprez*, Motetten, Bundel 12, S. 47–53, hrsg. von A. Smijers, Amsterdam 1954.
[46] Die Verbindung des *Englischen Grußes* mit dem PN wurde seit dem Jahre 1503 von den lothringischen *Benediktinern* und auf dem *Generalkapitel der Dominikaner 1266*, sowie auf der *Würzburger Synode 1287* beschlossen.
[47] J. A. Mattfeld, „Some Relationships between Texts and Cantus Firmi in the Liturgical Motets of Josquin des Pres", in: *Journal of the American Musicological Society 1961*, S. 177.
[48] Vgl. S. 4 Anm. 6 und 7.

und den Titel *Inni et Pater* tragen.[49] Wahrscheinlich wurden diese
Bücher ausschließlich in der Praxis verwendet, denn sie sind recht
abgegriffen und in schlecht erhaltenem Zustand.[50]Dagegen machen die gedruckten Chorbücher, die im *Civico Museo Bibliografico
Musicale* von Bologna und in der *Biblioteca Ambrosiana* von Milano
einen recht gut erhaltenen Eindruck.[51] Der Inhalt der handschriftli-
chen Chorbücher aus dem Mailänder Domarchiv ist nicht nur um-
fangreicher als derjenige der vier gedruckten Chorbücher, sondern
auch in hohem Grade identisch mit diesem, so daß wahrscheinlich
der Druck aus den Handschriften hervorgeht. Die gedruckten Bücher tragen den langen Titel:

Julii Caesaris Gabutii bononiensis olim, et Vincentii Pellegrini canonici pi-
saurensis nunc, in Metropolitana Ecclesia Musices Praefectorum. Libri
Quatuor, Primi & Secundi Chori. In quibus Hymni, Posthymni, et Lucerna-
lia in solemnitatibus totius anni secundum Sanctae Ambrosianae Ecclesiae
consuetudinem, quaternis, et quinis vocibus continentur ...

Außer PN-Vertonungen der beiden im Titel aufgeführten Meister,
*Gabussi* und *Pellegrini,* enthalten diese vier Chorbücher auch zahlreiche PN weiterer Musiker.[52]

Wie aus diesem Titel hervorgeht, sind die Kompositionen dem Bischof der *Ambrosianischen Kirche* gewidmet und zur feierlichen musikalischen Ausgestaltung des *Lucernariums*[53] gedacht. Hier ergibt
sich die Bestimmung des liturgischen Ortes nicht nur aus der Anordnung und Beschaffenheit der Quelle, sondern durch ausdrückli-
chen Hinweis in der Widmung des Gesamtwerkes. Der Ehrung
zweier Lokalgrößen, des verstorbenen *Giulio Cesare Gabussi*[54] und
des zur Zeit der Herausgabe (1619) noch lebenden Nachfolgers *Vincenzo Pellegrini,* ist es zu verdanken, daß ein solch umfangreiches

---

[49] Hier handelt es sich um Chorbücher, die auf ein Notenpult gestellt wurden, daß der gesamte Chor gleichzeitig daraus singen konnte. Die Stimmen sind in Blöcken je für sich auf eine *recto-* und *verso-Seite* in *grosso-
Schrift* gemalt, und zwar in folgender Anordnung:

| verso | recto |
|---|---|
| Cantus | Altus |
| Tenor | Bassus |
| Quintus | |

[50] S. o. S. 6 Anm. 26.
[51] In Bologna gibt es allerdings nur zwei statt vier Chorbücher.
[52] Siehe Anhang, alphabetisches Verzeichnis der Komponisten.
[53] *Lucernarium* = erster Teil der dreiteiligen *Vesper* nach ambrosianischem
Ritus.
[54] *Gabussi* war Schüler von *Constanzo Porta* und am Dom zu Milano bis
1611 Kapellmeister.

Sammelwerk an PN-Vertonungen ediert wurde und deren liturgische Bestimmung expressis verbis überliefert ist.[55]

Auch die Existenz von kleineren Sammlungen und Einzelausgaben weist auf den wohl speziell mailändischen Brauch hin, das PN innerhalb der *Vesper* aufzuführen.

*Michelangelo Grancini* schrieb in seinen *Sacri Concerti:* „espressi in Otto Magnificat et Otto Pater a quattro voci secondo il rito ambrosiano".[56] *Michelangelo* war um 1650 Kapellmeister (ab 1630 Organist) am Mailänder Dom und löste *Pellegrini* ab. Seine *Magnificat-Vertonungen* stehen in allen acht Psalmtönen, dazwischen jeweils ein PN.

Auch der Nachfolger *Grancini's, Giovanni Antonio Grossi*, ab 1669 Kapellmeister am Dom zu Mailand, schrieb sieben PN, die zusammen mit *Magnificat-Vertonungen* im „Libro primo de Magnificat et Pater noster a 4, 5, 6 voci per capella secondo il ritto ambrosiano, op. 9" überliefert sind.

Weitere einzelne Kompositionen italienischer Meister ruhen noch im *Archivio della Cappella del Duomo*.

Diese tiefverwurzelte Tradition, von Generation zu Generation ein oder mehrere PN für das *Lucernarium* bzw. die *Vesper* zu schaffen, ist auf den *ambrosianischen Ritus* zurückzuführen, was auch immer wieder von den Komponisten selbst in ihrem Vorwort betont wird.

In der *römischen Liturgie* dagegen fehlen solche Hinweise. Untersuchungen von bisher bekannten Sammelwerken mit für die *römische Liturgie* bestimmten *Vesper-Vertonungen* enthalten überhaupt kein PN.[57]

So kann bis jetzt zusammenfassend festgestellt werden, daß die Auswertung des Quellenmaterials kein einheitliches Bild ergibt. Die Vielfalt der Gebetsmöglichkeiten läßt sich auch auf die Auffüh-

---

[55] Interessant ist hier sowohl die Verteilung der Kompositionen auf Sommer- und Winterteil, als auch die Aufgliederung in zwei Chöre, *Primi Chori* und *Secundi Chori*. Jeder der beiden Chöre ist mit etwa der gleichen Anzahl von PN bedacht. Auf den Sommerteil entfallen doppelt so viele Werke wie auf den Winterteil. In beiden Teilen steht je eine Komposition von *Gabussi* und *Pellegrini* mit acht bzw. neun Stimmen, die auf beide Chöre gleichzeitig verteilt ist, sodaß jeder Chor gleich viel zu singen hat. Wahrscheinlich waren diese beiden Werke für besonders feierliche Anlässe bestimmt.

[56] Bologna, *Civico Museo Bibliografico Musicale*, Q 113, fol. 2–68; ein weiteres PN liegt in Milano, *Archivio della Cappella del Duomo*, Busta 20, n. 6.

[57] Z. B. *Adrian Willaerts Salmi Spezzati*, 1550, die nach venezianischer Gepflogenheit für den *Vespergottesdienst* bestimmt waren.

rungsmöglichkeiten des PN als polyphone Komposition übertragen: es scheint nicht einen liturgischen Ort allein, sondern mehrere zu geben.

In zwei Fällen ist der Nachweis eindeutig und sicher: für die *ambrosianische Liturgie* die Mailänder Quellen, die für das *Lucernarium* und in weiterem Sinne für die *Vesper* bestimmend sind und für die *römische Liturgie* die anonyme Komposition aus der *Sammlung Rhau*[58], wo das PN innerhalb des *Kommunionkreises* vorgetragen wurde.

Weitere Belege für die *römische Liturgie*, wie etwa zeitgenössisch-literarische Berichte oder direkte Hinweise im Vorwort von Kompositionen wären zur Bekräftigung der in diesem Bericht aufgestellten Hypothesen wünschenswert.

Vorerst muß man sich mit spärlichen Belegen bescheiden und eine weitergehende Klärung zukünftigen Forschungen anheim stellen.

Zum Prinzip *a solo sacerdote* ist zu sagen, daß es unter dem Zwang der Mehrstimmigkeit moderner Gebetsvertonungen modifiziert oder sogar aufgehoben wurde.

---

[58] Siehe S. 13 und 16 ff.

# VATERUNSER-BIBLIOGRAPHIE
## 1. Teil

# A

Aalders, Cornelis: Onze Vader. Over het volmaakte gebed. Amsterdam: Uitgevers Matschappij Holland 1957. 123 S.

Aalders, W. J.: Het Onze Vader. Zeist: Ploegsma 1928. 61 S.

Aarnio, Jussi u. a.: s. Give us this Day.

Aarts, Florens Gerard Antoine Marie: The Pater Noster of Richard Ermyte. A late Middle English exposition of the Lord's Prayer. Den Haag: Nijhoff 1967. CXIV, 174 S.
Anm.: Zugleich erschienen als Dissertation Nijmegen, ed. from Westminster School Library MS 3. With an introduction, variants, notes and glossary.
Ebenfalls erschienen in: Archivum linguisticum N. S. 1 (1970). S. 106 ff.

Abaelardus, Petrus: Expositio Orationis Dominicae. In: Migne, vol. 178, Sp. 611–618.

Abd-Ru-Shin (Oskar Ernst Bernhardt): Die zehn Gebote Gottes und das Vaterunser. Den Menschen gedeutet. München: Verlag Der Ruf 1930. VII, 95 S.
– The ten commandments and the Lord's Prayer as explained to mankind. Vomperberg: Bernhardt 1962 (rev. edition). 70 S.
– Das Vaterunser. In: Gralswelt. Schwäbisch Gmünd. 9 (1955). S. 247–252.

Abrahams, J.: The Lord's Prayer. In: Studies in Pharisaism and the Gospels II. Cambridge: 1924. S. 93–108.

Abramowski, R.: Neue Schriften Theodors von Mopsuestia. In: Zeitschrift für neutestamentliche Wissenschaft. Berlin 33 (1934), S. 66–84.

Adam, Adolf: Das Gebet des Herrn (in der Messe). In: Die Messe in neuer Gestalt (Pastorale Handreichungen, Band 10). Würzburg: Echter 1974. S. 85–88.

Adam, August: Der heilige Wille Gottes – Die Gotteskindschaft. In: Frömmigkeit und Gnade. Würzburg: Augustinus-Verlag 1957. S. 59 (–73) u. 74–87; (im besonderen S. 59 und 83 ff. ausdrückl. Bezug auf das Vaterunser).

Adam, Bernd: Katechetische Vaterunserauslegungen. Texte und Untersuchungen zu deutschsprachigen Auslegungen des 14. u.

15. Jahrhunderts (Münchener Texte u. Untersuchungen zur Deutschen Literatur des Mittelalters, Bd. 55). München – Zürich: Artemis 1976. VIII, 267 S.

**Adam,** Karl: Christus unser Bruder. Hierin zum Thema Vaterunser: S. 33, 36f., 120f. Regensburg: Habbel (5. Aufl.) 1938.
– Jesus Christus. Hierin zum Thema Vaterunser: S. 79, 157, 173. Augsburg: Haas & Grabherr (1.–7. Aufl.) 1933–1946; 8. Aufl.: Düsseldorf: Patmos 1949.

**Adelmann von Adelmannsfelden,** J. A. Graf: Das Vaterunser. In: Sendung Aktuelle Botschaft. Südwestfunk, Baden-Baden, 8. bis 13. August 1977. Das unveröffentlichte Manuskript der Sendung befindet sich in der Vaterunser-Bibliothek der Stiftung „Oratio Dominica".

**Adelung,** Johann Christoph (1732–1806): Mithridates oder Allgemeine Sprachen.;unde mit dem Vater Unser als Sprachprobe in bey nahe fünfhundert Sprachen und Mundarten. Fortgesetzt von Johann Severin Vater. Berlin: Voss 1806–1817; Nachdruck Hildesheim: Olms 1970.

**Adler,** Marian: Christus, der Weg zum Vater. Innsbruck: Felizian Rauch 1935. 84 S.

**Aegidius Romanus:** (1243–1316): ...In Orationem Dominicam (Romae 1555) ... Nachdruck Frankfurt (Main): Minerva 1968. 800 S.

**Ahern,** B. M.: Gathering the Fragments: The Lord's Prayer. In: Worship. Collegeville, Minn. 35 (1961). S. 424–429.

**Aimon d'Auxerre:** Homiliae aliquot de Sanctis ... Homilia XIII: Sermo de Oratione Dominica. In: Migne. vol. 118. Sp. 800–804.

**Albani,** Johannes: Vaterunser vor Verdun. Hirtenbriefe. Dresden: C. L. Ungelenk 1916. 48 S.

**Albertz,** Martin: Gebetsbüchlein. Teil 1: Das Gebet des Herrn. Berlin-Spandau: Wichern-Verlag 1947. 18 S.
– Die ökumenische Bedeutung des Gebets des Herrn. Berlin: Verlag Haus und Schule 1949. 39 S.
Anm.: Letzterer Beitrag auch in: Der Anfang. Berlin: Verlag Haus und Schule 1949. Heft 13, 40 S.

**Allen,** Charles Livingstone: The Lord's Prayer. An interpretation. Westwood N.J.: Revell 1963, 64 S.
Anm.: Beitrag auch enthalten in: Allen, Charles Livingstone: God's Psychiatry. The twenty-third Psalm. The Ten Commandments. The Lord's Prayer. The Beatitudes. Kingswood: World's Work 1960. 176 S.

**Alonso Diaz,** J.: El Padre Nuestro como oración actual. In: Sal Terrae. Santander. 63 (1975). S. 196–202.

– Padre Nuestro. Santander: Sal Terrae 1954. 112 S.
– El „Padre Nuestro" en el problema general de la Escatologia. In: Miscelánea Comillas. Collectanea Theologica 34/35 (1960). S. 297 bis 308.
– El problema literario del Padre Nuestro. In: Estudios Bíblicos. Madrid 1959. S. 63–75.

**Althoff,** Karl Friedrich: Das Vaterunser. Die Wortgestalt des Menschheitsgebets auf ihrem Weg durch die Kulturen der Völker. Stuttgart: Verlag Urachhaus Johannes M. Mayer 1978. 280 S., 15 Zeichn.

**Altmann,** Odilo OFM: Dreimal zwei Tägliches Brot. In: Schule des Opfers. München: Ars sacra 1958. S. 105–110.

**Amiot,** François: Pater noster und Libera (in der heiligen Messe). Geschichte der heiligen Messe. (Der Christ in der Welt. Reihe IX, Bd. 3. Aschaffenburg: Pattloch 1957 (²1961) [Reihe 9, Bd. 3] S. 109–112.
– Figure evangeliche: S. Giovanni Battista: Il discorso della montagna, **il Pater;** S. Pietro: Il discorso dopo la cena. A cura die Giovanni Montali. Siena: Ed. Cantagalli 1942. 198 S.

**Ammann,** Hans: Zur Form des Unser-Vaters. In: Kirchenblatt für die reformierte Schweiz. Basel: Reinhard 110 (1954). S. 55–56.

**Ammon,** Daniel: Geisteskräfte im Vaterunser. Unterwaissach (Württ.): Selbstverlag des Autors 1925. 52 S.

**Andacht über das Gebet des Herrn.** In: Gebets- und Gesangbuch für das Bistum Berlin. 1941. S. 454ff.

**André,** Philippe: Le Notre Père. Matériaux pour la catéchèse. In: Catechistes. Paris. 1966. S. 151–178.

**Andrieu:** Le „Carré SATOR". Etude nouvelle. In: Mémoires de l'Académie des Sciences, Arts et Belles Lettres de Dijon. Dijon 1937. S. XXX–XXXII.

**Aner,** Karl: Das Vaterunser in der Geschichte der evangelischen Frömmigkeit (Sammlung gemeinverständlicher Vorträge u. Schriften aus dem Gebiete der Theologie u. Religionsgeschichte Nr. 109). Tübingen: J. C. B. Mohr 1924. 48 S.

**Angela,** Schwester OSU: Vater unser! München: Ars sacra 1934. 29 S.

**Angénieux,** J.: Les différents types de structure du Pater dans l'histoire de son exégèse. In: Ephemerides Theol. Lovaniensis. Leiden: Brill 1970. Fasc. 1. 39 S.

**Anselm von Lucca:** Meditatio in Orationem Dominicam. In: Migne, vol. 149, Sp. 569–578.

**Antonius de Mathelica**: Expositio Orationis Dominicae. Parma: Francesco de Prato 1535.

**Die apostolischen Väter:** In: Bibliothek der Kirchenväter. Bd. 35, S. 11. München: Kösel 1918.

**Aravalles,** Juan: Von der Bitte. In: Wie beten? München: Arssacra-Verlag 1965. S. 69–73.

**Armenische Kirchenväter:** Ausgewählte Schriften. In: Bibliothek der Kirchenväter. Bd. 58, S. 277–285. München: Kösel & Pustet 1927.

**Aron,** Robert: Les origines juives du Pater. In: La Maison Dieu. Paris 85 (1966) I. S. 36–40.

**Artopoeus,** Johannes Georgius: Succincta Commentatio ad Orationis Dominicae Petitionem Quintam, Matth. 6,12. Straßburg: J. Pastorius 1689.

**Assmann,** Wolfgang: Beten wie der Meister. In: Dies Wort gilt heute. Hildesheim: Bernward-Verlag 1968. S. 13f.

**Atkinson,** Donald: The Origin and Date of the SATOR Word-Square. In: The Journal of Ecclesiastical History. London, 2 Nr. 1 (1951). Sp. 1–18.
– The SATOR-Formula and the Beginnings of Christianity. In: Bulletin of the John Rylands Library. Manchester, 22 (1938). S. 419–434.

**Attal,** F. S.: L'orazione domenicale. In: Miscellánea Franciscana. Roma 62 (1962). S. 135–154.

**Audin,** Amable: Le carré magique: s. **Couchoud,** Paul-Louis.

**Augagneur,** Marcel: Notre Père (Collection Blanche: Nouvelle Revue Française). Paris: Ed. Gallimard 1930. 242 S.

**Augustinus, Aurelius,** Der heilige: Ausgewählte Schriften. In: Bibliothek der Kirchenväter. Bd. 28 (1916): S. 423–425; Bd. 30 (1917): S. 27–30; Bd. 49 (1925):S. 496f. München: Kösel.

# B

**B.:** Die einheitliche Fassung des „Vaterunser" für das deutsche Sprachgebiet. In: L'Ami du Peuple, Straßburg vom 29.9.1968.

**Baarslag,** Derk Johan: Het „Onze Vader". Baarn: Bosch & Keuning 1946. 232 S.

24

**Bach,** Johann Sebastian: Vater unser im Himmelreich. In: Orgelwerke V-Urtext, Nr. 47 u. 48, S. 51 u. 52, 109/110. Frankfurt/London/New York: Edition Peters (Nr. 244a) 1952.

**Baesecke,** Georg: Unerledigte Vorfragen der althochdeutschen Textkritik und Literaturgeschichte. I. Die Vaterunser vor Notker. In: Beiträge zur Geschichte der deutschen Sprache und Literatur. Halle/Saale: Max Niemeyer vol. 69/II (1947). S. 361–365.

**Bahr,** Gordon J.: The Use of the Lord's Prayer in the Primitive Church. In: Journal of Biblical Literature. Philadelphia, Pa. 84 (1965). S. 153–159.

**Baker,** Aelred OSB: What sort of bread did Jesus want us to pray for? In: New Blackfriars. London: 54 (1973). S. 125–129.
– Lead us not into temptation. In: New Blackfriars. London: 52 (1971). S. 64–69.

**Balthasar,** Hans Urs von: Christliches Beten – Beten in der Kirche (Thema einer geistlichen Woche „Beten in einer weltlichen Welt"). Hier: Das Urgebet (Das Vaterunser). Bericht in: Herder-Korrespondenz. Freiburg: Herder 32 (1978). S. 402.
– Im Vater-unser steht kein Ich. In: Kirchenbote für das Bistum Osnabrück, Nr. 9 vom 26. 2. 1978.

**Bammel,** Ernst: Ein neuer Vater-Unser-Text. In: Zeitschrift für die neutestamentliche Wissenschaft und die Kunde der älteren Kirche. Berlin: 52 (1961). S. 280–281.
– A New Text of the Lord's Prayer. In: The Expository Times. Edinburgh: 72 (1961). S. 54.

**Bannach,** Horst: Das Vaterunser. In: Sonntagsblatt. Hamburg 1955. Nr. 27–31, jeweils S. 3.
– Das Vaterunser. Das Gebet der Jünger Jesu. Hamburg: Furche-Verlag (Furche-Bücherei Bd. 140) 1957. 46 S.

**Barbieri,** Sante Uberto: El Padre Nuestro. Buenos Aires: Editorial La Aurora 1967. 88 S.

**Barchewitz,** Alfred: Das Vaterunser in der Not unserer Zeit. Gastpredigt. Leipzig: P. Eger 1919. 12 S.

**Barclay,** William: The Beatitudes and the Lord's Prayer for everyman. New York: Harper & Row 1968. 256 S.
– The Plain Man looks at the Lord's Prayer. London: Collins 1964. 128 S.
– Wie sollen wir beten? Eine Einführung in das Gebet des Herrn. Aus dem Englischen von Wolfgang Müller. Kassel: J. G. Oncken Verlag 1968. 126 S.

**Barns,** J. W. B. / Zilliacus, H. (Hrsg.): The Antinoopolis Papyri part II (Matt 6,10 S. (Pater noster) saec. 3ᵖ. Egypt Exploration Society 1960. S. 6f., plate IV (verso).

**Barone,** Paolo M.: Pater noster: istruzioni sull'orazione domenicale. Casale Monferrato: Il Ministero della Parola 1917. 103 S.

**Barsotti,** Divo: Unterschied zwischen dem Gebet des einzelnen Christen und dem Gebet der Kirche. In: Christliches Mysterium und Gottes Wort. Einsiedeln: Benziger 1957. S. 307.

**Bartelt,** Wilhelm: Das Vaterunser. In: Das Evangelium nach Lukas (Die Heilige Schrift für das Leben erklärt, Bd. XII). Freiburg: Herder 1936. S. 122–126.

**Barth,** Karl: Das Vaterunser nach den Katechismen der Reformation. Zürich: EVZ-Verlag 1965. 114 S.
– La Prière d'après les catéchismes de la Réformation. Chap. 2: Explication de l'Oraison Dominicale d'après les Réformateurs. Neuchâtel: Delachaux & Niestlé 1953. S. 23–59.

**Barth,** Richard: Das Vaterunser-Evangelium. Die frohe Botschaft unseres Heilands im Rahmen des Vaterunser. Weimar: Kirchenbewegung „Deutsche Christen" 1934. 74 S.

**Bartmann,** Hans: Vater im Himmel! Geheiligt werde dein Name! In: Seele. Regensburg: Habbel, 34 (1958). S. 202f.

**Bartolomeo da Saluzzo:** Lux animae ad perfectionem anhelantis… Nunc recens ex Italico in Latinum conversum… Expositio orationis Dominicae: S. 444–451. Köln: Joannes Crith 1607 (italien. Ausgabe 1906, 390 S.).

**Basset,** Bernard SJ: Das erste Vaterunser des Glaubenszweiflers. In: Wir Glaubenszweifler (Herder-Bücherei Bd. 346). Freiburg: Herder 1969. S. 103, 114.

**Bassett,** F. Tilney: Give us this day our daily bread. In: Expository Times. vol. 3, Nr. 1 (1891–1892). S. 27–31.

**Bassó,** Federico, Pbro.: Padre Nuestro del Cielo. Cuaderno de catequesis para el curso de Primera confesión, Confirmación, Primera comunión. Ilustraciones del Autor. Vaterunser: S. 29. Barcelona: Editorial Teide 1968. 79 S.

**Bath,** V. C.: The Lord's Prayer in Daily Life. Chicago: Thoughts that inspire Publ. Co. 1962. 111 S.

**Bauer,** Erika (Hrsg.): s. **Paternoster-Auslegung.**

**Bauer,** H.: Das Gebet des Herrn. In: Jahrbücher für Deutsche Theologie. 13 (1868). S. 303–311.

**Bauer,** Johannes Bapt.: Libera nos a malo (Mt 6,13). In: Verbum Domini. Roma, 34 (1956). S. 12–15.

**Baumann,** Rolf: Vaterunser. Vorwort zu einem Vater-unser-Beitrag von Walter Dirks. In: Bibel heute. Stuttgart: Verlag Kath. Bibelwerk 1974. 1. Quartal, S. 98.
– Abba, lieber Vater. Zum biblischen Gottesbild. In: Bibel und Kirche. Stuttgart: Verlag Kath. Bibelwerk, 22 (1967). H. 3, S. 73–78.

**Baumgartner,** J.: Das Gebet der Einheit. Der neue französische Text des Vaterunser. In: Schweiz. Kirchenzeitung. Luzern, 134 (1966). S. 70–72, 94–96.

**Baur,** Andreas: Das Gebet des Herrn in der Katechese: s. **Smitmans,** Adolf.
– Vaterunser. Zum Gebet des Herrn heute. Mit Illustrationen von Gisela Fäustlin. Donauwörth: Auer 1969. 32 S.

**Baur,** Johannes: Pater noster – Gebet des Herrn. In: Kleine Liturgik der heiligen Messe. Innsbruck: Rauch 1957. S. 78–79.

**Baur,** Karl: Vaterunser. Erklärung. In: Die Messe in der Glaubensverkündigung. Hrsg. F. X. Arnold u. Balthasar Fischer. Freiburg: Herder 1950. S. 62.

**Bavel,** T. van: Inferas – Inducas. Apropos de Matth. 6,13 dans les œuvres de S. Augustin. In: Revue Bénédictine. Maredsous/Belgien 1959. S. 348–351.

**Bayer,** Oswald G.: Vater unser! Zürich: NZN-Verlag 1949. 14 S.

**Baylot:** Considérations sur le Pater d'après les Pères et autres maîtres de la vie spirituelle. Tours: Cattier 1883. 191 S.

**Beaucamp,** Évode / Relles, Jean-Pascal de: Israel attend son Dieu. Des psaumes aux vœux du Pater (Collection Bible et vie chrétienne). Paris / Bruges: Desclée de Brouwer 1967. 345 S.
– Israele attende il suo Dio. Dai salmi alle invocazioni del Pater (Collezione Sit pax et veritas). Milano – Bolzano: Ed. Paoline 1970. 500 S.
– Le Pater, prière des chrétiens d'action. In: Cahiers du Clergé rural. Paris 1960. Nr. 169, S. 67–68; 219–247; 533–544; 579–588.

**Becker,** Karl / Peter, Maria: Das Heilige Vaterunser. Ein Werkbuch. Freiburg: Herder 1951. 330 S.
– Das Vaterunser im Leben des Christen. (Auszug aus: Das Heilige Vaterunser). Leipzig: St. Benno-Verlag. 1959. 71 S.
– Our Father. A Handbook for Meditation. Transl. by Ruth Mary Bethell. Chicago: Regnery 1956. 334 S.

**Beer,** Norbert: Laß deine Augen offen sein. Bildmeditationen zum Vaterunser nach Lithographien von Otto Dix. München: Claudius-Verlag 1973. 64 S.

**Behr,** von: Das Vater unser für seine Feldsoldaten in Verse gebracht (1 Blatt). Saarbrücken: Ch. Clauss 1914.

**Beilner,** Wolfgang: Vaterunser. In: Jesus ohne Retuschen. Graz: Styria 1974. S. 222–224, 238f.

**Beissel,** Stephan SJ: Betrachtungspunkte für alle Tage des Kirchenjahres. Bd. 1: Das Gebet des Herrn und der Englische Gruß. Freiburg: Herder (Erstauflage 1900); 2. umgearb. Aufl. 1904. 133 S.; 3. verb. Aufl. 1919. X, 166 S.

**Bellet,** C.: Le „Pater" et l'„Ave Maria". Saint Maxime: Ed. de la Revue du Rosaire 1933. 55 S.

**Benedictus** Sanctus: Mönchsregel. In: Bibliothek der Kirchenväter. Bd. 20, S. 42f., 45. München: Kösel 1914.

**Bengsch,** Alfred Kardinal: So sollt ihr beten: Vater unser im Himmel. Meditationen über das Gebet des Herrn. In: Klerusblatt. Eichstätt, 53 (1973) S. 105–111.
– Vater Gott – nicht Weltmaschine. In: Der Glaube an die Auferstehung. Berlin: Morus-Verlag 1962. S. 13–18.

**Benoît,** Jean-Daniel: Le Notre Père dans le culte et la prière des Eglises protestantes. In: La Maison-Dieu. Paris: 85 (1966). S. 101 bis 116.

**Berger,** Fritz: Etwas über das Unser-Vater. Wydibühl, Brenzikofen (Schweiz): Selbstverlag des Verfassers. ca. 1940. 16 S.

**Berger,** Klaus: Vaterunser. In: Sacramentum mundi. Freiburg: Herder 1969. Bd. IV Sp. 1147–1152.
– The Lord's Prayer. In: Sacramentum mundi. Vol. 3, London / New York: Herder 1968. S. 343–346.

**Berger,** Rupert: Das Herrengebet (in der heiligen Messe). In: Tut dies zu meinem Gedächtnis. München: Don-Bosco-Verlag 1971. S. 75–80.
– Pater noster. In: Kleines liturgisches Wörterbuch (Herderbücherei Bd. 339–340). Freiburg: Herder 1969. S. 337–339.

**Bernard,** Aleth: Notre Père. Ill. de Serge Zagli (Coll. Clairs matins). Paris: Ed. Fleurus 1960. 30 S.

**Bernard,** Rogatien OP: Beten können: Vater unser. In: Das Mysterium Jesu. Freiburg: Herder 1959. S. 153–165.

**Berner,** Erwin: Unser Vater! Eine Betrachtung über das Gebet des Herrn. Hamburg: Advent-Verlag 1949. 93 S.

**Bertram,** Hans: Vaterunser – Trost in höchster Not. In: Flug in die Hölle. München: Desch 1951. S. 50, 75, 79, 89, 107.

**Bertrangs,** A.: Het Onze Vader. In: Bidden met de Schrift. Getuigenis 6.3 (1962). Roermond. S. 210–220.

**Besnard,** Fr. A.-M. OP: Mon Père et votre Père. Prière et paternité divine. In: La Vie spirituelle. Paris, vol. 102 (1960). S. 5–17.

**Betting,** Alfons: Das Vaterunser. In: Ambrosius. Zeitschrift für Prediger. Donauwörth: Auer 59 (1954). S. 36–49, 86–93, 140–152, 164–182.

**Betz,** Otto: Manifest der Christen in der Welt. Das Vaterunser heute. In: Bibel und Kirche (Sonderheft „Christsein im Lichte des Vaterunsers"). Stuttgart: Verlag Kath. Bibelwerk 22 (1967). S. 86 bis 92.
– Die vielen Worte tun es nicht. In: Die Humanität Jesu. Hrsg. Marianne Müssle (Pfeiffer-Werkbücher Nr. 98). München: Pfeiffer 1971. S. 59–73.
Anm.: Ausdrückl. Bezug auf das Vaterunser S. 63–65.

**Beuerle,** Herbert / Ruppel, Paul Ernst: Vaterunser-Lieder. Alte Kirchengesänge in Sätzen für zwei gleiche u. drei gemischte Stimmen. Neukirchen – Vluyn: Verlag Singende Gemeinde 1962. 32 S.

**Bezzel,** Hermann von: Das Gebet des Herrn. Letzte Katechismusstunden über das Vaterunser. Vorwort von Joh. Rupprecht. Stuttgart: D. Gundert 1929. 140 S.

**Bibelmission in Deutschland:** Darum sollt ihr also beten (Vaterunser nach dem kleinen Katechismus von Martin Luther und dem Heidelberger Katechismus). Wuppertal-Barmen 1962. 32 S.

**Bieder,** W.: „Dein Reich komme" oder: „Zu uns komme Dein Reich"? (Lk 11,2). In: Kirchenblatt für die reformierte Schweiz. Basel: Reinhardt 101 (1944). S. 23–24.

**Biel,** Gabriel: Das Herrengebet: s. **Damerau,** Rudolf.

**Bierbaum,** Athanasius OFM: Das Vaterunser (als Danksagung nach der Kommunion). In: Botschaft vom Vatergott, Bd. 2: Der Vatergott und die Menschennöte. Werl: Verlag der Franziskus-Druckerei 1938. S. 29–31.

**Bigu,** C. / Vidal, J.: Le contenu du Pater. In: Prière et Vie. Toulouse: November 1963. S. 531–537; Dezember 1963, S. 599–606; Januar 1964, S. 23–32.

**Billerbeck,** Paul: Kommentar zum Neuen Testament aus Talmud und Midrasch. s. **Strack,** Hermann L.

**Bindley,** T. Herbert: Eschatology in the Lord's Prayer. In: The Expositor. 8th Ser. vol. 18. 1919. S. 315–320.

**Binet,** Nicole: Le Notre Père ou la prière du Seigneur. Tours: Mâme 1956. 23 S.

**Bischöfe Deutschlands und Österreichs (Hrsg.):** Andacht über das Gebet des Herrn. In: Gotteslob. Kath. Gebet- u. Gesangbuch, hier: Ausgabe für das Erzbistum München u. Freising. München: Pfeiffer 1975. Nr. 782, S. 813–818.

**Bischoff,** A.: EPIOUSIOS. In: Zeitschrift für die neutestamentliche Wissenschaft. Berlin: Töpelmann Bd. 7, Nr. 3 (1906). S. 266–271.

**Bischoff,** Erich: Jesus und die Rabbinen. Jesu Bergpredigt und die Unabhängigkeit vom Rabbinismus (Schriften des Institutum Judaicum in Berlin N. 33). Zu Thema Vaterunser: s. 73–82: Mt 6,9f. Leipzig: J. C. Hinrichs 1905.

**Bismarck,** Klaus von: Was heißt denn eigentlich Täglich Brot? In: Kirche in der Zeit. Düsseldorf. 16 (1961). S. 11–16.

**Bittner,** Heinz: Kein anderes Vaterunser. In: Werkhefte. München, 22 (1968). H. 11, S. 325.

**Black,** Matthew: The Aramaic of τὸν ἄρτον ἡμῶν τὸν ἐπιούσιον (Matth. 6,11 – Luke 11,3). In: The Journal of Theological Studies. vol. 42 (1941). S. 186–189.

**Blakeney,** E. H.: Matthew VI, 13 – Luke XI, 4; cf. Mark XIV, 38. In: The Expository Times. Edinburgh 57 (1945). S. 279.

**Blarr,** O. G.: Neue geistliche Lieder. Melodiefassung u. Satz von O. G. Blarr (Bosse-Edition 236). Regensburg: Gustav Bosse 1974.

**Bläser,** P.: „Des Herrn Wort bleibt in Ewigkeit". Das Vaterunser Mt. 6,9–13, Luk. 11,1–4. In: Ut omnes unum. Paderborn 17 (1954). S. 15–18, 36–41, 83–85, 105–106.

**Blass,** Friedrich: EPIOUSIOS. In: Grammatik des neutestamentlichen Griechisch. Göttingen: Vandenhoeck & Ruprecht. 9. Aufl. 1954. § 123–124.

**Blatchford,** R.: Notre Père qui êtes aux cieux (Petite Bibliothèque libre-pens. et soc.). Herblay (Seine et Oise): Ed. de l'Idée libre 1923.

**Blattmann,** Georg: Das Vater Unser und Du. Begegnung mit einem Gebetstext. In: Die Christengemeinschaft. Stuttgart: Verlag Urachhaus 40 (1968). I. S. 229–232; II. S. 261–264; III. S. 297–299.

**Bleek,** Friedrich: Das Vaterunser. In: Synoptische Erklärung der drei ersten Evangelien, Bd. I. Hrsg. Heinrich Holtzmann. Leipzig: Wilhelm Engelmann 1862. S. 298–309.

**Blenkinsopp,** Joseph S. D. B.: Apropos of the Lord's Prayer. In: The Heythrop Journal. Oxford. 3 (1962) Nr. 1, S. 51–60.
– The Lord's Prayer and the Hill of Olives. In: The Heythrop Journal. Oxford. 3 (1962 Nr. 2, S. 169–171.

**Bloomfield,** M. W. / Guyot, B.-G. / Howard, D. R. / Kabealo, T. B.: Incipits of Latin Works on the Virtues and Vices, 1100–1500 A. D., including a section of incipits on the Pater Noster. Cambridge (Mass.): The Medieval Academy of America 1979. (18/26). XVI, 780 S.

**Blumhardt,** Joh. Christoph: Das Vaterunser. Stuttgart: Evang. Missionsverlag (5. Aufl.) 1960. 64 S.
– Der Sinn des Reichsgebets. In: Der christliche Sonntag. Freiburg: Herder, 1 (1949). S. 197.

**Bocchi,** Arrigo: Il Pater noster: carme. Venezia: Compositori tip. 1872. 12 S.

**Bock,** Johann Peter SJ: Nachträgliches zur Brotbitte des Vaterunsers. In: Zeitschrift für kath. Theologie. vol. 36 (1912). S. 654–664, 869–886.
– Die Brotbitte des Vaterunsers. Ein Beitrag zum Verständnis dieses Universalgebetes und einschlägiger patristisch-liturgischer Fragen. Paderborn: Bonifacius-Druckerei 1911. XVI, 339 S.
Anm: Dazu Besprechung von Emil Dorsch SJ in: Zeitschrift für kath. Theologie. 36 (1912). S. 134–136.
– Le pain quotidien du Pater ... Trad. par A. Villien. Paris: Lethielleux 1912.
– Panem nostrum quotidianum da nobis hodie. In: Zeitschrift für kath. Theologie. vol. 32 (1908). S. 776–782.

**Bodoni,** Giambattista: Bodonis „Vaterunser in 155 Sprachen": s. **Presser,** Helmut; s. **Eule,** Wilhelm.

**Boeckh,** Jürgen: Vaterunser. In: Mit ihm reden. Berlin: Christl. Zeitschriftenverlag. 1977.

**Boegner,** Marc: La prière de l'Eglise universelle. Six prédications de Carême 1951, prononcées en l'église réformée de Passy, suivies de la méditation de vendredi saint. Paris: Berger-Levrault. 148 S.
– Prayer of the Church Universal. Transl. by Howard Schomer. Nashville: Abingdon Pr. 1954. 128 S.

**Boehmer,** Julius: Die neutestamentliche Gottesschau und die ersten drei Bitten des Vaterunsers (Mühlmanns theologische

Taschenbücher Bd. 11). Halle/Saale: R. Mühlmann Verlag 1917. VIII, 211 S.
– Die vierte Bitte nicht nur Mittelpunkt, sondern Höhepunkt des Vaterunsers. In: Treuga Dei. 100 (1931). S. 12–14.

**Boff,** Leonardo: Vater unser. Das Gebet umfassender Befreiung. Aus dem Portugiesischen übersetzt von Horst Goldstein. Düsseldorf: Patmos Verlag 1981. 199 S. Anm.: Die Originalausgabe erschien 1979 bei Editora Vozes, Petrópolis (Brasilien).

**Bohatta-Morpurgo,** Ida: Vater unser, für die Kinder gemalt und erklärt. München: Ars sacra 1931. 10 Bl. mit Abb.
– El „Padre Nuestro". Friburgo – Barcelona: Herder 1935. 20 S. mit 9 farb. Ill.

**Böhlen,** Hippolytus OFM: Vaterunser. In: Dem Herrn entgegen. Eucharistische Monatsblätter für die weibliche Jugend. Wiesbaden: Hermann Rauch, 6 (1923). Nr. 11, S. 2–4.

**Bohren,** Rudolf: Das Unser Vater – heute. Zehn Vorträge. Zürich: Zwingli-Verlag 1957. 136 S.

**Bois,** Henri: Ne nous induis pas en tentation. In: La Foi et la Vie. vol. 3, Nr. 18 (1900). S. 273–277.

**Boll,** Jos. Alphons: Das Vaterunser. Eine bildliche Darstellung als Anschauungsmittel für den Unterricht (1 farb. Blatt auf Karton u. Text auf der Rückseite). Donaueschingen: O. Mory 1909.

**Bolliger,** Adolf: Die vierte Bitte des Unservaters. In: Schweizerische Theologische Zeitschrift. 30 (1913). Nr. 5, S. 276–285.

**Bommer,** Josef: Die Bitte. In: Vom Beten des Christen. München: Rex-Verlag 1966. S. 39–44.

**Bongioanni,** Fausto M.: Morale del „Padre Nostro". Interpretazione testuale dell'orazione domenicale. Torino: Soc. Ed. Internazionale 1947. 177 S.

**Bonhoeffer,** Dietrich: Dein Reich komme. Das Gebet der Gemeinde und Gottes Reich auf Erden. Die erste Tafel. Eine Auslegung der ersten drei Gebote. Hrsg. u. m. e. Nachwort v. Eberhard Bethge (Furche-Bücherei 146). Hamburg: Furche-Verlag 1957. 45 S.

**Bonnard,** Pierre / Dupont, J. / Refoulé, F.: Notre père qui est aux cieux. La prière œcuménique (Cahiers de la traduction œcuménique de la Bible Nr. 3). Paris: Ed. du Cerf 1968. 118 S.

**Bonsirven,** Joseph: Notre Père (Coll. „Le Témoignage Chrétien", Nr. 43). Le Puy: Xavier Mappus 1945. 32 S.
– Le règne de Dieu. Chap. IX: Religion du règne: En esprit et en vérité. La prière dans le règne de Dieu (Coll. Théologie, vol. 37). Paris: Ed. Aubier 1957. S. 153–173.

**Bopp,** Linus: Das Vaterunsergebet als Türe zwischen Opferhandlung und Opfermahl. In: Missa est. Buch der meßliturgischen Bildungswerte. Freiburg: Herder 1938 (2. Aufl. 1941). S. 202–205.

**Borchardt-Sattler,** Dodo: Die sieben Vaterunserbitten in sieben Kunstblättern. München: Rose-Verlag 1975.

**Bornhak,** Helmut: Wege zur Stille. Gebete zum Vaterunser. Stuttgart: Evang. Missionsverlag 1960. 171 S.

**Borning,** Walther: Das Vaterunser nach dem kleinen Katechismus Dr. Martin Luthers (Rüstzeug für den Bau der deutschen evangelischen Kirche, 3. Serie). Berlin: Warneck 1933. 28 S.

**Boros,** Ladislaus: Zur Deutung des Bittgebets (Mt 6,6–8). In: Über das christliche Beten. Mainz: Matthias-Grünewald-Verlag 1973. S. 51.

**Bösinger,** Rudolf: Vom Vaterunser betroffen. Begebenheiten. Lahr: Schauenburg-Verlag 1962. 45 S.

**Bosch,** van den s. **Van den Bosch**

**Boskamp,** Maria Friedrich Paul: Das gotische Vaterunser. Erinnerung an einen alten Lehrer. In: Echo der Zeit. Recklinghausen. 10. 10. 1954.

**Botha,** F. J.: Recent Research on the Lord's Prayer. In: The Sermon on the Mount. Essays on Mt. 5–7 (Proceedings of the 3rd Meeting of „Die Nuwe-Testamentiese Werkgemeenskap van Suid-Afrika. Univ. of Pretoria 1967. S. 42–50.

**Botto,** Guido: Richiesto dai discepoli Egli disse: „Pater noster..." Milano: Bompiani 1948. 295 S.

**Bourgoin,** H.: Epiousios expliqué par la notion du préfixe vide. In: Biblica 60 (1979). S. 91–96.

**Bourguet,** Pierre: Notre Père. Etudes et méditations sur l'Oraison Dominicale. Orné de 12 pl. reprod. les émaux de Colin Nohailler (XVI. siècle). Paris: Éd. Je sers 1941.

**Brändle,** Max: Warum kein Dank im Vaterunser. Die sechste Bitte im Vaterunser – Der Schluß des Vaterunsers. In: Bibel, Sakramente, Liturgie. Antwort auf Fragen katholischer und evangelischer Christen (Tyrolia-Taschenbuch Nr. 18). Innsbruck: Tyrolia-Verlag 1962. S. 67–70, 71–74, 75 f.

**Braun,** F.-M.: Le pain dont nous avons besoin (Mt 6,11; Lc 11,3). In: Nouvelle Revue Théologique 110 (1978) S. 559–568.

**Braun,** Heinrich Suso OFMCap: Jesus und das Vaterunser. In: Jesus als Mensch. München: Verlag Ars sacra 1960. S. 49.

**Braun,** Herbert: Predigtmeditation über Mat 6,5–13: s. **Weise,** M.

**Bremond,** Henri: Das Vaterunser beginnt mit Anbetung. In: Das wesentliche Gebet. Regensburg: Pustet 1939. S. 28f.

**Brems,** Alois / Mosshamer, Ottilie: Vater unser. In: Das Wort an die Jugend. Augsburg: Johann Wilhelm Naumann 1948. 2. Jahreskreis, S. 158f.

**Brentano,** Clemens von: Das Vaterunser. Übersetzt nach einem alten Manuskript. Hrsg. u. ergänzt von Maria Andrea Goldmann. Dülmen: Laumann 1948. 40 S.

**Brentz,** Johann: Das teglich Gebet. So unser Herr Jesus Christus selbst gelehret hat. Ausgelegt durch Herren Johan. Berentium und newlich mit fleisse verdeutscht durch Stephanum Agricolam. Erffurdt (sic): Wolffgangus und Geruasius Sthürmer 1550.

**Breucha,** Hermann: Vater unser, der du bist im Himmel. Predigten über das Herrengebet für die Fasten- u. Osterzeit. In: Gedanken zur Sonntagspredigt XIX, Nr. 27–41. Stuttgart: Verlag der religiösen Bildungsarbeit 1967. 56 S.

**Bridel,** Philippe: Explication de l'Oraison Dominicale. Lausanne: ca. 1870.

**Brinktrine,** Johannes: Die heilige Messe. §50: Das Gebet des Herrn. Paderborn: F. Schöningh 3. verb. Aufl. 1950 (1. Aufl. 1931).

**Bro,** Bernard: Parallelen des Vaterunsers zum Hohenpriesterlichen Gebet. In: Lerne beten. Freiburg: Herder 1964. S. 92–95; siehe auch S. 95 ff.

**Brocke,** Karl: Das Vaterunser, Das Gebet der Gotteskinder. Paderborn: Bonifacius-Druckerei 1956. 152 S.

**Brocke,** Michael / Strolz, Walter / Petuchowski, J. J. (Hrsg.): Das Vaterunser. Gemeinsames im Beten von Juden und Christen. Veröffentlichung der Stiftung Oratio Dominica. Freiburg: Herder 1974. 286 S.

**Broecker,** Arthur von: Das Vaterunser in Zeiten des Krieges. Predigt über Matt. 6,9–14, gehalten am 6.9.1914. Hamburg: Agentur des Rauhen Hauses 1914, 14 S.

**Brors,** Franz: Leiden und Beten. Betrachtungen in zwei Predigtreihen. Bd. II: Das „Gebet des Herrn", der Inbegriff allen Betens. Rottenburg: Bader'sche Verlagsbuchhdlg. 1932. 61 S.

**Brouwer,** Jelle Hindrik: It alderhillichst gebet yn fryske lûden. Mei ynlieding en oantekeningen fan J. H. Brouwer. Assen: Van Gorkum 1964. 125 S.

**Brown,** Raymond E.: The Pater Noster as an Eschatological Prayer. In: Theological Studies. New York 22 (1961). S. 175–208.
– The Meaning of the Our Father. In: Theological Digest. St. Mary's, Ka. vol. 10 (1962). Nr. 1, S. 3–10.
– Sentido escatologico del Padrenuestro. In: Selecciones de Libros de Teologia. San Cugat del Vallés (Barcelona). vol. 1 (1962), Nr. 1, S. 54–62.

**Brüggemann,** Theo: Das Gebet für Nichtkönner. In: Gebete zur Bergpredigt. München: Pfeiffer 1972. S. 49–51.

**Brugmann-Thumb:** Griechische Grammatik (Handbuch der klass. Altertumswissenschaft 2, 1) Darin S. 675: EPIOUSIOS. München: C. H. Beck 1913.

**Brun,** Lyder: Der Name und die Königsherrschaft im Vaterunser. In: Harnack-Ehrung. Beiträge zur Kirchengeschichte, ihrem Lehrer Adolf von Harnack zu seinem 70. Geburtstag dargebracht von einer Reihe seiner Schüler. Leipzig: J. C. Hinrichs 1921. S. 22–31.

**Bruppacher,** Hans: Zum ökumenischen deutschen Unservater. In: Kirchenblatt für die reformierte Schweiz. Basel: Reinhardt, 129 (1968) Nr. 10. S. 149–152.

**Bucher,** Theodor: Freiheit und Bindung. Betrachtungen zur dritten Bitte des Herrengebetes. In: Einheit in Christus. Evangel. u. kath. Bekenntnisse. Zürich / Einsiedeln: Zwingli-Verlag; Verlag Benziger 1960. S. 16–29.

**Buchrucker,** Armin-Ernst: Das Vaterunser als Begleiter auf dem christlichen Lebenswege. In: Kirchliches Monatsblatt f. d. evang.-luth. Gemeinden in Amerika. Philadelphia, Pa. 10 (1953). S. 223 bis 225.

**Buckley,** S.: The Pater Noster. In: Eucharist & Priest. Kerala: Alwaye 68 (1962). S. 151–161.

**Bühnert,** Franz: Kriegs-Vaterunser. Worte v. von Behr. In melodramatischer Weise für Orgel oder Harmonium. Leipzig: J. J. Weber 1917. 2 S.

**Büll,** Alma: Das Vater-Unser. Morgenandachten vom Sommer 1936. Reval: F. Wassermann 1936. 23 S.

**Bungeroth,** Anneliese: Das Reich und die Kraft. Gedanken zum Vaterunser. Stuttgart: Ehrenfried Klotz 1965. 44 S.

**Burbach,** Hermann Josef MSF: Vaterunser im Straßenverkehr. In: Klerusblatt. Eichstätt – München 1971. Nr. 14, S. 221.

**Buri,** Fritz: Gebot und Gebet. Ein Lesebuch zu den zehn Geboten und zum Unser-Vater. Zollikon: Evang. Verlag 1960. 124 S.

Burkitt, F.C.: „As we have forgiven" (Matth. 6,12). In: The Journal of Theological Studies. vol. 33 (1932). Nr. 131, S. 253–255.

Burrows, Millar: Thy Kingdom come. In: Journal of Biblical Literature. Philadelphia, Pa. vol. 74 (1955). S. 1–8.

Bussche, Henri van den: s, Van den Bussche, Henri.

Bussel, C. van: s. Van Bussel, C.

Bütler, Anselm OSB: Beten, wie der Herr es gelehrt hat. Eine kurze Erklärung des Vaterunsers. In: Mariastein (Zeitschrift der Benediktiner von Mariastein). Jahrgang 1979. I.: S. 126–129; II.: 152–155; III.: 206–208; IV.: 239–244; V.: 265–269.

Buttrick, George Arthur: So we believe – So we pray. Nashville, Tenn.: Abingdon Press 1962. 250 S.

Bynwalth, Matthias: Das Vaterunser. Ausgelegt durch Matthiam Bynwalth, Prediger zu Gdantzk (1525). Hrsg. von Hermann Freytag. In: Flugschriften aus den ersten Jahren der Reformation. Hrsg.: O. Clemen, Bd. 4. Leipzig: Rudolf Haupt 1910–1911. S. 135 bis 157.

# C

Cabodevilla, José Maria: Discurso del Padrenuestro. Ruegos y preguntas (Biblioteca de Autores Cristianos Nr. 319). Madrid: La Editorial Católica S. A. 1971. 457 S.

Cabrol, F.: Le chant du Pater à la messe III. In: Revue Grégorienne 14 (1929). S. 1–17.

Cambell, J.: S. François a-t-il composé une paraphrase du Pater? In: Franziskanische Studien. Paderborn 45 (1963). S. 338–342.

Campenhausen, Hans von: Sollen wir das Vaterunser gemeinsam sprechen: Unser Beten darf kein gedankenloses Mitplappern werden. In: Sonntagsblatt. Hamburg 6 (1953) Nr. 32, S. 10.
Anm.: Dazu Leserbriefdiskussion in Sonntagsblatt 6 (1953) Nr. 38, S. 19.

Camps, G. M.: Aportaciones per una nova versió catalana del Pere nostre. In: Questions de vida cristiá. Monserrat 27 (1965) S. 72–75.

Canini, Angelo: De locis S. Scripturae hebraicis commentarius... Kap. 12: De Dimitte nobis et aliis: S. 69–62; Kap. 14: De Pane quotidiano, in oratione Dominica: S. 69–75. Anvers: Veuve de J. Beller 1600.

**Capderoque,** Paul: L'Oraison Dominicale. In: Etudes Théologiques et Religieuses. vol. 4 (1929). S. 186–188.

**Carbo de Costaciaro,** Ludovicus: Orationis Dominicae ampla expositio. Venezia: Joh. Bapt. Somaschus 1590.

**Carcopino,** Jérôme: Le Christianisme du „carré magique". In: Museum Helveticum. Basel 5 (1948), S. 16–59.
Anm.: Ebenfalls erschienen in Études d'Histoire Chrétienne. Paris. 1953, S. 9–91.
– Encore le carré magique. In: Académie des inscriptions et Belles Lettres. Comptes rendus des séances de l'année 1955... séance du 9. 12. 1955. Paris. S. 500–507.

**Carley,** Royal V. The Lord's Prayer for today; together with other choice portions of Holy Scripture, Compiled and illustrated by R. V. Carley. Norwalk, Conn. C. R. Gibson 1974. 28 S.

**Carmignac,** Jean: Recherches sur le „Notre Père". Paris: Ed. Letouzey & Ané 1969. 608 S.
– À l'écoute du notre père (Abrégée de „Recherches sur le notre père"). Paris: Editions de Paris 1971. 117 S.
– „Fais que nous n'entrions pas dans la tentation". La portée d'une négation devant un verbe au causatif. In: Revue Biblique. Paris 62 (1965). Nr. 2, S. 218–226.
– Hebrew Translations of the Lord's Prayer. In: Biblical and Near Eastern Studies. Grand Rapids, Mich.: William, B. Eerdmans Publ. Co. 1978. S. 18–79.

**Carnelutti,** Francesco: Il poema di Gesù (Quaderni di San Giorgio Nr. 16). Firenze 1961. 105 S.
– Interpretazione del Pater noster. Nuova edizione aumentata. Bologna / Roma: C. Zuffi 1950. 69 S.

**Carnoy,** A.: À propos du carré magique SATOR. In: La nouvelle Clio, tomes X–XII, Nr. 4–6, S. 252.

**Carré,** Ambroise-Marie OP: Le Pater dans nos vies (Coll. „Conférences de Notre Dame de Paris"). Paris: Editions du Cerf 1964. 185 S.
– Das Vaterunser in unserem Leben. Predigten, gehalten in Notre Dame, Paris 1964. Rottenburg: Badersche Verlagshandlung (im Schwabenverlag, Stuttgart) 1965. 171 S.
– Le Pater pour le monde (Coll. „Conférences de Notre Dame de Paris"). Paris: Editions du Cerf 1965. 192 S.
– Das Vaterunser für die Welt. Predigten, gehalten in Notre Dame,

Paris 1965. Rottenburg: Badersche Verlagshandlung (im Schwabenverlag, Stuttgart) 1967. 168 S.
- Le Notre Père du Christ et des Chrétiens (Coll. „Foi Vivante" Nr. 142). Paris: Editions du Cerf 1971. 256 S.
- El padre nuestro rezado y vivido. Trad. por J. Aman. Bilbao: Verlag Mensajero 1968. 161 S.

**Carretto,** Carlo: Denn du bist mein Vater. Kapitel S. 165–166 in Buch gleichen Titels. Freiburg: Herder 1975.

**Casalis,** George: Le notre Père et la situation mondiale. In: Christianisme social. Paris 77 (1969) Nr. 3–6. S. 191–207.
- Das Vaterunser und die Weltlage. In: Evangelische Theologie. München 29 (1969). Nr. 7, S. 357–371.

**Casel,** Odo OSB: Das Beten vom Advent im Vaterunser. In: Der Advent als Lebensform des Christen. In: Das Wort in der Zeit. Regensburg: Manz 1934. S. 243.

**Casper,** Bernhard: Unser Vater – der Du in den Himmeln bist. Morgenansprachen im Rahmen des „Wort in den Tag". Sendung des Südwestfunk, Baden-Baden, MW + UKW I vom 24. bis 29. 3. 1980.

**Celada,** B.: El Padre Nuestro. Progresos en la inteligencia de la oración de los cristianos. In: Cultura Biblica. Segovia. vol. 22 (1965). S. 279–283.

**Celerin von Brixen:** Das Vaterunser. Erwägungen über das Gebet des Herrn. Brixen: A. Weger 1946. 32 S.

**Cellini,** Adolfo: Il „Pater noster": Questioni esegetiche sulla orazione domenicale, con speciali referenze alle esposizione fattane da S. Teresa. Roma: Tip. Unione edit. 1919. 28 S.

**Cerfaux,** Lucien: L'itinéraire du Règne de Dieu au Royaume des cieux. In: Bible et vie chrétienne. Paris. 1953. Nr. 3, S. 29–32.

**Ceruti,** Ant.: Studi sopra il Padre nostro, orazione del N. S. Gesù Cristo. Firenze: Sborgi 1885. 100 S.

**Chamberlaine,** Joannes: Oratio Dominica in diversas omnium fere gentium linguas versa ... Amsterdam: Typis Guilielmi et Davidis Goerei 1715.

**Charmot,** François SJ: Die Liebe des Vaters. In: Gebet ist Dialog. Wien: Herold-Verlag 1963. S. 21–25–28.

**Chase,** Frederic Henry: The Lord's Prayer in the Early Church (Coll. „Texts and Studies", vol. I, Nr. 3). Cambridge: University Press 1891.

**Chavasse,** Christopher Maude: A litany of the Lord's Prayer. London: S.P.C.K. 1962. 15 S.

**Chevrot,** Georges: Das Vaterunser (in der Messe). In: Unsere heilige Messe. Einsiedeln: Benziger 1953. S. 331–340.

**Chiminelli,** Piero: Il Padrenostro e il mondo moderno. Roma: Scuola teologica battista 1916. VIII, 200 S.
– La storia della preghiera immortale. Note di storia intorno al „pater noster". Torino: Società ed. internazionale 1942. 221 S.

**Cholmondeley,** F. G.: „Give us this Day our Daily Bread". In: The Expository Times. vol. 29, Nr. 3 (Dez. 1917) S. 139–140.

**Chopineau,** Jacques: Petit Midrache provisoire sur le Notre-Père. In: Foi et vie. Paris. 76 (1977) S. 1–6.

**Chosroae Magni** Episcopi Monophysitici explicatio precum missae. E lingua armeniaca in latinam versa per Dr. E. Vetter. Vaterunser-Bezug: S. 48–50. Freiburg: Herder 1880.

**Christsein im Lichte des Vaterunsers:** Sonderheft der Zeitschrift „Bibel und Kirche" mit Beiträgen von Rolf Baumann, Otto Betz u. Wolfgang Knörzer. Stuttgart: Verlag Kath. Bibelwerk (Heft 3) 1967.

**Cieszkowski,** August Graf: Ojcze-Nasz (Das Vaterunser). Bd. 1: Posen 1899; Bd. 2: Posen 1899; Bd. 3: Posen 1903; Bd. 4: Posen 1923. Anm.: Bd. 1 erschien 1848 anonym in einer polnischen Druckerei in Paris unter dem Titel „Das Vater Unser".
– Notre Père. Hrsg. August Graf Cieskowski jr, M. Gasztowth u. Paul Cazin. 4 Bde. Paris 1906–1929.
– The Lord's Prayer. Auszug aus allen 4 Bänden, zusammengestellt von John Rose. London 1919.

**Cipriano,** San: A Donato – L'Unità della Chiesa – La Preghiera del Signore. Traduzione, introduzione e note di Carmelo Failla (Coll. Collana Patristica, diretta da Carmelo Faulla). Roma: città nuova editrice 1967. S. 115–157 u. 161–163.
s. auch unter Cyprian von Karthago

**Clarke,** John Henry: William Blake (1757–1827) on The Lord's Prayer. New York: Haskell House Publ. Ltd. 1971. 174 S.

**Clarke,** William Kemp Lowther: The Lord's Prayer (Chichester pamphlets). London: S.P.C.K. 1959. 10 S.

**Claudel,** Paul: Zum Pater noster. In: Die Messe. Paderborn: F. Schöningh 1939. S. 42–45.

**Claudius,** Hermann / Winnig, August: Was wir dem Vaterunser verdanken (Auszug aus dem Buch „Das Vaterunser. Eine Auslegung, dargeboten von deutschen Dichtern). Berlin-Steglitz: Eckart-Verlag 1940. 15 S. (Beitrag Claudius: S. 5–9).

**Claudius,** Matthias: Über das Gebet (u. vor allem das Vaterunser). In: Sämtliche Werke. Stuttgart: J. G. Cotta'sche Buchhdlg. Nachf. (17.-24. Tsd.) 1962. S. 194–198.
– Vater unser. In: Der christliche Sonntag. Freiburg: Herder 3 (1951). S. 5.
– Das Vaterunser. In: Der Weinstock. Buch der jungen Familie. Hrsg. Helene Helming. Freiburg: Herder 1938. S. 176f.

**Clemen,** Otto: Das lateinische Original von Luthers „Vater-Unser vorwärts und rückwärts" vom Jahre 1516. In: Zeitschrift für Kirchengeschichte. Gotha: Leopold Klotz. Bd. 48, Neue Folge 11 (1929). S. 198–207.

**Clifford,** William: „Give us this Day our Daily Bread". A Prayer for the „meat that endureth". In: The Expository Times. vol. 28, Nr. 11 (1917). S. 523–524.

**Clough,** William A.: Father we thank Thee. Graces and Prayers for the Home. New York: Abingdon-Cokesbury 1949. 112 S.

**Coassolo,** O. M.: L'„Oratio Dominica" in S. Agostino. Diss. Torino 1948. In: Convivium Dominicum. Catania. 1959. S. 45–66.

**Coburn,** John B.: Deliver us from Evil. The Prayer of Our Lord. Photographs by Ray Ellis. New York: The Seabury Press 1976. 93 S.

**Cocks,** Harry Francis Lovell: The Lord's prayer. Broadcast in „Lift up your hearts", 3.–8. Aug. 1959 (Broadcast Talks Nr. 56). London: Independent Press Ltd. 1959. 15 S.

**Cohausz,** Otto: Zum Vaterunser. In: Die Frömmigkeit Jesu Christi. Kirnach – Villingen: Verlag der Schulbrüder 1930. S. 57–64.

**Collins,** R. J.: „Thy will be done on earth as it is in heaven" (Mt. 6,10). In: Bible today. Collegeville, Minn. 14 (1964). S. 911–917.

**Colubiew,** Antoni: Briefe an Freund Jan. Wenn man beten will (die drei ersten Vaterunser-Bitten). München: Ars sacra 1963. 256 S.

**Considine,** Daniel SJ: Vater unser. In: Gott liebt uns. München: Ars sacra 1962. S. 276f.

**Cook,** Albert S.: The Evolution of the Lord's Prayer in English. In: The American Journal of Philology. Baltimore, Md., vol. 12 (1891). S. 59–66.

**Cooper,** L.: Certain Rhythms in the English Bible. With illustrations from the Psalms, Ecclesiastes and the **Lord's Prayer**. Ithaca, N. Y. 1952. Diss. Cornell University Pr.

**Coppée,** François: Le Pater. 1 acte. Paris: Alphonse Lemerre (53. Aufl. in Französisch) 1889–1897.
Anm.: Ab 1915 auch in engl. Sprache erschienen.

**Coquerel,** Athanase: Notre Père. Etude de la prière enseignée par Jésus-Christ. Paris: Fischbacher 1875. 222 S.

**Corbach,** Liselotte: Jesus lehrt das Vaterunser. In: Die Bergpredigt in der Schule. Göttingen: Vandenhoeck & Ruprecht 1956 ($^2$1962). S. 149–154.

**Cornelius,** Peter: Das Vaterunser in seiner Oper „Cid". In: Ludwig Roll, Peter Cornelius, der Christ; erschienen in: Seele. Regensburg: Habbel 8 (1926). S. 371f.
Anm.: Peter Cornelius komponierte 1854 das Vaterunser zu eigenen Texten nach gregorianischen Weisen.

**Coste,** René: Notre Père sur le Monde. Paris: Ed. Montaigne, Aubier 1966. 254 S.
– Padre Nostro sul mondo. Trad. Benedettine di Rosano. Assisi: Ed. Cittadella 1968. 228 S.

**Couchoud,** Paul-Louis / Audin, Amable: Le carré magique. Une interprétation graphique. In: Latomus. Bruxelles. vol. 17 (1958). Nr. 3, S. 518–527.

**Couet,** Eugène: Notre Pain Quotidien, c'est-à-dire le T. S. Sacrement de l'Autel, par Jean Falconi, traduit et annoté par Eugène Couet. Appendice I; chap. I: Notre pain quotidien c'est l'Eucharistie (par Eugène Couet). Paris: Librairie Eucharistique 1893. S. 184–202.

**Cremer,** Ernst F. M.: Dein Reich komme! Kriegspredigten über das „Vater Unser". Gütersloh: Bertelsmann 1915. 94 S.

**Cremer-Kögel:** Biblisch-theologisches Wörterbuch der neutestamentlichen Gräzität. Darin Literatur über EPIOUSIOS bis 1913; S. 407f. Gotha 1915.

**Creutzberg,** H. W.: Het Gebed des Heeren. Den Haag: C. Cloomendaal 2de druck 1947. 34 S.

**Crosby,** Michael H. OFMCap: Thy will be done. Praying the Our Father as subversive activity. New York: Orbis Books, Maryknoll 1977. VIII, 254 S.

**Crozet,** Léon: Credo secret antique dans un carré magique. In: Bulletin de l'association Guillaume Budé. 4e série Nr. 4. Paris. Dezember 1960. S. 572–578.

**Curé,** Amédée Alexandre: L'Oraison dominicale, ses rapports avec les sept dons du Saint-Esprit, les sept péchés capitaux, les vertus théologiques et cardinales et les béatitudes. Paris: Librairie de l'Œuvre de Saint-Paul 1895–1898.
– L'Oraison dominicale. Ses rapports avec les sept dons du Saint-

Esprit, les Sept Péchés capitaux, les Vertus théologiques et cardinales et les Béatitudes. Instructions sur le „Pater" prêchées dans la chapelle royale de Frohsdorf. Paris: Librairie de l'Œuvre de Saint-Paul 1901–1906.

**Curot,** Abbé J: Le Notre Père au XIXe siècle. Bar-le-Duc: Guerin 1874.

**Curvers,** Alexis: Le carré magique. In: Itinéraires. Paris. Nr. 120 (1968) S. 33–52; Nr. 121 (1968) S. 168–190; Nr. 122 (1968) S. 329–341; Nr. 123 (1968) S. 87–100; Nr. 124 (1968) S. 93–118; Nr. 125 (1968) S. 258–270; Nr. 126 (1968) S. 117–146; Nr. 128 (1968) S. 111–148.

**Cusanus: s. Nicolaus von Cusa.**

**Cuttaz,** François: Le Pater et L'Ave. Sherbrooke (Canada): Ed. Paulines 1966. 31 S.

**Cuvier,** Louis: L'Oraison dominicale expliquée. Avec une notice biographique et portrait. Paris: Fischbacher 1902. 93 S.

**Cyprian von Karthago,** Der heilige: De dominica oratione 4–6. In: Neues Stundenbuch, Bd. 2 (Ergänzungshefte, Väterlesungen; Zeit im Jahreskreis 10.–18. Woche). Einsiedeln – Freiburg: Benziger/Herder 1973. S. 19–32.
– L'Oraison Dominicale, Texte, traduction, introduction et notes par Michel Réveillaud (Publications des Etudes d'histoire et de philosophie religieuses, vol. 58; Université de Strasbourg, Faculté de théologie protestante). Paris: Presses Universitaires de France 1964. 216 S.
– Des heiligen Bischofs und Martyrers Thascius Caecilius Cyprianus Unterweisung über das Gebet des Herrn. Aus dem Lateinischen übertragen von Thomas Michels OSB. Klosterneuburg: Volksliturgisches Apostolat 1935. 54 S.
– Siehe auch unter **Cipriano,** San.

**Cyrillus Hierosolymitanus:** Katechesen. In: Bibliothek der Kirchenväter, Bd. 41, S. 387–390. München: Kösel & Pustet 1922.

**Cyster,** R. F.: The Lord's Prayer and the Exodus Tradition. In: Theology. Edinburgh 64 (1961). S. 377–381.

# D

**D., J.**: Das gemeinsame Vaterunser (Leserbrief). In: Der christliche Sonntag. Freiburg: Herder 15 (1963), S. 192.
Anm.: Weitere Leserbriefe zu diesem Thema in Jhg. 1963, S. 96 u. 174.

**Dacquino,** Pietro: La preghiera del cristiano. In: Bibbia e Oriente. Milano. 5 (1963) Nr. 6, S. 201–205.

**Dali,** Salvador: Paternoster. Milano: Ed. Rizzoli 1966.

**Dalmais,** I.-H. OP: L'introduction et l'embolisme de l'Oraison dominicale dans la célébration eucharistique. In: Lai Maison-Dieu Nr. 85. Paris: Les Éditions du Cerf 1966. S. 92–100.

**Dalman,** Gustaf: Die Worte Jesu. Mit Berücksichtigung des nachkanonischen jüdischen Schrifttums und der aramäischen Sprache. Band I: Einleitung und wichtige Begriffe. Mit Anhang: A. **Das Vaterunser.** Darmstadt: Wissenschaftl. Buchgesellschaft 1965 (unveränderter reprographischer Nachdruck der 2. Aufl. Leipzig, Verlag J. C. Hinrichs, 1930). S. 283–365.

**Damerau,** Rudolf: Das Herrengebet. Nach einem Kommentar des Gabriel Biel (Studien zu den Grundlagen der Reformation, Bd. 3). Gießen: Wilhelm Schmitz 1964. 176 S.
– I. Der Herrengebetskommentar eines Unbekannten. Textkritische Ausgabe. II. 53 Auslegungen des Herrengebets des Karthäuserpriors Johannes Hagen (+1475). Textkritische Ausgabe (Studien zu den Grundlagen der Reformation, Bd. 4). Gießen: Wilhelm Schmitz 1966. 115 S.

**Damian,** Ludwig / Kautzsch, Andreas: Das ‚Vater Unser‘ – heute. Vortragszyklus an fünf Abenden in der Christuskirche Freiburg (Brsg.): 1. Abend (Pfarrer Damian), 9. Okt. 1980: Das Vaterunser in einer vaterlosen Gesellschaft; 2. Abend (Pfarrer Kautzsch), 14. Okt. 1980: Dein Reich komme; 3. Abend (Pfarrer Damian), 16. Okt. 1980: Unser täglich Brot – Überfluß produziert Hunger; 4. Abend (Pfarrer Damian), 21. Okt. 1980: Schuld vergeben?; 5. Abend (Pfarrer Damian), 23. Okt. 1980: Trotzdem loben.

**Daneau,** Lambert: Theses de Oratione Dominica. Leiden 1581. 20 S.

**Daniel-Rops,** Henry: Pater noster. In: Die heilige Messe. Innsbruck: Abendländ. Verlagsanstalt 1952.
– The Pater Noster. In: This is the Mass. New York: Ed. Hawthorn Books 1958. S. 120–123.

**Dante Alighieri:** Orazione domenicale (Divina commedia, Purgato-

43

rio XI, 1–24). Versioni in lingua maltese, sanscrita, siamese, siro-caldaica. Roma: Bibliotheca Besso 1920. jeweils 4 S.

**Darum sollt ihr also beten.** Hrsg.: Bibelmission in Deutschland, Wuppertal: Aussaat-Verlag (101.–135. Tsd.) 1962. 30 S.

**Dassmann,** E./Frank, K. S. (Hrsg.): Die Vaterunser-Erklärung der Magisterregel = pietas. Festschrift für B. Kötting. In: Münster 1980, S. 458–471.

**Dausch,** Petrus: Vaterunser – das Mustergebet. In: Die drei älteren Evangelien (Bonner Bibel, Bd. II). Bonn: Peter Hanstein 1932. S. 121–129.

**David,** Dom.: Il Pater: riflessioni nuove su cose vecchie. Novara: Tipografia Operaia 1893. 16 S.

**David von Augsburg:** Paternoster... s. **Schwab,** F. M.

**Davidson,** John.: The Lord's Prayer. Cleveland, Ohio: Ed. World Publications 1970. 60 S.

**Davies,** William David: Die Form des „Vater Unser". In: Die Bergpredigt. Exeget. Untersuchungen ihrer jüdischen u. früh-christl. Elemente. München: Claudius-Verlag 1970. S. 16 f., 102.
– The Setting of the Sermon on the Mount. London: Cambridge University Press. 1964. 547 S. Besonders zu beachten: S. 4–5, 11 bis 12, 309–313, 451–453.

**Day,** Gardiner Mumford: Lord's Prayer. An interpretation. Oxford / Toronto: Seabury 1954. 98 S.

**Daymard,** Abbé: Le Pater, ou instructions sur l'Oraison dominica-le. Paris: Lethielleux 1903.

**Deane,** Anthony Charles: Our Father. A Study of the Lord's Prayer (Coll. Little Books on the Christian Life). London: Hodder & Stoughton 1938. 128 S.

**Debrunner,** Albert: „Epiousios" und kein Ende. In: Museum Helveticum. Zürich: 9 (1952). S. 60–62.
– „Epiousios". In: Glotta. 4 (1913). S. 249–253.
– EPIOUSIOS. In: Glotta. 13 (1924). S. 167–171.
– Nochmals: „Unser tägliches Brot". In: Schweizerische Theolo-gische Zeitschrift. 30 (1914). S. 38–41.
– „Epiousios". In: Theologische Literaturzeitung. Leipzig. Nr. 5 (1925). Sp. 119.

**Decsy,** G.: Der älteste ungarische Text des Vaterunsers. In: Orbis scriptus. D. Tschizewskij zum 70. Geburtstag; Hrsg.: D. Gerhardt u. a. München: W. Fink 1966. S. 155–161.

**Dein Name werde geheiligt.** Wiesbaden: Wachtturm-Gesellschaft 1963. 383 S.

44

**Dein Wille geschehe auf Erden.** Wiesbaden: Wachtturm-Gesellschaft 1960. 383 S.

**Deissmann,** Adolf: „Epiousios". In: Neutestamentliche Studien. Georg Heinrici zu seinem 70. Geburtstag dargebracht. Leipzig: J. C. Hinrichs 1914. S. 115–119.
– Noch einmal „Epiousios". In: Reinhold-Seeberg-Festschrift, vol. I: Zur Theorie des Christentums. Leipzig 1929. S. 299–306.

**Delcor,** M.: A propos de la traduction œcuménique du „Notre Père". In: Bulletin de Littérature Ècclésiastique. Toulouse: 62 (1970). S. 127–130.

**Delcourt,** Raymond: „Notre Père". Meditations sur l'oraison dominicale. Paris: Ed. Altis 1969. 84 S.

**Delforge,** Frédéric: La Prière du Seigneur. 8 fiches sur le Notre Père. Paris: Christianisme au XX$^e$ siècle 1970. 32 S.

**Della Corte,** Matteo: I Cristiani a Pompei. In: Soc. Reale di Napoli. Rendiconti della Reale Accademia di Archeologia Lettere e Belle Arti. N.S. vol. 19 (1938–1939). S. 3–32.
– Il crittogramma del „Pater noster" rinvenuto a Pompei (con 2 figure). In: Atti della Pont. Accad. Romana di Archeologia (Ser. III). Rendiconti, vol. 12 (1936). S. 397–401.
– Il Crittogramma del „Pater noster". In: Società Reale di Napoli. Rendiconti della Reale Accademia di Archeologia, Lettere et Belle Arti. N.S. vol 17 (1937). S. 79–99.
– Una divinazione di G.B. Rossi, comprovata a Pompei. La presenza dei Cristiani nella città fatale. In: L'Osservatore Romano, Nr. 37 (23.317), S. 2, col. 2–3 (1937).

**Delorme,** J.: La Prière du Seigneur. Pour une catéchèse biblique du „Notre Père". A propos de la nouvelle traduction. In: L'Ami du Clergé. Langres. 75 (1966). S. 225–236.

**Delp,** Alfred SJ: Vater unser. Geschrieben zwischen Verurteilung und Hinrichtung im Gefängnis zu Tegel. Sonderdruck aus „Stimmen der Zeit" 72 (1946), Heft 1. Freiburg: Herder 1947. 23 S.
– – Lizenzausgabe Herder Wien 1947. 20 S.
– Vater unser. In: Im Angesicht des Todes. Frankfurt: Verlag Josef Knecht 1947. S. 115–129.
Anm.: „Im Angesicht des Todes" auch in der Herderbücherei als Lizenzausgabe (Bd. 30) 1958 erschienen.

**Denis-Boulet,** Noele-Maurice: Das Pater noster (Einführung des Pater noster in die Messe – Der Ort des Pater noster innerhalb der Messe seit Gregor d. Gr. – Das Pater noster als Vorbereitungsgebet auf die Kommunion. Libera). In: Aimé-Georges Martimort u.a.: Handbuch der Liturgiewissenschaft. Freiburg: Herder 1963.

– La place du Notre Père dans la liturgie. In: La Maison-Dieu. Paris: 1966. Nr. 85, S. 69–91.

**Denn Dein ist das Reich:** s. **Schimmel, Annemarie.**

**Denys le Chartreux:** Doctoris Ecstatici D. Dyonisii Cartusiani Opera Omnia. Tome XI: Enarratio in Evang. sec. Matthaeum, art. 13; Expositio Orationis Dominicae: S. 79–82; Tome XII: Enarratio in Evangelium sec. Lucam, art. 29: Expositio in Orationem Dominicam: S. 27–30. Montreuil: 1900–1901.

**Deuster, Adolf:** Das Wagnis des Vaterunsers. Freiburg: Herder 1952. 103 S.
– Erlöse uns von dem Übel (Leserbrief). In: Der christliche Sonntag. Freiburg: Herder 3 (1951). S. 288.

**Dhôtel, Jean-Claude:** Note sur les anciennes traductions françaises du „Pater". In: La Maison-Dieu. Paris: 1965. Nr. 83, S. 148–157.
– Richesse et infortunes de l'Oraison Dominicale dans l'histoire de la catéchèse. In: Catéchistes. Paris: 1966. S. 135–149.

**Díaz, Alonso SJ:** El Padre Nuestro dentro del Problema General de la Escatología. In: Collectanea Theologica. Miscelánea Comillas XXXIV–XXXV. Comillas: Universidad Pontificia 1960. S. 297–308.
– El problema literario del Padre Nuestro. In: Estudios Bíblicos. Madrid: vol. XVIII (1959). S. 63–75.

**Diaz, Esteban E.:** Confirmación hebrea de que hay una errónea traducción en la versión castellana del Padrenuestro (11 Q Ps°, Ps 155,11). In: Cultura biblica. Segovia, 25 (1968). S. 300–302.

**Dibelius, Martin:** Die dritte Bitte des Vaterunsers. In: Botschaft und Geschichte. Gesammelte Aufsätze von Martin Dibelius. Tübingen: J. C. B. Mohr 1953. Bd. 1. S. 175–177.
Anm.: Dieser Beitrag erschien auch in: Christliche Welt. 54 (1940). Sp. 52f.

**Dibelius, Otto:** Das Vaterunser. Umrisse zu einer Geschichte des Gebets in der alten und mittleren Kirche. Gießen: A. Töpelmann 1903. IX, 180 S.
– Das Vaterunser der deutschen Not. Halle: C. Ed. Müller 1921. 56 S. (2. Aufl. 1925, 67 S.).

**Di Capua, Francesco:** Il criptogramma di Pompei. In: L'Osservatore Romano. Nr. 74 (31. 3. 1937). S. 3, col. 2–6.

**Didaskalia** (1976) Heft 6: Die ganze Nummer der in Lissabon erscheinenden Zeitschrift behandelt das Vaterunser in der portugiesischen Literatur und bei den portugiesischen Mystikern.

46

**Dienemann,** Max (Rabbiner): „Kerngebet aller christlichen Kirchen ist das ‚Vaterunser'". In: Die Lehren des Judentums, Bd. III, Teil 5. Leipzig 1929, S. 428.
Anm.: Obiger Ausspruch auch zitiert in: Schalom Ben Chorin: Jesus im Judentum. Wuppertal, 1970, S. 41 u. f.

**Diepen,** Rudolf: Meditation zum Vaterunser. In: Christ in der Gegenwart. Freiburg: Herder 27 (1975). Nr. 21, S. 166.

**Diercks,** G. F. (Hrsg.): Tertullianus, Q.: Septimius Florus Tertullianus De Oratione. Critische uitgave met Prolegomena. Vertaling en philologisch-exegetisch-liturgische Commentaar door G. F. Diercks. Bussum: P. Brand 1947. Zum Thema „Vaterunser" s. 127 f.

**Dietzfelbinger,** Hermann: Das heilige Vaterunser. In: Bauer, Herbert: Die heiligen zehn Gebote. Der kirchliche Unterricht an der Volksschule. München: Evangel. Presseverband für Bayern 1954.
Anm.: Von obigem Beitrag erschien gekürzte Nachschrift in der Bibelwoche (als Ms. gedruckt). 1960. 62 S.

**Dillersberger,** Josef: Der Blick auf den Vater. In: Matthäus, Das Evangelium des heiligen Matthäus in theologischer und heilsgeschichtlicher Schau. Bd. II: Der Meister in Wort und Wunder. Salzburg: Otto Müller 1952. S. 102–113.
– Das Gebet des Herrn. In: Lukas, Das Evangelium des heiligen Lukas in theologischer und heilsgeschichtlicher Schau. Bd. IV: Auf dem Wege nach Jerusalem. Salzburg: Otto Müller 1941. S. 88 bis 97.

**Dini,** A.: Il „Padre Nostro" è preghiera pubblica? In: Aspernas. Organo dell'accademia ecclesiastica napolitana. Napoli, vol. 10 (1963). S. 391–407.

**Dinkler,** Erich: SATOR AREPO. In: Die Religion in Geschichte und Gegenwart. Tübingen: J. C. B. Mohr 1961. 3., völlig neu bearb. Aufl. Bd. 5, Sp. 1373–1374.

**Dion,** G. M.: Documents pour une nouvelle traduction en Kinyarawanda du „Notre Père". In: Théologie et Pastorale au Rwanda et au Burundi. Bujumbura, 8 (1968). S. 30–38.

**Dirichs,** Josef: Das frühchristliche lateinische Kreuzworträtsel SATOR AREPO zu Ende erklärt. In: Theologie und Glaube. Paderborn: Schöningh 40 (1950). S. 529–534.
– Nachtrag zu „Das frühchristliche lat. Kreuzworträtsel Sator Arepo…". In: Theologie und Glaube. Paderborn. F. Schöningh. 41 (1951). S. 339–340.

**Dirks,** Walter: Vaterunser. Mit Vorwort von Rolf Baumann (S. 98).
In: Bibel heute. Stuttgart: Verlag Kath. Bibelwerk. 1. Quartal
(1974). S. 100–107.
– Unser Vater und das Vaterunser (Kleine Schriften zur Theolo-
gie). München: Kösel 1972. 150 S.
– Unser Vater. Rand- und Vorbemerkungen zu einem aktuellen
Tatbestand. In: Hochland. München: Kösel 60 (1967–1968). S. 193
bis 200.
– Von der Vatergüte Gottes und dem Elend der Menschen. In:
Christliche Besinnung. Würzburg: Werkbund-Verlag 1951. S. 115
bis 136.

**Dit bidden wij … dit belijden wij.** De kern van ons christelijk geloof
(Het Onze Vader/Het Credo; Medewerkers: A. G. Barkey Wolf,
J. J. Buskes, W. I. Doude van Troostwijk e. a.). Zwolle: La Rivière &
Voorhoeve 1970. 184 S.

**Doane,** Pelagie / Talbot, Dorothy: The Lord's Prayer and The
Beatitudes. Illustrated. London: Foulsham 1955. 24 S.

**Dobschütz,** Ernst von: The Lord's Prayer. In: Harvard Theological
Review. vol. 7, H. 3 (Juli 1914). S. 294–321.

**Doehring,** Bruno: Das Vaterunser mitten ins Leben hinein.
Predigtreihe, im Dom zu Berlin gehalten. Berlin: Beenken 1938.
76 S.

**Dölger,** Franz-Joseph: „Unser tägliches Brot". Das eine Brot als
Tagesbedarf und das halbe Brot des Einsiedlers Paulus. In: Antike
und Christentum. Münster: Aschendorff. vol. 5 (1936). S. 201–210.
– Echo aus Antike und Christentum. 47.: Die SATOR-Formel ein
richtiger Krebs. In: Antike und Christentum, vol. 3 (1932). S. 278
bis 279.
– Die Fischdenkmäler in der frühchristlichen Plastik, Malerei etc.
In: Ichthys. Münster: Aschendorff. vol. V (1932). S. 57–64, 253–257.

**Domergue,** Marcel SJ: Notre Père (Coll. Prions). Toulouse: Ed.
Prière et Vie 1965. 64 S. (ill.).

**Donders,** Adolf: Gott, mein Vater. In: Gott im Alltag. Köln:
Katholische-Tat-Verlag 1932. S. 25–30.

**Dörig,** Bruno/Schäfer, Hans Ulrich: Meditationen zum Vater unser
und zum Meditationsbild des Bruder Klaus. Ökumenischer Medita-
tionstext, hrsg. Luzern: Zentralstelle Fastenopfer; Basel: Brot für
Brüder 1982. 16 S. mit farbiger Wiedergabe des Meditationsbildes
von Bruder Klaus.

**Dorn,** Käthe (d. i. Rosa Springer): Das Vaterunser in neun Erzählungen dargestellt. Stuttgart: Christl. Verlagshaus (36.–38. Ts.)
1934. 240 S.

**Dornseiff,** Franz: ἐπιούσιος im Vaterunser. In: Glotta. Göttingen: Vandenhoeck & Ruprecht vol. 5 (1956). S. 145–149.
Anm.: Außerdem erschienen in: Kleine Schriften. Leipzig: Köhler & Amelang 1964. Bd. II, S. 248–255.
– Das Rotas-Opera-Quadrat. In: Zeitschrift für die neutestamentliche Wissenschaft. vol. 36 (1937). S. 222–238.

**Dorr,** Karl Raphael: Wenn ihr betet... Suchet zuerst das Reich Gottes. In: Bergpredigt in dieser Zeit. Wien: Cura-Verlag 1966. S. 101 f.

**Dorries,** Bernhard: Erklärung des kleinen Katechismus D. Martin Luthers. Teil 3: Das Vaterunser und die Sakramente. Göttingen: Vandenhoeck & Ruprecht 1. u. 2. Aufl. 1926. IV, 132 S.

**Douen,** Emmanuel-Orentin: Essai sur l'Oraison Dominicale. Straßburg: Berger-Levrault 1853.

**Drake,** Hurd Allyn: Devotional Study of the Lord's Prayer: Our Father. Higley (Ind.): Butler 1950. 91 S.

**Dravins,** K.: Das Hasentöterische lettische Vaterunser. In: Studi Baltici. Firenze: NS 1 1952. S. 211–230.

**Dreissen,** Josef: Der du bist ... In: ,,Frohen Sonntag!". Leutesdorf: Johannes-Verlag 1978. Zitiert in: Christ in der Gegenwart. Freiburg: Herder 32 (1980), S. 15.
– ,,Wenn ihr nicht werdet wie die Kinder ...". Eine theologisch-missiologische Besinnung auf das Vaterunser. In: Katholische Frauenbildung. Paderborn: F. Schöningh 62 (1961). S. 333–350.

**Drouzy,** M. O. P.: Le ,,Pater", Prière du Christ. In: La Vie Spirituelle. Paris, 93 (1955). S. 115–134.

**Dryander,** D. E.: Das Vaterunser, in acht Predigten ausgelegt. Halle a. S.: Richard Mühlmann's Verlag (2. Taus.) 1912. 135 S.

**Dubor,** G. de: Le Pater au XIIe siècle. In: Bulletin archéologique et historique publ. sous la direction de la Société Archéologique de Tarn-et-Garonne. vol. 4 (1876). S. 99–100.

**Dulac,** Odette: Le Notre Père des Petits. Lyon: Mappus 1952. 24 S.

**Du läßt uns Vater sagen.** In: Der Weinberg. Mainz: Verlag der Oblaten. Heft 11, 1947.

**Dümling,** Werner (Hrsg.): s.**Vater unser im Himmelreich.**

**Dunkmann,** Karl: Das Gebet des deutschen Volkes. Akademische Reden über das Vaterunser. Dresden: C. L. Ungelenk 1915. 62 S.

**Du, unser Vater.** Jüdische Gebete für Christen. Ausgewählt u. übersetzt von Pnina Navè. Mit einem Vorwort des Bischofs von

Straßburg, Léon Arthur Elchinger (Veröffentlichungen der Stiftung „Oratio Dominica"). Freiburg: Herder 1975. IX, 114 S.

**Dunstan,** Ruth: Pray around the World; six stories across the world illustrating the Lord's Prayer; with notes for teachers etc. London: Society for the propagation of the Gospel 1963. 45 S.

**Dupont,** Jacques (en collaboration avec Pierre Bonnard): Le Notre Père: notes exégétiques. In: La Maison-Dieu Nr. 85. Paris: Les Éditions du Cerf 1966. S. 7–35.
Anm.: Ders. Beitrag auch enthalten in: Notre Père qui es aux cieux. La prière œcuménique (Cahiers de la Traduction Œcuménique de la Bible Nr. 3). Paris: Les Éditions du Cerf / Les Bergers et les mages 1968. S. 77–115.

**Dürig,** Walter: Das Vaterunser in der Messe. In: Gemeinde im Herrenmahl. Zur Praxis der Meßfeier. Hrsg. Theodor Maas-Ewerd u. Klemens Richter. Freiburg: Herder 1976. 2. Aufl. S. 323–330.
– Die Deutung der Brotbitte des Vaterunsers bei den lateinischen Vätern bis Hieronymus. In: Liturgisches Jahrbuch. Münster: Aschendorff 18 (1968). S. 72–86.
– Die Exegese der vierten Vaterunser-Bitte bei Augustinus. In: Liturgisches Jahrbuch, Münster: Aschendorff 22 (1972), S. 49–61.

# E

**E., A.:** Das Vaterunser auf der Straße. In: Der christliche Sonntag. Freiburg: Herder 1 (1949). S. 341.

**Ebeling,** Gerhard: Unser Vater. Predigt über Matt 6,9a. Bad Cannstatt: Müllerschön 1959. 12 S.
– Vom Gebet. Predigten über das Unser-Vater. Tübingen: J. C. B. Mohr 1963. 144 S.
Anm.: Auch als Siebenstern-Taschenbuch Nr. 89: München: Siebenstern-TB-Verlag 1967. 125 S. erschienen.
– On Prayer. Nine sermons. Philadelphia, Pa: Fortress 1966. 145 S.
– The Lord's Prayer in today's world. Transl. by James W. Leitch. London: SCM Press 1966. 140 S.

**Eberle,** Josef: „Das ‚Unser Vater' ein schoen Gebet…" In: „Hier irrt Goethe von A–Z". Stuttgart: DVA 1973. S. 21.

**Eckhart, Meister:** Opera latina. Auspiciis Inst. S. Sabinae in Urbe ad codicum fidem ed. Fasc. 1: Super oratione dominica. Ed. Raymundus Klibansky. Roma 1934. XVI, 17 S.

– Tractatus super Oratione Dominica. Hrsg.: Erich Seeberg. In: Die deutschen und lateinischen Werke II: Die latein. Werke, vol. 5. Stuttgart: W. Kohlhammer 1936. S. 101–129.

**Edwards,** J. K.: The word „Epiousios" in the fourth petition of the Lord's Prayer. In: Zeitschrift für wissenschaftl. Theologie. vol. 29 Nr. 3 (1886). S. 371–378.

**Eger,** Josef CSSR: Das ‚Gebet des Herrn' als ‚Form' christlichen Betens. In: Du darfst beten. Augsburg: Winfried-Werk 1961. S. 96 bis 104.
– Das Vaterunser keine Gebetsformel, sondern Form allen Betens. In: Wir dürfen beten. Freiburg: Seelsorge-Verlag 1971. S. 80.

**Ehrenberg,** W.: Was drückt das Vaterunser aus? In: Das edle Leben. Zeitschr. für prakt. Philosophie u. Lebensmeisterung. Stuttgart, 8 (1959). S. 3–6.

**Ehrhard,** Albert: Das Vaterunser. Akademische Predigten. Mainz: Kirchheim 1912. XI, 132 S.

**Eicher,** Peter: Das tägliche Brot. In: Christ in der Gegenwart (34) 1982, S. 73. Freiburg: Verlag Herder.

**Einiger,** Christoph (Hrsg.): Die schönsten Gebete der Welt. München: Südwest-Verlag 1964; 5. Aufl. 1973. 480 S.

**Einleitung in die Heilige Schrift.** Hrsg. André Robert / André Feuillet. Bd. II: Neues Testament. Zum Thema Vaterunser: S. 143, 697. Wien / Freiburg: Herder ²1965.

**Ein Schritt zur Wiedervereinigung im Glauben** (Das Gebet Vaterunser). In: Die Seele. Regensburg: 24 (1948). S. 344.

**Ein Vaterunser für die ganze Woche.** Auswahl der Gebete und Buchschmuck von Elisabeth Reuter. Berlin: Evangel. Verlagsanstalt. 5. Aufl. 1967. 8 Bl.

**Ein Zeichen.** Die Vaterunser-Kapelle im Ibental. Mit Einführung von Eugen Walter (Veröffentlichungen der Stiftung „Oratio Dominica"). Freiburg: Herder 1969 (2. Aufl. 1976). 347 S. mit zahlr. Abbildungen.

**Eisenberg,** Wilhelm: Unser Vater im Himmel. Acht Kriegspredigten über das Gebet des Herrn. Marburg: Elwertsche Verlagshdl. 1916. 71 S.

**Eisenhofer,** Ludwig: Vaterunser. In: Grundriß der Liturgik des römischen Ritus (5. Aufl. neu bearbeitet von Joseph Lechner). Freiburg: Herder 1950. S. 43 f.
Daraus:
– Vaterunser im Brevier: S. 326, 334;

– – in der Messe: S. 201, 222f.;
– – im Taufritus: S. 244f.;
– Zur Paternoster-Einleitung der römischen Messe. In: Archiv für Liturgiewissenschaft. Regensburg: 4 (1956). S. 325–340.

**Eisgruber,** Tilde: Das Vaterunser und Ave Maria. Eine farbige Bilderfolge. Begleitwort von Basilius Hermann. Nürnberg: Sebaldus-Verlag 1926. 39 S.

**Eissing,** Dieter: Gebetseinladungen zum Vaterunser. In: Gottesdienst. Freiburg: Herder. 15 (1981). S. 35–36.

**Eitrem,** S.: The SATOR AREPO Formula once more. In: Eranos. Zürich: Rhein-Verlag 48 (1950). Nr. 2, S. 73–74.

**Ejder,** Bertil: Om spräket i Herrens bön pa svenska i äldere tid. In: Svensk teologisk kvartalskrift. 54 (1978) Nr. 3, S. 110–118.

**Elbern,** Josef SJ: Das Vaterunser – Gebet der Christenheit. In: Frau im Leben. Augsburg: Verlag des Winfried-Werks Josef Hall. April 1978, S. 14.

**Elliott,** Norman K.: How to BE the Lord's Prayer. The Drift, Evesham, Worcs.: Arthur James Ltd. 143 S.

**Elsner,** Martin: „Dein Wille geschehe". In: Die Christengemeinschaft. Stuttgart: Verlag Urachhaus 39 (1967). S. 39–41.

**Emmanuel,** Pierre: Notre Père. Les Béatitudes. Poèmes. Suivi d'illustrations de Loo. Paris: Ed. du Seuil 1969. 62 S.

**Emmanuel,** S. M.: Notre Père qui êtes aux cieux. Lyon: I. A. C. 1944.

**Emminghaus,** J. H.: Artikel: „Satorformel". In: Lexikon für Theologie u. Kirche. Bd. IX, Sp. 343–344. Freiburg: Herder 1964.

**Engel,** J.: Maria lehrt uns das Vaterunser beten. In: Weihestunden. Gelegenheitsreden. Breslau: Aderholz 1931. 280 S.

**Englebert,** Omer: Die Grotte der Erleuchtung, auch Vaterunser-Grotte genannt. Deutsche Ausgabe. Jerusalem: Bermarome (o. J.). 20 S.

**Erasmus von Rotterdam:** Und vergib uns unsere Schuld. In: Christ in der Gegenwart. Freiburg: 27 (1975). S. 237.

**Erdmann,** G.: Gibt es ein aramäisches Ur-Vaterunser? In: Deutscher Forschungsdienst. Bad Godesberg: 9 (1962). H. 20. Bl. 1–2.

**Ermoni,** V.: Jésus et la Prière dans l'Evangile. Chap. 2: L'Oraison Dominicale (Science et religion, études pour le temps présent, vol. 404). Paris: Bloud 1907. S. 21–36.

**Espinassous,** Alphonse d': Philosophie de l'Oraison Dominicale. Liège: Ledoyen 1859.

**Esplugnes,** Miguel d': El Pare Nostro: gloses apologétiques. 4 volls. Barcelona: Ed. Poliglota 1923. 284, 270, 275, 285 S.
Anm.: Das Werk ist in katalan. Sprache erschienen.
– El Pare Nostro... In: Resena Eccles. vol. 15. Monserrat: 1923. 279 S.

**Essenwein,** Albert: Das Vaterunser, Neun Predigten. Stuttgart: Holland & Josenhans 1925. 47 S.

**Eßer,** Kajetan OFM.: Die dem hl. Franziskus von Assisi zugeschriebene Expositio in Pater Noster. In: Collectanea Franciscana. Roma, 40 (1970) S. 241–271.

**Eule,** Wilhelm: Zwei Jahrtausende Bibelbuch. S. 192–193: Das Vaterunser in 155 Sprachen. Gütersloh: Gerd Mohn 1960.

**Euringer,** Sebastian: Das Sator-Arepo-Quadrat. Aberglaube oder Arkandisziplin? In: Historisches Jahrbuch der Görres-Gesellschaft. München – Freiburg: Verlag Karl Alber 71 (1952). S. 334 bis 353.

**Evans,** Christopher F.: The Lord's Prayer (Seraph Books). London: S.P.C.K. 1963. 103 S.

**Evely,** Louis: Notre Père. Aux sources de notre fraternité (Coll. Action féconde). Paris: Ed. Fleurus 1956. 171 S.
– Manifest der Liebe: Das Vaterunser. Übersetzt von Maria Wahl. Freiburg: Herder 1958 (7. Aufl. 1967). 151 S.
– Entmythologisieren wir das Vaterunser. In: Das Gebet eines modernen Menschen. Graz: Styria 1969. S. 157–181.
– We dare to say Our Father, New York: Herder & Herder 1965; London: Burnes & Oates 2nd ed. 1967. 129 S.
– Padre nostro. – Alle sorgenti della nostra fraternità. Trad. G. Belleri. Milano – Torino – Roma: Ed. Ancora 5. ed. 1969. 152 S. –
– Nuestro Padre. Trad. M. M. Muñoz Jimenez Millas. Madrid: Ed. Atenas ODER 6. ed. 1967. 207 S.
– Unser Vater. In: Maria vom guten Rat. Würzburg 1969. Heft Juni/Juli. S. 32–35.

**Evertsbusch,** St. Friedr.: Das Vaterunser oder das Christenthum als Gebet. Lennep: Richard Schmitz 1861. 330 S.

**Exbrayat,** Idebert: Notre Père ou la prière révolutionnaire (Collection Croire – Penser – Espérer). Genève: Editions Labor et Fides 1955. 170 S.

# F

F.: Zur Gebetspraxis – Der göttliche Magnet (Fiat voluntas tua). In: Seele. Regensburg: Habbel 10 (1928). S. 60f.

**Failla,** Carmelo (Hrsg.): La Preghiera del Signore: s. **Cipriano, San.**

**Fangmeier,** Jürgen: Fünf Unservater-Predigten. Zürich: EVZ-Verlag 1965. 39 S.

**Farrar,** F. W.: Exegetic Studies on the Lord's Prayer. In: The Expositor. 4th ser. vol. 7 (1893). S. 38–49, 283–293.

**Fattinger,** Josef: Vaterunser. In: Der Katechet erzählt, Bd. II. Ried im Innkreis 1935. S. 273–278.

**Faulhaber,** Michael Kardinal von: Die vierte Vaterunser-Bitte. Hirtenbrief Fastenzeit 1948. München: Erzbischöfl. Ordinariat 1948. 5 S.
– Das Vaterunser am Silvesterabend. In: Zeitrufe, Gottesrufe. Gesammelte Predigten aus den Jahren 1922 bis 1932. Freiburg: Herder. (2. Aufl.) 1933. S. 222–231.
Anm.: In diesem Werk auch beachten: S. 16: Vaterunser, „das schönste aller Gebete"; S. 56: Vierte Vaterunserbitte; S. 145 f.: Ehrenplatz in der heiligen Messe.
– Das Vaterunser im Völkerkrieg. M.-Gladbach: B. Kühlen 1917. 24 S. m. 1 Abb.

**Faustmann,** Karl: Das Vaterunser, das beste Gebet. In: Aus tiefem Brunnen. Das deutsche Sprichwort. Freiburg: Herder 1920. Nr. 3163–3167, S. 307.

**Federer,** Heinrich: Vater unser, der du bist im Himmel. Eine Weihnachtsgeschichte aus dem Schneegebirge. Basel: Hess 1955. 159 S.

**Fedini,** Theofilo: Breve Discorso sopra l'Oratione Dominicale. Lyon: S. di Honorati 1559.

**Feesche,** Marie: Vater unser. Gedichte mit Dürerbildern. Hannover: Feesche 1933. 40 S.

**Feiten,** Josef: Vaterunser. Ein religiöses Spiel aus dem Jahr 1917. Paderborn: Junfermann 1925. 24 S.

**Feneberg,** Wolfgang: Persönliches Beten – aber wie? In: Wie heute beten? Hrsg. Georg Sporschill. Stuttgart: Verlag Kath. Bibelwerk 1973. S. 40, 43, 45 f.

**Fensham,** F. Charles: The Legal Background of Mt 6,12. In: Novum Testamentum. Leiden. vol. 4 (1960). S. 1–2.

**Ferrua,** A.: Sull' esistenza di christiani a Pompei. In: Civiltà Cattolica. 88 (1937). vol. 3, S. 127–139.

**Fertala,** F.: „Erlöse uns von dem Übel". Zum richtigen Verständnis der 7. Vaterunser-Bitte. In: Schweizerische Kirchenzeitung. Luzern, 117 (1949). S. 114–117.

**Fesenmayer,** Gebhard OFMCap: Das Beten zum Vater. In: Deine Zwiesprache mit Gott (Reihe Franziskanische Lebenswerte). Zürich: Thomas-Verlag; Paderborn – Wien: Schöningh 1956. S. 157 bis 161.

**Feuillet,** André (Hrsg.): s. **Einleitung in die Heilige Schrift,** Bd. 2.

**Fiebig,** Paul: Vater unser! Kriegsgebetstunden. Leipzig: M. Koch 1914. 31 S.
– Das Vaterunser. Ursprung, Sinn u. Bedeutung des christl. Hauptgebetes (Beiträge zur Förderung christl. Theologie, Bd. 30, H. 3). Gütersloh: Bertelsmann 1927. 106 S.

**Filson,** Floyd V.: Were there Christians in Pompeii? In: The Biblical Archeologist. vol. 2, Nr. 2 (1939). S. 14–16.

**Fink,** Stephan: Semina, Bd. IV: Inter spinas. Fasten- u. Sylvesterpredigten, darin auch zum Thema Vaterunser. Rottenburg: Bader 1931.

**Fischer,** Anton: Vater unser. In: Anwander, Anton: Wörterbuch der Religion. Würzburg: Echter 1962. S. 566f.
– Das eschatologische Vaterunser der Urkirche. In: Eine heilige Kirche. München: Ernst Reinhardt 23 (1942). S. 126–131.

**Fischer,** Balthasar: Warum hat das Pater noster einen Vorspruch und einen „Nachsatz"? In: Was nicht im Katechismus steht. Trier: Paulinus-Verlag 1952. S. 115–118.
– Formen privater Tauferinnerung im Abendland: Das Herrengebet als Tauferinnerung. In: Liturgisches Jahrbuch. Münster: Aschendorff 9 (1959). S. 161f.
– Unser Tischgebet. In: Volk Gottes um den Altar. Trier: Paulinus-Verlag 1960. S. 31–33.

**Fischer,** Carl: Die Zusammenhänge des heutigen Weltgeschehens mit dem Vaterunser und die Zusammenhänge des vierten Tieres und des kleinen Horns (Dan 7,8–11) mit dem Antichristentum der Endzeit. Gräflich Wiese, Oberschlesien. Selbstverlag des Verfassers 1930. 24 S.

**Fischer,** E.: Luther und das Vaterunser. In: Deutsch-evangelische Blätter. 30 (1905). Nr. 1, S. 35–65.

**Fischer,** Hermann: Das liebe Vaterunser. Vollständ. Gebetbuch für jedermann im Geiste und mit den Worten des Vaterunsers. Steyl / Kaldenkirchen: Missionsdruckerei 1920. VIII, 266 S.

**Fishwick**, Duncan: On the Origin of the Rotas-Sator Square. In: The Harvard Theological Review. Cambridge (Mass) vol. 57 Nr. 1 (1964). S. 39–53.

**Fleischmann**, Alfons: Das neue Vaterunser. Zwei Ansprachen im Bayerischen Rundfunk am 12. u. 19. Mai 1968 (Manuskript der Kath. Morgenfeier „Glauben heute", Abt. Kirchenfunk). 13 S.

**Flunk**, Matthias: ὁ ἄρτος ἐπιούσιος (Matth 6,11; Lk 11,3). In: Zeitschrift für kath. Theologie. 13 (1889). S. 210–212.

**Focke**, Friedrich: Sator arepo. Abenteuer eines magischen Quadrats. In: Würzburger Jahrbücher für die Altertumswissenschaft. Würzburg: Verlag Ferdinand Schöningh 3 (1948). S. 366–401. Mit vier Tafeln.

**Foerster**, W.: Artikel EPIOUSIOS. In: Kittel, Theologisches Wörterbuch zum Neuen Testament, Bd. II. Stuttgart: Kohlhammer 1935. Sp. 578–595.

**Fogle**, Willa: Notre Père. Trad. de l'anglais par Mary Stirling. Paris: Dangles 1959. 107 S.

**Ford**, J. Massingberd: The forgiveness Clause in the Matthean Form of Our Father. In: Zeitschrift für die neutestamentliche Wissenschaft und die Kunde der älteren Kirche. Berlin: Alfred Töpelmann 59 (1968). S. 127–131.
– Yom Kippur and the Matthean Form of the Pater Noster. In: Worship. Collegeville (Minn.). vol 41 (1967). S. 609–619.

**Förster**, Friedrich Karl: Was bedeuten eigentlich die Worte: „Dein Wille geschehe"? In: Die Friedensstadt. Paderborn: 14 (1951). S. 58–60.

**Foucauld**, Charles de: Deutung des Vaterunsers. In: Beten – Lieben – Glauben. Unveröffentlichte Meditationen. München: Rex-Verlag 1970. S. 12–22.

**Foucault**, J.-A. de: Notre pain quotidien. In: Revue des Etudes Grecques. Paris, 83 (1970). S. 56–62.

**Fourgez**, Jean Isaac: L'Oraison Dominicale expliquée et considerée comme la plus excellente des prières vocales, suivie de l'exposition de l'Ave Maria. Paris: Berche et Tralin 1870. 356 S.

**Fox**, Emmet: The Lord's Prayer. An interpretation. London: The Rally 1932. 63 S.
– Das Vaterunser (The Lord's Prayer, German Edition). Eine Auslegung (UNITY-Buchreihe). Pforzheim: Verlag Helmut Theodor Frick, Abt. UNITY (4. deutsche Auflage) 1978. 43 S.

**Fraine,** Jean de SJ: Prier avec la Bible. Les antécédents bibliques de grandes prières chrétiennes. Bruges / Paris: Ed. Beyaert 1961. 246 S.
– Art.: Oraison Dominicale. In: Dictionnaire de la Bible. Paris: Letouzey & Ané 1960. fasc. 33, Sp. 788–800.
– Praying with the Bible. The biblical Bases of great Christian Prayers. Transl. by Wynne Saul. Tournai: Desclée 1964. VIII, 182 S.
– Bijbelsbidden. De bijbelse achtersgrond van grote gebeden (Pater Noster, Magnificat etc). Brugge / Bruges: Beyaert 1960. 256 S.

**François de Sales:** Paraphrase de l'oraison dominicale adressée à une de ses filles spirituelles (Œuvres de Saint Francois de Sales, éd. complète, tome 26, opuscule 53). Annecy, Monastère de la Visitation 1932. S. 377–419.

**Frankenmölle-Stieler,** Renate u. a.: Das Herrengebet. In: Gebet für heute. Hildesheim: Bernward-Verlag 1970. S. 10f.

**Franz von Assisi:** Die Auslegung zum Gebet des Herrn. In: Jungclaussen, Emmanuel OSB: Beten mit Franz von Assisi. Freiburg: Herder 1976. S. 79–82.
– Pater noster. In: Otto Karrer, Gottesminne. München: Verlag Ars sacra 1929. S. 74–77.
– Expositio super orationem dominicam. In: Opera omnia (Medii Aevi Bibliotheca Patristica. Series prima, Bd. 6). Paris: Imprimerie de la Bibliothèque Ecclesiastique 1880. Sp. 253–254.

**Frei,** Hans: Herr, lehre uns beten. Acht Predigten über das Vaterunser. Schönewerd (Schweiz): Christkatholisches Schriftenlager 1952. 40 S.
Anm.: Die Broschüre ist im gleichen Umfang erschienen in Zürich: EVZ-Verlag 1965.

**Fresenius,** W.: Beobachtungen und Gedanken zum Gebet des Herrn. In: Evangelische Theologie. München: 20 (1960). S. 235 bis 239.

**Freudenberger,** Rudolf: Zum Text der zweiten Vaterunserbitte. In: New Testament Studies. London/New York. vol. 15 (1968–69) Nr. 4 (1969). S. 419–432.

**Freundorfer,** Joseph Bischof: Das Vaterunser. Predigtreihe während der St. Ulrichs-Festwoche 1957. In: Klerusblatt. Eichstätt/München: 37 (1957), Nr. 20–24: S. 340f., 357f., 373f., 393f., 410f.
– Unser Vater. In: Vorsehung, Leid und Krieg. Biblische Gedanken. Würzburg: 1940. S. 76f.

Frey, Jean-Baptiste: Le Pater est-il juif ou chrétien? In: Revue Biblique. Paris. vol. 12 (nouvelle série) (1915). S. 556–563.

Freytag, Hermann (Hrsg.): Das Vaterunser: s. Bynwalth, Matthias.

Fridrichsen, Anton: ΑΡΤΟΣ ΕΠΙΟΥΣΙΟΣ. In: Symbolae Osloenses. II (1924). S. 31–41.
– ARTOS EPIOUSIOS. Eine Nachlese. In: Symbolae Osloenses. IX (1930). S. 62–68.

Friedrich, Hans: Das Vaterunser in trüben Tagen. Gütersloh: C. Bertelsmann 1921. 120 S.

Fries, Nikolaus: Bilderbuch zum heiligen Vaterunser. Neun Erzählungen. Stuttgart: J. F. Steinkopf (20. Aufl.) 1927. 306 S.
– L'Oraison dominicale en action. Neuf récits. Trad. de l'allemand par Ch. Galopin-Schaub. Neuchâtel: Sandoz et Thuillier 1882.

Frohnmeyer, Karl: Art.: Vaterunser. In: Calwer Bibellexikon. Stuttgart: Calwer Verlag 3. Aufl. 1973. Sp. 1379f.

Frugoni, Arsenio: „Sator Arepo Tenet Opera Rotas". In: Rivista di Storia e Letteratura Religiosa. Firenze, vol. 1 (1965). Nr. 3. S. 433 bis 439.

Fry, McGregor: A Provisional New Translation of the Lord's Prayer. In: The Bible Translator. London: United Bible Societies. vol. 18 (1967). Nr. 3. S. 123–125.

Fuchs, Ernst: Gebet und Gebetssituation (dabei auch Vaterunser). In: Evangelische Theologie. München: Chr. Kaiser 29 (1969). S. 133–144.
– Unser Vater. Predigt über Luk 16,19–31. Stuttgart-Bad Canstatt: Müllerschön 1960. 7 S.

Fuchs, Friedrich: Vater unser – Das ewige Gebet des Christen. Zu den Vaterunser-Holzschnitten von Ruth Schaumann. In: Caritas-Kalender 1946. Freiburg: Caritas-Verlag. S. 25–42.
– Vaterunsergeist in der Gemeinde. In: Der Volksverein für das kath. Deutschland. M.-Gladbach 40 (1930). H. 2, S. 18–26.

Fuchs, Harald: AREPO. In: Theologische Zeitschrift. Basel: Reinhardt 5 (1949) Nr. 6, S. 468–469.
– Die Herkunft der Satorformel. In: Schweizerisches Archiv für Volkskunde. Basel: 47 (1951). S. 28–54.

Fuetterlin, Magdalena: Das Vaterunser an der Krippe. In: Walburgis-Blätter. Eichstätt. 1939. S. 134.
Anm.: Ist aus dem handgeschriebenen Gebetbuch der 1528 verstorbenen Klosterfrau von Abtei St. Walburg.

Fugel, Gebhard: Jesus lehrt beten: s. Lippert, Peter.

**Führich,** Joseph: Das Gebeth des Herrn. Neun Bleistiftzeichnungen zum Vaterunser. Mit einer Einleitung von Hans Geller. Als Privatdruck erschienen. Berlin: Verlag Gebr. Mann 1958.
– Das Vaterunser. Das Gebet des Herrn. In neun Blättern gezeichnet und radiert von Joseph Führich und mit einem ausführlichen Text begleitet von Anton Müller. Prag: P. Bohmanns Erben 1826.

**Funke,** Alexander: Unser aller Gebet. Gladbeck: Schriftenmissions-Verlag 1960. 1 gef. Blatt.

**Furberg,** Ingemar: Das Pater noster in der Messe (Bibliotheca Theologiae Practicae, Bd. 21). Lund: CWK Gleerups Förlag 1968. XXXIII, 275 S.

# G

**Gaber,** A.: Gotteskindschaft. In: Seele. Regensburg: Josef Habbel. 4 (1922). S. 173f.

**Gadient,** Rudolf: Vaterunser. In: Schweizerische Kirchenzeitung, Luzern; Datum der Veröffentlichung nicht bekannt. Zitiert in: Klerusblatt, Eichstätt / München 1968, Nr. 7, S. 118.

**Gaechter,** Paul SJ: Das Vaterunser. In: Das Matthäus-Evangelium. Ein Kommentar von Paul Gaechter. Innsbruck: Tyrolia 1963. S. 209–222.

**Gaglio,** A.: Le sette domande del Pater Noster. In: Rivista Liturgica. 15 (1928). S. 45–48.

**Gagov,** Giuseppe: La soluzione di un antico crittogramma Sator arepo. In: Miscellanea Francescana. Roma: 61 (1961). Nr. 2–3, S. 276–282.

**Galli,** Mario von: Unser Vater Unser. Zürich: Pendo Verlag 1977. 104 S.
– Die ganze Welt... im Vaterunser. Abdruck aus: „Unser Vater Unser". In: Ruhrwort, Essen, 19 (1977), Nr. 50, S. 9 vom 10. Dezember.

**Galot,** Jean SJ: Unser Vater. In: Gott unser Vater. Deutsch von Adolf Rodewyk SJ. Paderborn: Verlag der Bonifacius-Druckerei 1963. S. 41, 174–179.
– Il „Padre" nella preghiera liturgica. In: La Civiltà Cattolica. Roma: 1972. Quad. 2917 anno 123. vol. 1, Nr. 1, S. 8–17.

**Gäng,** Richard: Das Vaterunser in alemannischer Sprache. In: Badische Zeitung. Freiburg, 7./8. Dez. 1968.

**Gansfort,** Wessel: De oratione et modo orandi cum luculentissima dominicae orationis expositione. Erschienen Venedig 1614. Hiervon Bearbeitung von A. J. Persijn: Wessel Gansfort. De oratione dominica. In een dietse bewerking. Assen: Van Gorcum 1964. 178 S. Siehe auch unter **Persijn,** A. J.

**García Consuegra,** Manuel: Padre nuestro, version moderna. Santa Clara, Cuba 1963. 1 Bl.

**Garofalo,** Salvatore: Il „pater noster", (Quaderni della Radio Nr. 41). Roma: Ed. RAI Radio Italiana 1955. 109 S.

**Garreau,** Albert: Notre pain de chaque jour. Roman. Paris: Aubier, Éditions Montaigne 1953. 238 S.

**Garriga,** P.: Un nou Parenostre i la llibertat dels cristians. In: Questions de Vida Cristià. Monserrat. vol. 51 (1970). S. 112–119. Anm.: In katalanischer Sprache erschienen.

**Gatterer,** Michael SJ: Vom Gebet und vom Vaterunser. In: Das Religionsbuch der Kirche – Catechismus Romanus. Innsbruck: Felizian Rauch 1932. Seitenverweis nicht bekannt.

**Gay,** Teofilo: Il Padre nostro. 12 conferenze popolari. Firenze: Tipografia Cooperative 1885. 70 S.

**Gay,** Volney P.: Public rituals versus private treatment. Psychodynamics of prayer. In: Journal of religion and health. New York. 17 (1978). S. 244–260.

**Das Gebet des Herrn.** In Wort und Bild erklärt von Josef Wisdorf und Johannes Hohmann. Essen: Fredebeul & Koenen 1967. 31 S.

**Das Gebet des Herrn – unser Gebet.** In: Kirche und Leben, Münster. 14. März 1965.

**Das Gebet des Herrn.** In: Wunderbare Welt. Ein Bildungsbuch für Jungen und Mädchen. Freiburg: Herder 1958 (6. Aufl. 1963). S. 242 bis 246.

**Gebet des Herrn.** In: Leitfaden für das Studium der christlichen Wissenschaft. Verfaßt in Zusammenarbeit von Emmy Bütikofer, Max Kappeler, Milly Rudin, Betty Schurter. Teil 3: Gebote, Seligpreisungen, **Gebet des Herrn.** Zürich: E. T. Gramm 1949. 36 S.

**Das Gebet des Herrn.** Handreichung zur Jahresaufgabe der Evang. Reichsfrauenhilfe für 1939/40. Potsdam: Stiftsges.-Verlag 1939. 64 S.

**Das Gebet des Herrn,** ein Spiegel der Seele. München: Pfeiffer 1937. 4 Bl.

**Das Gebet des Herrn.** In Konferenzansprachen erklärt und ausgelegt. Hrsg.: Ernst Modersohn. Bad Blankenburg: Buchdruckerei u. Verlag „Harfe" 1927. 32 S.

**Das Gebet des Herrn in den Sprachen Rußlands.** Slavistische Studienbücher, VII. Photomechanischer Nachdruck der Ausgabe St. Petersburg 1870. Mit Nachwort hrsg. von Wolfgang Veenker. Wiesbaden: Otto Harrassowitz 1971. XII, 91 S.

**Gebetswoche für die Einheit der Christen 1973.** Darin: II. Zum Vaterunser. Freising: Kyrios-Verlag 1973. S. 3–4.

**Gebet- und Gesangbuch für das Bistum Berlin.** Darin: Andacht über das Gebet des Herrn. 1941. S. 454f.

**Gebser,** Augustus Rudolphus: De Oratione Dominica. Pars I et II. Königsberg: Georgius Greis 1830.

**Gedanken zu den Bitten des Vaterunsers.** Mit Graphiken von L. Holtz-Halfing. In: Missionskalender der Benediktinermissionare von St. Ottilien. St. Ottilien: Eos-Verlag 48 (1951). S. 33–34, 45–46, 55–56, 65–66, 77–78, 87–88, 97–98, 107–108.

**Geiss,** Gottlieb: Sieben Bitten zum Herzausschütten. Betrachtungen zum Vaterunser (Der Schatz im Acker, Bd. 10). Neukirchen-Vluyn: Verlag des Erziehungsvereins 1960. 107 S.

**Gennadius Scholarios:** Œuvres complèts. Tome IV: Paraphrase de l'oraison dominicale. Paris: Bonne Presse 1935. S. 344–348.

**Gennaro,** C.: Il Padre mio e il Padre vostro. In: E. Ancilli (ed.): Mistero del Dio vivente. Roma: 1968. S. 73–81.

**Genovesi,** Piero: Padre nostro que sei con noi. Romanzo. Milano: Casa Editrice Ceschina 1955. 100 S.

**George,** Augustin SM: Ne nous soumets pas à la tentation... Note sur la traduction nouvelle du Notre Père. In: Bible et Vie chrétienne. Paris: 71 (1966). S. 74–79.
– Jésus Fils de Dieu dans Saint Luc. 6: Les prières de Jésus. In: Revue Biblique. Paris: 72 (1965). S. 203–206.

**Gerbert,** Gustav: Das Vaterunser heute. In: Werkbuch Kanzelarbeit, Bd. V: Predigten über die Liebe. Innsbruck: Tyrolia 1961. S. 119–157.

**Gerhardsson,** Birger: Fader vär i Nya Testamentet. In: Svensk teologisk kvartalskrift. 54 (1978) Nr. 3, S. 93–102.

**Gerson-Kiwi,** Edith: Musik der Bibel (Schallplatte). Düsseldorf: Schwann.

**Geyer,** Margarete: Das Vaterunser still gebetet. Recklinghausen: Paulus-Verlag 1948. 2 Bl.

**Giacomo dalla Pieve:** Catechismi sopra l'orazione domenicale. Genova: Tipografia della Gioventù 1875. 108 S.

**Giavini,** G.: Abbiamo forse in Mt 6,19 – 7,11 il primo commento al „Pater Noster"? In: Rivista Biblica Italiana. Brescia, 13 (1965). S. 171–177.

**Gickler,** Dominicus OP: Ewigkeitswerte im Alltag. Gedanken über das Leben aus dem Gebete des Herrn. Kevelaer: Josef Bercker 1924. 142 S.

**Giesen,** Traugott: Was hält und trägt. Das Vaterunser für unsere Zeit. Gütersloh: Gütersloher Verlagshaus (GTB/Siebenstern, 1028) 1981. 64 S. m. zahlreichen Fotos.

**Giglinger,** Fritz/Heiss, Wolfgang: Lieber Bruder Franz. Einladung zum einfachen Leben. Das Buch ist nach dem Vaterunser gegliedert. Thaur/Tirol – Wien: Österreichischer Kulturverlag (1. Aufl.) 1979; (2. Aufl.) 1980. 280 S.

**Gihr,** Nikolaus: Gedanken über katholisches Gebetsleben im Anschluß an das Vaterunser und an das Ave Maria. Freiburg: Herder (5.–9. Tsd.) 1916. X, 326 S.
– Vaterunser. In: Das heilige Meßopfer, dogmatisch, liturgisch u. aszetisch erklärt. Freiburg: Herder (17.–19. Aufl.) 1922. S. 614–628.

**Gij, onze Vader.** Joodse gebeden voor christenen. Uitgekozen door Pnina Navè (holländisch-flämische Ausgabe von Du, unser Vater. Freiburg: Herder). Brugge: Uitgeverij Emmaus; Boxtel: Katholieke Bijbelstichting 1977. 124 S.

**Gilles de Rome:** Primus Tomus Operum: Expositio in Orationem Dominicam. Roma: apud Antonium Bladum 1565. S. 1–7.

**Gillet,** Grete von (Hrsg.): Vater unser im Himmelreich, der Du uns alle heißest gleich… Karlsruhe: Evang. Presseverband für Baden 1947. 24 S.

**Giordani,** Igino: Il „Padrenostro" preghiera sociale. Brescia: Morcelliana 1946. 83 S.

**Giuseppe Vincenzo dell'Eucaristia:** Il Pater Noster. In: Bibbia e Preghiera. Lezioni del 3º corso di Spiritualità sulla Preghiera (Fiamma Viva Nr. 3). Roma: Istituto di Spiritualità dei Carmelitani Scalzi di Roma 1962. XII, 270 S.

**Give us this Day**. A boy learns the meaning of the Lord's Prayer. Narrated and illustrated by Jussi Aarnio, Aarno Hammar, Pekka Kosonen, Eero Veneskoski. Camden, New Jersey: Thomas Nelson Inc. 1967. 72 S.

**Glötzle,** Ludwig / Knöpfler, Alois: Das Vater Unser im Geiste der ältesten Kirchenväter in Bild und Wort dargestellt. Mit 9 Heliogravüren. Freiburg: Herder (3. Aufl.) 1911 (Erstauflage 1899) VI, 46 S. Text.

**Gnilka,** Josef / Jungmann, Josef Andreas SJ: Vaterunser – das „Gebet des Herrn". In: Lexikon für Theologie u. Kirche, Bd. 10. Freiburg: Herder 1965. 2. Aufl., Sp. 624–629.

**Goetz,** Diego Hanns OP: Das Vaterunser der Liebenden. Wien: Herold-Verlag 1952. 342 S.

**Goldmann,** Maria Andrea (Hrsg.): s. **Brentano,** Clemens von: Das Vaterunser.

**Goltz,** Eduard Frh. von der: Das Gebet in der ältesten Christenheit. Leipzig: J. C. Hinrichs 1901. S. 35–53, 190.

**Goltzen,** Herbert: Das neue Vaterunser. In: Zeitwende. Die neue Furche. Hamburg: 39 (1968). H. 7, S. 471–477.

**Golubiew,** Antoni: Briefe an Freund Jan. Wenn man beten will (40 Betrachtungen im Anschluß an die drei ersten Vaterunser-Bitten). Aus dem Polnischen übersetzt von Elise Eckert u. Otto Karrer. München: Ars sacra-Verlag 1963. 255 S.

**Gomez,** M. Antonieta: ... Asì en la Tierra ... (Colección F, Bd. 5). Madrid/Barcelona: Editorial Magisterio Español, S. A. (2. Aufl.) 1969. 85 S.

**Gonnet,** J.: Les „Glosa Pater" cathares et vaudoises. In: Cathares en Languedoc (Cahiers de Fanjeaux, 3). Toulouse: E. Privat 1968. S. 59–67.

**Gordan,** Paul: Die Politik des Vaterunsers. In: Ruhrwort. Essen. Jg. 19, 8. Okt. 1977.

**Gore,** Charles: Prayer and the Lord's Prayer. With an introduction by Angus Dun. New York / London: Harper / G. Allen 1947. XV, 124 S.

**Gössmann,** Wilhelm u. Elisabeth: Das sei euer Gebet. In: Die Bergpredigt. München: Max Hueber 1965. S. 31 f.

**Götte,** Michaela: Die Vaterunser-Kapelle im Ibental. Zulassungsarbeit zur 1. Prüfung für das Lehramt an Grund- u. Hauptschulen. Dozent: Prof. W. Flamm. Freiburg: Frühjahr 1971.

**Götz,** Arnulf OFM: Vom Vaterunser. In: Münchener Kath. Kirchenzeitung, 32 (1939), 7. Mai, S. 290.

**Goulder,** M. D.: The Composition of the Lord's Prayer. In: The Journal of Theological Studies. New Series vol. XIV. Oxford: The Clarendon Press 1963. S. 32–45.

**Graber,** Rudolf: Das Vaterunser – eucharistisch. In: Für das Leben der Welt. Nürnberg: Johann Michael Sailer Verlag 1960. S. 109 bis 112.

**Gräf,** Richard CSSP: Macht des Gebetes. Darin zum Thema Vaterunser: S. 90f. Regensburg: Friedrich Pustet 1957.
– Herr, lehre uns beten. Darin zum Thema Vaterunser: S. 107, 263f., 267f. Regensburg: Friedrich Pustet 1939.
– Ja Vater. Alltag in Gott. Darin zum Thema Vaterunser: S. 15. Regensburg: Friedrich Pustet (6. Aufl.) 1937.

**Grässer,** Erich: Das Problem der Parusieverzögerung in den synoptischen Evangelien und in der Apostelgeschichte. In: Beihefte zur Zeitschrift für die Neutestamentliche Wissenschaft 22: S. 95 bis 113: Die Bitte um das Reich. Berlin: Töpelmann 2. Aufl. 1960 (1. Aufl. 1957).

**Grassi,** J. A.: Our Father. In: The New Catholic Encyclopedia. New York: vol. 10 (1967). S. 829–831.

**Gratry,** Alphonse: Das wesentlichste Gebet. In: Der christliche Sonntag. Freiburg: Herder 3 (1951). S. 213.

**Greet,** Kenneth Gerold: The Relevance of the Lord's Prayer today (Little Book of Kindly Light, 2. Ser. Nr. 20). London: Epworth (Methodist Publ. House) 1952. 18 S.

**Gregor von Nyssa:** Lord's Prayer (and the Beatitudes). Translated and annotated by Hilda Graef (Ancient Christian Writers, Bd. 18). London-Westminster: Longmans / Newman 1954. 210 S.
– Über das Gebet des Herrn. In: Bibliothek der Kirchenväter, Bd. 56: Des heiligen Bischofs Gregor von Nyssa ausgewählte Schriften. München: Kösel & Pustet 1927. Zum Thema Vaterunser: S. 89–150.

**Greiner,** Albert: Joie du Notre Père. Paris / Strasbourg: Editions luthériennes-Librairie Oberlin 1959. 63 S.
– Die Freude des Vaterunsers. Aus dem Französ. von Marie-Louise Leininger-Wolff u. Peter Göpfert. Hrsg. Theodor Heckel. München: Evang. Luth. Dekanat 1964. 31 S.

**Greinwald,** Josef: Herr, lehre uns beten. In der Gebetsschule des Vaterunsers (Mt 6,5–16; Lk 11,1–13). Privatdruck für die Bibelgemeinde von St. Martin in Landshut. 1945. 8 S.

**Grellner,** Cajus OFM: Vater unser. In: Vom Altar ins Leben. Werl: Dietrich-Coelde-Verlag 1960. S. 122, 131.

**Grelot,** Pierre: La quatrième demande du Pater et son arrière-plan sémitique. In: New Testament Studies. 25 (1979) S. 299–314.

**Grente,** Georges Kardinal: Notre Père. Paris: Librairie Arthème Fayard 1953. 268 S.
– Das Gebet der Brüderlichkeit. Vom Sinn des Vaterunsers für unsere Zeit. Aus dem Französ. von Dr. Martha Rohrbach. Paderborn: Bonifacius-Druckerei 1956. 225 S.
– Our Father. Dublin: Scepter 1959. 224 S.
– Padre nostro. Trad. di A. Belardinelli. Milano: Vita e Pensiero 1955. X, 198 S.

**Griebel,** Benno: Das gemeinsame Vaterunser. Leserbrief zu Streiflicht (SZ Nr. 260). In: Süddeutsche Zeitung, München, 24./25./26. Dez. 1965.

**Grillparzer,** Franz: Vater unser. In: Werke. Ausgabe des Hesse-Verlags, Leipzig, I, S. 44f.
Anm.: Zitiert in: Otto Karrer, Jahrbuch der Seele. 1951, S. 272f.

**Grimm,** Leonhard: Das Vaterunser. In: Der katholische Christ in seiner Welt, Bd. II. Freiburg: Herder 1947. 2. Aufl. S. 401f.

**Gros,** Erwin: Unser Lebensbekenntnis. Neun Andachten über das heilige Vaterunser. Stuttgart: Kohlhammer 1914. 25 S.

**Grosser,** Felix: Ein neuer Vorschlag zur Deutung der SATOR-Formel. In: Archiv für Religionswissenschaft. vol. 24, Nr. 1–2 (1926). S. 165–169.

**Grossouw,** W. K.: Das Reich Gottes – Der Geist der Kindschaft – Wie im Himmel, so auf Erden. – Vergib uns unsere Schuld. In: Das geistliche Leben. München: Ars sacra 1952. S. 11–13, 401–403, 471–473, 785–787.
– Der Vater im Himmel – Das Kommen des Reiches. In: Biblische Frömmigkeit. München: Ars sacra 1956. S. 21–34, 35–45.

**Grou,** Jean Nicolas (1731–1803): Marks of true devotion and the Christian Sanctified by the Lord's Prayer. London: Burns & Oates 1962. XI, 165 S.

**Gruber,** Andreas: Das erste Vaterunser (im neuen Jahr). In: Künde die Botschaft. München / Freiburg: Wewel 1974. S. 112–117.

**Grunau,** Simon: s. **Schmidt,** Wolfgang P.: Zu Simon Grunaus Vaterunser.

**Grundmann,** Walter: Das Evangelium nach Lukas. S. 227–235; Jesus lehrt seine Jünger beten (Lk 11,1–13; Mt 6,9–13; 7,7–11)

(Theol. Handkommentar zum NT, Bd. 3). Berlin: Evang. Verl. Anst. 6. Aufl. 1971. XV, 457 S.
– Das Evangelium nach Matthäus. S. 197–206: Die Gebetsdidaché des Matthäus 6,7–15; Lk 11,1–4; Mk 11,25f. (Theol. Handkommentar zum NT, Bd. 1). Berlin: Evang. Verl. Anst. 2. Aufl. 1971. XX, 580 S.

**Gryglewicz,** F.: Le texte primitif de l'oraison Dominicale (en polonais). In: Zesz Nauk KUL 5,2. 18 (1962). S. 17–31.

**Gspann,** Johannes Chr.: Das Vaterunser als Spiegel der katholischen Weltanschauung. In: Das Neue Reich. 6 (1924) S. 920–922.

**Guardini,** Romano: Der Herr. Betrachtungen über die Person und das Leben Jesu Christi. Vaterunser: S. 123, 281, 546. Würzburg: Werkbund-Verlag 13. erw. Aufl. 1964 (1. Aufl. 1937).
– The Lord. Transl. by Elinor Castendyk Briefs. Chicago: Regnery 1954. XI, 535 S.
– Le Seigneur. Méditations sur la personne et la vie de Jésus-Christ. Trad. par R. P. Lorson SJ. Paris/Colmar: Ed. Alsatia 1946.
– Il Signore. Meditazioni sulla persona e la vita di N. S. Gesù Christo. Trad. di Raffaele Forni. Milano: Vita e Pensiero 1949. XV, 573 S.
– Das Gebet des Herrn. Mainz: Matthias Grünewald Verlag (9. Aufl.) 1965; (1. Aufl. 1932) 112 S.
– The Lord's Prayer. Transl. by Isabel McHugh. London: Burns & Oates 1958. 125 S.; New York: Pantheon Books 1958.
– La prière du Seigneur. Trad. par J. Ancelet-Hustache (Collection „Livre de vie"). Paris: Edition du Seuil 1965. 128 S.
– Het gebed des Heren. Den Haag: Lannoo 1963. 144 S.
– Gebet und Wahrheit. Meditationen über das Vaterunser. Würzburg: Werkbund-Verlag 1960. 216 S.
– Prière et verité. Meditations sur le Notre Père. Trad. de Jeanne Ancelet-Hustache. Paris: Ed. du Cerf 1966. 236 S.
– Gebed en waarheid. Meditaties over het Onze Vader. Vertaling: Hans Wagemans. Bussum: P. Brand 1961. 226 S.
– Das Gebet zum Vater. In: Vorschule des Betens. Mainz: Matthias-Grünewald-Verlag 1948. S. 132–135.
– Das Pater noster: Gottes Weite: Die christliche Blickrichtung. In: Parochia. Hrsg. Karl Borgmann. Kolmar: Alsatia-Verlag 1935. S. 202–206.
– Der Wille Gottes. In: Vom lebendigen Gott. Mainz: Matthias-Grünewald-Verlag 1936. S. 47–56.

**Guarducci,** Margherita: Il misterioso „Quadrato magico": l'interpretazione di Jérôme Carcopino e documenti nuovi. In: L'Archeologia Classica. Roma: vol. 17 Nr. 2 (1965). S. 219–270.

**Guerry,** Emile-Maurice Erzbischof: Der Vater im Himmel. Kurze biblische Betrachtungen (Sammlung Licht vom Licht. Neue Folge Bd. XI). Darin: 78. Betrachtung: Das Vaterunser – Erster Teil: S. 238–240; 79. Betrachtung: Das Vaterunser – Zweiter Teil: S. 240–243. Einsiedeln: Benziger Verlag 1963.
Anm.: Die franzős. Originalausgabe erschien (11. Aufl. 1947) unter dem Titel „Vers le Père" im Verlag Desclée De Brouwer & Cie. in Paris).

**Guignebert,** Ch.: Le Pater. In: Mélanges G. Glotz, vol. I. Paris 1932. S. 417–430.

**Guillet,** Jacques SJ: Das Gebet des Sohnes als Quell des Betens im Evangelium – Das Gebet Jesu als Kraft des Gebetes der Apostel. In: Vom rechten Beten. Hrsg. Peter Henrici. Frankfurt: Josef Knecht 1965. S. 15–30.

**Gülden,** Josef: Mitherausgeber von „Der Mensch als Bruder" (mit Beitrag „Unser tägliches Brot heute"): s. **Unser tägliches Brot heute.**
– Jahr des Herrn 1970. Ein Hausbuch vom Vaterunser. Leipzig: St. Benno-Verlag 1970. 432 S.
– Gewissensbildung und Gewissenserforschung nach dem Vaterunser. In: Lehre uns beten. Regensburg: Josef Habbel 1948. S. 44 bis 53.
Anm.: Obiger Beitrag auch in Petrusblatt, Berlin 1948. S. 2.
– Gewissensbildung nach dem Vaterunser. In: Parochia. Hrsg. Karl Borgmann. Kolmar: Alsatia-Verlag 1935. S. 359–364.
– Pater noster (in der heiligen Messe). In: Volksliturgie und Seelsorge. Hrsg. Karl Borgmann. Kolmar: Verlag Alsatia 1942. S. 117 f.
– Lebenslauf nach dem Vaterunser. In: In den Tagen des Alters verlaß mich nicht. Regensburg: Josef Habbel 1963. Vater-unser-Bezug: S. 27, 28–30.

**Gundlach,** Anton: Gebet des Herrn. Cf. 63 Bildband. 46 Dias mit Text. Freiburg: Verlag der Calig 1940.

**Gunnarson,** Gunnar: Mein Vater im Himmel. Wuppertal-Barmen: Kiefel-Verlag 1970. 20 S.

**Günther,** Hans: Vater-Unser! Predigten mit einem Vorwort von Paul Conrad. Neuruppin: Evangel. Gemeindebund (3. Aufl.) 1925. 93 S.

**Die gute Adresse.** Meditationen zum Vaterunser. Mit Beiträgen von Johann Ev. Baumgartner, Hermann Dietzfelbinger u. a. Hrsg. Georg Heckel. München: Claudius Verlag 1977. 112 S.

**Gutzwiller,** Richard: Vater unser. In: Meditationen über Lukas. Einsiedeln: Benziger 1954 (hier: Sonderausgabe für die Bonner Buchgemeinde). II, S. 34–39.
– Das Vaterunser. In: Meditationen über Matthäus. Einsiedeln: Benziger 1934 (hier Sonderausgabe für die Bonner Buchgemeinde). I, S. 81–100.

**Guyot,** Bertrand Georges: A propos de quelques commentaires sur le Pater Noster. In: Revue des Sciences Philosophiques et Théologiques. Paris: Vrin 56 (1972). I.: S. 245–255; II.: S. 423–432.

**Gypkens,** Franz: Das Vaterunser. Frankfurt (Main): Main-Verlag 1961. 82 S.
– Vater unser. Erklärung in acht Predigten. In: Einkehr und Heimkehr. Hildesheim: Borgmeyer 1946. S. 47–87.
– Herr, dein Wille geschehe, wie im Himmel… In: Weinberg. Mainz: Verlag der Oblaten. H. 4, 1967.

# H

**Haag,** Herbert: Vater unser. In: Bibel-Lexikon (Hrsg. Herbert Haag). Einsiedeln: Benziger. (2. Aufl.) 1968. Sp. 1813–1815.
– Wenn ihr betet… (Reihe Theologische Meditationen, Bd. 16). Einsiedeln: Benziger 1967. 59 S.
– Zum neuen deutschen Vaterunsertext. In: Universitas. Stuttgart: 24 (1969). H. 5, S. 537–543.
– Zum neuen deutschen Vaterunser-Text. In: Neue Zürcher Zeitung vom 3. Nov. 1968.

**Haberl,** Hans: Die hohe Kunst. Zwölf Studien über das Gebet des Herrn. Wuppertal-Barmen: E. Müller 1929. 32 S.

**Habitz,** Franzjosef: Das neue Vaterunser. Zur Geschichte der Doxologie. In: Deutsche Tagespost. Würzburg: 8./9. Dez. 1967.

**Hadidian,** D. Y.: The Meaning of „Epiousios" and the Codices Sergii. In: New Testament Studies. London: vol. 5 Nr. 1 (Oktober 1958). S. 75–81.

**Haes,** Paul de: Op aarde als in de Hemel. Brugge: Beyaert 1963. 322 S.
– Quonam sensu Deus dicitur Pater noster? In: Collectanea Mechliniensia. Mechelen: vol. 38 (1953). S. 551–557.

**Hallam,** A. D.: Tradukoj de la Patro Nio Milla wa Milla. In: Biblia Revuo. Ravenna 4 (1968). S. 50.

**Haller,** Heinrich: s. **Paternoster-Auslegung.**

**Hamman,** Adalbert OFM: Le Notre Père dans la catéchèse des Pères de l'Eglise. In: La Maison-Dieu. Paris: Les Editions du Cerf 85 (1966). S. 41–68.
– Le Pater, expliqué par les Pères. Présenté et traduit par Adalbert Hamman OFM. Paris: Editions Franciscaines (1. Aufl. 1952); nouvelle édition 1961. 232 S.
– Il „Padre nostro" spiegato dai Padri della Chiesa. Trad. dal francese di Carlo Falconi. Milano: Edizione Comunità 1954. XII, 146 S.
– La Prière. vol. I: Le Nouveau Testament. 1959. Zum Thema Vaterunser: S. 94–134; vol. II: Les trois premiers siècles. 1963. Zum Thema Vaterunser: S. 275–279, 280–284, 308–314. Tournai – Paris: Desclée.

**Handreichung zur 23. Bibelwoche 1960/61 über das Vaterunser** (Matth. 6, 9–13): Herr, lehre uns beten. Ausgel. v. Paul Toaspern. Berlin: Evang. Verlags-Anstalt 1960. 91 S.

**Handschrift Andechs:** Pater noster. In: Otto Karrer, Wie unsere Väter beteten. München: Ars sacra 1927. S. 77–79.

**Hanhart,** Brigitte u. Bernadette: S Vatterunser. I d Mundart übertreit von Käthi Born. Mönchaltorf / Hamburg: Nord-Süd-Verlag 1971. 32 S.

**Hanne,** Johannes R.: Das Gebet des Herrn. In: Jahrbücher für deutsche Theologie. vol. 11 (1866). S. 507–522.
– Artikel: Gebet des Herrn. In: Bibellexikon. Hrsg. Daniel Schenkel. Bd. 2. Leipzig: F. A. Brockhaus 1869. S. 346–350.

**Hanß,** Josef: Vaterunser. In: Kurze und lehrreiche Beispiele für den neuen Katechismus. Limburg: Steffen 1925. S. 428f.

**Häring,** Bernhard CSSR: Gebet – Gewinn der Mitte. Graz: Styria 1975. Ausdrückliche Bezüge auf das Vaterunser: S. 12, 68, 135.
– Geheiligt werde dein Name. In: Liebe ist mehr als Gebot. Lebenserneuerung aus dem Geist der Bergpredigt. München – Freiburg: Wewel 1968. S. 46, 47–50.
– Lobpreis des Namens Gottes. In: Christ in einer neuen Welt. München – Freiburg: Wewel 1959. S. 276–278.
– Vaterunser (keine Gebetsformel!). In: Das Gesetz Christi, Bd. 2. München – Freiburg: Wewel, 7. Aufl. 1963. S. 245f.

**Harnack,** Adolf von: Die ursprüngliche Gestalt des Vaterunsers. In: Sitzungsberichte der Königl. Preuß. Akademie der Wissenschaften. Berlin: Reimer 7. 1. 1904. S. 195–208.

**Harner,** P. B.: Understanding the Lord's prayer. Philadelphia: Fortress 1975. 144 S.

**Härtel,** Alfons (Stuttgart): Unser täglich **Brot gib** uns heute und **vergib** uns unsere **Schuld,** wie auch wir vergeben unseren Schuldigern. Eine Betrachtung für heimatsuchende Menschen aller Art. Augsburg: Druck G. Weber 1947. 16 S.

**Hartmann,** Franz: Das Vaterunser und dessen mystische Bedeutung. In: Theosophie. Bd. 12 (1924). S. 321–327.

**Hasselbach,** Ulrich von: Änderung des Vaterunsers? Statt „Erlöse uns von dem Übel" – „Erlöse uns von dem Bösen". In: Christ und Welt. Stuttgart: 9 (1956). Nr. 25, S. 6.

**Hatzfeld,** Johannes: Vaterunsergeist in der Gemeinde. München: Ars sacra 1931. 30 S. m. Abbildungen.
– Das Vaterunser. In: Vom Reiche Gottes. Paderborn: Vlg. der Bonifacius-Druckerei 1940. S. 77–90.

**Hauck,** Friedrich: ἄρτος ἐπιούσιος. In: Zeitschrift für die Neutestamentliche Wissenschaft und die Kunde der älteren Kirche. Berlin: Töpelmann 33 (1934). S. 199–202.

**Haugg,** Donatus: Pater noster. In: Vom Geheimnis der heiligen Messe. München: Kösel 1936. S. 127 f.

**Häuser,** Erwin: Das gemeinsame Vaterunser (Leserbrief). In: Der christliche Sonntag. Freiburg: Herder 15 (1963), S. 96.
Anm.: Weitere Leserbriefe als Erwiderung in Jhg. 1963, S. 174 u. 192.

**Hauser,** Laurentius: Vater unser! Gebetbuch für kath. Christen. München: Kath. Volkskunst-Anstalten 1922. 320 S.

**Hausherr,** Irenée SJ: Prière de vie – vie de prière. Chap. III: Le Notre Père (Coll. Vie spirituelle et vie intérieure). Paris: Lethielleux (3. Aufl.) 1965. S. 75–88.
Anm.: Außerdem erschienen in: La vie spirituelle. vol. 113 (1965). S. 689–695.
– Das Vaterunser. In: Leben aus dem Gebet. Hrsg. Michel Olphe-Galliard SJ. Salzburg: Otto Müller 1969. S. 66–79, S. 93.

**Haussleiter,** Johannes: Artikel: Vaterunser. In: Realenzyklopädie für protestantische Theologie und Kirche. Leipzig: J. C. Hinrichs. (3. verb. u. verm. Aufl.) 1908. S. 431–445.

**Häussling,** Angelus OSB: In der Not des Endes. Die Funktion des Embolismus. In: Heiliger Dienst. Salzburg: 21 (1967) F. 2, S. 66–69.

**Hayer,** Gerold (Hrsg.): Pater-noster-Auslegung: s. **Pottenstein,** Ulrich von.

**Hebbel,** Friedrich: preist die einzigartige Schönheit des Vaterunsers in seinen „Tagebüchern" (zitiert in der „Schöneren Zukunft" vom 13.3.1938, S.615 u. im Sonntagsblatt zur „Kreuznacher Zeitung" vom 25. Sept. 1921).

**Hebestreit,** Wilhelm: Das Vaterunser unserer Zeit. In: Sonntagsblatt für die katholische Familie (Hrsg. Alfons Heilmann). 64 (1938), S. 402.

**Hecher,** Joseph: Predigten über das Vaterunser. Stuttgart: Joseph Roth'sche Verlagsbuchhdlg. 1898. VIII, 366 S.

**Heckel,** Georg: s. **Die gute Adresse.**

**Heggelbacher,** Othmar: Vater unser! Die Botschaft Christi in ihrer kürzesten Fassung (Werkstunden-Bücherei Nr. 57). Amorbach: Verlag Albert Burgmaier 1937. 16 S.

**Hegyi,** Pater SJ: Vater unser. Vorgetragen in den „Exerzitien für jedermann", gehalten in Fürstenried bei München vom 20. bis 24. September 1978. Als unveröffentlichtes Manuskript vorhanden.

**Das heilige Vaterunser:** s. **Becker,** Karl.

**Heimanns,** H.: Das Kriegs-Vaterunser der Heimgebliebenen. 8 S. – Das Kriegs-Vaterunser des Soldaten. 8 S. Beide: M.-Gladbach: B. Kühlen 1915.

**Heinen,** Anton: So sollt ihr beten: Vater unser, der du bist im Himmel. In: Die Bergpredigt Jesu Christi. M.-Gladbach: Volksverein-Verlag 1921. S. 102–133.
Anm.: Eine 2. Aufl. 1926 erschienen; hier S.109–145.

**Heinrici,** Georg: Beiträge zur Geschichte und Erklärung des Neuen Testaments, Bd. III, 1: Die Bergpredigt Matth. 5–7, Luk. 6,20–49 begriffsgeschichtlich untersucht. 2. Aus der Hinterlassenschaft des Petrus von Laodicea. Leipzig: Dürrsche Buchh. 1905. III, 120 S.

**Heinz-Mohr,** Gerd: Vater unser im Himmel... Die Anrede des Vaterunsers in der Geschichte der Auslegung. In: Deutsches Pfarrerblatt, Neukirchen-Vluyn. Januar 1969. S. 12–14.

**Heiss,** Wolfgang: Lieber Bruder Franz: s. **Giglinger,** Fritz.

**Heiter,** A.: s. **Montifontanus,** P. Luzian.

**Helbich,** Hans-Martin: Geborgen in allen Ängsten. Gedanken zum Vaterunser, weitergegeben für Menschen unserer Zeit. Berlin: Christl. Zeitschr.-Verlag 1966 (5. Aufl. um 1975). 95 S.

**Helewa,** G.: La Preghiera del cristiano „Abba! Padre!" In: Rivista di Vita Spirituale. Roma, 25 (1971).

**Heller,** Johannes: Die sechste Bitte des Vaterunsers. In: Zeitschrift für katholische Theologie. Wien, vol. 25 (1901). S. 85–93.

**Helmholdt,** W.: Das türkische Vaterunser in Hans Schiltbergs Reisebuch. In: 1): Folia Orientalia. Krakow: vol. 6 (1964 ed. 1965). S. 247–249; 2): Central Asiatic Journal. Den Haag / Wiesbaden: vol. 11 (1966). S. 141–143.

**Hemmerdinger,** Bertrand: Un élément pythagoricien dans le Pater. In: Zeitschr. für die neutestamentl. Wissenschaft. Gießen – Berlin, Bd. 63 (1972). S. 121.

**Hemmerle,** Klaus: Das Väter unser und die Frage nach dem Wofür unseres Lebens. In: Lebendiges Zeugnis. Paderborn 36 (1981). S. 30–34.

**Hengsbach,** Franz Bischof: Herr, lehre uns beten – Vater unser im Himmel. Fastenhirtenbrief u. sechs Predigten. In: glauben, hoffen, beten. Fastenpredigten. Paderborn: Verlag Bonifacius-Druckerei 1970. S. 135–180.
– Zu uns komme dein Reich. In: Pflüge einen neuen Acker (Dein Reich komme – Bitte um den Frieden). St. Augustin: Verlag Wort u. Werk 1972. S. 7–13.

**Henke,** Fritz: Auflösung der AREPO-Zeile in der SATOR-Formel. In: Theologische Zeitschrift. Basel: Friedrich Reinhardt 5 (1949). S. 316–317.
– Das Große Palindrom (Sator-Formel). Schmalenbek bei Ahrensburg 1949 (Privatdruck).

**Hennig,** John: Zur Stellung des Tischgebets in der Liturgie (das Vaterunser). In: Liturgisches Jahrbuch 18 (1968). S. 87, 91f.
– Our Daily Bread. In: Theological Studies. New York, vol. 4 (1943). S. 445–454.

**Henseler,** Ewald: Abba – Vater! Besinnliches zum Vaterunser. M.-Gladbach: B. Kühlen 1931. 87 S. m. Abb.

**Hensler,** Joseph: Das Vaterunser. Text- und Literaturkritische Untersuchungen (Sammlung Neutestamentliche Abhandlungen, Bd. 4, Nr. 5). Münster: Aschendorff 1914. XII, 96 u. III S.

**H(epding),** H.: Die Sator-Formel. In: Hessische Blätter für Volkskunde. vol. 34 (1935). S. 111–113.

**Herbst,** F.: Herr lehre uns beten. Betrachtungen über das Gebet des Herrn (Der Weg göttliche Zeugnisse, 12/15). Elberfeld: Buchhdlg. der evang. Gesellsch. für Deutschland 1911. 67 S.

**Herbst,** Joseph: Le Pater médité ou douze explications de l'Oraison Dominicale. Paris: A. René 1845.

**Heredia,** C. M. SJ: Bittet und ihr werdet empfangen. In: Eine Quelle der Kraft (vom Bittgebet, das Berge versetzt). Innsbruck: Marianischer Verlag 1952. S. 60–66.

**Hermann,** Basilius OSB: Begleitworte zu der farbigen Bilderfolge von Tilde Eisgruber: Das Vaterunser und Ave Maria. Nürnberg: Sebaldus-Verlag 1926. 40 S.

**Herr lehre uns beten!** (Gedanken über das Vaterunser). Hamburg: Advent-Verlag 1932. 24 S.

Das „**Herrengebet**" in chinesischen Schriftzeichen (in der wörtlichen Bedeutung „Gebet zum Himmelsherrn"). In: Erdkreis. Würzburg: Arena-Verlag 7 (1957), Februarheft.

**Herrmann,** Immanuel: Das neue Vaterunser. Kein hilfloses Gebet, sondern ein Vorsatz zu tätiger Arbeit. Jena: Jenaer Volksbuchhdlg. (2. Aufl.) 1921. 71 S.

**Herrmann,** Johannes: Der alttestamentliche Urgrund des Vaterunsers. In: Festschrift Otto Procksch zum 60. Geburtstag. Leipzig: A. Deichert 1934. S. 71–98.

**Hesse,** Hermann Albert: Göttliche und menschliche Anliegen. Betrachtungen über das Unser Vater. Elberfeld: Buchh. des Erziehungsvereins 1923. 30 S.

**Hessen,** Johannes: Das Herrengebet. Ausgelegt in Gebeten. München: Ars sacra 1952. 31 S.
Anm.: frühere Auflage bereits 1940 bei Ars sacra erschienen.
– Unser Vater. Gebete des Gotteskindes. Darin Vaterunser-Bezug: S. 17. Rottenburg: Bader'sche Verlagsbuchhdlg. (7. Aufl.) 1947); (6. verm. u. verb. Aufl. 1940).
– Unser Vater! In: Gotteskind (Bücher der Wiedergeburt, Bd. 10). Habelschwerdt: Frankes Buchhdlg. 1924. S. 29–36.

**Heyder,** P. Gebhard Maria a St. Laurentio O.C.D.: Vaterunser und Ave Maria, kurz erklärt. Neumarkt/Opf.: Buchdruckerei Gg. Schlierf 1944/47. 30 S.

**Heyn,** Wilhelm: Das Vaterunser in Kriegsnot. Kriegsandachten gehalten in der evangel. Kirche zu Nieder-Wiesa-Greiffenberg. Mit Vorwort von Walter Richter. Breslau: Evang. Buchh. 1915. 38 S.

**Hicks,** Roger: Wer wird herrschen? Das Gebet des Herrn und der moderne Mensch. Hrsg. von der Offensive Junger Christen. Wuppertal: Aussaat-Verlag 1973. 87 S.
– The Lord's Prayer and Modern Man. A contemporary approach. London: Blandford Press 1967. 96 S.

**Higgins,** A. J. B.: „Lead us not in Temptation". In: Expository Times. Edinburgh, vol. 58 (1946–47). 250 S.

**Hilber,** Jakob: Enquête über das Verständnis des „Vater Unser" auf Formosa. In: Neue Zeitschrift für Missionswissenschaft. Beckenried: 21 (1965). H. 3, S. 213–220.

**Hildebrand,** Dietrich von: Die Botschaft des „Pater noster". In: Der verwüstete Weinberg, II. Teil, 2. Kap. Regensburg: Josef Habbel 1973. S. 228–238.

**Hilger,** Hans (Hrsg.): Das Gebet des Herrn. In: Gottes Wort und unsere Antwort. Handbuch für den Bibelunterricht, Bd. II. Freiburg: Herder 1966. S. 193–203.

**Hiller,** Friedrich: „Auf Adelers Fittichen". Vaterunser-Geschichten. Feuchtwangen: Frankenverlag Sommer & Schorr 1931. 175 S.

**Hinz,** Friedhelm: Die slovinzischen und kaschubischen Fassungen des Vaterunsers. In: Zeitschrift für Slavistik. Berlin, Bd. 11 (1966). H. 2, S. 205–213.

**Hirsch,** Emmanuel: Frühgeschichte des Evangeliums. Zweites Buch: Die Vorlagen des Lukas und das Sondergut des Matthäus. Tübingen: J. C. B. Mohr 1941. S. 101–102.

**Hirsch,** Ernst: Das Mariendorfer Vaterunser (Waldenser u. Franzosen in Hessen). In: Zeitschrift für französ. Sprache u. Literatur. Wiesbaden. Bd. 75) (1965); Nr. 1, S. 27–30.

**Hirschmann,** Hans: Vater unser – erlöse uns. Betrachtungen zum Gebet des Herrn. Würzburg: Edition Kolb, im Echter-Verlag 1979. 55 S. m. 10 Illustrationen.

**Hoare,** J. N.: „Lead us not into temptation". In: The Expository Times. vol 50 (1939). S. 333.

**Hoch,** Dorothee: Wenn ihr betet… Eine Hilfe zum Beten an Hand des Vaterunsers (Schriftenfolge zum Weitergeben, 24). Lahr: Kaufmann 1962. 56 S.

**Hodgson,** Leonhard: The Lord's Prayer. 6 Sermons. (Cathedral of Winchester). London: Longmans 1934. 80 S.

**Hoduem,** A.: De introductione orationis Dominicae in missa. In: Collationes Brugenses. 1938. S. 375–378.

**Hofer,** Alfons SJ: Vater unser im Himmel. In: Pastoralblatt für die Diözesen Aachen, Berlin, Essen, Köln, Osnabrück. Köln: Juli 1977. S. 197–199.

**Hoffmann,** Georgius: De Oratione Dominica. Breslau: Otto Gutsmann 1884.

**Hofius,** O.: Artikel: Vater. In: Begriffslexikon zum NT in drei Bänden. Hrsg. Lothar Coenen. Wuppertal: R. Brockhaus (3. Aufl.) 1972. Bd. 3, Sp. 1241–1247.

**Hohmann,** Johannes: s. **Das Gebet des Herrn.**

**Holbein,** Hans: Bilder zum „Vaterunser". Mit Einführung von Dr. Hanspeter Landolt. Gedruckt im Auftrag von Dr. h. c. Richard Doetsch-Benziger für seine Freunde. Druck: Conzett & Huber, Zürich 1953. 5 S. Einführung, 7 Bildtafeln.

**Holländische Bischöfe:** Arbeiten in Hoffnung. Deutung des Vaterunsers. In: Schreiben „Macht, Ohnmacht, Hoffnung" Dezember 1974. Sonderdruck in „Publik Forum" (wohl ähnl. Datums), S. 12–16. Niederländ. Originalfassung hrsg. Sekretariat van de R. K. Kerkprovincie in Nederland, 1974.

**Hollis,** Gertrude: After this manner: the Lord's Prayer. London: Mowbray 1936. 86 S.

**Hölscher,** To: Het Onze Vader. Ill. van Claude Benoy. Bruxelles: Minerva 1949. 80 S.

**Holzinger,** Karl: Zur Lösung der Epiousios-Frage. In: Philologische Wochenschrift. vol. 51, Nr. 27 (1931). col. 857–863.

**Hönnicke,** Gustav: Neuere Forschungen zum Vaterunser bei Matthäus und Lukás. In: Neue Kirchliche Zeitschrift. vol. 17, Nr. 1, 2 u. 3 (1906). S. 57–67, 106–120, 169–180.

**Hopfner,** Isidoro: Ancora più luce sul cryptogramma di Pompei. In: L'Osservatore Romano (23.334) 6. 3. 1937, Nr. 54, S. 3, col. 3–4.

**Hophan,** Otto OFMCap: Wir wagen zu sagen: Vater... In: Die Frohe Botschaft. Leben und Lehren unseres Herrn (Hrsg. Drittordenszentrale Schwyz) Einsiedeln: Benziger 1943. S. 161–165.

**Horna,** L. de: Vater unser. Mit Bildern von L. de Horna (Müllers Bilderbogen). München: Ars sacra 1975. 20 S.

**Horstmann,** Erwin: Die Satorformel. Aus: Das Goetheanum. Wochenschrift für Anthroposophie. Dornach: 47 (1968) Nr. 24, S. 187–188.

**Horwil,** H. W.: Our „Daily" Bread. In: The Expository Times. vol. 2 Nr. 11 (1891). S. 254–255.

**Houk,** Cornelius B.: Peirasmos. The Lord's Prayer and the Massah Tradition. In: Scottish Journal of Theology. London, vol. 19 (1966). Nr. 2, S. 216–225.

**Hoyle,** R. B.: The Lord's Prayer in History. In: Biblical Review. vol. 17 (1932). S. 210–226.

**Hülster,** P. A.: So sollt ihr beten. Das Gebet des Herrn, von den Kirchenvätern erklärt (Klosterneuburger Hefte Nr. 43. Hrsg. Pius Parsch). Klosterneuburg: Verl. Volksliturg. Apostolat 1936. 32 S.

**Hünermann,** Wilhelm: Vaterunser. In: Wir haben seine Herrlichkeit gesehen. Ein Leben Jesu. Innsbruck: Tyrolia 1956. S. 157f.

**Hurdes,** Felix: Vater unser, Gedanken aus dem Konzentrationslager, Wien: Herder 1950. 159 S.

**Huschens,** Jakob: Der Sonntag der katholischen Familie. Volkstümliche Erklärungen des Vaterunser etc. Einsiedeln: Benziger 1916. XXX, 669 S., ill.

**Husemann,** Friedrich: Das Vaterunser. In: Der Ewige Name. Sechs Vorträge. Buchenbach bei Freiburg: Selbstverlag C. M. Husemann 1963. S. 59–83.

**Hussey,** Maurice: The Petitions of the Paternoster in Mediaeval English Literature. In: Medium Aevum. Oxford, vol. 27 Nr. 1 (1958). S. 8–16.

# I

**Ibn Saba:** Commentarius in orationem dominicam. (Margarita pretiosa, cap. 33, ed. J. Périer). In: Bibl. Orientalis. vol. 16. Paris 1922. S. 683–708.

**Iersel,** B. van: Pater Noster. In: Het Heilig Land. Nijmegen: vol. 13 (1960). S. 55–59, 65–69, 122–124, 137–139, 154–156, 165–167.

**Imbach,** Josef: Vaterunser-Parodien. In Beitrag „Die Lästerungen und unser Glaube. Zur Parodie religiöser Texte in der deutschen Gegenwartsliteratur. In: Christ in der Gegenwart. Freiburg: Herder 29 (1977). S. 413–414.

**Ingle,** George Ernest: The Lord's Creed. An examination of the Lord's prayer. London Collins: 1964. 223 S.

**Irmler,** Rudolf: Das wichtigste Gespräch. Meditation über das Vaterunser. Gießen – Basel: Brunnen-Verlag 1966. 22 S.

# J

**Jacky,** Philip: Unser Vater, dein ist das Reich. 52 Sonntagsworte. Teil 1: 1934. 158 S.; Teil 2: 1935. 156 S. Weinfelden: Neuenschwander.

**Jacobi,** Gerhard: Vaterunser-Predigten. Stuttgart: Calwer Verlag 1968. 88 S.

**Jacquemin,** Dom Edmond OCR: La Portée de la troisième Demande du „Pater". In: Ephemerides Theologicae Lovanienses. Bruges: C. Beyaert 25 (1949). S. 61–76.
– Etude Biblique (Mt 6,9–13; Lk 11,2–4). La Prière du Seigneur. In: Assemblée du Seigneur. Bruges: Jahr des Erscheinens nicht bekannt. S. 47–64.

**Jaeger,** Charles: A propos de deux passages du sermon sur la montagne: 1 Matthieu 6,13 ... In: Revue d'Histoire et de Philosophie religieuse. vol. 18 (1938). S. 415–417.

**Jaeger,** Paul: Vaterunser-Andachtsbüchlein für vier Wochen (Sonntagsgedanken, H. 10). Stuttgart: Quell-Verlag 1962. 46 S.

**Jäger,** Rudolf: Pater noster. In: Meine heilige Messe. Freundesbriefe. Paderborn: Bonifacius-Druckerei 1936. S. 131–134.

**Jahr des Herrn.** Ein Hausbuch vom Vaterunser. Leipzig: St. Benno-Verlag 1970. 432 S.

**James,** D. T.: Epiousios (Luke 11,3; Matt. 6,11). In: The Expository Times. vol 32 Nr. 9 (1921). S. 428.

**Jannaris,** A. N.: The English Version of the Lord's Prayer. In: The Contemporary Review. Nr. 346 (1894). S. 580–591.

**Jannasch,** W.: Vaterunser: s. **Jeremias,** Joachim.

**Jean de la Foi:** Notre Père. Anvers: L. Opdebeek 1911. 87 S.

**Jehle,** Edmund: Das Vater Unser und Ave Maria in Wort und Bild. Paderborn: F. Schöningh 1929. 48 S. m. Abb.

**Jenny,** Markus: Zum „ökumenischen" Vaterunser-Text. In: Kirchenblatt für die reformierte Schweiz. Basel: Reinhardt 124 (1968) Nr. 12, S. 182–183.

**Jeremias,** Joachim: Abba. Studien zur neutestamentlichen Theologie und Zeitgeschichte. Darin S. 152–171: Das Vater-Unser im Lichte der neueren Forschung. Göttingen: Vandenhoeck & Ruprecht 1966. 371 S.
Anm.: Derselbe Beitrag in: Tradition u. Gegenwart. Fünf Gastvor-

lesungen anläßl. des 150jähr. Bestehens der Berliner Theol. Fakultät. Berlin: 1962. S. 7–34; Zeichen der Zeit. Berlin: 16 (1962). S. 1–13.
– Kennzeichen der Ipsissima vox Jesu. In: Synoptische Studien, Alfred Wikenhauser zugeeignet. München: Zink 1953. S. 86–93. Ebenso in: Abba. Studien zur neutestamentl. Theologie u. Zeitgeschichte. Göttingen: Vandenhoeck & Ruprecht 1966. S. 145–152, 152–171.
– Neutestamentl. Theologie I: Die Verkündigung Jesu. Das Vaterunser. Gütersloh: Mohn 1971. 313 S.
– Das Vater-Unser im Lichte der neueren Forschung (Calwer Hefte Nr. 50). Stuttgart: Calwer Verlag. 1. Aufl. 1962; 4. revid. Aufl. 1967. 31 S.
– The Lord's Prayer in Modern Research. In: The Expository Times. Edinburgh: vol. 71 (1960). S. 141–146.
– The Prayers of Jesus. Trad. by J. Bowden. Napperville / London: A. R. Allenson / SCM Press 1967. 124 S.
– Le Pater et la recherche moderne sur le Nouveau Testament. In: Nouvelles chrétiennes d'Israel. Jerusalem: vol. 14 (1963). S. 9–13.
– Abba – Jesus et son Père (Coll. Parole de Dieu, Nr. 8). Paris: Ed. du Seuil 1972. 142 S.
– Paroles de Jésus ... Le sermon sur la montagne. Trad. française par Dom Marie Mailhé (Collection Foi vivante Nr. 7). Paris: Ed. du Cerf 1965. 103 S.
– Fader var i den nyare forskningens (Pater noster in luce investigationis recentioris). In: Svensk Exegetisk Arsbok. Uppsala: vol. 27 (1962). S. 33–54.
– Palabras de Jesus. El sermón de la montaña. El Padre Nuestro (Trad. de la 5. y 3. ed. alemana por José Maria Bernáldes Montalvo. Madrid: Fax 1968. 185 S.

**Jeremias,** Joachim / Jannasch, W.: Art.: Vaterunser. In: Die Religion in Geschichte und Gegenwart, Bd. 6 Tübingen: J. C. B. Mohr 1962. Sp. 1235–1238.

**Jerphanion,** Guillaume de: La formule magique SATOR AREPO ou ROTAS OPERA. Vieilles théories et faits nouveaux. In: Recherches de Science Religieuse. vol. 25, Nr. 2 (1935). S. 188–225.
– Encore la formule SATOR AREPO. In: Les Etudes Classiques. vol. 4, Nr. 3 (1935). S. 438–440.
– La formule magique SATOR-AREPO ou ROTAS OPERA. Vieilles théories et faits nouveaux. In: La Voix des Monuments. Etudes d'Archéologie. N. S. Rome – Paris 1938. S. 38–76; dazu 77–94.
– Du nouveau sur la formule magique ROTAS OPERA (et non SATOR AREPO). In: Recherches de Science Religieuse. vol. 27, Nr. 3 (1937). S. 326–335.
– Osservazione sull'origine del quadrato magico „Sator Arepo".

In: Atti della Pontif. Academia Romana di Archeologia (Ser. III) Rendiconti vol. 12 (1936). S. 401–404.

**Jette,** Thérèse de: Notre Père. Ill. de P. Franceschini. Grenoble: Dardelet 1945. 19 S.

**Jiriczek,** Otto Luitpold: Das Adelsberger althochdeutsche Vaterunser. In: Beiträge zur Geschichte der deutschen Sprache u. Literatur. Halle: Niemeyer 43 (1917). S. 470–489.

**Johannes Chrysostomus** (Pseudó): Ausgewählte Schriften. Bd. 2. In: Bibliothek der Kirchenväter. Bd. 25, S. 10–18. München: Kösel 1916.
– Œuvres complètes ... ed. J. B. Jeannin. vol. IV, S. 21–24: Homélie au sujet de la conduite selon Dieu, sur la „Porte étroite" et l'explication de la prière „Notre Père", chap. 3–5. Bar-le-Duc: L. Guérin 1864.

**Johanny,** Raymond: La prière du Seigneur chez les Pères. In: Parole et Pain. Paris: 12 (1966). S. 5–33.

**Jones,** Mary Alice: The Lord's Prayer. Comments. Ill. by Dorothy Grider. London: Collins 1968. 45 S.

**Jordan,** Gerald Ray: Life-giving-Words. Anderson, Ind: Warner Press 1964. 112 S.

**Joüon,** Paul: Quelques aramaismes sous-jacents au grec des Evangiles ... Matt. 6, 11. In: Recherches de Science Religieuse. vol. 17 (1927). S. 219–221.

**Jousse,** Marcel: Les Formules targoûmiques du „Pater" dans le Milieu ethnique palestinien. Paris: Geuthner 1950. 51 S.

**Jubilate Deo.** Cantus Gregoriani... nach den Constitutionen des Zweiten Vatikanischen Konzils. Pater noster: S. 20–22. Typis Polyglottis Vaticanis 1974.

**Jüchen,** Aurel von: Lob des Vaterunsers. Gütersloh: Verlag Der Rufer 1947. 52 S.

**Jung,** Carl Gustav: Antwort auf Hiob. Zum Thema „Vaterunser" S. 59. Zürich: Rascher Verlag 1952 (4. revid. Auflage 1954). 169 S.

**Jungandreas,** Wolfgang: Zur Überlieferung und Sprache der deutschen Vaterunser-Auslegung des Nikolaus von Kues. In: Mitteilungen und Forschungsbeiträge der Cusanus-Gesellschaft, Bd. 7. Mainz: Matthias-Grünewald-Verlag 1969. S. 67–88.

**Jungmann,** Josef Andreas SJ: Das Pater noster in der römischen Liturgie. In: Messe im Gottesvolk. Freiburg: Herder 1970. S. 82–84.
– Pater noster. In: Christliches Beten in Wandel und Bestand. München: Ars sacra 1969. S. 197.

- **Vaterunser,** das „Gebet des Herrn". Artikel in: Lexikon für
Theologie und Kirche. Freiburg: Herder (2. Aufl., Bd. 10) 1965.
Sp. 624–629.
- Pater noster (im Stundengebet). In: Wortgottesdienst. Regens-
burg: Friedrich Pustet 1964. S. 94f.
- Pater noster (auf dem Hintergrund seiner Geschichte). In: Der
Gottesdienst der Kirche. Innsbruck: Tyrolia 1962. S. 22, 53, 85, 93,
156f., 178f., 184, 186, 190f., 220.
- Pater noster. In: Liturgisches Erbe und pastorale Gegenwart.
Innsbruck: Tyrolia 1960. S. 179, 185 193, 198, 203, 206, 234f., 236,
268, 281.
Außerdem: Die Verbindung des Kyrie mit dem Pater noster:
S. 240–252; Das Gebet des Herrn im Brevier: S. 252–264.
- Das Gebet des Herrn im römischen Brevier. In: Zeitschrift für
kath. Theologie. Wien – Innsbruck 73 (1951). S. 85–92 u. S. 347–358.
- Pater noster. In: Missarum Sollemnia, Bd. II. Wien – Freiburg:
Herder 1949. S. 343–363.
- Pater noster (Arkandisziplin). In: Liturgie der christlichen Früh-
zeit bis auf Gregor den Großen. Freiburg (Schweiz): Universitäts-
verlag 1967. S. 146, S. 281 (Pater noster als Vorbereitungsgebet zur
Kommunion).
- Das Vaterunser im Kommunionritus. In: Gewordene Liturgie.
Innsbruck: Felizian Rauch 1941. S. 137–164.
- Das Pater noster im Kommunionritus. In: Zeitschrift für kath.
Theologie. Wien – Innsbruck 56 (1934). S. 552–571.
- Pater noster und Credo im Breviergebet, eine altchristliche
Tauferinnerung. In: Gewordene Liturgie. Innsbruck: Felizian
Rauch 1941. S. 165–172.
- Pater noster und Credo im Breviergebet, eine altchristliche
Tauferinnerung. In: Zeitschrift für Aszese und Mystik. 1934.
S. 259–264.
- Vaterunser. In: Frohbotschaft und unsere Glaubensverkündi-
gung. Regensburg: Friedrich Pustet 1936. S. 45.
Anm.: Hier auch Verweis auf den Aufsatz „Paternoster im
Breviergebet..." in Zeitschrift für Aszese und Mystik 9 (1934).
S. 109, 152f., 155, 157, 211f.
- Die Stellung Christi im liturgischen Gebet. In: Liturgiege-
schichtliche Forschungen. Münster. 8 (1925). Seitenangabe nicht
bekannt.

# K

**Kaefer,** Herbert: Aktion und Feier der Buße. Neue Bußgottesdienste. Kapitel 7 (S. 67–77): Vater unser. Freiburg: Herder 1981.

**Kaim,** Emil: Das letzte Vaterunser am Sylvesterabend. In: Alles wird geheiligt durch Gottes Wort, Bd. III. 1941. S. 31–37.
– Predigtreihe über das Vaterunser. In: Alles wird geheiligt durch Gottes Wort, Bd. X. 1941. S. 163–256.

**Kaiser,** Isabella: Vater unser ... Roman. Köln: Bachem (15. Aufl.) 1932. 189 S.

**Kaiser,** Paul: Kriegsgebet. Eine Vaterunserbetrachtung für daheim und im Felde. Predigt am Sonntag Rogate 1915. Leipzig: Serigsche Buchh. 1915. 14 S.

**Kalt,** Edmund: Jesus lehrt das Vaterunser als Reichgottesgebet. In: Werkbuch der Bibel, Bd. II: Neues Testament. Freiburg: Herder 1941. S. 123–127.
– Vater unser. In: Biblisches Reallexikon, Bd. II. Paderborn: F. Schöningh 1931. Sp. 919–924.

**Kalt,** Gustav: Das Vaterunser. In: Die Feier der heiligen Eucharistie. Luzern: Rex-Verlag 1959. S. 154–158.

**Kammelberger,** Karl: Das Paternoster. In: Die Quelle des Lebens. Wien: Herder 1959. S. 100–102.

**Kamphausen,** Adolf Hermann Heinrich: Das Gebet des Herrn. Elberfeld: R. L. Friederichs 1866.

**Kappeler,** A.: Die vierte Bitte im Unservater. In: Schweizerische Theologische Zeitschrift. vol. 31 (1914). S. 147–156.

**Karner,** Karl: Die SATOR-Inschrift von Aquincum. In: Theologische Literaturzeitung. Berlin – Leipzig, Bd. 82 Nr. 5 (Mai 1957). Sp. 391–394.

**Kärntner Vaterunser-Auslegung** (Handschr. A). Hrsg. Franz-Joseph Mone. In: Anzeiger für Kunde der teutschen Vorzeit. 8 (1839). S. 39–44.

**Karrer,** Otto: Kurzkommentare zu Mt 6,9–13 u. Lk 11,1–4. In: Neues Testament. München: Ars sacra 1967. S. 38f. u. 202f.
– Vater im Himmel. Zu Lk 11,2 u. Mt 6,9 u. Traditionszeugnissen von Augustinus Maximus dem Bekenner, J. H. Newman u. Otto Karrer. München: Ars sacra 1963. S. 127–134.
– Das Beten zum Vater. In: Biblische Meditationen. München: Ars sacra 1958. S. 197 u. 202f.

– Vater Unser, auch Fürbitte aller füreinander. In: Das Reich Gottes heute. München: Ars sacra 1956. S. 264.
– Vater im Himmel. In: Schicksal und Würde des Menschen. Einsiedeln: Benziger 1940. S. 54f.
– Die Gotteskindschaft. Darin Vaterunser-Bezug: S. 79f. München: Ars sacra 1934.
– Das Vater unser. In: Erklärung des Matthäusevangeliums, T. 3: Die frohe Botschaft. München: Ars sacra 1953. S. 69–76

**Kasteren,** Joh. Peter van S.J.: Was Jesus predigte. Eine Erklärung des Vaterunsers. Deutsche Bearbeitung von Johs. Spendel S.J. Freiburg: Herder 1920. VII, 163 S.

**Kauchtschischwili,** S.: Ein Beitrag zur Epiousios-Frage. In: Philologische Wochenschrift. vol. 50 (1930). col. 1166–1168.

**Kaufmann,** Ludwig: Das Vaterunser auswendig und inwendig. In: Orientierung. Zürich: 32 (1968). Nr. 3, S. 35–36.
– Vom Wert der halben Schritte. Anmerkungen zum „ökumenischen" Vaterunser. In: Orientierung. Zürich: 32 (1968). Nr. 1, S. 3 bis 4.

**Kaulen,** Franz: Brot der Engel. Katholisches Gebetbuch. Thema Vaterunser: S. 118–122. Freiburg: Herder 1911.

**Kautzsch,** Andreas: Das ‚Vater Unser' – heute (Vortragszyklus an fünf Abenden): s. **Damian,**Ludwig.

**Kay,** W.: On the Derivation and Meaning of Epiousios. In: The Journal of Philology. vol. 5 (1874). S. 48–51.

**Kehrein,** Joseph (Hrsg.): Pater Noster u. Ave Maria in deutschen Übersetzungen. Nebst einem Anhang: Die altdeutschen Namen Gottes u. Marias. Unveränderter Nachdruck d. Ausg. v. 1865. Walluf b. Wiesbaden: Sändig 1973. 101 S.

**Kelber,** Wilhelm: Christus im Vaterunser. In: Die Christengemeinschaft. Stuttgart: Verlag Urachhaus 24 (1952). S. 136–137.

**Keller,** Hermann: Das Vaterunser. In: Herr lehre uns beten. Als Manuskript gedruckt. Kempen: Abtei Mariendonk 1972. S. 61–194.

**Keller,** Joh. Emil: Unser Vater. Berlin-Lichtenberg: Verlag „Weg zur Wahrheit" Joh. E. Keller 1931. 54 S.

**Kellog,** A. L./Talbot, E. W.: The Wycliffite Pater Noster and Ten Commandments with Special Reference to English MSS 85 and 90 in the John Rylands Library (editio). In: Bulletin of the John Rylands Library. Manchester: 42 (1960). S. 345–377.

**Kerning,** J. B.: Die Grundzüge der Bibel. Das Gebet des Herrn und das kanonische Gesetz. Lorch (Württ.): Renatus-Verlag 1928. 168 S.

Kerr, Clarence Ware: Pattern for Powerful Praying. Los Angeles: Cowman 1958. 155 S.

Kieffer, René: Fader vår i äldere kyrklig tradition. In: Svensk teologisk kvartalskrift. 54 (1978), Nr. 3, S. 103–109.

Kiel, Elfriede: s. Unser tägliches Brot heute.

Kielmann, Heinrich Adolf: Der ΑΡΤΟΣ ΕΠΙΟΥΣΙΟΣ in der Brotbitte des Herrengebetes. Eine sprachwissenschaftliche Untersuchung. Bad Kreuznach: Reinhard Schmithals 1883.

Kierkegaard, Sören: Vater im Himmel. In: Die Tagebücher. Hrsg. Theodor Häcker. S. 103, 108. Zitiert in: Otto Karrer: Jahrbuch der Seele. München: Ars sacra 1951. S. 275.

Kilian, Augustinus: Das Gebet des Herrn. Nach dem hl. Thomas von Aquin erklärt. Wiesbaden: Hermann Rauch 1925. 189 S.

Kilpatrick, Dunbar: The Origins of the Gospel acc. to S. Matthew. Oxford: Clarendon Press 1946. Behandlung des Vaterunsers: S. 21 u. 76f.

Kind: Das Gebet des Herrn. In: Theologische Zeitschrift aus der Schweiz (später: Schweiz. Theol. Zeitschrift). vol. 6, Nr. 4 (1889). S. 210–226.

King, Robert: The Lord's Prayer. An esoteric interpretation. Chatham: Golden Hind Press 1949. 16 S.

Kirchberg, Johs.: Das Vater unser eines Landpfarrers. Liederzyklus. Regensburg: vorm. G. J. Manz 1913. 30 S.

Kirchenväter, Die: Cyprian, Chrysologus, Origines, Gregor von Nyssa, griechische Liturgie; Elisäus Wardapet: Zum Vaterunser. In: Birgit Weiß (Hrsg.): Gebete u. Betrachtungen der Kirchenväter. München: Kösel 1963. S. 277–286.

Kirchenväter, Texte der (Hrsg. Heinrich Kraft): München: Kösel 1966. Bd. II, S. 56–58: Zitat von Augustinus: Bd. IV, S. 287f.: Zitat von Cyrill von Jerusalem.

Kirchesch, Franz: Soziale Lehren des Vaterunsers (Auf Franziskus-Pfaden. Braunes Heft Nr. 2). Mayen (Rhld.): Ständehaus-Verlag 1927.

Kirchgässner, Alfons: Vater (Bezug auf Vaterunser). In: Geistliches Wörterbüchlein. Frankfurt: Josef Knecht 1958. S. 45f.

Kirchgässner, Ernst: Das Vaterunser als Einreisevisum. In: Rettet den Menschen. Regensburg: Pustet 1967. S. 45–47.

**Kirchhoff,** Hermann: Beispiel Herrengebet. In: Gottesdienst. Freiburg / Einsiedeln: Herder / Benziger 20 (1975).

**Kistemaker,** Simon J.: Lord's prayer in the first century. In: Journal of the Evangelical Theological Society. Jackson, Miss. 21 (1978), S. 323–328.

**Klaffenbach,** G.: EPIOUSIOS: „Kommender, nächster Tag". In: Museum Helveticum. (Lindos Inscr. A. D. 22). Basel: 6 (1949). S. 216–225.

**Klaver,** Richard: When you pray. An Analysis of the Our Father. Westminster: Newman Press 1956. 209 S.

**Kleber,** A.: The Lord's Prayer and the Decalog. In: Catholic Biblical Quarterly. vol. 3 (1941). S. 302–320.

**Klein,** G.: Die ursprüngliche Gestalt des Vaterunsers. In: Zeitschrift für die neutestamentliche Wissenschaft und die Kunde des Urchristentums. Berlin: Alfred Töpelmann 7 (1906). S. 34–50.

**Kleine,** Erwin: Sinneswandel im Gebet. Ein Hinweis zum Vaterunser. In: Bayerisches Sonntags-Blatt. München: 82 (1964) Nr. 7, S. 98.
– Lobgesang von dunklen Ufern. Ökumenische Gedanken zum Vaterunser. Frankfurt: Main-Verlag 1962. 131 S.

**Kleine-Natrop,** Johannes: Das Vaterunser als Tischgebet der Opfergemeinde. In: Unser Opfer am Altar und im Alltag. Dülmen: Laumann 1937. S. 118–126.

**Kleinheyer,** Bruno: Wir wagen zu sprechen. In: Der Altar ist die Mitte. Limburg: Lahn-Verlag 1962. S. 104–107.

**Klopstock,** Friedrich Gottlieb: Psalm zu den einzelnen Bitten des Vaterunsers. In: Die Christengemeinschaft. Stuttgart: Verlag Urachhaus 48 (1976), Heft 6, S. 177–178.

**Klostermann,** Erich: Das Matthäusevangelium. (Handbuch zum NT, Bd. 4; 2. völlig neubearb. Aufl.). Zum Thema Vaterunser (Mt 6,9–13): S. 54–59. Tübingen: J. C. B. Mohr 1927.
– Das Lukasevangelium. (Handbuch zum NT, Bd. 5; 2., völlig neubearb. Aufl.). Zum Thema Vaterunser: § 36: Vom Gebet (1c 11, S. 123f.) Tübingen: J. C. B. Mohr 1929.

**Kner,** Anton: Unser tägliches Brot gib uns heute. In: Jeder Tag hat seine Chance. Freiburg: Seelsorge-Verlag 1968. S. 34–36.

**Knieriem,** Rolf: Das Vaterunser. Ausgelegt. (Metanoia, 1). Marburg, Lahn: Theol. Arbeitsgemeinschaft der Studentenmission in Deutschland 1960. 67 S.

**Knoke,** Karl: Eine Auslegung des Vaterunsers aus dem Jahre 1522. In: Zeitschrift für Kirchengeschichte. vol. 20, Nr. 1 (1899). S. 19–36.

**Knöpfler,** Alois: Das Vater Unser im Geiste der ältesten Kirchenväter…: s. **Glötzle,** Ludwig.

**Knörzer,** Wolfgang: Unser Vater im Himmel. Das Gebet des Herrn als Inbegriff des Evangeliums. In: Bibel und Kirche. Stuttgart: Verlag Kath. Bibelwerk 22 (1967). S. 79–86.
– Thesen zur Praxis des Vaterunserbetens. In: Bibel und Kirche. Stuttgart: Verlag Kath. Bibelwerk 22 (1967). S. 93–94.
– Vaterunser. In: Bibel im Jahr '68: „Unsere Antwort das Gebet". Stuttgart: Verlag Kath. Bibelwerk 1968. S. 70–76.
– Das Vaterunser: Mitte der Bergpredigt – Mitte des Evangeliums. In: Die Bergpredigt (Biblisches Forum, Bd. 2). Stuttgart: Verlag Kath. Bibelwerk 1968. S. 69–82.
– Vaterunser. Das Gebet der Christenheit – Mitte von Frömmigkeit und Leben. Gebets- u. Lebensordnung des Christen nach Mt 6, 1–18 u. Lk 10, 25 – 11, 13. Stuttgart: Verlag Kath. Bibelwerk 1966. 130 S. 2., völlig neubearb. Aufl. 1969. 119 S.

**Kobbe,** Ursula: Sie brauchen Liebe. Religiöse Erfahrungen mit geistig behinderten Kindern im Lichte des Vaterunsers (Veröffentlichungen der Stiftung „Oratio Dominica"). Freiburg: Herder 1977. 189 S.

**Koberger,** Franz: Das Vaterunserspiel. Für die neue Jugend frei nach einem Märchen. Nürnberg: Kath. Bücherstube 1927. 6 Bl. Schreibmaschinenschrift.

**Köberle,** Adolf: Das Vaterunser als Schule des Gebets. In: Evangelischer Digest. Stuttgart: 3 (1961). H. 7, S. 23–28.
– Das Vaterunser und der Mensch der Gegenwart. Stuttgart: Quell-Verlag 1940. 16 S.

**Koch,** Anton SJ: Das Vaterunser. In: Homiletisches Handbuch. 1. Abt., Bd. 5–6 III, S. 81–84; Bd. VIII, S. 86–89. Freiburg: Herder 1938.

Anm.: Das Werk enthält außerdem zahlreiche Querverweise u. Literaturangaben.

**Koch,** J. / Teske, H. (Hrsg.): Die Auslegung des Vaterunsers in vier Predigten: s. **Nicolaus von Cusa.**

**Koch-Doll,** Maria: Betrachtungen zum Vaterunser. In: Seele. Regensburg: Josef Habbel. 11 (1929): 1f., 48f., 97f., 244f., 257f., 304f.; 12 (1930): 18f., 47f.

**Kolb,** Eduard: Das Gebet des Herrn. Eine Auslegung des „Unser Vater". Zürich: Taubstummen-Pfarramt 1956. 32 S.

**Kondrinewitsch,** Josef: „Vater unser". In: Visitkarten Gottes. Kurzbetrachtungen für den christlichen Alltag. Wien – Freiburg: Herder 1971. S. 121–133.

**König,** Franz Kardinal: Gemeinsam beten können. „Vaterunser" und „Ave Maria" in der neuen Textfassung. In: Wiener Kirchenzeitung, 21. März 1968.

**König,** Sebastianus: Devota et orthodoxa consideratio Orationis Dominicae. Straßburg: Johann Rapp 1626.

**Könn,** Josef: Die Stellung des Vaterunsers in der Messe (Vaterunser als Krönung des Opferakts, Zusammenhang von Vaterunser und Opferteilnahme). In: Die heilige Messe. Essen: Verlagsges. Augustin Wibbelt 1941. S. 204–265 (3. Aufl. 1949).

**Kortholt,** Christianus: De pane EPIOUSIOS, quem in oratione dominica petimus, exercitatio salmasiana. Kiel: Joachim Reumann 1677.

**Kösters,** Ludwig SJ: Vater im Himmel. In: Unser Christusglaube. Freiburg: Herder 1937. S. 71f.

**Kothe,** Hermann: Nochmals Epiousios. In: Neue Jahrbücher für Philologie und Pädagogik. vol. 60 (= 2. Abt. Bd. 36) (1890). S. 586 bis 587.

**Kraemer,** Franz Maria: PATER NOSTER. In: Geistliche Sonette. Bonn: Verlag Götz Schwippert 1947. S. 25–33.

**Kramp,** Joseph SJ: „Vater unser..." In: Stimmen der Zeit. Freiburg: Herder 52 (1922). S. 354–368.

**Kranječ,** Heinrich: Soldaten-Vaterunser. Graz: Styria (7. Aufl.) 1916. 21 S.

**Kraus,** Annie: Das Brot, das uns sättigt. Wie sollen wir die Vaterunser-Bitte verstehen? In: Michael. Kath. Wochenzeitung. Düsseldorf: 9 (1951). Nr. 39.
– Die vierte Bitte. In: Theologische Quartalschrift. Rottenburg: Bd. 129 (1949). S. 127f.
– Die vierte Bitte. Versuch einer Auslegung. Frankfurt: Josef Knecht 1948. 72 S.
– Zeit der Liebe. Eine Betrachtung zur vierten Bitte des Vaterunsers. Meitingen: Kyrios-Verlag 1970. 62 S.

**Krause,** G.: Sch'ma Iisrael – Sch'mone Esre – Pater noster. Glaubensbekenntnisse und Pflichtgebete in klingenden Äußerungen. In: Deutsches Pfarrerblatt. Neukirchen-Vluyn, 70 (1970). S. 273–277.

**Krauss,** Meinhold / Lundbeck, Johannes (Hrsg.): Die vielen Namen Gottes. Gerd Heinz-Mohr zum 60. Geburtstag. Zum Thema „Vaterunser" S. 13, 15, 98f. Stuttgart: J. F. Steinkopf 1974.

**Kristeller,** Paul (Hrsg.): Exercitium super pater noster. Nach der ältesten Ausgabe der Bibliothèque Nationale zu Paris in 8 Lichtdrucktafeln u. 7 S. Text (Veröffentlichung der Graphischen Gesellschaft, Nr. VI). Berlin: Bruno Cassirer 1908.

**Kroeker,** Jakob: Im Heiligtum des Vaterunsers. Erbauliche Gedanken u. Reden über das Gebet des Herrn nach Mt 6,9–13. Metzingen: Brunnquell-Verlag 1951. 112 S.

**Kroening,** G.: Was bedeutet ΑΡΤΟΣ ΕΠΙΟΥΣΙΟΣ? In: Gymnasium. Bd. 22 Nr. 5 (1905). S. 165–168.

**Krömler,** Hans: Unser aller Gebet. Eine ökumenische Besinnung über das Gebet des Herrn (Übersetzung des „Vaterunsers" von Otto Karrer) (Kleine Kostbarkeiten der Aldus-Manutius-Drucke. 12). Zürich: Aldus-Manutius 1958. 49 S.

**Kruse,** Heinz S.J.: „Pater Noster" et Passio Christi. In: Verbum Domini. Roma: Pontificium Institutum Biblicum 46 (1968). S. 3–29.

**Kubiak,** Marianus OSB: Meditation über das Vaterunser (zum Jahresschluß). In: Der Prediger und Katechet. München – Freiburg: Wewel 114 (1975). S. 94–97.

**Kuhaupt,** Hermann: Vaterunser-Gebet in Christi Namen. In: Abba, Vater! Christliche Lehre vom Gebet. Freiburg: Herder 1948. S. 108.

**Kuhlmann,** Edward: God's Children at Prayer. Narratives for children in interpretation of the Lord's Prayer. Columbus, Ohio: Wartburg Press 1947. 64 S., ill.

**Kuhlmann,** Jürgen: Gott – unser Vater. Eine Betrachtung. In: Christ in der Gegenwart. Freiburg: Herder 25 (1973.) S. 150–151.

**Kuhn,** G.: Zum Verständnis des Wortes ἐπιούσιος im Unservater. In: Schweizerische Theologische Zeitschrift. vol. 31 (1914). S. 33 bis 38.
– Unser tägliches Brot. In: Schweizerische Theologische Zeitschrift. vol. 36, Nr. 5–6 (1919). S. 191–196.

**Kuhn,** Karl Georg: Neues Licht auf Versuchung, Sünde u. Fleisch im NT (Titel unsicher). In: Zeitschrift für Theologie und Kirche. Tübingen: J. C. B. Mohr: Bd. 49 (1952). S. 200–222.
– New Light on Temptation, Sin and Flesh in the New Testament. In: The Scrolls and the New Testament. London: SCM Press 1958. S. 94–113, bes. S. 109, 111.
– Achtzehngebet und Vaterunser und der Reim. Wissenschaftli-

che Untersuchungen zum Neuen Testament, hrsg. von J. Jeremias u. O. Michel, Bd. 1. Tübingen: J. C. B. Mohr 1950. III, 51 S.

**Kühnel,** Josef: Das Vaterunser. (Gedanken.) Düsseldorf: Gesellschaft für Buchdruck u. Verlag 1939. 15 S.
– Vater unser. Düsseldorf: Bastion Verl. 1946. 15 S.
– Zitate über das Vaterunser. In: Weisheit aus vier Jahrtausenden. Düsseldorf: Ges. f. Buchdr. u. Verl. 1940. S. 25, 146.

**Kukowski,** Leon von: Das Gebet des Herrn. Bücherschau im „Klerusblatt". Eichstätt / München: 44 (1964). Nr. 1, S. 14f.

**Künsberg,** Sofie Freiin von: Vater unser und andere Erzählungen. Innsbruck: Felizian Rauch 1926. 202 S.

**Kunte,** Josef: Welches sind die wichtigsten Gebete? In: Goldene Worte über ein wichtiges Kapitel (dort verwiesen auf Spirago, Kath. Volks-Katechismus). Klagenfurt: Carinthia 1919. S. 28.

**Kuss,** Otto: Das Vaterunser. In: Auslegung und Verkündigung, Bd. II: Biblische Vorträge in Meditationen. Regensburg: Pustet 1967. S. 275–333.
Anm.: Obiger Beitrag teilweise enthalten in: Theologie u. Glaube. Paderborn: Schöningh Bd. 42 (1952) u. Bd. 44 (1954), S. 64–66.

# L

**L., R.:** Erlöse uns von dem Übel. In: Schweizerische Kirchenzeitung. Luzern: 117 (1949). S. 137–138.

**Labourt,** Jérôme: Six entretiens sur le Pater. Paris: Gabalda 1924.

**La Croix,** Paul Marie de s. **Paul Marie de la Croix.**

**Lahitton,** José: Le Pater de Sainte-Thérèse de l'Enfant Jésus. Paris: Ed. Spes 1937. 239 S.
– El „Pater Noster" de Santa Teresita del Niño Jesus. Traducción del P. Bruno de San José, C. D. Burgos: Edit. „El Monte Carmelo" 1952. 269 S.

**Lahusen,** Friedrich: Die 5. Bitte des Vaterunsers und England. Predigt. Dein Wille geschehe auf Erden wie im Himmel. Unser Vater in dem Himmel, Dein Name werde geheiligt. Predigt. Und führe uns nicht in Versuchung, sondern erlöse uns von dem Übel. Predigt. Unser tägliches Brot gib uns heute. Predigt. Berlin: M. Warneck 1915. je 8 S.
– Das Vaterunser in 7 Predigten. Ausgelegt im Kriegsjahr 1915. Berlin: M. Warneck 1915. 71 S.

**Lahusen,** Hermann: Das Vaterunser. Eine Erklärung als Hilfe zum täglichen Gebet. Stuttgart: Quell-Verlag 1946. je 2 Bl.

**Lallinger,** Alfons OSB: Das Vaterunser. Der Weg zur Heiligkeit. Erbauungsbüchlein für innerliche Seelen. Aschaffenburg: Pattloch 1973. 190 S.
– So sollt ihr beten! Das Vaterunser, der Weg zur Heiligkeit. Konstanz: Verl. des Kanisiuswerkes 1933. 218 S.

**Lambot,** D. C.: Le „Pater" dans la Liturgie Apostolique d'après Saint Grégoire. In: Revue Bénédictine. Abbaye de Maredsous (Belgique): 13 (1930). S. 265–269.

**Lampert,** Johann Baptist: Gebet des Herrn. In: Exempel-Lexikon für Prediger und Katecheten. Bd. II. Freiburg: Herder (2. Aufl.) 1907. S. 157–216.

**Lang,** Hugo OSB: Das heilige Vaterunser. Rundfunkansprachen. München: Glocken-Verlag Dr. Martin Lurz 1946. 77 S.
– Das Vaterunser (Gedanken zum 4. Fastensonntag). In: Augsburger Postzeitung vom 9. März 1934.

**Langbehn,** Julius: Vaterunser. In: Der Geist des Ganzen. Freiburg: Herder 1930. S. 129.

**Langer,** Alois: Das Vater Unser. Fetischismus oder Christentum? (Volksschriften zur Umwälzung der Geister, H. 62). Bamberg: Handels-Druckerei 1907. 80 S.

**Langfors,** Arthur: Les traductions et paraphrases du Pater en vers français du moyen âge. In: Neuphilologische Mitteilungen. Bd. 14 (1922). S. 35–45.

**Läpple,** Alfred: Das Gebet des Herrn. In: Die Botschaft der Evangelien heute. München: Don Bosco-Verlag 1965. S. 350.
– Reich Gottes. In: Die Kernwahrheiten des Glaubens. Ein Kurzkatechismus für den heutigen Christen (bezogen auf die 2. u. 3. Bitte des Vaterunsers). München: Don-Bosco-Verlag 1973. S. 20 f.
– Das Vaterunser hier und heute (sieben Fastenpredigten). In: Der Prediger und Katechet. München – Freiburg: Wewel 96 (1957). H. 4–5, S. 234–292.

**Laros,** Matthias: Das Vaterunser als Gewissenserforschung. Regensburg: Friedrich Pustet 1956. 40 S.
– Dein Wille geschehe. In: Neue Zeit und alter Glaube. Eine Schriftenreihe über religiöse Fragen der Zeit. Freiburg: Herder 1936. S. 189.

**Lassaulx,** Hubert von: Das Heilige Vaterunser. In: Der christliche Sonntag. Freiburg: Herder 4 (1952). S. 404.

**Last,** Hugh: The ROTAS-SATOR Square: Present Position and Future Prospects. In: The Journal of Theological Studies. New Series 3 Nr. 1 (1952). S. 92–97.

**Lattey,** C. C.: The Our Father. In: Clergy Review. London, 31 (1949). S. 158–165.

**Laubarède,** Stéphane SJ: Notre Père, formule-clé du salut de l'univers (Coll. Quéstions posées aux catholiques). Toulouse: Editeur Privat 1966. 108 S.

**Laubscher,** Friedrich: Die Tür ist offen. Das Vaterunser als Anleitung und Hilfe zum Beten. Ein Stundenbuch. Stuttgart: Verlag Junge Gemeinde 1966. 142 S., 12 Tafeln.

**Lauck,** Willibald: Erklärung des Vaterunsers. In: Das Evangelium des hl. Matthäus u. des hl. Markus (Die Heilige Schrift für das Leben erklärt, Bd. XI). Freiburg: Herder 1935. S. 80–86.

**Laur,** Elred O.Cist: „So sollt ihr beten". Eine Gebetsschule unseres Herrn (Matth. 6,5–13 u. Luk. 11,2–18). Limburg: Gebr. Steffen 1925. 224 S.

**Laverdière,** Eugène: La Prière de la nouvelle alliance. In: Parole et Pain. Paris: 1966. Nr. 16, S. 397–420.

**Laymon,** Charles M.: The Lord's Prayer in its Biblical Setting. Nashville, Tenn.: Abingdon Press 1968. 160 S.

**Leaney,** Robert: The Lucan Text of the Lord's Prayer (Lk 11,2–4). In: Novum Testamentum. Leiden: E. J. Brill 1 (1956). S. 103–111.

**Lebourlier,** Jean: „Ne nous soumets pas à la tentation". In: Lettre de Ligugé. 123 (1967). Nr. 3, S. 3–18.

**Leclercq,** Henri: Article: SATOR-AREPO. In: Dictionnaire d'Archéologie chrétienne et de Liturgie. Paris: Letouzey et Ané. vol. XV (1949). S. 1, col. 913–915.
– Article: Oraison Dominicale. In: Dictionnaire d'Archéologie chrétienne et de Liturgie. Paris: Letouzey et Ané vol. 12, S. 2 (1936). col. 2244–2255.

**Ledrus,** Michele / Sartori, Remo: Padre nostro, che sei nei cieli. In: Parole di Vita. Brescia: Editrice Paideia 15 (1970). S. 94–108.

**Légasse,** Simon OFMCap: Jésus et l'enfant. „Enfants", „petits" et „simples" dans la tradition synoptique (Etudes Bibliques). Paris: Gabalda 1969. 376 S. s. S. 325.

**Leicher,** Alois SJ: Mein Vaterunser. Wir müßten das Vaterunser erst wieder entdecken. München: J. Pfeiffer 1953. 16 S.

**Leitheiser,** Ludwig / Pesch, Christ.: Jesus lehrt seine Jünger beten. In: Handbuch zur katholischen Schulbibel NT. Düsseldorf: Patmos-Verlag 1960. S. 174–178.

**Lemke,** Henry E.: Our Father. A Discussion of the Lord's Prayer. Philadelphia: Dorrance 1958. 46 S.

**Lengeling,** Emil Joseph: Vater unser. In: Die neue Ordnung der Eucharistiefeier (Reihe Lebendiger Gottesdienst, Bd. 17–18) Münster: Regensbergsche Buchhdlg. 1970. S. 21, 238, 240; s. Register S. 490.

**Lentzen-Deis,** Fritzleo SJ: Beten kraft des Gebetes Jesu. In: Geist und Leben. Würzburg: Echter 48 (1975). H. 3, S. 164–178.

**Léon-Dufour,** Xavier: Das Gebet, wie Jesus es gelehrt hat. In: Wörterbuch zur biblischen Botschaft. Freiburg: Herder 1964. S. 212f.
– Les Evangiles et l'histoire de Jésus (Coll. Parole de Dieu). Paris: Ed. du Seuil 1963. 528 S.
– Die Evangelien und der historische Jesus. Aschaffenburg: Pattloch 1966. Vater unser: S. 218, 370, 372, 406, 452, 453, 461.

**Leppich,** Johannes: In grüner Hölle. Ein brasilianisches Vaterunser. Düsseldorf: Bastion-Verlag 2. Aufl. 1967. 112 S.

**Lessmann,** Paul G.: The Lord's Prayer and the Lord's Passion. St. Louis, Mo.: Concordia 1966. 109 S.

**Letonnelier,** G.: Une interprétation du carré magique SATOR AREPO. In: Bulletin Archéologique du Comité des Travaux historiques et scientifiques. Paris, 1951–1952. S. 168–169.

**Lewis,** C. S.: „Girlanden" um Bitten des Vaterunsers. In: Briefe an seinen Freund. Einsiedeln: Benziger 1966. S. 24–55.

**Leyen,** Friedrich von der: Das Freisinger Paternoster und verwandte altdeutsche kirchliche Literatur. In: Walhalla. Bücherei für vaterländ. Geschichte, Kunst u. Kulturgesch. 3. München 1907. S. 68–78.

**Lhande,** Pierre: Le Pater (L'Evangile par dessus les toits). Paris: Ed. Spes 1931. 113 S.

**Lightfoot,** Joseph Barber: On a fresh Revision of the English New Testament (2. Aufl.). Appendix: On the words epiousios... London: Macmillan 1872. S. 195–242, S. 217f.

**Ligier,** Louis SJ: Le sens du Notre Père dans la liturgie de la messe. In: Parole et Pain. Paris: 12 (1966). S. 34–59.

**Limbeck,** Meinrad: Von Jesus beten lernen. Eine Auslegung des Vaterunsers auf dem Hintergrund des A. T. Stuttgart: Verlag Religiöse Bildungsarbeit 1980. 133 S.

**Lindau,** Hans: Das schöne Strahlenband der heiligen sieben Bitten des Paternoster. In: Seele. Regensburg: Habbel 1923. S. 118–120.

**Link,** Helen Kendall: Our Father. Thoughts and Prayers for Children. Ill. by Harold Minton. Philadelphia: Christian Education Press 1952. 96 S.

**Lipman,** Armand: Les origines juives de l'Oraison Dominicale ou Pater Noster, avec une introduction par Maurice Vernes. Paris: Fischbacher 1921. 47 S.

**Lippert,** Peter SJ: Jesus lehrt beten. In: Gotteswerke und Menschenwege. Biblische Geschichten in Bild und Wort, geschildert von Gebhard Fugel (und Peter Lippert). München: Ars sacra 1924. S. 52; Bildwiedergabe S. 51.

**Littmann,** Enno: Torreys Buch über die vier Evangelien. In: Zeitschrift für die neutestamentl. Wissenschaft. Bd. 34, Nr. 1 (1935). S. 20–34; bes. S. 29–30.

**Loeschcke,** Gerhard: Die Vaterunser-Erklärung des Theophilus von Antiochien. Eine Quellenuntersuchung zu den Vaterunser-Erklärungen des Tertullian, Cyprian, Chromatius u. Hieronymus (Sammlung Neue Studien zur Geschichte der Theologie u. der Kirche, 4). Berlin: Trowitzsch 1908. 51 S.

**Loheyde,** Gerhard: Das Vaterunser im Kriege und in schweren Notzeiten. Gütersloh: Verlag Der Rufer 1947. 26 S.

**Lohmeyer,** Ernst: Das Vater-Unser. Göttingen: Vandenhoeck & Ruprecht (5. unveränd. Aufl.) 1962 (Erstaufl. 1946) 216 S.
– The Lord's Prayer. Transl. from the German by John Bowden. London: Collins 1965. 320 S. (with bibliography).
– Our Father. An Introduction to the Lord's Prayer. New York: Harper & Row 1966. 320 S.
– Das Vater-Unser als Ganzheit. In: Theologische Blätter. vol. 17, Nr. 9–10 (1938). col. 217–227.

**Lord's Prayer.** Seven Prayers: The Lord's Prayer in seven languages: English French – German – Swedish – Spanish – Dutch – Indonesian. London: Narbulla Agency 1971. 20 S.

**Lord's Prayer** (Polyglott): The Lord's Prayer in the principal languages, dialects and versions of the world printed in type and vernaculars of the different nations. Compiled by G. F. Bergholtz. Chicago. 1884. 200 S.

**Lotz,** Johannes B.: Der siebenfache Weg. Das Herrengebet von seinem Ende her. Frankfurt: Verlag Josef Knecht 1980. 111 S.

– Wenn ihr heute Vater unser betet. Meditationen. (Veröffentlichungen der Stiftung „Oratio Dominica"). Freiburg: Herder 1978. 125 S.
– Das Vater unser – als Beispiel für die verweilende Wortmeditation. In: Einübung in das Meditieren am Neuen Testament. Frankfurt: Verlag Josef Knecht (2. Aufl.) 1965. S. 159–187.

**Lotz,** Theo: So betet der Christ. Gedanken in 12 Predigten zum Gebete des Herrn und zum Englischen Gruß, Paderborn: F. Schöningh 1938. 124 S.

**Louismet,** Sabinian: Anmutungen über das Vaterunser. Aus dem Englischen übersetzt von Chrysostomus Schmid OSB. St. Ottilien: Missionsverlag 1925. 99 S.

**Lowe,** John: The Lord's Prayer. London – New York: Oxford University Press 1962. 68 S.

**Lowrie,** W.: Abba Father. A comment on the Lord's Prayer. London: Longmans 1968. XVI, 232 S.

**Lucas,** Josef: So sollt ihr beten. Besinnliches über das Vaterunser. Limburg: Lahn-Verlag 1955. 335 S.

**Ludwig von Granada:** Vater unser. Betrachtungen über das Gebet des Herrn. Neu bearb. von Josef Nepp. München: Ars sacra 1936. 30 S. m. Abb.

**Lundbeck,** Johannes (Hrsg.): Die vielen Namen Gottes: s. **Krauss,** Meinhold (Hrsg.).

**Luther,** Martin: Auslegung des Vaterunsers. Sermon von den guten Werken (Calwer Luther-Ausgabe 3, erschienen als Siebenstern-Taschenbuch Nr. 40). Hrsg. Wolfgang Metzger. München u. Hamburg: Siebenstern Taschenbuch Verlag 1965. 223 S.
– Hingabe an den Vater (Auslegung deutsch des Vaterunsers für den einfältigen Laien). Ein Unterricht Luthers über eine alte Sache. Wiedergegeben von Harro Schoeneich. Gütersloh: Verlag Der Rufer 1949. 47 S.
– Das Vaterunser (Auszug aus Luthers Großem Katechismus). Berlin: Evang. Verlags-Anstalt 1949 (Lizenzausgabe). 24 S.
– Vater unser (Auslegung deutsch für den einfältigen Laien; Auszug: Luther lehrt es beten (zusammengestellt von Walter Koopmann). Bielefeld: Bechauf 1948. 28 S. m. Abb.
– Eine kurze Form der 10 Gebote, eine kurze Form des Glaubens, eine kurze Form des Vaterunsers (1520 erstm. erschienen). Dessau: Dünnhaupt 1934. 31 S. m. Zeichn.
– Auslegung deutsch des Vater unser für den einfältigen Laien. Hrsg. Walther von Loewenich (Klassische Erbauungsschriften des Protestantismus 2). München: Chr. Kaiser 1929. 82 S.; 3. Aufl. 1937. 67 S.

93

– Vater Unser. Aus Luthers Großem Katechismus. Zwickau: J. Herrmann 1927. 24 S. (2. Aufl. 1939; spätere Ausgabe Berlin: Evang. Verlags-Anstalt 1960).

– **Luther-Monumente.** Eine Sammlung hervorragender Schriften Dr. Martin Luthers. Hrsg. B. Schubert. Bd. 3: Sendbrief an den Papst Leo X.: Von der Freiheit eines Christenmenschen. Kurze Form der 10 Gebote, des Glaubens und des Vater Unser. Elberfeld: Luther. Bücherverein 1913. 110 S.

**Lüthi,** Kurt: Eine Traurede über das Vaterunser. In: Kirchenblatt für die reformierte Schweiz. Basel: 116 (1960). S. 289–290.

**Lüthi,** Walter: Das Unservater. Eine Auslegung. Basel: Reinhardt 15.–17. Tsd. 1963. 139 S.
– The Lord's Prayer. An Exposition. Transl. by Kurt Schoenenberger. Richmond, Va.: John Knox Press 1962. VII, 103 S.

**Lutz,** Joseph Maria: VATER UNSER. Sonette. München: Ehrenwirth 1948. 32 S.

**Luyapaert,** L.: Apprendre à dire „Notre Père". In: Revue diocésaine Tournai. Tournai 1961. S. 183–185.

**Luzi,** Pietro: Il Paternoster. Commento. Urbino: Ed. Chiara (2. Aufl.) 1960. 66 S.

**Luzzi,** G.: Il „Padrenostro". Firenze: Sansoni 1939. 80 S.

**Lyons,** H. P. C.: Und vergib uns unsere Schuld – Erlöse uns von dem Übel. In: Karl Färber (Hrsg.): Zum inneren Leben, Bd. III). Frankfurt: Josef Knecht 1967. Beide Stellen S. 269f.

# M

**m:** Das Vaterunser in der Meßfeier. In: Christ in der Gegenwart. Freiburg: Herder 30 (1978) S. 331.

**Macartney,** C. E.: The Lord's Prayer. New York: Fleming H. Revell 1942. 87 S.

**Macaulay,** Joseph Cordner: After this Manner. Thoughts on the Lord's Prayer. Grand Rapids, Mich.: Eerdmans 1952. 86 S.

**MacGee,** John Vernon: Prayer the Lord did not Pray. Wheaton, Ill.: van Kampen Press 1953. 95 S.

**Machoveć,** Milan: Jesus für Atheisten. Mit einem Geleitwort von Helmut Gollwitzer. Stuttgart: Kreuz-Verlag 1972. s. S. 104f., 117, 122f.

**MacKenna,** J.: The Our Father in the Middle Ages Mass-Commentaries. Dissertation Lic. theol. Trier 1968.

**Mackenzie,** Kenneth (Donald), Bishop of Brechin: The Divine Prayer. London: Mowbray 1956. 71 S.

**Maclaren,** Alexander: Our Father. Devotional Studies on the Lord's Prayer. Grand Rapids, Mich: Eerdmans (Home Devotional Library) 1946. 93 S.

**Madey,** Johannes: Das Gebet des Herrn. In: Wir beten unseren Glauben. Brücken zu Gott. München: Joseph Pfeiffer 1962. S.7f.

**Maertens,** Thierry / Frisque, Jean: Vater unser. Kurze Auslegung: In: Kommentar zu den neuen Lesungen der Messe. Freiburg: Herder 1970. Bd. 3: S.55f. (zu Mt 6,7–15) u. Bd. 6: S.80–81.

**Magdalena, Sr.** (Op gen Oorth): Tonfilm über die Vaterunser-Kapelle im Ibental. 1978 hergestellt.

**Magne,** Jean: Répétition de mots et exégèse dans quelques psaumes et le Pater. In: Biblica. Roma, 39 (1958). Fasc. 2, S.177 bis 197.

**Magnin,** Silvia: Das Vaterunser. Eine Meditation in Emailbildern von Silvia Magnin u. Texten von Ernst Steiger. Vaduz: Leben-Verlag 1976. 59 S.
Anm.: Das obige Buch diente als Vorlage für die Dia-Meditation „vaterunser". München: impuls studio 1979.

**Mai,** Angelo: Orationis Dominicae Explanatio ex codice saeculi circiter XI. In: Scriptorum veterum nova collectio e Vaticanis codicibus edita, vol. IX. Roma: Typ. Collegii Urbani 1837. S.377 bis 384.

**Maier,** Carl: Das Gebet des Herrn. In: Das Geheimnis des Glaubens. Eine Meßauslegung für das christliche Volk. Freiburg: Herder 1946. S.140–191.
Anm.: In der 3. Aufl. 1958 befindet sich diese Auslegung auf den Seiten 157–215.

**Maiuri,** Amedeo: Sulla datazione del „Quadrato magico" o criptogramma cristiano a Pompei. In: Rendiconti della Accademia di Archeol. Lett. e Belle Arti. Napoli: vol. 28 (1953). S.101–111.
– La Croce di Ercolano. In: Atti della Pontif. Accademia Romana di Archeologia. Rendiconti vol.15 (1939). S.193–218.

**Malessa,** Friedrich: Das Vaterunser in erbaulicher und prophetischer Deutung. Reutlingen: Philadelphia-Buchhandlung August Fuhr. 2. Aufl. 1952 (1. Aufl. 1938). 79 S.

**Manaranche,** André: Le Pater. In: 17ᵉ Dimanche Ordinaire. Assemblée du Seigneur 48, Paris: Les Éditions du Cerf 1972. S. 63 bis 69.

**Mangold,** Jörg: „Dein Name werde geheiligt!" Predigt über Matthäus 6,9. Basel: Reinhardt 1948. 10 S.

**Manson,** T. W.: The Lord's Prayer. In: Bulletin of the John Rylands Library. Manchester: vol. 38 (1955–56). S. 99–113, 436–448.
– The Lord's Prayer. In: The Sayings of Jesus as recorded in the Gospels according to St. Matthew and St. Luke. London: S.C.M. Press 1949 (repr. 1950). S. 167–171, 265–266.

**Marböck,** Johannes: „. . . . . wie auch wir vergeben". In: Christ in der Gegenwart (Reihe „Alttestamentliche Lesungen"). Freiburg: Herder 33 (1981). S. 303.

**Marchal,** Witold: Abba, Vater! Die Vaterbotschaft des Neuen Testaments. Düsseldorf: Patmos 1963. 126 S.
– Dieu Père dans le Nouveau Testament. Trad. par M. Cè. (Coll. Lire la Bible, 7). Paris: Ed. du Cerf 1965. 144 S.
– Abba, Père! La Prière du Christ et des Chrétiens. Nouvelle édition entièrement refondue (Analecta Biblica, 19 A.). Roma: Pontificio Istituto Biblico 1971. 272 S.
– Abba Vader! Studie over de oorsprong en de betekenis van het christelijk gebed „Abba, Vader" (Uit het Frans vertaald door W. Goll). Gent: Kolv 1964. 144 S.
– Abba, Pater! Oratio Christi et Christianorum. In: Verbum Domini. Roma: vol. 39 (1961). S. 240–247.

**Marchetti,** Ottavio: L'orazione domenicale. Meditazioni. Roma: Ferrari 1949. 435 S.

**Marckius,** Johannes: Exercitationes Juveniles... S. 357–454: De Pane EPIOUSIOS. Groningen: Dominicus Lens 1686.

**Marcos Abajo,** José Maria de: El reino de Dios. Curso 1º Nuestro Padre Dios. Salamanca: Anaya 1966. 67 S.

**Marcotte,** Marcel: Notre pain quotidien. Montréal: Bellarmin 1966. 141 S.

**Maresch,** Gustav: Zur SATOR-Formel. In: Commentationes Vindobonenses. vol. 1 (1935). S. 94–97.

**Maria Teresa (Suor) di Gesù:** Meditazioni sopra l'orazione domenicale. Napoli: Tip. pia casa dell'Addolorato 1890. 47 S.

96

**Maritain,** Raissa (Oumansoff): Notes sur le Pater. Paris–Bruges: Desclée de Brouwer 1962. 161 S.
– Notes on the Lord's Prayer. Arranged and ed. by Jacques Maritain. Foreword by Thomas Merton. New York / Toronto: Kenedy / Nelson 1964. 122 S.
– El Padre Nuestro. Trad. del Francès por M. Pastor. Madrid: Ed. Narcea 1972. 124 S.

**Marmion,** Columba OSB: Vaterunser, Gebet des Gotteskindes. In: Christus, das Leben der Seele. Paderborn: F. Schöningh 1937. S. 54, 541.

**Mar Osthathios,** Geevareghese: Cosmic, communitarian and kenotic dimensions of the new man in Christ. In: Indian Journal for Theology. 27 (1978), S. 177–185.

**Marshall,** J. T.: Our Morrow's Bread. In: The Expository Times. Nr. 1 (1891). S. 25–27.

**Martimort,** Aimé-Georges: Das Pater noster (in der liturgischen Feier). In: Handbuch der Liturgiewissenschaft, Bd. 1. Freiburg: Herder 1963. S. 143–146.

**Martin,** Bernhard: Das Vater-Unser. Ein Spruchbuch. Kassel: Johannes-Stauda-Verlag 1949. 50 S.

**Martin,** Eleanor Holman (Hrsg.): Our Father... the children offering in Lent (A book of praise and prayer and teaching for the children of the church etc. Book 2). London: SPCK (= Society for Promoting Christian Knowledge) 1951. X, 44 S. ill.

**Martin,** Hugh: The Lord's Prayer. New York / London: S.C.M. Press / Macmillan 1951. 128 S.

**Marty,** Martin E.: The Lord's Prayer. In: The Hidden Discipline. A Commentary on the Christian Life of Forgiveness in the Light of Luthers's Large Catechism. St. Louis, Mo.: Concordia Publishing House 1962. S. 65–87.

**Mases,** José Antonio: Los padre nuestros y el fusil. Barcelona: Plaza & Janes 1973. 272 S.

**Masser,** A.: Die althochdeutschen Übersetzungen des Vaterunsers. In: Beiträge zur Geschichte der deutschen Sprache u. Literatur, Bd. 85. Tübingen: 1963. S. 35–45.

**Massler,** Paul: Heimkehr zum Vaterunser. Drossen (Oder): P. A. Collrepp 1920. 149 S.

**Matthews,** Frances: Addresses on the Lord's Prayer. London: Allenson 1932. 79 S.

**Matthews,** Walter Robert: The Lord's Prayer. An exposition for today. London: Hodder & Stoughton (3. Aufl.) 1964. 59 S.

**Maurer,** Christian: Auf dem Wege zu einer einheitlichen deutsch-sprachigen Fassung des Herrengebets. In: Kirchenblatt für die reformierte Schweiz. Basel: Reinhardt 124 (1968). Nr. 12. S. 182 bis 183.
– Auf dem Weg zum gemeinsamen Vaterunsertext. In: Gottesdienst. Freiburg/Einsiedeln: Herder–Benziger 2 (1968), S. 41–42.

**Maurer,** Konrad: Das Unser Vater (Kleine Bibelauslegung 1). Zürich: Verlag Junge Kirche. 3. Aufl. 1947. 24 S.

**Mauriac,** François: Vaterunser. In: Leben Jesu. Aus dem Französ. von Robert Scherer. Freiburg: Herder 1936 (2. Aufl. 1937). S. 165 f. Anm.: 1955 erschien die 5., erw. Auflage; hier Vaterunser-Bezug S. 158.

**Maurice de Sully.** Maurice of Sully and the Medieval Vernacular homily: S. 83–87. With the text of Maurice's French Homilies from a Sens Cathedral Chapter Ms. By Charles Alan Robson. Oxford: B. Blackwell 1952. 219 S.

**May,** William John: Talk for young church members: The Lord's Prayer, the Beatitudes, the Apostles' Creed. London: Epworth Press 1955. VI, 79 S.

**Mayer,** Erika: Das Vaterunser lernen (Beitrag zum Thema ‚Beten im Religionsunterricht'. In: Anzeiger für die Seelsorge. Freiburg: Herder 90 (1981). S. 221, 224, 226.

**Mayer,** Josef Ernst: Wagnis und Bindung. Das Gebet des Herrn. Salzburg: Verlag Rupertuswerk, Erzabtei St. Peter 1952. 55 S.

**Mayr,** Resl: Das Weihnachtsspiel vom Vaterunser. (Unsere Weihnachtsspiele, Heft 10). Graz: Verlag Spiel und Fest 1961. 11 S.

**Mbunga,** Stefan (Tanganyika): Misa Baba Yetu. Schallplatte: Vater-Unser-Messe (Geschenk der Cathedral Bookshop in Dar Es Salam, Tanzania, Ostafrika). o. J.

**McBride,** Will: Das Vaterunser (Text-Bild-Band). Wuppertal: Jugenddienst-Verlag 1979. 122 S.

**McClellan,** J. B.: On the Rendering „Daily Bread" in the Lord's Prayer. In: The Expository Times. vol. 2, Nr. 8 (1890–91). S. 184 bis 188.

**Mechow,** Karl Benno von: Ursula betet das Vaterunser. In: Vorsommer. Roman. München: Albert Langen / Georg Müller 1935. S. 63 f.
Anm.: Der Roman wurde 1956 vom Verlag Herder übernommen.

**Meditationen zum Vater unser:** s. **Dörig,** Bruno.

**Megiser,** Hieronymus: Das Vaterunser. In 40 Sprachen. Mit einem Nachwort von Branko Berčič (Litterae Slovenicae, IV). München: Dr. Rudolf Trofenik 1968. Nachdruck der Ausg. Frankfurt 1593.

**Megivern,** J.: Forgive us our Depts. In: Scripture. London: 18 (1966). S. 33–47.

**Mehl,** Johannes G.: Gemeinsames Vaterunser und gemeinsames Apostolisches Glaubensbekenntnis. In: Gottesdienst u. Kirchenmusik. München: 1966. Nr. 6, S. 192–196.

**Mehl,** O. J.: Die Betonung des „Vater unser". In: Die Christenlehre. Berlin: 12 (1959). S. 52.

**Meinertz,** Max: Das Vaterunser. In: Theologische Revue. Münster: 45 (1949). Sp. 1–6.

**Meinhold,** Monika / Nickel, Rainer: Ironie, Parodie, Satire von Lucilius bis Loriot. Darin Text 4: Das Vaterunser (Fructus, Arbeitsmaterialien Latein). Freiburg / Würzburg: Ploetz-Verlag 1977. S. 56–59.

**Melchers,** Paulus Cardinal: Das Gebet des Herrn. Köln: Bachem 1883. 118 S.

**Melhardt,** Trude: Dein Wille geschehe. In: Seele. Regensburg: Josef Habbel 13 (1931). S. 132f.

**Mendelsohn-Bartholdy,** Felix: Vater unser im Himmelreich. Sonate VI. Schallplatte „Oberrheinische Orgeln. Freiburg: Christophorus-Verlag 1978. Seite B, 2. Teil.
– Vater unser im Himmelreich. In: Orgelwerke. Sonata VI. Frankfurt – New York – London: C. F. Peters o. J. S. 102.

**Meneghini,** Bentivoglio OFM: La preghiera dettataci da Gesù: Il „Padre Nostro". Brescia: La Queriniana 1940. 348 S.

**Menghin,** Oswald: Kriegs-Vaterunser und Verwandtes. München: Verlag Natur und Kultur 1916. 38 S.

**Merk,** K. Josef: Vater unser. Pater noster. In: Die heilige Messe in ihrer Feier. Stuttgart-Degerloch: Otto Schloz 1948. S. 155–159.

**Mertes,** Johannes: Das Vaterunser als Tischgebet. In: Gotteslob im Kirchenlied. Merzig: Vlg. der Merziger Druckerei 1962. S. 203 u. 208.

**Meßner,** Johannes: Gebet in der Kraft des Leidens. In: Das Wagnis des Christen. Innsbruck: Tyrolia 1960. S. 139–142 über die drei letzten Bitten des Vaterunsers.

**Metzger,** Bruce M.: How Many Times Does „EPIOUSIOS" Occur Outside the Lord's Prayer? In: The Expository Times. Edinburgh: vol. 69 (Nov. 1957). Nr. 2, S. 52–54.
Anm.: Ebenso enthalten in: NT Tools and Studies. Leiden: Brill 1968, S. 64–66.

**Metzger,** Max Josef: Für Frieden und Freiheit. In diesem Buch zum Thema „Vaterunser" die Seiten 13f., 67f., 92, 103, 106, 134f. beachten. Meitingen: Kyrios-Verlag 1964.
– Abba – guter Vater. In: Karl Färber (Hrsg.): Zum inneren Leben III. Frankfurt: Josef Knecht 1967. S. 85f.

**Metzler,** Veronika: Vater unser. In: Walburgis-Blätter. Eichstätt 1938. S. 2.

**Meyer,** Leo: EPIOUSIOS. In: Zeitschrift für vergleichende Sprachforschung. vol. 7, Nr. 6 (1858). S. 401–430.
– Über das griechische EPIOUSIOS. In: Nachrichten von der Königl. Ges. der Wissenschaften u. der Georg-August-Universität zu Göttingen. Nr. 7 (1886). S. 245–259.
– Über die vierte Bitte des Vaterunsers. Vortrag am 2. Jan. 1886. Dorpat: Karow 1886. 22 S.

**Meyer,** Paul: Ancienne glose du Symbole et du Pater (Teil V des Beitrages „Bribes de littérature anglo-normande"). In: Jahrbuch für romanische und englische Literatur. Leipzig: F. A. Brockhaus 7 (1866). S. 51–55.

**Meysing,** Jacques: Introduction à la numérologie biblique. Le diagramme SATOR-AREPO. In: Revue des sciences religieuses. Strasbourg: vol. 40 (1966). S. 321–352.

**Michaelis,** Joannes David: Commentatio de Battologia ad Matth. 6,7. Göttingen: Victorinus Bossigel 1753.
Anm.: Eine Neuausgabe erschien in: Syntagma Commentationum, pars secunda: Göttingen: Vandenhoeck 1767. S. 55–88.

**Michaelis,** Wilhelm: Das Unser-Vater (Mt 6,9–13(14f.). In: Das Evangelium nach Matthäus, Teil 1, Kap. 1–7. Zürich: Zwingli-Verlag 1948. S. 300–332.

**Michel-Jean,** Charles: Un nouveau texte du Notre Père. In: Parole et Pain. Paris: 12 (1966). S. 1–4.

**Michels,** Thomas OSB (Hrsg.): De dominica oratione: s. **Cyprian von Karthago.**

**Miegge,** G.: Le „Notre Père" du temps présent. In: Etudes théologiques et religieuses. Montpellier, vol. 35 (1960). H. 4, S. 237 bis 253.

**Minichthaler,** Josef: Das Paternoster mit seiner Erweiterung. In: Schönheit und Wert des heiligen Messopfers. Wien: Mayer & Co. 1937. S. 124–126.
– Vaterunser, das erste und vorzüglichste liturgische Gebet. In: Messe und Leben. Katechetische Behandlung des heiligen Messopfers. Innsbruck: Tyrolia 1935. S. 69–74.

**Mithridates:** s. **Adelung,** Johann Christoph.

**Modersohn,** Ernst: Das Vaterunser des Apostels Paulus. Biblische Betrachtungen über Epheser 3,14–21. Freiburg i. Br.: O. Fleig 1922. 100 S.
– In der Gebetsschule Jesu. Betrachtungen über das Gebet des Herrn. Blankenburg (Thür.): Buchdr. u. Verlag „Harfe" 1929. 119 S.
– (Hrsg.): s. **Das Gebet des Herrn.**

**Moffatt,** James: Tertullian on the Lord's Prayer. In: The Expositor. 8th Ser. Nr. 103 (1919). S. 24–41.
– Cyprian on the Lord's Prayer. ibidem. Nr. 105. S. 176–189.
– Augustine on the Lord's Prayer. ibidem. Nr. 106. S. 259–272.

**Moldaenke,** Theodor: Das Vater Unser. 10 Betrachtungen für besinnliche Leute. Berlin: M. Warneck 1928. 60 S.

**Moll,** Anna: Herr, lehre uns beten... In: Seele. Regensburg: Habbel 27 (1951). S. 60f.

**Möller,** Sebastian Heinrich: Über das Vater-Unser (Matth. 6,9; Luk. 11,1ff.). In: Theologische Monatsschrift für das Jahr 1802. vol. 1. S. 23–36.

**Molo,** Walter von: Vier Bitten des Vaterunsers. In: Zeitwende. München: 19 (1947). S. 382–384.

**Mone,** Franz-Joseph (Hrsg.): s. **Kärntner Vaterunser-Auslegung.**

**Monod,** W.: Le plan du „Notre Père". In: Revue Biblique. Paris: April 1965. S. 16.

**Montero,** Alonso J.: Dos versiones gallegas del Padrenuestro en el siglo XVIII. In: Compostellanum. Santiago de Compostela. vol. 10 (1965). S. 355–357.

**Montifontanus,** P. Luzian: Das Heilige Vater Unser. Neubearbeitet u. herausgegeben von Dr. A. Heiter. Buffalo, N.Y.: Druck u. Verlag der „Aurora und Christliche Woche" 1907. XI, 313 S.

**Moppert,** Oscar: Ein Helfer für Predigten über das Unser Vater: Ernst Lohmeyer: Das Vaterunser. In: Kirchenblatt für die reformierte Schweiz. Basel: Reinhardt: 113 (1957). S. 245–246.

**Morando,** Luigi: Lezioni catechistiche sul Pater noster e sull'Ave Maria. Roma: Tipografia Salesiana 1906. VIII, 112 S.

**Morison,** E. F.: „Hallowed be Thy Name". In: The Expository Times. vol. 28, Nr. 7 (1916–1917). S. 298–300.

**Morris,** Richard: Old English Homilies and Homiletic Treatises of the 12th and 13nd Centuries. First Series, VI: Pater Noster, London: N. Trübner 1868. S. 54–71.
– Old English Homilies of the 12th Century. Second Series V: Pater Noster. London: N. Trübner 1873. S. 24–31.

**Moss,** Harry George: Lord's Prayer in the Bible. With a Foreword by the Bishop of Blackburn. London: Longmans 1948. XI, 197 S.

**Mosshamer,** Ottilie: Vater unser: s. **Brems,** Alois.

**Mowinckel,** S.: Artos Epiousios. In: Norsk Teologisk Tidsskrift. vol. 40 (1939). S. 247–255.

**Muckermann,** Friedrich: Gedanken über das Vaterunser. In: Im Kampf zwischen zwei Epochen. Lebenserinnerungen. Mainz: Matthias-Gründewald-Verlag 1973. S. 556–557.

**Mühle,** Hans: Tägliche Kraft durch das Vaterunser. Eine Lebenshilfe und ein Zeugnis. Berlin: Christl. Zeitschriftenverlag (8. Aufl.) 1974 (1. Aufl. 1940). 104 S.
– Vaterunser der Arbeit. Arbeiter-Sprechchor (Reihe der Sprechchöre, 5). Berlin: E. Bloch 1934. 2 Bl.

**Müller,** Karl: Gott hat ein Ohr. Unser-Vater-Predigten in Südwest-Rheinhessen. Offenheim: Evang. Pfarramt Offenheim (Rheinhessen) 1977. 56 S.

**Müller,** Vollrath: Das Vaterunser – ein Kriegsgebet. Deutschlands Kämpfern und Betern gewidmet. Leipzig: P. Eger 1914. 16 S.

**Müller-Schwefe,** Hans-Rudolf: Schrittmacher des Lebens. Das Vaterunser. Hamburg: Agentur des Rauhen Hauses 1969. 127 S.

**Münscher,** Friedrich Wilhelm: Noch einmal über Epiousios. In: Neue Jahrbücher für Philologie und Pädagogik. vol. 16 (1890). S. 112–115.

**Münster,** M. Birgitta zu, OSB: Das Vaterunser. In: Walburgis-Blätter. Eichstätt 1940. S. 90–93.

**Murray,** J. O. F.: The Origin and Meaning of the Lord's Teaching in Prayer. Abbey House Westminster: Central Readers' Board Office 1941. 30 S.

**Murray,** Ralph L.: The Other Dimension. Meditations on the Disciples' Prayer. Nashville, Tenn: Broadman 1966. 96 S.

**Muschiol,** Felicitas: Das gemeinsame Vaterunser (Leserbrief). In: Der christliche Sonntag. Freiburg: Herder 15 (1963), S. 174.
Anm.: Weitere Leserbriefe zu diesem Thema in Jhg. 1963, S. 96 u. 192.

**Mussner,** Franz: Das Vaterunser als Gebet des Juden Jesus. In: Traktat über die Juden. München: Kösel 1979. S. 198–208.

# N

**Nar,** Johannes: Frohbotschaft. Kurzpredigten und Lesungen über das Vaterunser und die christliche Liebe. Freiburg: Caritasverlag 1936. 44 S.
– Das Vater unser, das liebreiche Gebet des Herrn. In: Vom Geiste Gottes. Augsburg: Vlg. des Caritasverbandes 1934. S. 60–83.

**Navè,** Pnina: s. **Du, unser Vater;** s. **Gij, onze Vader.**

**Nepp,** Josef (Bearb.): s. **Ludwig von Granada:** Vater unser.

**Nestle,** Eberhard: Zum Vaterunser. In: Zeitschrift für die neutestamentl. Wissenschaft und die Kunde des Urchristentums. 6 (1905). S. 107–108.
– Unser täglich Brot. In: Zeitschrift für die neutestamentl. Wissenschaft und die Kunde des Urchristentums. 1 (1900). S. 250–252.
– Epiousios in Hebrew and Aramaic. In: The Expository Times. 21 (1909). S. 43.
– Artikel: „Lord's Prayer". In: Encyclopaedia Biblica, vol. III. London: A. & C. Black 1902. Sp. 2816–2823.

**Neun,** Manfred (Hrsg.): Vaterunser. Acht Predigten – acht Standpunkte (Konrad Eissler, Ulrich Fick, Friedrich Gölz, Peter Kreyssig, Manfred Neun, Theo Sorg, Eberhard Stammler, Albert Sting). Stuttgart: Quell-Verlag 1973. 77 S.

**Nève,** Thomas: La nouvelle traduction française du „Notre Père". In: Paroisse et Liturgie. Bruges: 48 (1966). S. 73–78.

**Neville,** Derek: Nature and the Lord's Prayer. Northam, Sx.: Davenport & Neville 1954. 56 S.

**Nickel,** Rainer: s. **Meinhold,** Monika.

**Nicolas,** Waltraud: Dein ist die Kraft. Vaterunser-Meditationen (Kleine Burckhardthaus-Bücherei Bd. 5). Gelnhausen: Burckhardthaus-Verlag 1959. 46 S.

**Nicolaus von Cusa:** Cusanus-Texte I: Predigten... 6): Die Auslegung des Vaterunsers in vier Predigten. Hrsg. u. untersucht von Josef Koch u. Hans Teske. (Sitzungsberichte der Heidelberger Akademie der Wissenschaften, Philosoph.-histor. Klasse. Jg. 1938–39, 4. Abhandlung). Heidelberg: Carl Winter 1940. 320 S.

**Nicolmann,** Margarete: Das Gebet des Herrn im Mutterleben. Berlin: Sonnenweg-Verlag 1937. 19 S.

**Nicolussi,** Johann: Vater unser. Innsbruck: Felizian Rauch 1955. 91 S.

**Nielen,** Josef Maria: Unser Vater. In: Karl Färber (Hrsg.): Zum inneren Leben, Bd. III. Frankfurt: Josef Knecht 1967. S 92f.
– Gebet des Herrn. In: Gebet und Gottesdienst im Neuen Testament. Freiburg: Herder 1937. S. 10, 28, 29, 65, 67, 154, 156, 158, 169.

**Nienhaus,** Heinrich: Das Vater unser. Eine belehrende Erzählung für die reifere Jugend. Mit 8 Tondruckbildern. Einsiedeln: Benziger 1883. 159 S.

**Nikolaus von der Flüe:** Pater noster. In: Otto Karrer, Wie unsere Väter beteten. München: Ars sacra 1927. S 101–103; desgleichen in: Otto Karrer, Gottesminne. München: Ars sacra 1929. S 57–59.

**Nißl,** Karl: So sollt ihr beten! Erwägungen zum Vaterunser und Englischen Gruß. München: A. Huber 1940. 16 S.

**Noesgen,** D.: Das ursprüngliche Vaterunser nach D. Harnack. In: Evangelische Kirchenzeitung. vol. 78, Nr. 17 u. 18 (1904). Sp. 389 bis 398 u. Sp. 417–426.

**Noesselt,** Jo. Aug.: Exercitationes ad Sacrarum Scripturarum Interpretationem I: Observationes ad Orationem quam vocant Dominicam (Matth. VI,9 seq. et Lucae XI, 2 seq. S. 1–46. Halle: Curt 1803.

**Nola,** Alfonso M. di (Hrsg.): Religiöse Zeugnisse aller Zeiten und Völker (Titel der Originalausgabe: La preghiera dell'uomo). Deutsche Bearbeitung von Ernst Wilhelm Eschmann. Darin zum Thema Vaterunser: S. 278–279, 305. Düsseldorf–Köln: Eugen Diederichs Verlag 1963.

**Nothomb,** Pierre: Le Pater alterné. Poème. Bruges: Desclée de Brouwer 1950. 51 S.

**Notre Père.** Ill. de Raymond Gid. Avec 3 dessins. Paris: Revue des Jeunes 1943.

**Notre Père des Cieux.** Première Année d'Initiation Chrétienne. Bourges: Impr. Tardy 1946. 60 S.

**Le Notre Père des Enfants.** Hrsg.: Commission de l'enseignement religieux protestant, Taizé: Imprimerie de Taizé (Rencontres pédagogiques) (La première partie est signée: René Voeltzel). Taizé 1961. 32 S.

**Notre Père qui es aux Cieux.** La prière œcuménique. Beiträge von P. Bonnard, Jacques Dupont u. F. Refoulé. (Cahiers de la Traduction Œcuménique de la Bible, Nr. 3). Paris: Les Editions du Cerf / Les Bergers et les mages 1968. 118 S.

**Nyerere,** Julius: Das Vaterunser des Ministerpräsidenten. In: Welt in Christus. Feldkirch: 3/4 (1961) Nr. 32.
Anm.: Zitiert in Gottes Wort im Kirchenjahr, hrsg. Bernhard Willenbrink OMI, Bd. II, S. 272. Würzburg: Echter-Verlag.

# O

**O.,** E.: Vater unser (Leserbrief). In: Der christliche Sonntag. Freiburg: Herder 3 (1951). S 32.

**O.,** M. Vaterunser-Gedanken. In: Seele. Regensburg: Habbel 9 (1927). S 282f.

**Oberhammer,** Josef SJ: Eine vortreffliche Erklärung des Vaterunsers in katechetischen Predigten. In: Zeitschrift für katholische Theologie. Innsbruck: 32 (1908). S. 782–786.

**O'Donnell,** Clement M.: St. Cyprian on the Lord's Prayer. An Abstract of a Dissertation (Studies in Sacred Theology 2nd Ser. Nr. 124 A). Washington, D. C.: Catholic University of America Press 1960. XV, 52 S.

**Oehler,** Wilhelm Jos.: Das Vaterunser. 9 Heinrichsbader Predigten. Herisau (Appenzell): Selbstverlag Kurhaus Heinrichsbad 1929. 37 S.

**Oehler,** Willy Johannes: Herr, lehre uns beten. Zehn Kurzbetrachtungen zum Vaterunser. Basel: H. Majer 1948. 48 S.

**Oer,** Sebastian von OSB: Das Vaterunser. Zehn Betrachtungen. Freiburg: Herder 1910. 255 S. (3. u. 4. verb. Aufl. 1912; 5. u. 6. Aufl. 1923).

**Ohlmeyer,** Albert OSB: Sieben begnadete Sorgen. Das Vaterunser als Wort in den Tag. Freiburg: Herder 1957 (2. Aufl. 1958). 100 S.

**Olivi,** Pierre-Jean: L'explication littérale du Pater selon Pierre-Jean Olivi. With an introduction and notes by F. M. Delorme. In: Archivio italiano per la storia della pietà. Roma: vol. 1 (1951). S. 181–203.

**Olivier,** V. L. SJ: Conférences sur l'Oraison Dominicale. Liège: H. Dessain 1895.

**Onze Vader.** Kerkboekje voor de jeugd bevattende o. a. Gebeden onder de H. Mis, Biecht en Communiegebeden. Kevelaer: Butzon & Bercker. 3e druk 1956. 80 S.

**Ooteghem,** J. van: Le rébus SATOR. In: Les Etudes Classiques. vol. 3 Nr. 4 (1934). S. 557–558.

**Oppen,** Dietrich von: Der sachliche Mensch. Frömmigkeit am Ende des 20. Jahrhunderts. S. 150–154: Das „Vaterunser" – Das Reden mit dem Unbegreifbaren. Stuttgart: Kreuz-Verlag (2. Aufl.) 1969. 202 S.

**ORATIO DOMINICA.** Schallplatte (zwei Stück) vom Anno Santo 1975. Torino: Editrice Marietti.
– Reproduktion nach dem Original der Congregatio Propaganda Fide 1870 in 250 Sprachen mit den entsprechenden Schriftzeichen einschließl. Schallplatte „Gebet des Herrn" von Papst Paul VI. Torino: Marietti 1974.

**ORATIO DOMINICA:** s.: **Reuter,** Johannes

**Orcibal,** Jean: „Dei agricultura": le carré magique SATOR AREPO, sa valeur et son origine. In: Revue de l'Histoire des Religions. Paris: vol. 145 (1954). Nr. 1, S. 51–66.

**Origines:** Ausgewählte Schriften. Bd. 1. In: Bibliothek der Kirchenväter. Bd. 48, S. 64–137. München: Kösel & Pustet 1926.

**Osiander,** Andreas: Ein Sermon auss dem 6. capit. Matthei uber das heilige Vater unser... die er die letzte gethan den 2. Octobris jm. 1552 ja. Königsperg: 1552.

**Osmont,** Anne: Le Pater, commentaires ésotériques. Paris: Ed. des Champs Elysées 1949. 27 S.

**Otto,** Gert (Hrsg.): Praktisch theologisches Handbuch. Vaterunser: S. 42, 49, 61, 108f., 288, 297f. Hamburg: Furche-Verlag. 2. vollst. überarb. Aufl. 1975.

**Our Father.** The text of the Lord's Prayer with additional prayers by Princess Ileana. London: Faith Press 1960. 17 S.

**Owen,** E. C. E.: Epiousios. In: The Journal of Theological Studies. vol. 35 Nr. 140 (1934). S. 376–380.

# P

**P. R.:** Die Urfassung des Vaterunsers. In: Christ in der Gegenwart. Freiburg: Herder 22 (1970), S. 32.

**Page,** Thomas Ethelbert: Critical Notes on the Lord's Prayer. In: The Expositor. 3rd Ser. vol. 7 (1888). S. 433–440.

**Paldele,** P.: „Gib uns heute unser tägliches Brot". Gedanken über die Brotbitte in Krieg und Frieden. Innsbruck: Tyrolia 1916. 151 S.

**Papini,** Giovanni: Vater unser. In: Lebensgeschichte Christi. München: Allgem. Verlagsanstalt 1924–25. S. 160–163.

**Paracelsus,** Theophrastus von Hohenheim: Das Mahl des Herrn und Auslegung des Vaterunsers. Nach den Handschriften neu hrsg., übertr. u. erläutert von Gerhard Deggeller. Dornach – Basel: Hybernia-Verlag 1950. 171 S.

**Parkinson,** John: Kingdom come. With a foreword by the Bishop of London. London: Bles 1970. 93 S.

**Parsch,** Pius: Das Paternoster (biblisch-exegetisch). In: Meßerklärung im Geiste der liturgischen Erneuerung. Klosterneuburg: Verlag Volksliturg. Apostolat 1935. S. 279–285.
– Das Vaterunser. Klosterneuburg: Verlag Volksliturg. Apostolat o. J. 24 S.
– Das Vaterunser. Eine Bibelstunde. Heilige-Schrift-Karthotek u. Evangelien-Harmonie. Immenstadt: Verlag Georg Moser o. J. (mit Imprimatur Augsburg vom 4. 11. 29).

**Parsons,** Martin: Praying the Lord's Prayer. A brief introduction for personal use. (Christian Living Series; a Falcon Booklet). London: Church Pastoral-Aid Society 1964. 20 S.

**Parvillez,** Alphonse de, SJ: Le Notre Père (Coll. Les belles prières). Paris: Procure générale du Clergé 1948. 47 S.

**Pascher,** Josef: Das eine Vaterunser aller Getauften. Rundfunkvortrag im Bayerischen Rundfunk / Kirchenfunk (unter dem Titel KATHOLISCHE WELT) vom 21. 4. 1968. Ms. 11 S.
– Das Vaterunser der Christen des deutschen Sprachgebietes. In: Liturgisches Jahrbuch. Münster: Aschendorff 18 (1968). S. 65–71.
– Das neue Vaterunser. Das einheitliche Gebet der Christen im deutschen Sprachraum. In: Passauer Bistumsblatt 33 (1968), Nr. 12 vom 24. März.
– Das Vaterunser der einen Kirche im deutschen Sprachraum. In: Klerusblatt. Eichstätt / München 1968. Nr. 7, S. 106 f.
– Vaterunser (in der Messe). In: Eucharistia. Gestalt und Vollzug. Münster: Aschendorff 1947. S. 260.

– Vaterunser keine Gebetsformel. In: Inwendiges Leben in der Werkgefahr. Krailing vor München: Wewel 1940. S. 39f.

**Paslack,** H. Ewald: Exegetische Bemerkungen zu Matt. 6,9–13 u. Luk. 11,2–4. Ein Vortrag, teilweise gehalten auf der Fellinschen Sprengelsynode am 1. Juni 1904. Straßburg: Ed. J. Heitz 1905.

**Le Pater Noster** (en sept langues: français – anglais – allemand – américain – hollandais – suédois – espagnol). Paris: C.N.A.C. 1966.

**Pater noster.** La traduction commune du „Notre Père". In: Documentation Catholique. Paris: 63 (1966). S. 181–184; Informations Catholiques Internationales. Paris: 1966, S. 6; Questions liturgiques et paroiss. Louvain: 1966. S. 141–145.

**Pater noster: s. Handschrift Andechs.**

**Paternoster-Auslegung.** Zugeschrieben Jakob von Jüterbog. Verdeutscht von Heinrich Haller. Hrsg. Erika Bauer (Lunder Germanistische Forschungen, 39). Lund: CWK Gleerup / Kopenhagen: Ejnar Munksgaard 1966. 299 S., 4 Faks.

**Patfoort,** A. O. P.: Prière de Vie, Vie de Prière. In: La Vie Spirituelle. Paris: 113 (1965). S. 689–695.

**Pauleser,** Saturnin OFM: Vater unser! In: Messfeier – Lebensfeier. Miltenberg: Vlg. des Christkönigsbundes 1957. S. 24–26.
– Das Vaterunser – das Gebet der Christenheit. Eine Mahnung zur Einheit. Würzburg: F. Schöningh 1947. 36 S.

**Paul-Marie de la Croix OCD:** Méditations du „Pater" (Coll. Vie et Prière). Bruges / Paris: Desclée de Brouwer 1961 (3. Aufl. 1966). 302 S.
– Das Vaterunser. Betrachtet für Christen von heute. Aus dem Französ. von M. Maria-Petra Desaing OSU. Luzern: Räber 1964. 254 S.
– Meditación del Padrenuestro. Madrid: Ed. Rialp 1962. 399 S.

**Pearson,** E. M.: The Lord's Prayer. A course of lessons for children aged 8–10 years. London: S.P.C.K. 1947. 48 S.

**Pechstein,** H. Max: Das Vater Unser. Holzschnitte. Ausgabe A: Holzschnitte mit der Hand koloriert; Ausgabe B: Einfarbige Holzschnitte. Berlin: Propyläen-Verlag 1921. 12 Tafeln.

**Péguy,** Charles: Quelques Poèmes. Le Pater: S. 16–24. Utrecht / Anvers: Het Spectrum 1953.
– Das Vaterunser. Vorbemerkung von Dr. Heinrich Kahlefeld. In: Akadem. Bonifatius-Korrespondenz 50 (1935). Nr. 3, S. 121–128.
– Vater unser. In: Das Mysterium der unschuldigen Kinder. Wien, München: Verlag Herold 1958. 190 S.

**Peignot,** Gabriel: Quelques recherches sur d'anciennes traductions de l'Oraison Dominicale... Dijon: V. Lagier 1839.

**Pelletier,** R.: La deuxième demande du Pater d'après la tradition. Roma: Diss. Pontificia Università Gregoriana 1952.

**Persijn,** A. J. (Hrsg.): Wessel Gansfort. De oratione dominica. In een dietse bewerking. Assen: Van Gorcum 1964. 178 S.
Siehe auch unter **Gansfort,** Wessel.

**Pesch,** Christ.: Jesus lehrt seine Jünger beten: s. **Leitheiser,** Ludwig.

**Pesch,** Otto Hermann: Das Gebet zum Vater – Das Bittgebet. In: Das Gebet. Augsburg: Verl. Winfried-Werk 1972. S. 44 f, S. 113 f.
– Pater noster oder Vater unser, das Beten in der Muttersprache. In: Sprechender Glaube. Mainz: Matth.-Grünewald-Verlag 1970. S. 78.

**Petau,** Denis: Dissertationum Ecclesiasticarum Libri Duo... Liber II, caput 9: De petitione quarta Orationis Dominicae. In: J. B. Fournials ed.: Dogmata Theologica. vol. 7. Paris: Louis Vivès 1867 (1re éd. en 1641). S. 463–468.

**Peter,** Maria: Vaterunser-Betrachtungen. In: Herders Haus-Kalender für Zeit und Ewigkeit, Jahrgang 1951. Freiburg: Herder 1950. S. 48, 51, 66, 69, 84, 87, 102, 105.
– (Hrsg.): Das heilige Vaterunser: s. **Becker,** Karl.

**Petersmann,** Werner: The Gospel in the Lord's Prayer. Lecture-Sermon. In: Bibliotheca Sacra. vol. 87, Nr. 347 (1930). S. 284–297.

**Peterson,** Erik: Frühkirche, Judentum und Gnosis. Zum Thema „Vaterunser": S. 18 u. 164. Freiburg: Herder 1959.

**Pétré,** Hélène: Les leçons du „panem nostrum quotidianum". In: Recherches de science religieuse (Mélanges J. Lebreton II). Paris, vol. 40 (1951–52). S. 63–79.

**Petrus Chrysologus:** Ausgewählte Predigten. In: Bibliothek der Kirchenväter. Bd. 43, S. 75–105. München: Kösel & Pustet 1923.

**Pettitt,** (Charles) Ian: Sermon outlines on the Lord's Prayer. With a Commentation by the Archbishop of York. London: Mowbray 1957. 32 S.

**Petuchowski,** J. J. (Hrsg.): Das Vaterunser: s. **Brocke,** Michael.

**Petzold-Heinz,** Irma: Vaterunser. Acht Claudius-Geschichten nach Bildern von Ludwig Richter. Stuttgart: Christl. Verlags-Haus 1954. 83 S. (ill.).

**Peuntner,** Thomas: Betrachtungen über das Vaterunser…: s. **Rudolf,** Rainer SDS (Hrsg.).

**Peysson,** Abbé: Le Parfum du Pater. Paris: (2. Aufl.) 1881.

**Pfältzer,** Norbert: Die deutschen Vaterunser-Auslegungen von den Anfängen bis ins zwölfte Jahrhundert. Vergleichende Studie auf Grund von quellenkritischen Einzelinterpretationen (Bibliographie S. 183–193). Frankfurt: Inaugural-Dissertation 1959.

**Pfannkuche,** Heinrich Fridrich: Über die Gebetsformel der Messiasschüler Matth VI, 9–13 u. Luc XI, 2–4. In: Allgem. Bibliothek der bibl. Litteratur von Johann Gottfr. Eichhorn, Bd. 10. Leipzig: Weidmann 1800. S. 846–878.

**Pfannschmidt,** C. G.: Die sieben Bitten des Vater Unser. 8 Kupferätzungen nebst erläuterndem Text des Künstlers. Berlin: R. Schuster 1908.

**Pfeifer,** Hermann: Das Vaterunser. Leipzig: Dürrsche Buchh. 1913. V, 96 S.

**Pfeiffer,** W.: Gleicher Wortlaut des Vaterunsers. In: Deutsches Pfarrerblatt. Neukirchen–Vluyn: 53 (1953). S. 347.

**Pfendsack,** Werner: Unser Vater. Eine Auslegung des Gebets der Christenheit. Basel: Fr. Reinhardt 1961. 113 S.

**Pfenningsdorf,** Oskar: Praktisches Christentum im Rahmen des kleinen Katechismus Luthers, Teil II: Der christl. Glaube und das Gebet des Herrn. 2. u. 3. Hauptstück. Schwerin: F. Bahn (5. neubearb. Aufl.) 1909. 287 S.
– Der christliche Glaube und das Gebet des Herrn. Ein kurzer Leitfaden in Anlehnung an „Praktisches Christentum", Teil 2. Schwerin: F. Bahn (2. Aufl.) 1920. 50 S.

**Piccon-Schultes,** Helga: Vater unser. In: Christ in der Gegenwart. Freiburg: Herder 28 (1976). S. 310.

**Pichenot,** A.: Il Pater, ovvero istruzioni sopra l'orazione domenicale. Versione di Angelo Acquarone. Sampierdarena: Libr. Salesiana 1904. 368 S.

**Pichery,** E.: La Prière du Seigneur. In: La Vie Spirituelle. vol. 13, Nr. 73 (1925). S. 25–50; Nr. 74 (1925). S. 142–165.

**Pieper,** Josef: Weistum – Dichtung – Sakrament. Aufsätze und Notizen. Zum Thema „Vaterunser": S. 322f. München: Kösel 1954.

**Pierre,** Abbé: Vaterunser, die Gott lächerlich machen. In: Regensburger Bistumsblatt vom 17. März 1957.

**Pierret,** Theodore: Conférence sur l'Oraison Dominicale et traduction du traité de Saint Cyprien sur le même sujet. Paris: Sarlit. 1862. 336 S.

**Pies,** Otto SJ: Das Große Gespräch. Winke für das innerliche Leben. Darin Vaterunser-Bezug: S. 20, 62, 134. Kevelaer: Butzon & Bercker 1956.
– Teilnahme an Gottes Gespräch. In: Das große Gespräch. Kevelaer: Butzon & Bercker 1955. S. 20.

**Piguet,** Gabriel Emmanuel Joseph: Notre Père qui êtes aux cieux... Méditations quotidiennes d'après les temps liturgiques. 2 Bde. Paris: Maison de la Bonne Presse 1951. 382 u. 386 S.

**Pilgrim:** Vaterunser – Des Friedens Weg. In: Reihe Evangelium im Taschenformat. „Welch tiefe innere Beziehung: Himmelfahrt und Vaterunser". Ausgedeutet in „Vaterland", Luzern, 12. Mai 1956.

**Pistelli,** Ermenegildo: Il Pater noster. Firenze: Ariani 1907. 25 S.

**Planck,** Heinrich von: Predigt... über die 6. Bitte des Vaterunsers. Stuttgart: Quell-Verlag der evang. Gesellschaft 1915. 12 S.
– Das Vaterunser. 9 Predigten 1914–1915. Stuttgart: Calwer Verlag 1915. 154 S.

**Plassmann,** J. O.: Eine alte Formel und ihre neue Deutung. In: Germanien. Sept. 1937, Nr. 9. S. 284–285.

**Plotzke,** Urban OP: Das Vaterunser. In: Bergpredigt. Von der Freiheit des christlichen Lebens. Frankfurt: Josef Knecht 1960. S. 168–216.
– Das Gebet des Herrn als Gebot der Zeit. Köln und Vechta: Albertus-Magnus-Verlag 1938. 118 S.; 3. Aufl. 1940. 104 S.

**Plummer,** Alfred: Artikel: „Lord's Prayer". In: A Dictionary of the Bible... ed. by James Hastings, vol. III. Edinburgh: T. & T. Clark 1905. S. 141–144.

**Plus,** Raoul SJ: Zu Gott, dem Vater. München: Ars sacra 1936. 32 S.
– Paternité divine. Fraternité humaine. Toulouse: Apostolat de la prière 1935. 15 S.

**Prodhradsky,** Gerhard: Vaterunser (im Stundengebet, bei der Taufe, in der Messe). In: Lexikon der Liturgie. Innsbruck: Tyrolia 1962. S. 394f.

**Poeppig,** Fred: Das Vaterunser als Menschheits- und Erkenntnisgebet. Basel: Verlag Die Pforte 1956. 116 S.

**Pöhlmann,** D. J. P. (Hrsg.): Geist und Kraft des Vaterunsers. Ein Andachtsbuch für christliche Familien, die sich gern nach Jesu

Sinn und Vorschrift mit Gott unterhalten. Erlangen: Palmsche Verlagshandlung 1825. 222 S.

**Poirine,** J.: Le Pater et l'heure présente. Paris: Lethielleux o.J. (zw. 1920 u. 1930). 305 S.

**Polaert,** André: La catéchèse du Notre Père aux hommes d'aujourd'hui. In: La Maison-Dieu. Paris: Nr. 85 (1966). S. 117–139.

**Polanus von Polansdorf,** Amandus: Syntagma Theologiae Christianae... Tomus II, Buch IX, Kap. 17: De oratione Dominica. Genf: Pierre Aubert 1612. Sp. 759–775.

**Ponte,** Ludwig de SJ: Vaterunser (14. Betrachtung). In: Betrachtung über die vorzüglichen Geheimnisse unseres Glaubens. Neue deutsche Ausgabe von Max Schmid SJ. Bd. III. Regensburg: Manz 1930. S. 212–237.

**Pöppinghaus,** Josef SJ: das vaterunser. Kleine Abendmeditation zur Eröffnung (des ND-Bundestages). In: Hirschberg, Frankfurt a. M. 1971 Nr. 6/7, S. 140–142.

**Portmans,** Fr.: La science du Pater ou l'Oraison Dominicale appliquée aux Mystères du saint Rosaire, aux grandes fêtes de l'année etc. Liège: Dessain 1884.

**Pottenstein,** Ulrich von (ca. 1360–1420): Paternoster-Auslegung. Nach der Handschrift a X 13 des Erzstifts St. Peter zu Salzburg kritisch herausgegeben u. eingeleitet von Gerold Hayer. Dissertation Salzburg 1972. Bd. 1; 89+103 S.; Bd. 2: 422 S. Mit Literaturverzeichnis Bl. 82–89.

**Pottwin,** Lemuel S.: Does the Lord's Prayer make mention of the Devil? In: Bibliotheca Sacra. vol. 48, Nr. 190 (1891). S. 332–339.
– Further on τοῦ πονηροῦ in the Lord's Prayer. In: Bibliotheca Sacra. vol. 48, Nr. 192 (1891). S. 686–691.
– EPIOUSIOS. In: Journal of Biblical Literature. vol. 12, Nr. 1 (1893). S. 15–22.
– The Old Syriac Version of the Lord's Prayer: Its Rendering of EPIOUSIOS. In: Bibliotheca Sacra. vol. 51, Nr. 201 (1894). S. 165 bis 168.

**Prentice,** William K.: Our „Daily" Bread, τὸν ἄρτον ἡμῶν τὸν ἐπιούσιον , In: The Review of Religion. New York: vol. 11 (1947); Nr. 2. S. 126–131.

**Presser,** Helmut: Bodonis „Vaterunser in 155 Sprachen (Giambattista Bodoni, Buchdrucker 1740–1813). In: Der Druckspiegel. Stuttgart: 21 (1966). Nr. 9, S. 569–571.

**Preve,** Maurizio: Armonie del Padre Nostro. Alba: Ed. Paoline 1948. 128 S.

112

**Price,** George: A Life-changing Prayer. Stockwell: Ilfracombe 1961. 37 S.

**Prime,** Derek: Tell me the answer about the Lord's Prayer. London: Victory Press 1965.

**Probst,** Jakob: Das Unservater. Betrachtungen und Lieder. Basel: Kober / Majer 1912. 72 S.

**Prochnow,** Herbert Victor: Meditations on the Lord's Prayer. Natick, Mass.: Wilde 1959. 60 S.

**Projektgruppe Glaubensinformation:** Dein Wille geschehe. In: Wer glaubt, denkt weiter (Herderbücherei, Bd. 550). Freiburg: Herder 1977. S. 123f.

**Przybylski,** Lothar: Das Vaterunser für die deutsche Not. Cottbus: H. Differt 1923. 47 S.

**Pugsley,** Clement Harry Horrell (Hrsg.): After this manner. 31 meditations on the Lord's Prayer (Epworth devotional book series). London: Epworth; Chicago: Allenson 1952. XII, 180 S.

**Puniet,** Pierre de: Les trois homélies catéchétiques du sacramentaire gélasien … III: L'Expositio Orationis Dominicae. In: Revue d'Histoire Ecclésiastique. vol. 6 (1905). S. 304–318.

**Pury,** Roland de: Notre Père … (Collection L'actualité protestante). Neuchâtel: Delachaux et Niestlé (2. Aufl.) 1959. 95 S.

**Puzik,** Erich: Das Vaterunser des Flüchtlings. Weiden / Opf.: Verl. Der neue Tag / Königstein: Priesterreferat 1948. 62 S.

**Pytel,** J.: Adveniat regnum tuum – Historia Interpretacij prosby (orationis Mt 6,9 ss. par. resc. franc.). In: Roczniki Teologiczno-Kanoniczne. Lublin: 11 (1964). H. 1, S. 57–69.

# R

**Radecki,** Sigismund von: Die sieben Bitten – Der Wille Gottes. In: Wort und Wunder. Salzburg / Leipzig: Verlag Otto Müller 1940. S. 99–161.

**Ragaz,** Leonhard: Von der Revolution der Bibel. 1. Das Unservater. Zürich: Relig. soz. Vereinigung der Schweiz 1943. 28 S.

**Rahner,** Karl: Das Gebet kein Hymnus, sondern sieben Bitten. In: Sendung zum Gebet. Schriften zur Theologie, Bd. III. Einsiedeln: Benziger 1956. S. 250.

– Das Gebet der Schuld. In: Von der Not und dem Segen des Gebetes. Innsbruck: Felizian Rauch 1949. S. 118–139. Ebenda: Vaterunser als Bittgebet. S. 83 f.
Anm.: Von der Not und dem Segen des Gebetes 1958 als Bd. 28 in der Herderbücherei erschienen (S. 116–137), später, 1978, als Bd. 647 der Herderbücherei.
– Gott, unser Vater. In: Gnade als Freiheit (Herderbücherei Bd. 322). Freiburg: Herder 1968. S. 24–29.

**Ramsay,** R. Guy: The Lord's Prayer in modern Life. London: Kingsgate Press 1936. 82 S.

**Rathgeber,** Alphons M.: Das Paternoster. In: Das heilige Meßopfer. Nürnberg: Sebaldus-Verlag 1946. S. 322–326.

**Rattenbury,** J. E.: Our Father and His Family. A devotional and social study of the Lord's Prayer. London: Epworth 1928. 96 S.

**Rau,** Christoph: Unser täglich Brot. In: Christengemeinschaft. Stuttgart: Verlag Urachhaus 35 (1963). S. 201–205.
– Das Vaterunser und die Neugliederung des Matthäus-Evangeliums. In: Die Christengemeinschaft. Stuttgart: Verlag Urachhaus 45 (1973). Nr. 5, S. 146–150.

**Rau,** Johann Wilhelm: Festum Jesu Christi Natalitium... Praemittuntur nonnulla de quaestione: An oratio dominica praecipue apostolis fuerit destinata. Erlangen: Jung 1804.

**Raynald,** Volanda: Biography of a prayer. An explanation of the power, efficacy and insight resulting from the use of the Lord's Prayer as an exercise in devotion. Los Angeles: Commonwealth Press 1945. XVI, 94 S.

**Read,** David H. C.: The Lord's Prayer for today. Holy Common Sense. Nashville and New York: Abingdon Press 1968. 96 S.

**Reatz,** August: Das Vaterunser. In: Jesus Christus. Sein Leben, seine Lehre, sein Werk. Freiburg: Herder 1925. S. 181 f.

**Rechenberg,** Friedrich Georg Frh. von: Wenn ihr betet. Gedanken über das Vaterunser. Gießen: Brunnen-Verlag 1929. 70 S.

**Recker,** Klaus: Das Gebet des Herrn. In: Einheit und Frieden. Gedanken zu den Grundgebeten. Kevelaer: Butzon & Bercker 1973. S. 47–52.

**Redlich,** Herbert (Hrsg.): s. **Vater unser im Himmelreich.**

**Redpath,** Alan: Victorious Praying. Studies in the Family Prayer. London: Pickering 1957. 151 S.; Paperback-Edition 1971. 151 S.

114

**Redslob** (anonymes Werk, jedoch Zuschreibung gesichert): Das Gebet des Herrn (1. Aufl. 1692). Straßburg: Berger-Levrault 1847.

**Refoulé,** François: La prière des chrétiens. I. Le Notre Père dans la tradition chrétienne; II. Le Notre Père et l'exégèse moderne.
– La prière du Seigneur et le Mouvement œcuménique.
Beide Beiträge in: Notre Père qui es aux cieux. La prière œcuménique (P. Bonnard, J. Dupont, F. Refoulé) (Cahiers de la Traduction Œcuménique de la Bible, Nr. 3). Paris: Les Éditions du Cerf / Les Bergers et les mages 1968. S. 9–51 u. S. 53–75.

**Rehn,** Walter: Das Vaterunser. 17 Federzeichnungen. Mit einer Einführung von Walther Kalbe. Wülfingerode / Sollstedt: Treue-Verlag 1927. 6 S., 17 Tafeln.

**Reichert,** Franz Rudolf (Hrsg.): Die älteste deutsche Gesamtauslegung der Messe. S. 172–175: Von dem Pater noster bis auf die Collecten (Corpus Catholicorum Nr. 29). Münster: Aschendorff 1967 (1. Aufl. Nürnberg 1480). CXXXII, 233 S.

**Reinmann,** Wilhelm: Das Gebet des Herrn. Predigt über Lukas 11, 2–4. Berlin: Hutten-Verlag 1925. 13 S.

**Relles,** Jean-Pascal de: Israel attend son Dieu: s. **Beaucamp, Évode.**

**Rendtorff,** Rolf: Der Staat Israel und die Christen (zum Thema „Vaterunser" S. 183–196). In: Zeitwende. Gütersloh: Gerd Mohn 1974. H. 3.

**Rengstorf,** Das Vaterunser in seiner Bedeutung für unser Zusammenleben. In: Kerygma und Melos. Festschrift C. Mahrenholz. Kassel: Bärenreiter-Verlag 1970. S. 13–26.

**Renhardt,** Josef: Das Vater unser. In: Der Seelsorger. Wien: 21 (1950–51). S. 118–119.

**Reuter,** Elisabeth (Hrsg.): Ein Vaterunser für die ganze Woche. Berlin: Evang. Verlagsanstalt. 5. Aufl. 1967. 8 Bl.

**Reuter,** Johannes: Oratio Dominica XL linguarum. Collecta a Joh. Reuter. Rostochii, anno MDCLXXV. Editio nova phototypis expressa. Kopenhagen: Imanta 1954. 46 S.

**Réveillaud,** Michel (Hrsg.): Saint Cyprien: L'Oraison Dominicale: s. **Cyprian von Karthago.**

**Reyero,** A.: Algo muy importante acerca del Padre Nuestro y la oración en general. Con el P. Alonso Diaz y otros profesores de Comillas. In: Cultura biblica. Madrid. 32 (1975), S. 137–142.

115

**Rheinfelder,** Hans: Dante als Beter. In: Serta Romanica. Festschr. für Gerhard Rohlfs zum 75. Geburtstag. Tübingen: Max Niemeyer Verlag 1968. S. 219–236.
– Dantes Paternoster. In: Estudis Romànics. Barcelona: Institut d'Estudis Catalans 9 (1967). S. 241–249.

**Rich,** Joseph Walter: Lord's Prayer: Ill. by Stanley Dunlap jr. Washington, D. C.: Review & Herald 1956. 127 S.

**Richard Ermyte: s. Aarts,** F. G. A. M. (Hrsg.)

**Richardson,** R. D.: The Lord's Prayer as an Early Eucharistia. In: Anglican Theological Review. Evanston, Ill.: 39 (1957). S. 123–130.

**Richstätter,** Karl SJ: Herz-Jesu-Paternoster. In: Deutsche Herz-Jesu-Gebete. München: Kösel 1930. S. 101 f.

**Richter,** Klemens: Zum „Embolismus" nach dem Vaterunser. In: Christ in der Gegenwart. Freiburg: Herder 33 (1981). S. 339.

**Richter,** Ludwig: Bilder zum Vaterunser. Geleitwort von Matthias Claudius (hrsg. auf Veranlassung der Evang.-Luth. Freikirche). Berlin: Evang. Verlagsanstalt 1966. 8 Bl. u. Abb.
– 12 Bilder zum Vaterunser. Geleitwort von Matthias Claudius. Zwickau (4. Aufl.) 1935. 9 Bl.
– Unser Vater in dem Himmel. 9 eingedruckte farbige Bilder mit Andachten von Gottfried Herbers. Lahr: Verlag für Volkskunst u. Volksbildung R. Keutel ca. 1922. 23 S.
– Vater Unser in Bildern. Leipzig: A. Dürr (20. Aufl.) 1908. 8 Bl. u. Titelbild (Volksausgabe 1913).
– Vater Unser in Bildern. In Holzschnitt ausgeführt von August Gaber. Dresden: Verlag Gaber u. Richter (1. Ausg.) 1856. 9 Bdl.

**Richter,** Wilhelm: Ein deutsches Vaterunser. 5 Predigten. Berlin: Röttger 1933. 31 S.

**Rienecker,** Fritz: Das Evangelium nach Matthäus. Zum Vaterunser: Mt 6,9–15, S. 72–76. (Wuppertaler Studienbibel). Wuppertal: R. Brockhaus 1974.

**Rimaud,** Didier: Le Notre Père et les psaumes. In: La Vie Chrétienne. Paris: Nr. 85 (mars 1966), S. 9–13; Nr. 86 (avril 1966), S. 8–14; Nr. 87 (mai 1966), S. 13–16.

**Rittelmeyer,** Friedrich: Das Vaterunser als Menschwerdung. Stuttgart: Verlag Urachhaus (8.–11. Tsd.) 1952. 184 S.
Anm.: Eine frühere Ausgabe des Werkes erschien im Verlag Christengemeinschaft Stuttgart 1935. 204 S. u. trat als neues Werk an die Stelle eines Buches gleichen Titels, das zuletzt 1923 erschien.
– Das Vaterunser. Zehn Kanzelreden. München: Chr. Kaiser 1923 (12. Tsd.). IV, 88 S.

116

- The Lord's Prayer, Transl. from the German. London: Macmillan 1931.

**Ritter,** Karl Bernhard: Das Vaterunser. Hamburg: Hanseat. Verl.-Anst. 1925. 72 S.

**Ritz,** Emil MS: Das Vaterunser, betend erklärt. Ulm/Donau / Mörschwil (Schweiz): La Salette-Verlag 1967. 126 S.

**Robert,** André (Hrsg.): s. **Einleitung in die Heilige Schrift,** Bd. 2.

**Robinson,** Arthur Willam: The Way to Pray. A Study of the Lord's Prayer. London: SCM Press 1931. 127 S.

**Robinson,** J. A.: The Lord's Prayer in the Early Church. Cambridge 1891.

**Rocca,** Annette di: Vater unser! Freiburg / Schweiz: Kanisius-Druckerei 1951. 80 S.

**Rocc(h)a,** Angelo de Camerino: Bibliotheca Apostolica Vaticana... Commentario... Appendix... De Oratione Dominica variis linguis et characteribus conscripta. Roma: Typ. Apostolica Vaticana 1591. S. 365–376.

**Rodriguez,** Alphonse SJ: Explication des demandes du Pater. Opuscule traduit de l'Espagnol. Lille: Desclée de Brouwer 1893.

**Roennecke,** Carlo: Il Paternostro overro l'orazione domenicale: dodici meditazioni. Firenze: Tipografia Claudiana 1878. 228 S.

**Roetzer,** W.: Des hl. Augustinus Schriften als liturgiegeschichtliche Quelle. München: Huber 1930. Zum Thema Vaterunser: S. 128f.

**Rogg,** Michael: Das Gebet des Herrn. Ausgelegt und gepredigt im hohen Dom zu Augsburg. Kempten u. München: Verlag Joseph Kösel 1909. 58 S.

**Rogge,** Christian: 'Επούσιος und kein Ende. In: Philologische Wochenschrift. Leipzig: O. R. Reisland 47 (1927). Sp. 1129–1135.

**Roguet,** A.-M.: Le nouveau texte français du „Notre Père". In: La vie spirituelle. Paris: 114 (1966). S. 5–24.

**Rohde,** Maria: Vater unser... In: Kirchenzeitung für das Bistum Hildesheim. Nr. 50 v. 13. Dez. 1959.

**Romberg,** Wilhelm: Hier legt mein Sinn sich vor Dir nieder. Das Gebet des Herrn betend entfaltet (Schule des Gebets, 2). Berlin: Furche-Verlag 1935. 101 S.

**Rönsch,** Hermann: Wie und aus welchem Grundgedanken ist die griechische Fassung der vierten Bitte im Vaterunser zu erklären? Exegetische Studie. In: Zeitschrift für wissenschaftliche Theologie. Leipzig: R. Reisland 27 (1884). S. 385–393.

117

Rordorf, W.: „Wie auch wir vergeben unseren Schuldnern" (Mt 6,12b). In: Studia Patristica. Berlin: vol. 10,1 (1970). S. 236–241.

Roser, Henri: Le Notre-Père expliqué par Luther, Zwingli et Calvin. Rouen: Cagniard 1894.

Rössler, Helmut: Das Vaterunser als Tischgebet vor der Opfermahlzeit. In: Messe verständlich gemacht. Regensburg: Friedrich Pustet 1967. S. 132f.

Rössler, Max: Herr, lehre uns beten. In: Den ihr nicht kennt. Christus-Meditationen (Arena-Taschenbuch 43–44). Würzburg: Arena-Verlag 1961. S. 182–188.
Anm.: Vgl. auch Ausgabe des Echter-Verlags, Würzburg. 1955, S. 170–175.

Rostovtzeff, M. I.: Il rebus SATOR. In: Annali della R. Scuola Normale Superiore di Pisa. Lettere, Storia e Filosofia. Ser. II, vol. 3 (1934). S. 103–105.

Rousseau, O.: Le „Pater" dans la liturgie de la messe (Cours et Conférences VII, 1928). Löwen / Louvain 1929. S. 231–241.

Rousset, A.: Notre pain quotidien. Paris: Maison de la Bonne Presse 1912. 86 S. avec figures.

Roux, Hébert: L'Evangile du Royaume. Commentaire sur l'Evangile selon S. Matthieu. Genève: Labor et Fides 1956. S. 73 bis 76: La Prière.

Rudberg, Gunnar: Zusatz zu Anton Fridrichsen: ARTOS EPIOUSIOS. In: Symbolae Osloenses II. 1924. S. 42.

Rudl, Siegmund: Kriegs-Vaterunser. Andenken an den Weltkrieg für alle Mitkämpfer und ihre Angehörigen, Prag: Druck- u. Verl.-Anst. Bonifatia 1918. 8 farb. Bilder u. 2 S. Text.

Rudolf, Rainer SDS: Thomas Peuntners Betrachtungen über das Vaterunser und das Ave Maria. Nach österreichischen Handschriften herausgegeben u. untersucht. Wien: Verlag des Notringes der wissenschaftl. Verbände Österreichs 1963. 120 S.

Rüger, Leo: So dürfen wir nun sagen: „Abba, lieber Vater!" In: Der Werktagsheilige in unserer Zeit. Paderborn: F. Schöningh 1939. S. 37–42.

Ruhland, Gustav: Unser tägliches Brot gib uns heute. Die Wirtschaftspolitik des Vaterunsers. Berlin: Deutsche Verlagsges. (2. Aufl.) 1933. 95 S.

Ruland, Ludwig: Das Vaterunser. Sieben Fastenpredigten. Breslau: Aderholz 1910. 90 S.

118

**Ruler,** Arnold Albert van: Het onze Vader. Nijkerk: G. F. Callenbach 1953. 48 S.

**Rumoldus van den H. Elias:** Heer leer ons bidden. Overweegingen op het Onze Vader (Karmel-Bibliothek). Heide-Kalmthout (Belgien): Soverdi-pers. 1946. 83 S.

**Rupp,** Hans: Vom rechten Beten. Betrachtungen über das Gebet des Herrn. Kaiserslautern: Buchhandl. des Evang. Vereins für die Pfalz 1933. 44 S.

**Ruppel,** Paul Ernst: Vaterunser-Lieder: s. **Beuerle,** Herbert.

# S

**Sabourin,** L.: Il vangelo di Matteo. In: Teologia e esegesi, Roma 1976. S. 425–457.

**Sailer,** Johann Michael: Das Vaterunser der Kranken. In: Hermann Gilhaus (Hrsg.): Ich bin nicht mehr allein. München: Ars sacra Verlag 1971. S. 50.
– Das Vaterunser. In: Gebete des Christen. Olten: Walter-Verlag 1947. S. 112–141.
– Das Vaterunser. Für Kinder erklärt. Mit Bildern von Ida Bohatta-Morpurgo. München: Ars sacra Verlag 1937. 62 S.

**Sainsaulieu,** Helmut: Das Paternoster. In: Et cum spiritu tuo. Die Antwort des Gläubigen. Wien: Herold-Verlag 1960. S. 135–141.

**Saliège,** Jules-Geraud Kardinal: Jesus und das Gebet. In: Schriften zum geistlichen Leben. Würzburg: Arena-Verlag 1963. S. 75–85, insbes. S. 77f. zum Thema „Vaterunser".

**Salisbury,** Frank O.: Lord's Prayer. 7 Pictures. The text apart from the authors own symbolism, was written by Robert Evans with the cooperation of Horace Shipp. London: Evans 1948. 46 S.

**Salvaneschi,** Nino: Dein Reich komme... In: Karl Färber (Hrsg.): Zum inneren Leben, Bd. III. Frankfurt: Verlag Josef Knecht 1967. S. 264.
– Vater unser. Deutung der einzelnen Bitten zur Bittprozession. Übersetzt von Franziska Friedrich. In: Münchener Kath. Kirchenzeitung, 41 (1948), S. 9.

**Samwaies,** Peter: Devotion digested: In several Discourses and Meditations upon the Lord's most holy Prayer... London: Richard Royston 1652.

**Sanders,** John Oswald: The World's Greatest Sermon. London: Marshall, Morgan & Scott 1972. 160 S.
– Maßstäbe, die herausfordern. Die Bergpredigt als Lebensprogramm. Aus dem Englischen von Gerlind Krause. Gießen / Basel: Brunnen-Verlag 1974. 127 S., zum Thema Vaterunser: S. 81–91: Wie wir beten sollen.

**Sandmel,** Samuel: A Jewish Understanding of the New Testament. Cincinnati: Hebrew Union College 1956. Zum Thema „Vaterunser": S. 150.

**Santmire,** H. Paul: Retranslating „Our Father". The urgency and the possibility. In: Dialog. St. Paul, Minn. 16 (1977), S. 101–106.

**Santo,** Joseph: Le „Notre Père" de l'heure présente. Préface de M. l'Abbé L. Ducrocq. Paris: chez l'auteur 1911. 192 S.

**Saphir,** A.: Het gebed des Heren (Lectures on the Lord's Prayer). Naar het Engels door A. R. Zalman-Marda. Amsterdam: Kirchner 1949. 206 S.

**Sarda,** Honoré MDF: Notre pain quotidien ou L'Evangile au jour le jour à la portée des petits et des grands. Paris: Les Editions Ouvrières 1961. 183 S. bes. S. 77.

**Sartori,** Remo: Padre nostro: s. **Ledrus,** Michele.

**Sattler,** Heinrichjoseph: Das Gebet, die verborgene Großmacht der Welt. Darin Hinweise auf das Vaterunser: S. 11, 32, 59f., 72. Köln: Lahn-Verlag für rel. Schrifttum Sattler & Co. 1940. 81 S.

**Sauer,** Paul: Das heilige Vaterunser. St. Louis, Mo.: Concordia 1949. 64 S.

**Schaefer,** Franz: Vaterunser oder Herrengebet. In: Anzeiger für die kath. Geistlichkeit. Freiburg: Herder. H. 5, 1968, S. 194.

**Schäfer,** Dina: Das Vaterunser für Kinder und Jugendliche (Bildband; 57 Bilder christlicher Kunst mit Kurztext). Freiburg: Christophorus-Verlag [um 1940].

**Schäfer,** Hans Ulrich: Meditationen zum Vater unser und zum Meditationsbild des Bruder Klaus: s. **Dörig,** Bruno

**Schäfer,** Peter: Das Vaterunser als Gebet in unserer Zeitenwende. 16 Predigt-Vorschläge (Predigten u. Vorträge, Bd. 37). Wiesbaden: Matthias-Grünewald-Verlag 1934. 158 S.

**Schanz,** Paul: Commentar über das Evangelium des heiligen Matthäus. 2. Das Gebet. 5–15. Freiburg: Herder 1879. S. 211–221.

**Schauer,** Friedrich: Das Vaterunser für unsere Notzeit erklärt. Königsberg, Pr.: Evangel. Jungmännerbund Ostpreußen 1924. 14 S.

**Schauerte,** Heinrich: Volkskunde des Vaterunsers. In: Theologie und Glaube. Paderborn: F. Schöningh 51 (1966). S. 449–459.

**Schawaller,** Fritz: Ein Vaterunser an den Gräbern. Predigt. Hrsg. Evangelischer Trostbund. Berlin: Schriftenvertriebsanstalt 1913.

**Scheele,** Paul-Werner: Vater, die Stunde ist da. Gebete der Ökumene (Herderbücherei Nr. 194). Darin zum Thema Vaterunser: S. 39–41, 150–152, 156. Freiburg: Herder 1964. 192 S.
– Opfer des Wortes. Gebete der Heiden aus fünf Jahrtausenden. Nach den Bitten des Vaterunsers zusammengestellt. Paderborn: Schöningh 1960. 288 S.

**Schell,** Hermann: „Zu uns komme dein Reich". In: Verherrlichung und Gemeinschaft. Hrsg. Paul-Werner Scheele. Paderborn: Schöningh 1957. Nr. 646 f.

**Schellbach,** Martin: Vater unser. Predigten für die Gegenwart. Lieder, Zeugnisse und Gebete zum Vaterunser aus 18 Jahrhunderten der Kirche. Berlin: Evang. Verlags-Anstalt 1950. 136 S.

**Schempp,** Otto: Das Vaterunser mit Lichtbildern. Gottesdienstliche Experimente beim 11. Deutschen Evang. Kirchentag in Dortmund. In: Badische Zeitung. Freiburg: Nr. 171: 27./28. Juli 1963, S. 3 f.

**Schempp,** Paul: Der Anruf Gottes. Eine Erklärung der ersten Bitte des Vaterunsers. München: Chr. Kaiser 1949. 151 S.

**Schenck,** Ernst von: Das Vaterunser (geschrieben 1937–1939). Aarau: Verlag der AZ-Presse 1945. 31 S.

**Scherding,** Pierre: Culte chrétien. In: Revue d'histoire et de philosophie religieuses. Strasbourg. 57 (1977), Nr. 1, S. 53–64.

**Scherer,** Robert: Das Vaterunser. Unseres Lebens täglich Brot. Beiträge zu einer Auslegung. Für Herrn Dr. Theophil Herder-Dorneich zum 60. Geburtstag. Freiburg 1958. 114 Schreibmaschinenseiten.

**Schieder,** Julius: Das Vaterunser in schwerer Zeit. Predigt. Augsburg: Schlossersche Buchhdlg. 1919.
– Das Vaterunser heute. Vortrag. München: Evangel. Buchhandlung 1938. 8 S.

**Schiller,** Gertrud: Das Vaterunser – Pater noster. In: Ikonographie der christlichen Kunst, Bd. 4,1, Die Kirche. Gütersloh: Gütersloher Verlagshaus Gerd Mohn 1976. S. 147–153.

**Schiller,** Margarete: Das Vaterunser. Ein Deklamatorium für Familien-, Werbe- u. Gemeinschaftsabende. Mit einem Anhang: Stoff für die angeführten Ansprachen. Berlin-Friedrichshagen: Jugendbuch-Buchhdlg. 1921. 32 S.

**Schimmel,** Annemarie: Denn Dein ist das Reich. Gebete aus dem Islam (nach dem Vaterunser gegliedert) (Veröffentlichungen der Stiftung „Oratio Dominica"). Freiburg: Herder 1978. 125 S.

**Schinle,** Gertrudis OCSO: Unser Vater in den Himmeln. Meditationen zum Vaterunser. Leutesdorf: Johannes-Verlag (2. Aufl.) 1973. 86 S.

**Schlags,** Willibrord: Herr, lehre uns beten. Alte und neue Hilfen, das Vaterunser andächtig zu beten. Trier: Paulinusdruckerei 1924. 16 S.

**Schlatter:** Der Kampf ums „tägliche Brot". In: Der Kirchenfreund. Blätter für evangelische Wahrheit und kirchliches Leben. Basel: 47 (1913). S. 385–391.

**Schlatter,** Adolf: Das Unser Vater und unsere gegenwärtige Lage. (Aus der Welt der Bibel, Nr. 5). Berlin: Furche-Verlag (3. Aufl.) 1930. 30 S.
– Das Unser Vater. Auslegung des Herrengebetes. Berlin: Furche-Verlag 1938. 43 S.

**Schlette,** Heinz Robert: Skeptisches Vaterunser. Hermeneutische Meditationen. In: Skeptische Religionsphilosophie. Zur Kritik der Pietät. (rombach hochschul paperback). Freiburg: Verlag Rombach 1972. S. 84–117.

**Schlig,** Hans: Das Vaterunser. In: Seele. Regensburg: Josef Habbel 1949. S. 146f.

**Schlunk,** Martin: Eine Predigtreihe über das Vaterunser. Stuttgart: Quell-Verlag 1949. 76 S.

**Schmid,** Chrysostomus OSB (Übers.): Anmutungen über das Vaterunser: s. **Louismet, Sabinian.**

**Schmid,** H. Christliches Beten und christliche Tat. In: Seele. Regensburg: Habbel 10 (1928). S. 14–17.

**Schmid,** Josef: Das Vaterunser. In: Das Evangelium nach Lukas (Regensburger Neues Testament). Regensburg: Friedrich Pustet 1940. S. 150–153.
– Das Vaterunser. In: Das Evangelium nach Matthäus (Regensburger Neues Testament Bd. 1). Regensburg: Gregorius-Verlag, vorm. Friedrich Pustet 1948. S. 89–98.
Anm.: In der 5. Aufl. 1965 befindet sich der Beitrag über das Vaterunser auf S. 121–135.

**Schmid,** W.: EPIOUSIOS. In: Glotta. Zeitschr. für griechische u. lateinische Sprache. vol. 6 (1915). S. 28–39.

**Schmidkonz,** Theo SJ: Jesus sagt: So sollt ihr beten... In: Tischgebete – Bergprdigt Jesu. München: Rex-Verlag 1976. S. 22 bis 28.
Anm.: Vgl. Sonderausgabe Meditative Gebete – Bergpredigt Jesu. München: Rex-Verlag 1977. S. 21–27.

**Schmidt,** Friedrich: Ihr sollt also beten. Bitten und Gedanken zum Vaterunser. Gütersloh: Verl. Kirche und Mann 1961. 12 S.

**Schmidt,** Heinrich: Und lehret sie! Eine Handreichung zum Katechismus-Unterricht – Das heilige Vaterunser (3. Hauptstück). Neuendettelsau: Freimund-Verlag 1954. 95 S.

**Schmidt,** Hermann SJ: Bidden onderweg van 1960 tot 1970. Documentaire studie met bibliografie en citatenselectie. Vater-unser: S. 45 f. + Bibliographie. Haarlem: J. H. Gottmer 1971. 195 S.
– Wie betet der heutige Mensch? Dokumente und Analysen (Übersetzung von „Bidden onderweg") (Pastoralliturgische Reihe in Verbindung mit der Zeitschrift „Gottesdienst"). Freiburg: Herder; Einsiedeln: Benziger 1972. Vaterunser: S. 58 f + Bibliographie.

**Schmidt,** Karl Ludwig: Artikel: Basileus, Basilea. In: Kittel: Theologisches Wörterbuch zum NT, Bd. I. Stuttgart: Kohlhammer 1933. Sp. 573–595.

**Schmidt,** Wolfgang P.: Zu Simon Grunaus Vaterunser. In: Indogermanische Forschungen. Berlin: 67 (1962). S. 261–273.

**Schmidt-Pauli,** Elisabeth von: Pater Noster. In: Missa sollemnis eines Lebens (Kardinal Faulhaber). Augsburg: Johann Wilh. Naumann 1949. S. 179–302.
Anm.: In diesem Buch auch Zitate aus Ansprachen des Kardinals, bes. S. 182 u. 183.

**Schmiedel,** Paul Wilhelm: Unser tägliches Brot. In: Schweizerische Theologische Zeitschrift. 30 (1913). S. 204–220.
– Nochmals „Unser tägliches Brot". ebendort. 31 (1914). S. 41–69.
– „Unser tägliches Brot". In: Der Kirchenfreund. Blätter für evang. Wahrheit u. kirchl. Leben. 48 (1914). S. 12–14.
– Die vierte Bitte im Vaterunser. In: Protestantische Monatshefte. 18 (1914). S. 358–364.
– Nochmals EPIOUSIOS. In: Philologische Wochenschrift. Nr. 50 (1928). Sp. 1530–1536.

**Schmitz,** Johannes: Das alte Vaterunser für die neue Zeit (Liga-Broschüren, F2). Kaldenkirchen: Missionsdruckerei in Steyl 1928. 32 S.

123

**Schnackenburg,** Rudolf: Gottes Herrschaft und Reich. Eine biblisch-theologische Studie. Freiburg: Herder 1959. Jüd. Gebete: S. 25; Matth 6,10: S. 54f., 72, 110; Luk 11,2: S. 54, 110.
– Vaterunser. In: Christliche Existenz nach dem Neuen Testament. München: Kösel 1967. Bd. 1, S. 145f.

**Schneider,** ?: Zum Gebet des Herrn. In: Schweizerische Theol. Zeitschrift, 20 (1903). S. 123–124.

**Schneider,** Gerhard: Das Vaterunser. In: Botschaft der Bergpredigt (Der Christ in der Welt VI, 8a). Aschaffenburg: Pattloch 1969. S. 70–77.

**Schneider,** Oda: So sollt ihr beten... In: Gott und Mensch im Gebet. Regensburg: F. Pustet 1939. S. 61–70.

**Schneider,** Reinhard: Die Macht des Vater unser. Jestetten: Miriam-Verlag 1976. 80 S.

**Schneider,** Reinhold: Und führe uns nicht in Versuchung. In: Macht und Gnade. Leipzig: Insel-Verlag 1941. S. 112–141.
– Führe uns nicht in Versuchung. In: Macht und Gnade. Ausg. 1949. S. 317–320.
Anm.: zitiert in Otto Karrer: Jahrbuch der Seele. 1951. S. 273.
– Das Vaterunser. In: Das Kreuz in der Zeit. Freiburg: Herder 1947. 58 S.
Anm.: Außerdem erschien eine Ausgabe (o. J.), 72 S., im Alsatia-Verlag in Colmar.
– Das Kreuz in der Zeit – Das Vaterunser – Der Kreuzweg – Die sieben Worte am Kreuz. Freiburg: Herder 1947. 149 S.
Anm.: Erschien auch in drei Einzelbändchen.
– Das Vaterunser. Neuausgabe mit einem Nachwort des Verfassers u. acht Illustrationen von Hans Holbein d. J. Freiburg: Herder 1957 (2. Aufl. 1959). 99 S. (4. Aufl. 1968)
– Doch viel geschieht, wenn zwei Hände sich falten. In: Worte aus der Tiefe (Hrsg. Curt Winterhalter). Freiburg: Herder 1976. S. 44f.
– Het Onzevader. Vertaald door A. Geerardijn. Antwerpen: Uitgev. Patmos 1960. 83 S.
– Das Vaterunser (mit begleitenden Worten zu den einzelnen Bitten). Hrsg. als erste Veröffentlichung vom Freundeskreis der Stiftung „Oratio Dominica". Freiburg: Herder [um 1963]. 10 S.

**Schnitzler,** Theodor: Das Vaterunser (in der heiligen Messe). Die Geschichte der Einfügung – Brückencharakter des Vaterunsers. In: Was die Messe bedeutet. Freiburg: Herder 1976. S. 173–176.
– Das Paternoster als Abschluß des Hochgebets und als Kommuniongebet. In: Die Messe in der Betrachtung, Bd. II. Freiburg: Herder 1957. S. 224–238.

Anm.: Von diesem Werk ist auch je eine englische, italienische u. spanische Ausgabe erschienen.
– Paternoster als Volksgebet. In: Kommuniongebet im Geist der Liturgie, erschienen im Liturgischen Jahrbuch. Münster: Aschendorff 9 (1959). S. 154f.

**Scholz,** Gustav: Vater unser, der du bist im Himmel. Kriegspredigten über das Vaterunser. Gotha: Engelhard-Reyhersche Hofbuchdruckerei 1914. 65 S.

**Schomerus,** Hans: Fülle der Welt. Das Vaterunser in unserer Zeit. München: Claudius-Verlag 1969. 149 S.
– Das Gebet des Herrn. In: Im Horizont des Christen. Stuttgart: Evang. Verlagswerk 1962. S. 76–88.

**Schopin,** Eugène: Notre Père qui es aux cieux. Imité de l'Anglais. Avec gravures. Toulouse: Soc. de livres religieux 1901.

**Schöttler,** Hans: Das Christentum des Vaterunsers. Die Wahrheit des 20. Jahrhunderts. Bremen: Verlag kommende Kirche 1938. 21 S.

**Schousboe,** J.: La Messe la plus ancienne: Recherches sur les origines du christianisme. In: Annales du Musée Guimet. Revue de l'histoire des religions. Paris: Librairie E. Leroux 48 (1927). S. 193 bis 256. Zum Thema „Pater noster" bes. S. 233–237.

**Schouwenburg,** P. N. van: Zeven beden en levenspractijk (Brandende kaarsen Nr. 69). s'Gravenhage: J. N. Voorhoeve 1949. 30 S.

**Schrader,** Fr. Io.: Oratio Dominica historice et dogmatice proposita praecipue autem Iudaismo opposita. Helmstedt: Stanno Hammiano 1723.

**Schräder,** Albrecht OFM: Ihr aber sollt also beten: „Vater unser …" (Buchausgabe der Schriftreihe Heiliges Wort, Nr. 21 bis 23). Freiburg: Herder 1938 (2. Aufl. 1939). 71 S.

**Schreiber,** Benedikt: Das Gebet der Reserve. Charles Péguy und das Vaterunser. In: „Der Pilger", Speyer, 17.5.1964.

**Schrenk,** Elias: „Priez ainsi". Etude sur l'Oraison Dominicale. Traduit librement de l'allemand par A. R. Paris: Fischbacher 1901.

**Schreyer,** Lothar: Oremus. Beter und Gebet. Mit 20 Bildern. Vaterunser: S. 62–66 (Reihe Vom Reichtum christl. Wirklichkeit, Bd. 12). Düsseldorf: Bastion-Verlag 1949. 203 S.

**Schrijnen,** Joseph: Geef ons heden ons dagelijk brood. In: Stud. Cath. vol. 4 (1927–28). S. 106–123.
– „Unser tägliches Brot gib uns heute". In: Collectanea Schrijnen. Nijmegen / Utrecht: Dekker Van de Vegt 1939. S. 303–320.

**Schrijvers,** Jos.: Notre Père qui êtes aux cieux. Entretiens spirituels. Bruxelles – Paris – Bruges: Desclée de Brouwer 1942. 318 S.

**Schroeder,** Hans Werner: Beten ist mehr als Bitten – Unser alltägliches Brot (Bitte u. Vollzug im zweiten Teil des Vaterunsers) – Führe uns nicht in Versuchung – Die Schuld und das Böse. In: Das Gebet. Übung und Erfahrung. Stuttgart / München: Verlag Urachhaus / Verlag die Christengemeinschaft 1977. S. 22: (Text des Vaterunsers), S. 32f., 39, 42, 77. Ebd.: Das Vaterunser bei Kindern und für Verstorbene. Fürbitte. S. 81–85.
– Bitte und Vollzug im Vaterunser. In: Die Christengemeinschaft. Stuttgart: Verlag Urachhaus 46 (1974). Nr. 11, S. 346–348.
– „Führe uns nicht in Versuchung". In: Die Christengemeinschaft. Stuttgart: Verlag Urachhaus 47 (1975). Nr. 2, S. 37–39.
– „Führe uns nicht in Versuchung". Im Gespräch mit dem Leser. In: Die Christengemeinschaft. Stuttgart: Verlag Urachhaus 48 (1976), Heft 6. S. 175–177.
– Das Gebet. Übung und Erfahrung. Stuttgart: Verlag Urachhaus 1977. 115 S.
– Sprechen und Hören des Vaterunsers. In: Die Christengemeinschaft. Stuttgart: Verlag Urachhaus 46 (1974). Nr. 3, S. 76–77.
– Das Vaterunser – mehr als ein Bittgebet. In: Die Christengemeinschaft. Stuttgart: Verlag Urachhaus 46 (1974). Nr. 9, S. 275 bis 277.

**Schröder,** Rudolf Alexander: s. **Vaterunser,** Das.

**Schröer,** Gustav: Der Vaterunser-Acker. Zwei Erzählungen. Berlin: Acker-Verlag 1936. 24 S.

**Schulte,** Joseph: Ein hebräisches Paternoster in einem Missale des 9. Jahrhunderts. In: Biblische Zeitschrift. 6 (1948). S. 48.

**Schulz,** Siegfried: Das Vaterunser: Mt 6,9–13 / Lk 11,1–4. In: Q Die Spruchquelle der Evangelisten. Zürich: tvz Theol. Verlag 1972. S. 84–93.

**Schulze,** Wilhelm: Das Vaterunser bei Rudolf Steiner. In: Evangelische Theologie. München: Chr. Kaiser 16 (1956). S. 427–432.

**Schumaker,** H.: A strange adventure of the „Our Father". In: Catholic World. New York: vol. 160 (1945). S. 342–349.

**Schümer,** Georg: Die dritte Bitte des Vaterunser. In: Christliche Welt. 1940. Heft 1, Sp. 16.

**Schupp,** Volker: Septenar und Bauform. Studien zur „Auslegung des Vaterunser", zu „De VII Sigillis" und zum „Palästinalied" Walthers von der Vogelweide (Philologische Studien u. Quellen, 22) (Diss. Freiburg i. Br.). Berlin: Erich Schmidt Verlag 1964. 195 S.

– Die „Auslegung des Vaterunsers" und ihre Bauform. In: Der Deutschunterricht. Stuttgart: Ernst Klett Verlag 11 (1959). S. 25–34.

**Schürmann,** Heinz: Das Gebet des Herrn. Aus der Verkündigung Jesu erläutert. Freiburg: Herder 1958. 142 S. (3. Aufl. 1965).
– Das Gebet des Herrn. Neubearbeitete u. erweit. Auflage. Freiburg: Herder 1978. 144 S.
– Das Gebet des Herrn als Schlüssel zum Verstehen Jesu (4. verbesserte u. erweiterte Auflage). Freiburg: Herder 1981. 192 S.
– Das Gebet des Herrn. Ein Übertragungsversuch. In: Bibel und Leben. Düsseldorf: 1 (1960). S. 261–265.
– Gottes mächtige Hilfsbereitschaft – gläubig bitten. In: Worte des Herrn. Mainz: Matthias-Grünewald-Verlag 1956. S. 159.
– Kurz-Erklärung des Vaterunsers. In: Worte des Herrn (Herderbücherei, Bd. 89). Freiburg: Herder 1961. S. 81 f.
– Worte des Herrn. Jesu Botschaft vom Königtum Gottes. Aufgrund der synoptischen Überlieferung zusammengestellt. Leipzig: St. Benno-Verlag 3. Aufl. 1960. 438 S. (1. Aufl. Mainz 1956).
– Praying with Christ. The „Our Father" for today. New York: Herder & Herder 1964. VI, 141 S.; Montreal: Palm Publ. 1964. 142 S.
– La Prière du Seigneur à la lumière de la prédication de Jésus (Études théologiques, 3). Paris: Ed. de l'Orante 1965. 117 S.
– Het gebed des Heren. Toegelicht uit de prediking van Jezus. Naar de 4de druk vertaald door Jules Verstaeten. Roermond – Maaseik: J. J. Romen & Zonen 1961. 127 S.
– Il Padre Nostro alla luce della predicazione di Gesù. Trad. di P. Vicentin. Roma: Città Nuova 1967. 172 S.
– Padre Nuestro. Madrid: Pax 1961. 216 S.

**Schütz,** Julius Franz: Das Vaterunser des Schaffenden. Gedichte. Graz: Leykam-Verlag 1917. 13 S.

**Schütze,** Alfred: Das Vaterunser und die Sakramente. In: Die Christusgemeinschaft. Stuttgart: Verl. Urachhaus: 22 (1950). H. 7 bis 8, S. 196–197.
– Das Vaterunser in den Sakramenten und in den Jahreszeiten. In: Die Christengemeinschaft. Stuttgart: Verl. Urachhaus 24 (1952). S. 138–140.

**Schwab,** Sr. Francis Mary: David of Augsburg's „Paternoster" and the Authenticity of his German Works (Diss. Univ. of California, Los Angeles) (Münchner Texte u. Untersuchungen zur deutschen Literatur des Mittelalters, 32). München: C. H. Beck 1971. VIII, 231 S.

**Schwartz,** J.: A propos du carré SATOR chez les Ethíopiens. In: Les Annales d'Ethiopie. Addis-Abeba / Paris: vol. 2 (1957). S. 219–223.

127

**Schwarz,** Günther: Matthäus 6,9–13 / Lukas 11,2–4. Emendation u. Rückübersetzung. In: New Testament Studies. London: vol. 15 (1969). Nr. 2, S. 233–247.

**Schwarz,** Leopold: Vaterunser. In: Steh' fest im Glauben, Bd. 5. München: Verlag Kath. Schrifttum Josef Schinner o. J. S. 433–440.
– Das Vaterunser als Gebet in unserer Zeitenwende. In: Kath. Familienkalender für das schaffende Volk in Stadt u. Land, Jhg. 1938.

**Schweitzer,** Albert: Die Mystik des Apostels Paulus. Darin S. 232 bis 236: Brotbitte. Tübingen: J. C. B. Mohr. 2. Aufl. 1954 (1. Aufl. 1930).

**Schweitzer,** C. G.: Hat Jesus selbst das Vaterunser gebetet? In: Deutsches Pfarrerblatt. Essen: 55 (1955). S. 265–266.

**Schweitzer,** Eduard: Das Unservater 6,7–13; vgl. Lk. 11,1–4. In: Das Evangelium nach Matthäus (Das Neue Testament Deutsch. Neues Göttinger Bibelwerk, Teilband 2). Göttingen: Vandenhoeck & Ruprecht (13. Aufl., 1. Aufl. der neuen Fassung) 1973. S. 91–100.

**Scott,** Ernest Findlay: The Lord's Prayer. Its character, purpose and interpretation. New York: Scribner 1. Aufl. 1951; Toronto: Saunders 1962. 126 S.

**Scott,** John Frank: Religion of the Lord's Prayer. Nashville, Tenn.: Abingdon Cokesbury 1946. 124 S.

**Scriba,** Otto: Das liebe Vaterunser, die Sprachlehre für die Kinder Gottes. Heilbronn: Eugen Salzer 1924. 80 S. m. Abb.

**Seale,** Ervin: Great Prayer. An interpretation of the Lord's Prayer. New York: Delhi publications 1947 (3., verb. Aufl.), 61 S.

**Seeberg,** Alfred: Vaterunser und Abendmahl. In: Neutestamentl. Studien. Georg Heinrici zu seinem 70. Geburtstag. Leipzig: J. C. Hinrichs 1914. S. 108–114.
– Die vierte Bitte des Vaterunsers. Rektoratsrede. Rostock: H. Warkentien 1914. 16 S.
– Die vierte Bitte des Vaterunsers. In: Reinhold Seeberg (Hrsg.): D. Alfred Seeberg: weiland ord. Prof. in Kiel, Worte des Gedächtnisses etc. Leipzig: A. Deichert'sche Verlags-Hdlg. 1916, S. 69–82.

**Seeburg,** Franz von (Pseudonym für Franz Xaver Hacker): Immergrün. Volkserzählungen Bd. 1: ... Vater Unser; Bd. 2: ... Und führe uns nicht in Versuchung; Bd. 3; ... Zu uns komme Dein Reich. Regensburg: Kösel-Pustet (4. Aufl.) 1919.

**Seeger,** Dora: Das Vaterunser. Zwei Weihnachtsfeiern. Potsdam: Stiftungsverlag 1930. 21 S.

**Seemann,** Margarete: Vater unser. Bilder von Tilde Eisgruber (Nürnberger Bilderbücher I/2). Nürnberg: Sebaldus-Verlag 1937 (neue Aufl. 1947). 12 Bl., 24 S.

**Seidel,** Uwe (Hrsg.): Vaterunser (Foto-Text-Heft 6). Gladbeck: Schriftenmissions-Verlag 1969. 24 S., 12 Bl. Abb. im Text.
Anm.: Gleichzeitig ebd. erschienen neun Schriftplakate zum Vaterunser.

**Seligmann,** S.: Die Satorformel. In: Hessische Blätter für Volkskunde. Leipzig: Teubner 13 (1914). S. 154–183.
– Ananisapta und Sator. In: Hessische Blätter für Volkskunde. Marburg: Kommissions-Verlag Elwert'sche Verlagsbuchhdlg. 20 (1921) S. 1–14.

**Sellmair,** Josef: Gewissenserforschung im Anschluß an das Vaterunser. In: Der Priester in der Welt. Regensburg: Friedrich Pustet 1939. S. 114–116.

**Senger,** Basilius OSB: Das Vaterunser (in der Messe). In: Laienliturgik. Kevelaer: Butzon & Bercker 1962. S. 104–106.

**Sequeira,** A. Ronald: Spielende Liturgie. Bewegung neben Wort und Ton in der Liturgie am Beispiel des Vaterunsers (Veröffentlichungen der Stiftung ,,Oratio Dominica''). Freiburg: Herder 1977. 223 S.

**Serrano de Haro,** Agustín: El Padre nuestro meditado por los niños. Para niños y niñas de 11 a 14 años. Madrid: Escuela Española 1961. 96 S.

**Sestili,** Alesandro: Pater noster. Ave Maria. Roma: Tip. E. Pappagallo 1957. 14 S.

**Seuffert,** Josef: Vaterunser – Gebet und Aufgabe. Eine Gebetsstunde oder sieben kurze Besinnungen. In: Wortgottesdienste 4. Düsseldorf: Verlag Haus Altenberg 1968. S. 50–59.

**Shearman,** Thomas G.: ,,Our Daily Bread''. In: Journal of Biblical Literature'' vol. 53 Nr. 2 (1934). S. 110–117.

**Sheen,** Fulton J.: Das Vaterunser. In: Leben Jesu. Freiburg: Herder 1961. S. 375.

**Sheward,** C. G.: The Lord's Prayer. A Study in Sources. In: The Expository Times. vol. 52, Nr. 3 (1940). S. 119–120.

**Shriver,** Donald W. jr.: The prayer that spans the world. An exposition: Social ethics and the Lord's Prayer. In: Interpretation. Richmond, Va.: vol. 21 (1967). Nr. 3, S. 274–288.

**Sickenberger,** Josef: Unser ausreichendes Brot gib uns heute! Akademische Rede. Habelschwerdt: Frankes Verlag 1923. 16 S.
– Das Vaterunser. In: Leben Jesu nach den vier Evangelien. Münster: Aschendorff'sche Verlagsbuchhdlg. 1932. § 52, II, S. 29 bis 32.

**Siewerth,** Gustav: Christi Reichsgebet. In: Der christliche Sonntag. Freiburg: Herder 4 (1952). S. 37–38.
– Das Gebet in der Ordnung des täglichen Lebens. Teil II,1: Das Vaterunser. In: Der christliche Sonntag. Freiburg: Herder 2 (1950). S. 53.

**Sikorsky,** Igor Ivan: The Message of the Lord's Prayer. New York: Obolensky 1963. 87 S.

**Sillevis Smitt,** Johannes Hendrik: Onze Vader die in de hemelen zijt. Den Haag: J. N. Voorhoeve 1958. 4. dr., 102 S.

**Simcox,** Carroll Eugene: Living the Lord's Prayer. A Study of Basic Christianity. New York: Morehouse 1951 / London: Dacre 1955 108 S. (New York); 94 S. + tables (London).

**Simovic,** Boniface: Le Pater chez quelques Pères latins. In: La France franciscaine. 21 (1938). S. 192–222 u. 245–264.

**Slack,** Kenneth: Praying the Lord's Prayer today. London: SCM Press 1973. 123 S.

**Smitmans,** Adolf: Vaterunser. In: Grabner-Haider (Hrsg.): Praktisches Bibellexikon. Freiburg: Herder 1969. Sp. 1145 f.

**Smitmans,** Adolf / Baur, Andreas: Das Gebet des Herrn in der Katechese (Werkhefte zur Bibelarbeit, 13). Stuttgart: Verlag Kath. Bibelwerk 1971. 141 S.

**Smukal,** G. M.: The Lord's Prayer – the Pastor's Prayer. In: Concordia Theological Monthly. St. Louis, Mo.: vol. 16 (1945). S. 145–153, 236–248, 301–306, 396–404, 456–472, 505–513, 583–590, 666–672, 842–847.

**Snowden,** Rita Frances: The Lord's Prayer: the Living Word. London: Epworth (Methodist Publ. House) 1968. 62 S.

**Sockman,** Ralph Washington: Lord's Prayer. An interpretation. London: Pilgrim's Press 1947. 20 S.
Anm.: Weitere Ausgabe erschienen: Nashville, Tenn.: Abingdon 1962.

**Soden,** Hermann Freiherr von: Die ursprüngliche Gestalt des Vaterunser. In: Die Christliche Welt. vol. 18, Nr. 10 (1904). S. 218 bis 224.
– Die älteste Form des Vaterunsers. In: Monatsschrift für Gottesdienst und Kirchliche Kunst. 1904. S. 333–345.

**Soiron,** Thaddäus OFM: Beten nur vor Gott (zu Mt 6,5–15). In: Die Bergpredigt Jesu. Freiburg: Herder 1941. S. 321–369.
– Das Vaterunser. In: Kirche und Kanzel. Paderborn: F. Schöningh 1927. S. 333–351.

**Sölle,** Dorothee: Meditation über das Vaterunser. In: Bibel heute. 1. Quartal 1974, S. 108.

**Solowjow,** Wladimir: Unser tägliches Brot gib uns heute. In: St. Nikolausbote. Berlin: 9 (1958).
Anm.: Obiger Beitrag entnommen dem Buch: Solowjow: „Die geistlichen Grundlagen des Lebens".

**Sonderegger,** Hugo: Das Gebet der Armen. Eine Anleitung zu evangelischem Beten an Hand des Unser Vater. Zürich: Zwingli-Verlag 1957. 111 S.

**Sonnenschein** Carl: Berliner Vaterunser. In: Notizen, Bd. XI. Berlin: Germania-Verlag 1928.

**Sorg,** Theo: Wenn ihr aber betet...: Über das Vaterunser. Stuttgart / Berlin: Kreuz-Verlag 1973. 157 S.

**So sollt ihr denn beten: Vater unser.** In: Die Worte des Herrn. Gebete und Reden, Gespräche und Sprüche Jesu. Hrsg. Friedrich Streicher. Zürich: Manesse-Verlag Conzett & Huber 1948. S. 20 u. 84.

**Spaemann,** Heinrich: Die Anrede Gottes. Einleitung einer Betrachtungsfolge über das Herrengebet. Meitingen: Kyrios-Verlag 1966. 24 S.
– Brot für den Tag. In: Orientierung am Kinde. Düsseldorf: Patmos-Verlag 1967. S. 101f.
– Das Gebet zum Vater. In: Wege ins Beten. München: Kösel-Verlag 1972. S. 48–52 (s. a. „Lehre uns beten" zu Lk 11,1–13, S. 35).
– Jesu Gebetslehre bei Lukas. In: Wege ins Beten. München: Kösel 1972. S. 35–52.
Anm.: Beachten auch Vaterunser-Hinweis in: Feuer auf die Erde zu werfen ... Freiburg: Herder 1961. S. 22.

**Spee,** Friedrich von: Das Vaterunser. In: Josef Borst, Lobsinge dem Herrn, meine Seele. Gebete deutscher Dichter. Würzburg: Rita-Verlag 1935. S. 120f.

**Spence,** R. M.: EPIOUSIOS. In: The Expository Times. vol. 2 Nr. 11 (1890–1891). S. 255–256.

**Speyr,** Adrienne von: Lumina. Darin Hinweise auf das Vaterunser: S. 20, 21, 42. Einsiedeln: Johannes-Verlag 1969. 63 S.
– Die Kraft des Vaterunsers und Ave Maria. Gebetszettel Nr. 200 mit Imprimatur Freiburg / Schweiz. 1931. 3 bzw. 8 S.

131

**Spitta,** Friedrich: Die älteste Form des Vaterunsers. In: Monatsschrift für Gottesdienst und kirchliche Kunst. vol. 9 Nr. 11 (1904). S. 333–345.

**Spitta,** Martin: Das Vaterunser. Madrid: Selbstverlag 1967. 55 S.

**Spoerri,** Th.: Onze Vader (Notre Père). Amsterdam: Ten Have 1947. 32 S.

**Springer,** Emil: Unser tägliches Brot gib uns heute. Die Brotbitte des Vaterunsers nach ihrem eucharistischen Sinne. Paderborn: Bonifacius-Druckerei 1912. 95 S.

**Staab,** Karl: Erklärung des Vaterunsers. In: Das Evangelium nach Matthäus (Echterbibel). Würzburg: Echter-Verlag 1951. S. 37–40.
– Das Vaterunser. In: Das Evangelium nach Lukas (Echterbibel). Würzburg: Echter-Verlag 1956. S. 71f.

**Stach,** Ilse von: Das Vaterunser der Armen Seelen. In: Regensburger Bistumsblatt. Regensburg: Nr. 44 vom 4. 11. 1951. S. 3.

**Stadler,** Hans: Pater noster. In: Mein Sonntag. München: Ars sacra 1937. S. 149f.

**Stäger,** Robert: Das Vaterunser. Gedichte. Luzern: Josef Stocker 1944. 19 S.

**Stählin,** Wilhelm: Der Mensch, der das „Vaterunser" betet. In: Evangelische Jahresbriefe der Michaelsbruderschaft. Kassel: Bärenreiter-Verlag 16 (1951–1952). S. 2–7, 41–45, 81–85, 121–127, 185 bis 188.

**Stamm,** R. T.: On Earth, as it is in Heaven. In: Lutheran Church Quarterly. vol. 12 (ca. 1939?). S. 168–182.

**Stano,** Gaetano: Artikel: Pater Noster. In: Enciclopedia Cattolica. Firenze: Sansoni vol. IX (1952). col. 943–946.

**Stapfer,** J. F.: Dissertatio epistolica ad V. Cl. Joannem Georgium Altmannum, de Nexu et Sensu Orationis Dominicae Prophetico. In: Tempe Helvetica. Tomi primi, sectio tertia. Zürich: Heidegger 1736. S. 351–363.

**Stapper,** Richard: Vaterunser u. Englischer Gruß. In: Grundriß der Liturgik. Münster: Aschendorff, 3. u. verb. Aufl. 1922. S. 77 u. S. 177.

**Starcky,** Jean: La quatrième demande du Pater. In: Harvard Theological Review. Cambridge, Mass. vol. 64 (1971). Nr. 2–3. S. 401–409.

**Stark,** Franz: Das Vaterunser. In: Alfons Schrodi OMI (Hrsg.): Gottes Wort im Kirchenjahr. Würzburg: Echter 1970. Bd. 2, S. 30f.

**Staudinger,** Josef SJ: Das Vater-Unser. In: Die Bergpredigt. Wien: Herder 1957. S. 147–182, dazu S. 288f.

**Steege,** Heinrich: Das Vaterunser in unserer Zeit. Versuch einer Deutung (Evangelische Zeitstimmen Nr. 54). Hamburg: Herbert Reich, Evang. Verlag 1970. 46 S.

**Stegmann,** Anton: Das Vaterunser in sieben Fastenpredigten. Wangen i. A.: Buchdruckerei J. Walchner 1954. 57 S.

**Stehmann,** Maria: Katechismusfreude. Betrachtungen mit Kindern über die Bilder des „Schäfer-Katechismus". Teil 3: Das Vaterunser. Potsdam: Stiftges.-Verlag 1935. 30 S.

**Steidle,** Basilius: Das Gebet des Herrn. Auswahl und Übertragung der Texte (der Kirchenväter). (Veröffentl. des Inst. für neuzeitl. Volksbildungsarbeit Dortmund). Leipzig: Jakob Hegner 1938. 83 S.

**Steiger,** Ernst: Das Vaterunser: s. **Magnin,** Silvia.

**Stein,** Otto: Das Gebet des Herrn, in Kriegsgebetsstunden ausgelegt. Hildenbach: Neuzeitverlag v. L. Wiegand 1915. 31 S.

**Steiner,** Josef (Hrsg.): Wenn wir beten: Vater unser (Gemeindekatechismus I). Freiburg: Herder 1981. 96 S.

**Steiner,** Rudolf: Das Vaterunser. Eine esoterische Betrachtung. Nachschrift eines Vortrages vom 28. 1. 1907 in Berlin. Nach einer vom Vortragenden nicht durchgesehenen Nachschrift hrsg. von der Rudolf-Steiner-Nachlaßverwaltung. Dornach: Verlag Rudolf Steiner-Nachlaßverwaltung (11. Aufl.) 1968. 27 S. (12. Aufl. 1976). Anm.: Derselbe Text erschien in Freiburg: Novalis-Verlag 1954. 31 S. u. in Berlin: Philosophisch-Anthroposophischer Verlag (15. bis 19. Tsd.) 1921. 42 S.
– The Lord's Prayer. An esoteric study; revision by M. Cotterell. London: Anthroposophical Publ. Co. 1958. 30 S.
– The structure of the Lord's Prayer. Lecture given at Karlsruhe 4th February 1907. Transl. by A. H. Parker. London: Rudolf Steiner Press 1971. 29 S.
– Notre Père qui êtes aux cieux. Paris: Presses Univ. de France 1926. 32 S.

**Steinmetz,** Franz Josef SJ: „Dein Reich komme!" Zur zweiten Bitte des Vaterunsers. In: Geist und Leben. Würzburg: Echter Verlag 41 (1968). S. 414–428.

**Stendahl,** Krister: The Scrolls and the New Testament: An introduction and a perspective. S. 11: EPIOUSIOS. In: The Scrolls and the New Testament. Ed. K. Stendahl. New York: Harper & Row 1957. IX, 308 S.

133

**Steuart,** Robert Henry Joseph: The Our Father. With an introduction by Conrad Pepler. London: Blackfriar Publ. 1955. X, 36 S.

**Steuernagel,** Carl: Die ursprüngliche Zweckbestimmung des Vaterunsers. In: Wissenschaftliche Zeitschrift der Karl-Marx-Universität Leipzig. Gesellschafts- u. Sprachwissenschaftl. Reihe. Leipzig: 3 (1953–1954). Heft 2/3, S. 217–220.

**Stiebitz,** Ferd.: Zu EPIOUSIOS. In: Philologische Wochenschrift. vol. 47, Nr. 29 (1927). Sp. 889–892.

**Stiefvater,** Alois: Das Vaterunser des Autofahrers. Augsburg: Verlag Winfried-Werk 1963. 4 S.
– Das Vaterunser als Fragebogen. In: Die Anregung. Köln: Verlag Wort und Werk 1.2.1963.
– Erziehungslehren aus dem Vaterunser. In: Seelsorge in der Zeit. Freiburg 6 (1951). S. 15–16.
– Das Vaterunser des Vaters. Freiburg: Verlag des Erzbischöfl. Missionsinstituts 1940. 16 S.
– Vom Gebet des Herrn. Recklinghausen: Paulus-Verlag 1940. 20 S.

**Stier,** Fridolin: Das Vaterunser. Illustrationen von Paul König. Kevelaer: Butzon & Bercker 1967. 24 S., 12 Bl.

**Stiglmayr,** J.: Das „Gebet des Herrn" nach der Ausdeutung des hl. Gregor von Nyssa. In: Akadem. Bonifatius-Korrespondenz. Bd. 41 (1927). S. 50–53.

**Stiller,** Wolfgang: „Geheiligt werde dein Name". Biblische Erwägungen. In: Theologie und Glaube. Paderborn: F. Schöningh 44 (1954). S. 64–66.
– „Vater unser". Biblische Erwägungen. In: Theologie und Glaube. Paderborn: F. Schöningh 42 (1952). S. 49–52.

**Stockmayer,** Otto: Das „Vater Unser". Unveränderter Abdruck einiger Andachtsnachschriften vom Mai 1904. Hrsg. Reiner-Friedemann Edel. Marburg / Lahn: Verlag R. F. Edel 1958. 36 S.

**Stöger,** Alois: Das Vaterunser. In: Ich aber sage euch. Die Bergpredigt lebendig gemacht. München: Josef Pfeiffer 1952. S. 80–98.
– das neue gebet. In: das evangelium nach lukas (Geistl. Schriftlesung, Bd. 3,1). Düsseldorf: Patmos-Verlag 1964. S. 308–313.

**Stoks,** M.: Jezus' hoogpriesterlijk gebed. Roermond: J. J. Romen 1946. 87 S.

**Stolberg,** Balthasar: Exercitationum graecae linguae tractatus, de soloecismis et barbarismis graecae novi foederis dictioni falso tributis ... Dissertatio tertia **De Pane** (EPIOUSIOS). Frankfurt/Leipzig: J. Chr. Wohlfart 1688. S. 220–250.

**Stolz,** Alban: Gesammelte Werke, Bd. 3: Das Vaterunser und der unendliche Gruß. Freiburg: Herder. Neuer Abdr. 1926 (1. Aufl. 1898). VIII, 526 S.

**Strack,** Hermann L. / Billerbeck, Paul: Kommentar zum Neuen Testament aus Talmud und Midrasch. Bd. 1: Das Evangelium nach Matthäus. Über Matth. 6,9: S. 406–424. München: C. H. Beck 3.–5. Aufl. 1969.

**Strathmann,** Hermann: Christen in Pompei und Herkulaneum (Sator-Arepo). In: Theologische Blätter. vol. 19, Nr. 1 (1940). S. 107 bis 108.

**Ströbele,** Georg: Das Gebet des Herrn. Gottesgedanken fürs Menschenleben. Mit Originalillustrationen von Willy Jakob. Bad Mergentheim: Verlagsbuchh. Karl Ohlinger. 1926. VI, 150 S.

**Strolz,** Richard: Das Gebet des Christen. Erwägungen zum heiligen Vaterunser. In: Die Quelle. Wien: April 1952. S. 77–79.

**Strolz,** Walter (Hrsg.): Das Vaterunser. s. **Brocke,** Michel (Hrsg.).

**Stuart,** McDonald: The Revelation of God in the Lord's Prayer. London: Stockwell 1931. 247 S.

**Stuhlfauth,** Georg: Die Sinnzeichen der altchristlichen Kunst (Sator-Arepo). In: Theologische Blätter. vol. 18, Nr. 8–9 (1939). Sp. 210–212.

**Sullivan,** John F.: Das Gebet des Herrn. In: Die äußeren Formen der katholischen Kirche. Aschaffenburg: Paul Pattloch 1958. S. 439f.

**Sully,** Maurice de: s. **Maurice de Sully**

**Sundwall,** Joh.: L'enigmatica iscrizione „Rotas" in Pompei. In: Acta Academiae Aboensis. Ser. A: Humaniora. Åbo: vol. 15 (1947 bis 1948) Nr. 5. S. 1–17.

**Sutphin,** Wyn Blair: Thine the Glory. Foreword by Norman Victor Hope. New York: Dutton; Toronto: Clarke 1962. 121 S.

**Suys,** E.: La formule SATOR est-elle chrétienne? In: Les Etudes Classiques. vol. 4, Nr. 2 (1935). S. 291–294.

**Swetnam,** James: Hallowed be Thy Name. In: Biblica. Roma: 52 (1971). S. 556–563.

**Sykes,** Marjorie H.: And do not bring us to the test. In: The Expository Times. Edinburgh: vol. 73 (1962). Nr. 6, S. 189–190.

**Sylveira,** Ioannes da: Commentariorum in Textum Euangelicum. Tom. II: Editio tertia ab Authore recognita et emendata... IV, cap. 15: Oratio Dominica. Lyon: Laurent Anisson 1660. S. 397–411.

**Sylvester,** Gussi (Auguste): Sieben lebende Bilder zum Heiligen Vaterunser. Berlin: Neuer Berliner Buchverlag 1933. 12 S.

**Szilágyi,** J.: Ein Ziegelstein mit Zauberformel aus dem Palast des Statthalters in Aquincum. In: Acta Antiqua Academiae Scient. Hungaricae. Budapest: 2 (1954). S. 305–310. 1 Abb.


# T


**Talbot,** Dorothy: The Lord's Prayer and The Beatitudes. s. **Doane, Pelagie.**

**Tanner,** Fritz: Sein Wille und mein Wille. In: Worte auf den Weg, hrsg. Bommer– Meier– Tanner. München: Rex-Verlag 1959. S. 113–115.

**Taylor,** Charles: Sayings of the Jewish Fathers... Excursus V: The Lord's Prayer. Cambridge University Press 1877. S. 138–145.

**Taylor,** Florence M.: Thine is the Glory. Ill. by Mary Royt. London: Collins 1963. 49 S.

**Techel,** Karl Arnd: Leiden macht das Wort verständlich (Das Vaterunser als Gebet des Trostes nach einem Todesfall). Neuffen: Sonnenweg-Verlag (3. Aufl.) 1972. 32 S.

**Tecklenburg,** Walter: Das „Vater unser" um 1490 im Münsterlande. In: Auf roter Erde. Heimatblätter der Westfäl. Nachrichten. Münster: 13 (1955). Nr. 13, S. 102–103.

**Teich,** Hans von: Das vollkommenste Gebet. In: Seele. Regensburg: Josef Habbel 4 (1922). S. 62.

**Ten Kate,** R.: Geef ons heden ons „dagelijk" brood. Epiousios een crux interpretum. In.: Nederlands theologisch tijdschrift. s'Gravenhage. 32 (1978), S. 125–139.

**Teresa von Ávila (von Jesus), Die heilige:** Padre nuestro teresiano. Madrid: Espiritualidad (Erscheinungsjahr nicht bekannt).
– Sept méditations sur le Pater Noster. Traduit du Père Cyprien.

Wittmann: Editions d'Histoire et d'Art 1946. 71 S.
- Le Pater. Montreal: Fides 1944. 32 S.
- Siete meditaciones sobre el Pater noster. Modena: Tipografia dell'Immacolata Concezione 1894. 67 S.

**Teresia Benedicta a Cruce OCD:** Vaterunser vor der heiligen Kommunion. In: Das Gebet der Kirche. Paderborn: Vlg. der Bonifatius-Druckerei 1937. S. 6.

**Ternant,** Paul: Le Père exauce la prière filiale. In: Assemblées du Seigneur 48 17e Dimanche ordinaire Année A. Paris 1972. S. 61 bis 72.

**Tertullianus,** Quintus Septimus Florens: Ausgewählte Schriften. Bd. 1. In: Bibliothek der Kirchenväter. Bd. 7, S. 249–256. München: Kösel 1912.
- s. **Diercks,** G. F. (Hrsg.).

**Tescari,** O.: L'orazione del Signore interpretata da S. Agostino. Torino: Soc. Ed. Internazionale 1939. 116 S.

**Teske,** H. (Hrsg.): Die Auslegung des Vaterunsers in vier Predigten: s. **Nicolaus von Cusa.**

**Thalhammer,** Dominikus SJ: Das Vaterunser. In: Der Große Entschluß. Wien: 13 (1957). S. 40–48; 14 (1958): S. 281–288, 537 bis 544.
- Gelebtes Gebet. Gedanken zum Vaterunser. Wien: Herder 1959. 126 S.

**Thalmann,** Richard: Brücke zwischen Himmel und Erde. Das Vater unser. St. Gallen: Rat-Verlag; Meitingen/Freising: Kyrios-Verlag 1979. 36 S. mit Bildern.

**Thedering,** Franz: Vater unser. Zeitgedichte. Vechta: Vechtaer Druckerei u. Verlag 1917. 16 S.

**Thellier de Poncheville, Abbé:** Le Pater et l'Ave du temps du guerre. Paris: Ed. Spes 1939. 33 S.

**Theodor von Mopsuestia:** On the Lord's Prayer and Sacraments. Ed. by A. Mingana (Woodbrook Studies 6). Cambridge: Heffer 1933. 291 S.

**Theodoricus von Paderborn:** Commentatio in Orationem Dominicam. In: Migne. Bd. 123 Sp. 333–340.

**Thibaut,** R.: Que votre Règne advienne. In: Nouvelle Revue Théologique. vol. 49, Nr. 12 (1922). S. 555–558.

**Thiele,** Wilhelm: Das Vaterunser zur Kriegszeit. Stuttgart: Verlag der evang. Gesellschaft 1914. 14 S.

137

– Für die daheim zum 2. Kriegsjahr, Heft 3: Das Vaterunser im Kriege. Berlin-Dahlem: Burckhardhaus-Verlag 1916. 12 S.

**Thielicke,** Helmut: Das Gebet, das die Welt umspannt. Reden über das Vaterunser aus den Jahren 1944/45. Stuttgart: Quell-Verlag 1945. 150 S.; 13. durchges. u. erweit. Aufl. 1973. 207 S.
Anm.: Außerdem im Quell-Verlag als Taschenbuch erschienen: 1980. 207 S.
– Our Heavenly Father. Sermons on the Lord's Prayer. Transl. with an introduction by John W. Doberstein. New York: Harper & Row 1960; London: Clarke 1965. 157 S. Repr. 1974: Baker Book House, Grand Rapids, Mich.

**Thieme,** Karl: ,,Erlöse uns von dem Bösen" (Leserbrief). In: Der christliche Sonntag. Freiburg: Herder 3 (1951). S. 312.

**Thiersch,** Heinrich W. J.: Das Gebet des Herrn nach der Heiligen Schrift ausgelegt. Basel: Felix Schneider 1889.

**Thilo,** Anna (Hrsg.): Das Vater Unser mit Worten aus den Hl. Schriften (Biblia Ausz.) zusammengestellt von Anna Thilo. Dresden: Anna Thilo 1927. 134 S.

**Thils,** Gustave: Die Vaterschaft Gottes. In: Christliche Heiligkeit. München: Manz 1961. S. 77 f.

**Thirtle,** James W.: The Lord's Prayer. An Interpretation, critical and expository. London: Morgan & Scott 1915.

**Thomas von Aquin:** Katechismus oder Erklärung des apostolischen Glaubensbekenntnisses, des **Vater unser,** Ave Maria u. der zehn Gebote Gottes. Übersetzt u. mit Anmerkungen versehen von A. Portmann u. X. Kunz. Kirchen (Sieg): Petrus-Verlag 1971 (unv. Nachdruck der 1. Aufl.). 259 S.
– Ich glaube an Gott. Eine Erklärung des Glaubensbekenntnisses u. der Schriften über das Vaterunser u. den Englischen Gruß. Hrsg. Willi Reich. Olten / Freiburg: Otto Walter 1958. 133 S.
– Vater unser (Compendium theologiae 251). Zitiert in: Otto Karrer, Jahrbuch der Seele. München: Ars sacra-Verlag 1951. S. 274.
– Erläuterungen zum Vaterunser. In: Thomas-Fibel. Hrsg. Heinz Raskop. Köln: J. P. Bachem 1936. S. 95–134.
– Le Pater et L'Ave. Introduction et traduction par un moine de Fontgombault (Collection Docteur Commun). Texte latin et français. Paris: Nouvelles Editions Latines 1973. 187 S.
– Il Padre nostro... e l'Ave Maria. Commenti alla ,,Preghiera del Signore" e al ,,saluto angelico" a cura di S. Maggiolini. Vicenza: Ed. di Vicenza 1967. 72 S.
– Expositio devotissima orationis dominicae videlicet Pater No-

ster. In: Opuscula omnia... cura et studio Petri Mandonnet. Tomus Quartus, Opusculum XXXIV. Paris: P. Lethielleux 1927. S. 389–411.

**Thomas,** Joan Gale: Our Father. Arranged in picture and rhyme for people who are still very young. New York: Lee and Shephard 1952.

**Thomé,** Josef: Unser Vater. Recklinghausen: Paulus-Verlag 1948. 1 Bl.
– Unser Vater. In: Einführung in den Geist der Messe. Regensburg: F. Pustet 1939. S. 83–85.

**Thompson,** G. H. P.: „Thy Will be Done in Earth, as it is in Heaven" (Mt 6,11). A Suggested Re-Interpretation. In: Expository Times. Edinburgh: vol. 70 (1958–59) Nr. 12. S. 379–381.

**Thornton,** Edward E.: Lord teach us pray. In: Review and expositor. 76 (1979), S. 219–239.

**Thumann,** Paul: Vaterunser in Bildern. Mit einer Dichtung von Martin Luther. Leipzig: A. Titze (7. Aufl.) 1908. 7 Bl. m. 19 Tafeln Text.

**Thurén,** J.: Huomisen leipä („Cratini diei panis Epiousios). In: Teologinen Aikakauskirja. Helsinki: vol. 75 (1975). S. 76–91.

**Thurner,** Martin: Vater, dein Reich komme – Dein Wille geschehe. In: Gebete aus der Gemeinde: Gebetszettel der Pfarrei Maria Königin, Baldham vor München. 1974. 5 S.

**Tibaldo,** Maria Fidelis H. S. P.: Padre Nuestro (Bilderbuch) (Colección Camino, Verdad y Vida). Buenos Aires: Ediciones Paulinas (7. Aufl.) 1971. 62 S.

**Tilborg,** S. van: A Form-Criticism of the Lord's Prayer. In: Novum Testamentum. Leiden: E. J. Brill 14 (1972), fasc. 2, S. 94–105.
– Een exegeet buigt sich over het Onze Vader. In: Jan Peters (Hrsg.): Bidden nu. Roermond: Romen 1971. Kap. 2, S. 83f.

**Tillard,** J.: Le Notre Père. La prière des Chrétiens. In: Lumière et Vie. Bruges: Abbaye de S. André. vol. 14 (1965). Nr. 5, S. 39–84.

**Tilmann,** Klemens: Abba – Vater. In: Leben aus der Tiefe. Einsiedeln: Benziger 1975. S. 36–39.
– Das geistliche Gespräch. Darin Vaterunser-Hinweise S. 129, 132. Würzburg: Echter 1956.
– Das Vaterunser. Erklärung. In: Lehre uns beten. Hrsg. Josef Gülden. Regensburg: Habbel 1948. S. 683–687.
– Das Vaterunser. In: Täglich beten, aber wie? Recklinghausen: Paulus-Verlag 1948 (3. erw. Aufl.). S. 32–37.

139

– Wie der Herr uns beten lehrte. In: Täglich beten, aber wie? Recklinghausen: Paulus-Verlag 1940. S. 32–37.
Anm.: Beide Texte sind gleich.

**Tittmann,** Martin: Das geistige Frühelement im gotischen Vaterunser. In: Die Drei. Stuttgart: 27 (1957). S. 123–126.

**Tod,** Marcus N.: Our Daily Bread. In: Church Quarterly Review. London: vol. 158 (1957). Nr. 326, S. 49–51.

**Tolzien,** Gerhard: Das Vaterunser im Kriege. Mit Zeichnungen von P. Rische u. E. Thomsen. Schwerin: F. Bahn (4. Aufl.) 1916. 88 S.

**Torrance,** Thomas Forsyth: The eternal ten commandments and the immutable Ten words of the Lord's Prayer... Edinburgh: J. Thin's Bookstore 1958. 19 S.

**Torrey,** Charles C.: The Translations made from the Original Aramaic Gospels. In: Studies in the History of Religions, pres. to C. H. Roy. New York: Macmillan 1912. S. 269–317.
– A possible metrical original of the Lord's Prayer. In: Zeitschrift für Assyrologie. vol. 28, Nr. 2–4 (1914). S. 312–317.

**Tóth,** Tihamér: Padre Nuestro. Trad. del hungaro por Antonio Sancho Nebot. Madrid: ODER. 3a ed. 1958.
– Onze Vader. Sermoenen uitgespr. in de kerk van de Pazmany-Universiteit te Budapest ged. het schooljaar 1936–37. Averbode ‹België›: Goede pers. 1942. XII. 432 S.

**La traduction commune du „Notre Père".** In: Les questions liturgiques et paroissiales. Louvain: Abbaye du Mont César: H. 2–3 (1966). S. 141–145.

**Trautvetter,** Paul: Sieben Predigten über das Unser Vater. Zürich: K. Neidhart & Co. 1943. 46 S.

**Trefzer,** Friedrich: Das Vaterunser. In: Betrachtungsbuch für alle Tage des Jahres. München: Ars sacra 1959. S. 149–159.

**Treib,** Ewald: Ihm ist das Reich (II. Teil Vaterunser) Johannes-Verlag, Leutesdorf 1977.

**Trepte,** Adolf: Das Vaterunser, seine Sendung und seine Welt. Berlin: Evangel. Presseverband für Deutschland 1938. 23 S.

**Tria,** Luigi: „Sator Arepo" formula magica o professione di fede? In: La Scuola Cattolica. vol. 63, fasc. 6 (1935). S. 698–714.
– Ancora sul crittogramma di Pompei. In: L'Osservatore Romano. Nr. 58 (1937). S. 3 col. 6.

**Trilling,** Wolfgang: Das Vaterunser. In: das evangelium nach matthäus (Geistliche Schriftlesung 1/1). Düsseldorf: Patmos-Verlag 1962. S. 146–151.

**Trillon de la Bigottière,** C.: Le Pater et l'Ave appris aux enfants. Avec six gravures. Paris: Roblot 1912. 85 S.

**Trueblood,** David Elton: The Lord's Prayer. New York: Harper & Row 1965. 128 S.

**Tuzson,** Emmi von (ill.): Das Vaterunser für unsere Kleinen. In Bildern und Versen. Feldkirch: Kreissl 1946. 12 Bl.


# U


**Ude,** Johann: Die Rettung. Die Gegenwartsnöte im Lichte des Vaterunsers. Graz: Styria 1921. 93 S.

**Umberg,** J. P. SJ: Rezension des Werkes von J. P. Bock SJ, „Die Brotbitte des Vaterunsers". In: Stimmen aus Maria Laach. Freiburg: Herder 1912. H. 1. S. 85–87.

**Underhill,** Evelyn: Fruits of the Spirit (and) Light of Christ (and) Abba: Meditations on the Lord's Prayer. 3 vols in 1 vol. London: Longmans 1956. 271 S.

**Unger,** Io. Godofr.: Meletema Antiquario Sacrum, De Antiquitate ΔΟΞΟΛΟΓΙΑΣ in Oratione Dominica, ad Matth. 6,13. In memoriam pacis religiosae secularem anno 1755 conscriptum. Leipzig: Breitkopf 1755.

**Unser tägliches Brot heute.** In: Der Mensch als Bruder – im Werk – im Fest – im Leid – in der Freundschaft vor Gott; hrsg. Elfriede Kiel u. Josef Gülden. Leipzig: St. Benno-Verlag 1973. S. 52–56.

Artikel: **Unser Vater.** In: Lexikon zur Bibel. Hrsg. Fritz Rienecker. Wuppertal: R. Brockhaus 3. Aufl. 1974. Sp. 1438–1440.

**Urban,** Paul: Das Vaterunser im Spiegel des Lebens (Schriftenreihe des „Linzer Kirchenblattes" 1) Linz / Donau: Verlag der Kath. Schriftenmission 1947. 40 S.

**Ussani,** Vincenzo: Per un esemplare cassinese di „Rotas Opera". In: Studi Medievali. N. S. Torino: vol. 16 (1943–1950). S. 237–241.

# V

**Van Bussel,** C.: Zo zult gij bidden... (Mt 6,9). In: Ons Geestelijk Leven. Tilburg: vol. 34 (1957). S. 72–80.

**Van den Bosch,** A. C. D.: Het Onze Vader Vandáág. Waageningen: Zomer & Keunings 1970. 110 S.

**Vandenbroucke,** F.: Le Pater (bibliographie). In: Questions liturgiques et paroissiales. Louvain: vol. 47 (1966). S. 176–178, 776–789.

**Van den Bussche,** Henri: Donne-nous aujourd'hui notre pain quotidien. In: Bible et Vie Chrétienne. Paris: vol. 32 (1960). S. 42 bis 46.
– Le „Notre Père". (Coll. Etudes religieuses, Nr. 747). Bruxelles / Paris: La Pensée Catholique / Office gén. du Livre 1960. 108 S.
– Das Vaterunser. Aus dem Französischen von Sigrid Loersch. Mainz: Matthias Grünewald Verlag 1963. 127 S.
– Understanding the Lord's Prayer. Transl. by Charles Schaldenbrand (Übers. von Het Onze Vader). London: Sheed & Ward 1964. 144 S.
– Het Onze Vader. Gent: Boekh. „Die Grael" 1960. 78 S. 2. Aufl. 1963. 96 S.
– „Padre Nuestro". Bilbao: Desclée de Brouwer 1965. 154 S.

**Vandeur,** Eugène OSB: L'Abandon à Dieu. Voie de la Paix. Commentaire du Pater. Maredsous: Editions de Maredsous (4. Aufl.) 1946. 247 S.
– Living the Lord's Prayer. Translated by M. Angelina Bouchard. London: Herder / Burns & Oates 1961. 192 S.
– Pater noster. In: Das heilige Meßopfer. Regensburg: F. Pustet 1930. S. 225–251.

**Vann,** Gerald: Das Vaterunser (in der Messe). In: Der Lebensbaum. Studien zur christlichen Symbolik. Einsiedeln: Benziger 1962. S. 277–281.

**vaterunser.** eine dia-meditation. Mit 24seitigem Textheft u. 8 Dias. München: impuls studio 1979.
Anm.: Als Vorlage zu dieser Dia-Meditation diente das Buch „Das Vaterunser". Eine Meditation in Emailbildern von Silvia Magnin mit Texten von Ernst Steiger. Siehe auch unter **Magnin.**

**Vater unser.** Überlieferung nach Matthäus. Erklärung im neuen Wochentags-Schott, Teil 1, zur 1. Woche am Dienstag in der Fastenzeit. Freiburg: Herder (5. Aufl.) 1978. S. 455–456.

142

**Vaterunser:** Parodistische Texte. In: Meinhold, Monika / Nickel, Rainer: Ironie, Parodie, Satire von Lucilius bis Loriot (Reihe: Fructus, Arbeitsmaterialien Latein). Freiburg–Würzburg: Ploetz 1977. S. 56–58.

**Das Vaterunser** (und der Vatergedanke im N. T.). In: Das Vaterbild in Mythos und Geschichte. Hrsg. H. Tellenbach. Stuttgart: W. Kohlhammer 1976. S. 141f.

**Das Vaterunser.** Gemeinsames im Beten von Juden und Christen. Hrsg. Michael Brocke, Jakob J. Petuchowski u. Walter Strolz (Veröffentlichungen der Stiftung „Oratio Dominica"). Freiburg: Herder 1974. 285 S.
Anm.: Dazu auch ausführl. Besprechung von Alfons Weiser in: Lebendiges Zeugnis. Schriftenreihe der Akadem. Bonifatius-Einigung. Paderborn: 30, H. 4 (1975). S. 68–70.

**Vaterunser.** Acht Predigten. Acht Standpunkte. Hrsg.: Manfred Neun. Stuttgart: Quell-Verlag 1973. 77 S.

**Vater Unser.** Chorheft (Bosse Edition 804). Regensburg: Gustav Bosse-Verlag 1970. 47 S.

**Das Vaterunser.** Katholisches Hausbuch. Bearb. von Josef Gülden u. Elfriede Kiel. Leipzig: St. Benno-Verlag 1969. 432 S.

**Vaterunser** (Foto-Text-Heft 6). Hrsg.: Uwe Seidel. Gladbeck: Schriftenmissions-Verlag 1969. 24 S., 12 Bl. Abb. im Text.
Anm.: Gleichzeitig ebd. erschienen neun Schriftplakate zum Vaterunser.

**Vaterunser.** Sondernummer der Zeitschrift „Ferment". Gossau: Pallottiner-Verlag. H. 11, Nov. 1967.

**Das heilige Vaterunser.** Unser tägliches Gebet auch heute. 9 Predigten. Berlin: Evang. Verlags-Anstalt 1965. 60 S.

**Das Vaterunser.** In: Gebete der Menschheit. Religiöse Zeugnisse aller Zeiten und Völker. Hrsg. Alfonso M. di Nola. Aus dem Italienischen von Ernst Wilhelm Eschmann. Düsseldorf–Köln: Eugen Diederichs Verlag 1963. S. 278–279.

**Vater unser.** Nach einem Pax-Christi-Text. In: Freiburger Katholisches Kirchenblatt. Freiburg: Herder 1961. 24. Sept., S. 877.

**Das „kleinste Vaterunser".** Das Vaterunser in 7 Sprachen. Format 2×2 mm. 14 S. Hrsg. Wiederaufbaufonds des Mainzer Gutenberg-Museums. München: 1958 / Fotokop, Darmstadt.

**Das Vaterunser – gemeinsam gesprochen.** In: Evangelische Welt. Bethel: 7 (1953). S. 605–606.

**Vater unser.** Gebet- und Gesangbuch der Diözese Linz. Hrsg. Jos. Cal. Fliesser vom Bischöfl. Ordinariat Linz. Linz / Donau: Oberösterreich. Landesverlag 6. Aufl. 1953. VIII, 560 S.

**Vaterunser.** Altdeutsche Erklärung des Vaterunsers bei Müllenhoff-Scheerer, Denkmäler I, 1958; zitiert in: Otto Karrer: Jahrbuch der Seele. München: Ars sacra 1951. S. 270.

**Vater unser.** Illustriert nebst Erklärung. Klosterneuburg: Volksliturg. Apostolat 1949. 8 S., 8 Taf.

**Vaterunser.** Gedanken eines Flüchtlings. In: Freiburger Kath. Kirchenblatt. Freiburg: Herder 15. Aug. 1948.

**Vater Unser.** Gebete aus einer Kirche in Not. Zollikon / Zürich: Evangel. Verlag 1943. 16 Bl.

**Vaterunser** – Was wir dem Vaterunser verdanken. Eine Auslegung deutscher Dichter. Hrsg. Hermann Claudius u. August Winnig. Berlin: Eckart-Verlag 1940. 15 S.

**Das Vaterunser.** Eine Auslegung. Dargeboten von deutschen Dichtern. Berlin-Steglitz: Eckart-Verlag 1940. 152 S.

**Das Vaterunser.** Eine Auslegung. Mit Beiträgen von Rudolf Alexander Schröder, Otto von Taube, Friedrich Bischoff, Jochen Klepper u.a. Witten / Berlin: Eckart-Verlag (Erstaufl. 1940), 2. veränd. Aufl. 1963. 132 S.

**Das Vaterunser:** als Motiv u. Thematik. In: Katholischer Familienkalender für das schaffende Volk, Jhg. 1938. München: Verlag des Verbandes süddeutscher kath. Arbeiter- u. Arbeiterinnenvereine 1937. 106 S.

**Das Vaterunser.** Erinnerungen an die Grundwahrheiten der Exerzitien. Leutesdorf: Verlag des Johannesbundes 1932. 2 Bl.

**Vater unser!** Blattkalender Jahrg. 12/1932. Verse von Marie Feesche. Künstlerische Photoaufnahmen: Jean Gaberell. Hannover: Feesche 1931. 9 Bl. m. Abb.
Anm.: Die früheren Jahrgänge erschienen mit wechselnden Themen.

**Das Vaterunser** oder die heiligen sieben Bitten. Zum Gebrauch beim 40stündigen Gebete und bei der Ewigen Anbetung. Rottweil: Verlag Emmanuel 1927. 47 S.

**Das Vaterunser** einer Seele, die eben kommuniziert hat. Berlin: Germania 1917. 8 S.

**Das Vaterunser.** Mit Worten von Reinhold Schneider. Hrsg.: Freundeskreis der Stiftung „Oratio Dominica". Freiburg: Herder um 1963. 10 S.

**vater unser.** Kurztonbild (Reihe SIGNALE Nr. 200). 36 Farbdias. München: SVD Steyler Verlag Film u. Ton. Erscheinungsjahr nicht bekannt.

**Das Vaterunser als Gebet und Lebensschule.** In: Die Anregung. Korrespondenz- und Werkblatt für den Klerus. Köln. 9 (1957): Nr. 18, S. 12; Nr. 20, S. 8; Nr. 22, S. 14; Nr. 23, S. 14, Nr. 24, S. 8–9; 10 (1958): Nr. 2, S. 9; Nr. 3, S. 10; Nr. 4, S. 8; Nr. 5, S. 8; Nr. 6, S. 12–13; Nr. 7, S. 7–8; Nr. 8, S. 15–16; Nr. 9, S. 20–22; Nr. 10, S. 16; Nr. 11, S. 10–11; Nr. 12, S. 19–20; Nr. 13, S. 10; Nr. 14, S. 6–7; Nr. 15/16, S. 14; Nr. 17, S. 8; Nr. 18, S. 6–7; Nr. 20, S. 16; Nr. 21, S. 10–11; Nr. 22, S. 12; Nr. 23, S. 11–12; Nr. 24, S. 11; 11 (1959): Nr. 1, S. 11; Nr. 2, S. 10–11; Nr. 3, S. IV1; Nr. 4, S. 10; Nr. 5, S. 11–12; Nr. 6, S. 8; Nr. 7, S. 9; Nr. 8, S. 11–12; Nr. 10, S. 11–12; Nr. 11, S. 8; Nr. 12, S. 9; Nr. 15, S. 11; Nr. 16, S. 12–13; Nr. 17, S. 12.

**Vaterunser-Gebete.** In: Kirchengesangbuch. Kath. Gesang- u. Gebetbuch der Schweiz. Vaterunser-Gebete: S. 684–687. Einsiedeln: Benziger 1966.

**Vaterunsergeist in der Gemeinde.** In: Der Volksverein. München – Gladbach: Volksvereinshaus 40 (1930), S. 18–26.

**Vater unser im Himmel.** In der neuen Fassung mit Noten. Gebetszettel. Hrsg.: Liturg. Institut in Trier. Freiburg: Christophorus-Verlag / Verlag Herder 1968. 4 S.

**Vater unser im Himmelreich.** Ein Ruf zum Gebet. Hrsg. Herbert Redlich. Symbol- u. Schriftzeichnungen von Christian Rietschel. Berlin: Evang. Verlagsanstalt 1949. 216 S.

**Vater unser im Himmelreich.** Gebetbüchlein für die evangelische Jugend. Hrsg. Werner Dümling. Wuppertal: Verlag des Kinderboten 1939. 54 S. m. Abb.

**Das Vater Unser in Bildern unserer Zeit.** Fotos von Horst Baumann u. a. Leporelloform. Gelnhausen: Burckhardthaus-Verlag 1963.

**Das Vaterunser in Liturgie und Meditation.** Schallplatte, hergestellt durch den Christophorus-Verlag Dezember 1968 als Widmung zum 70. Geburtstag von Dr. Theophil Herder-Dorneich (war im Handel nicht erhältlich).

**Die Vaterunser-Kapelle:** s. **Ein Zeichen**

**Vaterunser-Lieder:** s. **Blarr,** O. G.: s. **Beuerle,** H. / **Ruppel,** P. E.

**Vaterunser-Parodien:** s. **Imbach,** Josef

**S Vatterunser.** Mit Bildern von Brigitte Hanhart u. Bernadette. I d Mundart übertreit von Käthi Born. Text S. 32 von Brigitte Hanhart u. Kurt Baumann. Mönchaltorf+Hamburg: Nord-Süd-Verlag 1971. 32 S.

**Veenker,** Wolfgang (Hrsg.): Das Gebet des Herrn in den Sprachen Russlands. Photomechanischer Nachdruck der Ausgabe St. Petersburg 1870 (Slavistische Studienbücher, VII). Wiesbaden: Otto Harrassowitz 1971. XII, 91 S.

**Venantius Fortunatus:** Miscellanea, Liber X, Cap. 1: Expositio Orationis Dominicae. In: Migne. Bd. 88. Sp. 313–322.

**Vendryès,** Joseph: Une hypothèse sur le carré magique. In: Académie des Inscriptions et Belles Lettres. Comptes Rendus des séances de l'année 1953. Paris. S. 198–207.

**Verity,** G. B.: „Lead us not into temptation but..." In: The Expository Times. Edinburgh, vol. 58 (May 1947). Nr. 8, S. 221–222.

**Vernon,** Edward T.: The Lord's Prayer in Wartime. London: J. Clarke 1941. 96 S.

**Verschaeve,** Cyriel: Johannes meditiert das Vaterunser. In: Jesus, der Menschensohn. Freiburg: Herder 1957. S. 159–164.
Anm.: Obiger Beitrag auch zitiert in: Seele. Regensburg: Josef Habbel 33 (1957). S. 139.

**Verweyen,** Johannes Maria: Das Vaterunser. Betrachtungen und Gedanken. Breslau: Frankes Verlag 1936. 84 S.

**Verzel,** Comtesse de: Le Pater. Son efficacité. Issoudun (Indre): Dillen 1946–48. 20 S.

**Veuthy,** Léon OFMCap: Le Notre Père des âmes intérieures. Paris: Ed. Franciscaines 1947. 92 S.
– Das Vaterunser. Gebetswort und Gebetshaltung. Übers. von Jos. Hosse. Düsseldorf: Patmos-Verlag 1951. 80 S.
– Our Father. Transl. by James Meyer (Coll. Franciscan Spirituality Nr. 1). Chicago: Franciscan Herald Press 1955. 92 S.

**Veyne,** Paul: Le carré SATOR ou beaucoup de bruit pour rien. In: Bulletin de l'association Guillaume Budé, Supplément, Lettres d'Humanité Tome XXVII 4e série Nr. 4. Paris 1968. S. 427–460.

**Vianney,** Hl. Johannes Maria: Das Los einiger ist unentschieden. Ein Vaterunser und ein Ave Maria können sie retten. In: Unter der Kanzel von Ars. Hrsg. Walter Christoph Koch. Freiburg (Schweiz): Verlag des Kanisiuswerks 1948. S. 41.

**Vicedom,** Georg Friedrich: Gebet für die Welt. Das Vater-Unser als Missionsgebet. München: Chr. Kaiser 1965. 141 S.

– A Prayer for the World. The Lord's Prayer – A Prayer for Mission. Transl. by E. u. M. Schroeder. St. Louis, Mo.: Concordia 1967. 168 S.

**Vidal,** J.: Le contenu du Pater, s. **Bigu,** C.

**Vielhauer,** Philipp: Vaterunser-Probleme. Zu Ernst Lohmeyer: Das Vater-Unser. In: Verkündigung und Forschung. München: Kaiser 1949 bis 1950. S. 219–224.

**Vila,** David: El Padre Nuestro. Tarrasa (Barcelona): Selbstverlag des Verfassers 1973. 56 S.

**Vincent-Fumet,** Odette: Notre Père. Ill. par l'auteur. Montréal: Ed. du Lévrier 1946. 16 S.

**Vinci,** Luigi: La Coscienza del „Pater noster". Chiusi: S. Gentilini 1942. 101 S.

**Viollet,** Abbé Jean: Le ‚Notre Père'. Paris: Ed. Mariage et Famille 1934. 128 S.

**Visser,** H. A.: Onze Vader. s'Gravenhage: Boekencentrum 1952. 94 S.

**Visser,** L. L. J.: Só moet julle dan bid (Onse Vader). Kaapstad: N. G. Kerk-Uitgewers 1969.

**Vives,** J. C. (ed.): Doctorum angelici, seraphici, melliflui, extatici in orationem dominicam et salutationem angelicam expositiones. Roma: Tip. Artigianelli 1902. XII, 400 S.
– Expositio in Orationem Dominicam iuxta traditionem patristicam et theologicam. Roma: Typis Artificum a S. Josepho 1903.

**Voeltzel,** René: s. **Notre Père,** Le, des enfants.

**Vogel,** Heinz: Und führe uns nicht in Versuchung (Theologische Existenz heute, 62). München: Evangel. Verlag A. Lempp 1939. 62 S.

**Vogt,** Ernst: ὁ ἄρτος ἐπιούσιος = ὁ ἄρτος ὁ τῆς ἐπιούσης. In: Biblica. Roma: vol. 35 Nr. 1 (1954). S. 136–137.

**Vögtle,** Anton: Der eschatologische Bezug der Wir-Bitten des Vaterunsers. In: Jesus und Paulus. Festschrift für Werner Georg Kümmel zum 70. Geburtstag. Göttingen: Vandenhoeck & Ruprecht 1975. S. 344–362.

**Vokinger,** Konstantin: Mein Vater – Vater unser. Kriens (Schweiz): Großhof-Verlag 1953. 8 S.

**Volkes,** F. E.: The Lord's Prayer in the first three centuries. In: Studia Patristica. Berlin: vol. 10 (1970). S. 253–260.

**Völter,** Daniel: „Unser täglich Brot". In: Protestantische Monats-hefte. vol. 18, Nr. 7 (1914). S. 274–276.

**Vona,** C.: La quarta petitio dell'Oratio Dominica nell'inter-pretazione di antichi scrittori cristiani. In: Convivium Domini-cum. Catania 1959. S. 215–255.

**Von dem Pater noster biß auf die Collecten.** In: Corpus Catholico-rum. Werke kath. Schriftsteller im Zeitalter der Glaubensspaltung, Teil 3. Hrsg. u. eingeleitet von Franz Rudolf Reichert. Münster: Aschendorff 1967 (Erstausgabe ca. 1480). S. 172–175.

**Voronca,** Ilarie: Pater Noster. Suivi de: Ebauches d'un poème. Paris: Corréa 1938. 89 S.

**Vorwerk,** Dietrich: Gebet und Gebetserziehung. Probleme und Praxis des Gebetslebens u. e. Jahrgang Konfirmandenunterricht auf psychologischer Grundlage über das **Vaterunser.** Zwei Teile in einem Band. Schwerin: F. Bahn (2. Aufl.) 1913. VII, 655 u. 238 S.

**Vos,** Dom Cornelis OSB: Pater noster. In: Der Meßritus – Ein Beitrag zur sinnvolleren Formgestaltung. Salzburg: Verlag der Abtei St. Peter 1963. S. 110.

**Vosté,** J.: The Doxology of the Our Father (Matth. 6,13). In: Homiletic and Pastoral Review. New York: vol. 42 (1941–42). S. 368–369.

**Vreugdenhil,** Dirk (Hrsg.): Het Onze Vader. Enschede: Het Lande-lijk Verbond van de Evangelisatiecommissies van de Gereformeer-te Kerken in Nederland 1965. 18 S.

**Vries,** Anne de: Het Onze Vader (Bijbelboekjes voor de kleuters, Nr. 11). Kampen: J. H. Kok 1968. 32 S., ill.
– Das Unser Vater für die Kinder erklärt. Mit Bildern von Hans Deininger. Konstanz: Christl. Verlags-Anstalt 1961. 31 S.

**Vykoukal,** Ernst OSB: Vaterunser. In: Lexikon für Theologie und Kirche, Bd. X. Freiburg: Herder 1938. Sp. 498–501.

# W

**Wabnitz,** A.: Le vrai sens de la quatrième demande de la prière Dominicale. In: Revue de Théologie et des Quéstions Religieuses. vol. 11 (1902). S. 380–385.

**Wachter,** Petrus OSB: Das Vaterunser. In: An den Quellen der Andacht oder: Wie bringe ich gute Betrachtung fertig? Regensburg: Verlagsanstalt vorm. G. J. Manz 1921. S. 95–124.

**Walker,** F. W.: The Lord's Prayer: The voice and the presence. London: Stockwell 1934. 92 S.

**Walter,** Eugen: Das Gebet des Herrn. In: Das Kommen des Herrn, Bd. II. Freiburg: Herder 1947. S. 114–121.
– Das Gebet des Herrn (Reihe Die biblische Schatzkammer). Freiburg: Herder 1948. 45 S.
– Vaterunser. In: Die zweifache Geburt (Herderbücherei, Bd. 198). Freiburg: Herder 1965. S. 38f.

**Walter,** Hermengild OSB: Das Vaterunser. In: Kalender für das Jahr 1951. St. Ottilien: Eos-Verlag.

**Walter,** Piers: Lehre uns beten: s. **Zinzendorf,** Nikolaus Ludwig Graf von.

**Walther,** Georg: Untersuchungen zur Geschichte der griechischen Vaterunser-Exegese (Texte u. Untersuchungen zur Geschichte der altchristlichen Literatur. Reihe 3, Bd. 10, H. 3). Leipzig: J. C. Hinrichs 1914.
– Vaterunser-Erklärungen Griechischer Kirchenväter kritisch untersucht. Greifswald: Julius Abel 1914. 72 S.

**Walther,** Hans: Versifizierte Paternoster und Credo. In: Revue du Moyen Age Latin. Strasbourg: vol. 20 (1964). Nr. 1–2, S. 45–64.

**Wandzeitung für den christlichen Unterricht.** Hrsg. in Verbindung mit Kurt Frör. Reihe 3: Der Katechismus; Folge 12: Das Vaterunser. München: Evang. Presseverband für Bayern 1959. 6 Bl. m. Abb.

**Warth u. Löckle:** Über ἄρτος ἐπιούσιος im Vaterunser. In: Theologische Studien und Kritiken. vol. 57, Nr. 4 (1884). S. 769–777.

**Wasserzug-Traeder,** Gertrud: Unser Vater in dem Himmel. Eine Hilfe zum Gebet. Beatenberg (Schweiz): Verlag Bibelschule 1965. 11 S.

**Wassner,** Walter: Das Vater-Unser. Predigten gehalten in der Stadtkirche zu Neustadt in Holstein. Hamburg: Nölke 1946. 44 S.

**Watson,** Thomas: The Lord's Prayer. Reprinted from the 1890 ed. 1960. Revised edn. 1965. Reprinted 1972. London: Banner of Truth Trust. 332 S.

**Wehner,** Josef Magnus: Das große Vaterunser. Legenden um die sieben Bitten. München: Max Hueber Verlag 1935. 137 S.

**Weiger,** Joseph: Der Glaube an Gott den Vater. In: Der Charakter der altchristlichen Gebete. Erschienen in: Seele. Regensburg: Josef Habbel 1923. S. 147.

**Weigle,** Elisabeth: Das Vaterunser. Text und Original-Scherenschnitte. Göppingen / Stuttgart: Boccarius 1947. 6 Bl.

**Weil,** Simone: Betrachtungen über das Vaterunser. In: Zeugnis für das Gute. Traktate, Briefe, Aufzeichnungen. Olten – Freiburg: Walter-Verlag 1976; ebenso in: Das Unglück und die Gottesliebe. München: Kösel 1961. S. 235–248.
– Attente de Dieu. La Colombe: Ed. du Vieux Colombier 1950. 189 S.

**Weinrich,** Franz Johannes: Der Psalter des Herrn. Psalmen zu Bildern aus der Vaterunser-Kapelle im Ibental (Veröffentlichungen der Stiftung „Oratio Dominica"). Freiburg: Herder 1972. 283 S. mit 62 Illustrationen.

**Weirich,** Wilhelm: Das Gebetsleben des Christen im Lichte des Vaterunsers. Bibelkurs. Wuppertal: E. Müller 1939. 46 S.

**Weise,** M.: Das Vaterunser in „konsequent"-existentieller Interpretation. Zur Predigtmeditation über Mat 6,5–13 von H. Braun. In: Wort und Welt. Festschrift E. Hertzsch. Berlin: Evang. Verlagsanstalt 1968. S. 299–311.

**Weisheit der Väter.** Ein Kirchenväter-Brevier. Ausgewählt u. übertr. von Heinz Kraft. Zum Thema „Vaterunser": S. 146f. Hamburg: Agentur des Rauhen Hauses 1957.

**Weiß,** Franz: Jesu Reichsgebet (Reihe Tiefer und treuer. Schriften zur religiösen Verinnerlichung u. Erneuerung, Bd. 9). Einsiedeln: Benziger 1917. 88 S.

**Weiss,** Hugo: Die Bergpredigt Christi in ihrem organischen Zusammenhange. Darin: Das Gebetsformular des Vaterunsers S. 70–83. Freiburg: Herder 1892.

**Wells,** R. (d.i. Anna Weissauer): Vater unser. Konstanz: Kanisiuswerk 1941. 80 S.

**Welte,** Bernhard: Gedanken zum Vaterunser. In: Erhelltes Leben. Ein besinnliches Lesebuch. Hrsg. Alice Scherer. Freiburg: Herder 1978. S. 127–129.

150

– Vom Geist des Christentums. Darin zum Thema Vaterunser: S. 21f, 66, 69f. Frankfurt: Verlag Josef Knecht 1955.

**Wendel,** Carl: Das ROTAS-Quadrat in Pompeji. In: Zeitschrift für die neutestamentliche Wissenschaft. vol. 40 (1941). S. 138–151.

**Wenn wir beten: Vater unser.** Gemeindekatechismus I. Hrsg. Josef Steiner. Freiburg: Verlag Herder 1981. 96 S.

**Werlin,** Josef: Das Fragment einer gebetsartigen Betrachtung des Paternoster. In: Neuphilologische Mitteilungen 65 (1964). S. 45–53.

**Wesson,** Jeanne: Our Father. Ill. by Gordon Stowell. London: Scripture Union 1966. 46 S.

**Wester,** Manfred: Ein eigenes Vaterunser. In: Konkrete Verkündigung. Schritte zu einer praxisbezogenen Gemeindearbeit. Stuttgart / Berlin: Kreuz-Verlag 1974. S. 201–203.

**Whiston,** Charles Francis: When ye pray say Our Father. A devotional study of the Lord's Prayer. London: Pilgrim Press 1960. 117 S.

**White,** Ellen Gould: Het Gebed des Heeren. Den Haag: Boekenhuis „Veritas" 1947. 12 S.
– Gedanken vom Berg der Seligpreisungen. Hamburg: Vollmer & Bentlin. 16. Aufl. 1946 (Original-Ausg.: Thoughts of the Mount of Blessing. 1896).
– „Herr, lehre uns beten!" (deutscher Auszug von „Thoughts from the Mount of Blessing"). Gedanken über das Vaterunser. Hamburg: Advent-Verlag 1948. 23 S.

**White,** Walter Grainge: Annotated analysis of the Christian's Family prayer, commonly called the „Our Father", from Aramaic Sources. Stowmarket (Suffolk): The Vicarage Haughley: Rev. W. G. White 1956. 29 S.
– The Lord's Prayer. In: Expository Times. vol. 36, Nr. 2 (1924). S. 90–91.
– Thy kingdom come! In: Expository Times. vol. 33 (1921–22). S. 523f.

**Whitewell,** Richard: The Prayer of the Ages. Ashingdon, Rochford, Essex: The C. W. Daniel Company Ltd. 1956. 167 S.

**Wiéner,** Claude: La nouvelle traduction française de la prière du Seigneur: Signification pastorale et œcumenique. In: La Maison-Dieu. Paris: I 1966. Nr. 85. S. 140–152.

**Wiesnet,** Joseph: Das Gebet des Herrn. Neun Skizzen über das Vaterunser. In: Heilige Saat, Bd. 5. Hrsg. Nikolaus Gengler. Regensburg: F. Pustet 1933. S. 169–186.

**Wilkes,** J.: Das ökumenische Gebet des Herrn Jesus Christus, seine inhaltliche Erarbeitung und formale Gestaltung für Gehörlose. In: Neue Blätter für Taubstummenbildung. Heidelberg: 22 (1968). H. 8–9, S. 260–268.

**Willam,** Franz Michel: Die Welt vom Vaterunser aus gesehen. Freiburg: Herder 1961. 144 S.
– Le Pater, prière moderne. Traduction de René Virrion. Mulhouse: Salvator 1963. 136 S.

**Willcox,** Frederick: The Lord's Prayer for today. London: Epworth (Methodist Publ. House) 1950. 60 S.

**Williams,** A. Lukyn: ‚My Father' in Jewish Thought of the First Century. In: The Journal of Theological Studies. Oxford: 21 (1930). S. 42–47.

**Willis,** G. G.: The Lord's Prayer in Irish Gospel Manuscripts. In: Studia Evangelica vol. III (Texte u. Untersuchungen, vol. 88). Berlin: Akademie-Verlag 1964. S. 222–228.
– „In Earth as it is in Heaven". In: Studies in Church History. London / Edinburgh: vol. 3 (1966). S. 254–257.

**Wilmee,** Hyazinth M.: Vaterunser-Kirche (in Jerusalem). In: Lauda Jerusalem Dominum. Werl: Kommissariat des Heiligen Landes 1964. S. 128f.

**Wimmerer,** R.: EPIOUSIOS. In: Glotta. 16 (1928). S. 137.
– Noch einmal EPIOUSIOS. In: Glotta. 12 (1923). S. 68–82.

**Winckley:** Das Gebet des großen Heilers. In: Die weiße Fahne. Wegweiser zur erfolgreichen Lebensführung. Pfullingen: 30 (1957). S. 358–363.

**Winnig,** August: Das Vaterunser. In: Die goldene Stunde. Geschichten und Gedichte, heiter und besinnlich ausgewählt von Curt Winterhalter. Freiburg: Herder 1976. S. 188–190.
– Was wir dem Vaterunser verdanken: s. **Claudius,** Hermann.

**Winterswyl,** Ludwig A.: Das Vaterunser (in der Messe). In: Laienliturgik, I. Teil. Kevelaer: Butzon & Bercker 1938. S. 42–46.
– Die Zwölfapostellehre. Eine urchristliche Gemeindeordnung. Aus dem Griechischen übertragen, eingeleitet u. erklärt (Reihe Zeugen des Wortes). Darin zum Thema Vaterunser S. 21f., 52f. Freiburg: Herder 1939.

**Wisdorf,** Josef: s. **Das Gebet des Herrn.**

**Wisdorf,** Josef / Heinen, Anton: Das Vaterunser. In Wort und Bild gedeutet. Essen: Fredebeul & Koenen 1951. 12 Bl.

**Wisdorf,** Josef / Hohmann, Johannes: Das Gebet des Herrn. In Wort und Bild erklärt. Essen: Fredebeul & Koenen 1967. 31 S., ill.

**Wissemann, H.**: Die altslavischen Versionen der vierten Bitte des Vaterunsers. In: WeltSlav. 14 (1969). S. 393–405.

**Wissmann,** E.: Das Vaterunser. In: Weg und Wahrheit. Frankfurt / Darmstadt: 2 (1948): 2.–4. Bitte: Nr. 3/4, S. 24–26; 5. Bitte: Nr. 7/8, S. 52; 6. u. 7. Bitte: Nr. 9/10, S. 62–63; Schluß: Nr. 11/12, S. 79–81.

**Witsius,** Hermann: Exercitationes in Orationem Dominicam. Franecker: J. Gyselaar 1689.

**Wittig,** Josef: Das verlorene Vaterunser. Acht Geschichten. Heilbronn: Eugen Salzer 1933. 157 S.

**Witzel,** August: Das Vaterunser. In: Deutsches Pfarrerblatt. Essen: 55 (1955). S. 251.

**Wöhrmüller,** Abt Bonifaz OSB: Dein Wille geschehe. In: Gottes Lieblingsandacht. München: Josef Pfeiffer 1922 (4. Aufl. 1928). S. 7.

**Woike,** Fritz: Das Gebet der Gemeinde Jesu. Das Vaterunser in Gedichtform. Stuttgart-Sillenbuch: Verlag Goldene Worte 1962. 15 S.

**Worlitscheck,** Anton: Der Gemeinschaftsgedanke im Vaterunser. Freiburg: Herder 1927. 99 S.
Anm.: „Der Gemeinschaftsgedanke…" ist außerdem erschienen (gekürzt?) in: Zeitschrift für kath. Theologie. Bd. 51 (1927). S. 470f. u. Verbum Domini, Rom. vol. 7 (1927). S. 255f.

**Wörmann,** Eduard: Das Vaterunser. Andachten. Bethel: Schriftenniederlage der Anstalt Bethel 1933. 24 S.

**Woworsky,** Jos. Rud.: Das Vaterunser. Zehn Predigten über das „Gebet des Herrn". Graz: Styria 1913. 96 S.

**Wragg,** Arthur: Lord's Prayer in black and white. With drawings. London / Toronto: J. Cape / Irwin Clarke 1946. 26 S.

**Wratislaw,** A. H.: New Evidence as to the Origin and Meaning of EPIOUSIOS in the Lord's Prayer. In: The Churchman. N. S. vol. 2 (1888). S. 525–530.

**Wright,** R. F.: Our Daily Bread. In: Church Quarterly Review. vol. 157 (1956). S. 340–345.

**Wroblewska,** Krystyna: Ojze nasz: jedenáscie drzeworytów. Warszawa: Pax 1950. 11 plates.

**Wuite-Van Maasdijke,** Anne: Het Onze Vader. Kampen: J. H. Kok N. V. 1952. 227 S.

**Wulf,** Berthold: Das Reich Gottes. Zur Doxologie des Vaterunsers. In: Die Drei. Stuttgart: 31 (1961). S. 99–101.

**Wulf,** Friedrich SJ: Jesus lehrt beten. In: Michael Schmaus u. Alfred Läpple (Hrsg.): Ich kann nicht mehr beten. Wahrheit und Zeugnis. Düsseldorf: Patmos-Verlag 1964. S. 318.
– Vaterunser – ein vorbildliches Gebet. In: Handbuch theologischer Grundbegriffe. Hrsg. Heinrich Fries, Bd. 1. München: Kösel 1962. S. 434.
– Vater unser im Himmel. Meditationen über das Gebet des Herrn. Würzburg / Zürich: Echter / NZN 1969. 108 S.

**Wulff,** Ludwig: Dekalog und Vaterunser. Parchim: H. Wedemann 1907. IV, 68+4 S. m. 1 Fig.
– Über das Vaterunser als Jesu Grundzehnwort und über Mosis Sinaidekalog. Mit zwei Bucheinlagen: Dekalog u. Vaterunser 1907. Für die Echtheit von Dekalog u. Vaterunser 1908. Parchim: H. Wedemann 1917. 8, IV, 68,4 u. V. 69 S. m. 1 Fig.

**Würzburger,** Karl: Sie verharrten in den Gebeten. Auslegung des Vaterunsers. In: Erziehung nach dem Evangelium. Olten: Roven-Verlag 1965. S. 93–146.

**Wyszyński,** Stefan Kardinal: „Ojcze nasz..." Paris: Editions du Dialogue. Société d'Editions Internationales 1971. 134 S.

# Y

**Yaegly,** Arthur: Retranslation „Our Father". A response to H. Paul Santmire. In.: Dialog. St. Paul, Minn. 16 (1977), S. 296–297.

**Yamauchi,** Edwin M.: The „Daily Bread" Motif in Antiquity (Mt 6,11 par Epiousios). In: Westminster Theological Journal. vol. 28 (1966). S. 145–156.

# Z

**Zahler,** A.: Vater unser 1918. Gedicht. Wien: H. Kneplers Nachf. 1919. 1 Blatt.

**Zahn,** Theodor: Das Vaterunser eines Kritikers. In: Neue kirchliche Zeitschrift. vol. 2 (1891). S. 408–416.

**Zatzmann,** V.: Die Sator-Formel und ihre Lösung. In: Hessische Blätter für Volkskunde. Gießen: Selbstverlag der hessischen Vereinigung für Volkskunde 24 (1926). S. 98–105.

**Zecchini,** Stefano Pietro: Di due probabili errori di amanuense del Pater noster e proposta di correzione. Torino: Unione Tipografia 1882. 14 S.

**Zehrer,** Franz: Das Vaterunser. In: Synoptischer Kommentar, Bd. 11. Klosterneuburger Buch- u. Kunstverlag 1963. S. 62–71.

**Zerwick,** Max SJ: Vivere ex verbo Dei. 10): Oratio Dominica (Lk 11, 1–4). In: Verbum Domini. Roma: vol. 28, fasc. 3 (1950). S. 176 bis 180.
– Vivere ex verbo Dei. 11): perseveranter orare (Lk 11,5–13). In: Verbum Domini. Roma. vol. 28 (1950). S. 243–247.
– Vaterunser-Predigten 8–10. In: Der Weg. Wien: Bd. 14 (1960). S. 238–241; Bd. 15 (1961): S. 6–9, 27–30.
– Das Vaterunser. Sein Ort im Evangelium. In: Christlich-Pädagogische Blätter. Wien: Bd. 81 (1968). S. 139–141, 323–325.

**Ziegler,** Leopold: Menschwerdung (auf der Grundlage des Vaterunsers). Olten: Summa-Verlag (Hegner-Bücherei) 1948. Bd. 1: 380 S.; Bd. 2: 399 S.
Anm.: In dem von Karl Färber herausgegebenen Brevier „Zum inneren Leben" ist aus dem oben genannten Werk ein Auszug erschienen: Frankfurt: Josef Knecht 1967, Drittes Brevier, S. 91 f.

**Ziegner,** Oskar: Welche Stellung hat Luther dem Vaterunser im kleinen Katechismus gegeben? In: Domine dirige me in verbo tuo. Festschrift zum 70. Geburtstag von Landesbischof D. Moritz Mitzenheim. Berlin: Evang. Verlags-Anstalt 1961. S. 126–131.

**Zielinski,** Johannes: Dein Reich komme! In: Gott spricht. München: Ars sacra 1968. S. 174 f.

**Zilliacus,** H. (Hrsg.): The Antinoopolis Papyri: s. **Barns,** J. W. B.

**Zimmer,** Otto: Das Vaterunser. Untersuchung auf seine leitenden Grundgedanken. Berlin: Runge 1931. 44 S.

**Zimmermann,** Heinrich: Das Gebet Jesu – das Gebet der Christen – Gebet und Gotteskindschaft. In: Bibeltheologisches Wörterbuch. Hrsg. Johannes B. Bauer. Graz: Styria 1967. S. 459–467.

**Zimmermann,** Paul von: Das Vaterunser. Betrachtungen. Dresden: C. L. Ungelenk 1912. 211 S.

**Zimpel,** C. F.: Il Padre nostro. Milano: Gattinoni 1868. 84 S.

**Zink,** Jörg: Wie wir beten können. Darin zum Thema Vaterunser: S. 85, 100, 151, 208, 236f. Stuttgart – Berlin: Kreuz-Verlag 1970.
– Deine Zeit und alle Zeit. Darin zum Thema Vaterunser: S. 90f. Stuttgart – Berlin: Kreuz-Verlag (2. Aufl.) 1965; (4. Aufl.) 1972.
– Erfahrung mit Gott. Einübung in den christlichen Glauben. Darin zitiert: Hemingway mit Worten des Vaterunsers: S. 152f. Stuttgart – Berlin: Kreuz-Verlag 1974.
– Vater unser im Himmel. Der Spießer in uns betet das Vaterunser so – Sollten wir es hin und wieder nicht so beten? In: KOLPING. Verbandszeitschrift des Schweizer Kolpingwerkes. Zürich, 61 (1978), Nr. 2, S. 9.

**Zinzendorf,** Nikolaus Ludwig Graf von: Lehre uns beten (12 Reden über das Gebet des Herrn; Auszug). Das Vater Unser nach Zinzendorfs Auslegung bearbeitet von Piers Walter. Bad Salzuflen: MBK-Verlag 1938. 16 S.

**Zito,** Carlo: Pregate così... Il Pater, meditato ai piedi di Gesù in sacramento. Martina Franca: Tipografia Dragonetti 1957. 180 S.

**Zöllner,** Wilhelm: Das Vaterunser. Eine Auslegung. Potsdam: Stiftungsverlag 1930. 56 S.

**Zorell,** Franz: EPIOUSIOS. In Biblica. Rom. vol. 6, Nr. 3 (1925). S. 321–322.

**Zundel,** Maurice: Das Gebet des Herrn. In: das hohelied der heiligen messe. Wien: Seelsorger-Verlag 1937. S. 189–192.

**Zyro,** Ferd. Fr.: Noch einmal Matth. 6,11. In: Theologische Studien und Kritiken. vol. 25, Nr. 4 (1872). S. 709–715.

# ERGÄNZUNG

Die nachstehenden Hinweise sind fast ausschließlich der „Vater-unser-Mappe" von Monsignore Leon von Kukowski entnommen. Neben seiner reichhaltigen Vaterunser-Bücherei sammelte der Verstorbene alle erreichbaren Vaterunser-Beiträge in Zeitschriften und Blättern jeglicher Art, wie sie ihm in seiner langjährigen Redaktionstätigkeit (und noch früher) begegneten. Die bibliographischen Angaben sind großenteils lückenhaft; wir wollten auf die Aufnahme dieser Beiträge dennoch nicht verzichten.

**A., Fr.**: Unser tägliches Brot gib uns heute (gesprochen in die Situation unserer Zeit). Keine nähere Angabe.

**Agathon, Pater**: Das „Vater unser" des hl. Franz. In: Kirchenzeitung für das Erzbistum Köln, 6. Okt. 1957.

**Benedicta, M. OSB**: Vater Unser – Ich bin Dein Kind... Spruchkarte des St. Walburgis-Verlags, Eichstätt (P 23).

**Bloy, Léon**: Im Herrengebet werden wir belehrt... In einem Kirchenblatt (Name u. Datum nicht mehr feststellbar) zitiert.

**Bosco, Don, Der heilige**: „Die einzig richtige Politik ist die des Vaterunsers" (zitiert von Bundespräsident Miklas, mitgeteilt in „Ewige Anbetung", Altötting, Heft 6, 1934.

**Braun, Maria von**: VATER unser, der Du in dem HIMMEL bist... (aus einer großformatigen Spruchkarte, keine näheren Angaben).

**Burger, Martin**: Notre Père... Vater unser (eine Erinnerung aus dem Jahre 1940; keine nähere Quelle).

**Claudius, Matthias**: Das „Vaterunser" ist ein für allemal das beste Gebet...: Zitiert in verschiedenen Blättern (u.a. „Paulinus", Trier); nähere Angaben nicht mehr feststellbar.

**Daneffel, O. SJ**: Vater unser, der du bist in dem Himmel (geschrieben als geistliche Unterweisung für die Novizen im Noviziat Tisis bei Feldkirch; handgeschriebener Zettel älteren, nicht mehr feststellbaren Datums).

**Eisele, Hans** († 1944): Vater Unser. Ein Sonettenkranz (13 S. maschinengeschrieben; keine näheren Angaben.

**-er**: Vater unser... In: Blüte. Donauwörth: Verlag Ludwig Auer Pädagogische Stiftung Cassianeum, Heft 11 (1966), S. 326.

**Federer, Heinrich**: Vater unser (in dem Gedichtband „Ich lösche das Licht", 1930).

157

**Fehling,** H. M.: Geliebte im Herrn... und wir lächeln hochmütig (Gedanken über das Vaterunserbeten). In: Bildpost (Bödefeld), 24. 2. 1963.

**Fick,** Ulrich / Knoch, Otto: Vaterunser-Meditation. Gebetszettel; Hrsg.: Informationszentrum Berufe der Kirche, o. J., 4 S.

**Fischer,** Balthasar: „Nachgebet" zum Vaterunser: Folge 5 einer Artikelreihe „Die wichtigsten Neuerungen bei der Meßfeier (keine näheren Angaben).

**Frank,** Dankmar M.: Unser täglich Brot gib uns heute: Vorabdruck aus einem Gedichtzyklus; veröffentlicht in der „Bayerischen Rundschau" (Erscheinungsdatum nicht mehr feststellbar).

**Franz von Assisi,** Der heilige: Das Vaterunser des heiligen Franz. Veröffentlicht (vermutlich) in der „Kirchenzeitung für das Bistum Aachen (mit Bild von Assisi) vom 9. 6. 1963.

**Das Gebet der Russen** bei dem Gedanken an den Zaren, oder das Vater unser. Als Flugblatt gedruckt während des Ersten Weltkriegs (Erscheinungsjahr nicht bekannt) im Verlag J. B. Schulz, Nürnberg.

**Das Gebet des Herrn** – ein Spiegel der Seele. Gebetszettel. München: J. Pfeiffer 1937. 8 S.

**Das Gebet des Herrn – unser Gebet.** In: Kirche und Leben, Münster, Nr. 11, 14. März 1965.

**Das Gebet des Herrn.** Meditationen über das Vaterunser. Als Beitragsreihe unter der Rubrik „Einübung und Unterweisung" erschienen in: Geist und Leben. Würzburg: Echter-Verlag 31 (1958). Vorhanden sind die Beiträge I.: „So nun sollt ihr beten", S. 299–302; II.: „Geheiligt werde Dein Name", S. 380–383.

**Geulen,** Jakob: Völker-Vaterunser in der Pfingstnacht (erschienen vermutlich im „Würzburger Kath. Sonntagsblatt, Datum nicht feststellbar).

**Grillparzer,** Franz: Vater unser („Hör uns, Gott, wenn wir rufen! ...) (Zeitungsausschnitt, ohne nähere Angaben).

**Groß,** Werner: Vor und nach dem Vaterunser. Zum Verständnis des neuen Meßbuches (17). Entnommen einem kath. Kirchenblatt (für die Diözese Augsburg?) (27/1977, Nr. 9).

**Gruber,** Andreas: Das Vaterunser. Vervielfältigung des Stadtpfarramtes Rosenheim für seine Pfarrangehörigen. Keine Jahresangabe.

**Gülden,** Josef: Gewissensbildung im Vaterunser (Vortragsreihe). Maschinengeschriebenes Ms., 8 S., keine näheren Angaben.

**W. H.:** Eine kleine Gewissenserforschung zu den einzelnen Vaterunserbitten (keine näheren Angaben).

**Hasenkamp,** Gottfried: Vaterunser (keine näheren Angaben; wohl erschienen im Raum Münster – Kirchenblatt „Kirche und Leben"?).

**Hengsbach,** Franz Bischof: Der heilige Name Gottes. Wort des Bischofs zur Bitte: „Geheiligt werde dein Name" (keine näheren Angaben; vermutlich erschienen in „Ruhrwort", Essener Bistumsblatt).

**Das Hitlersche Vaterunser.** Zitiert in der evangelischen „Täglichen Rundschau". Keine näheren Angaben.

**Karrer,** Otto: „Vater" sagen in ganzem Vertrauen. (Aus einer Zeitschrift; keine näheren Angaben.)

**Kirchgässner,** Ernst: Vaterunser in Jazz? Gedanken zum Kirchengebet am 3. Sonntag nach Pfingsten (erschienen in einem Kirchenblatt, keine näheren Angaben).

**Kirschner,** Max: Seit 1600 Jahren „Vater unser" auf deutsch. Die älteste deutsche Übersetzung stammt vom westgotischen Bischof Wulfilas. Erschienen in einem diözesanen Kirchenblatt (möglicherweise für München-Freising?); Erscheinungsdatum nicht festzustellen.

**Kiss,** Melchior: Vaterunser. Deutsch von Karl Muth. In: Kompass. Winterthur, H. 3, 11 (1948).

**Knoch,** Otto: Vaterunser-Meditation: s. **Fick,** Ulrich.

**Knörzer,** Wolfgang: Abba – Lieber Vater. Folge 10 der Beitragsserie „Zur Gottesfrage des heutigen Menschen. In: Katholisches Sonntagsblatt, Stuttgart. Erscheinungsdatum nicht bekannt.

**Die Kraft des Vaterunser und Ave Maria.** Gebetszettel (Nr. 200) mit Imprimatur Freiburg / Schweiz vom 7. Mai 1931. 7 S.; Vaterunser: S. 1–3.

**Krämer,** Eugen: Vater Unser (in Gedichtform). In: Neubau. München: I, I – November 1946.

**Leitgeb,** Guido B.: Gebetszettel. Tägliche Gebete: Vater unser und Ave Maria. Rosenheim. Obb. Druckerei. Mit Imprimatur München–Freising vom 14. 11. 1945. 6 S.

**Nyassa-Vaterunser.** In: Kolpingsblatt, Köln. Erscheinungsdatum nicht sicher feststellbar (1960?).

**Pauli,** Bruder Johannes: Das Vaterunser – Wie ein reicher Mann das Vaterunser lernte. Nach dem Volksbuch „Schimpf und Ernst" 1952 nachgeschrieben und in kath. Kirchenblättern (Titel nicht bekannt) erschienen.

**Péguy,** Charles: Das Vaterunser. Übersetzt von Ida Coudenhove. Keine näheren Angaben.

**Pleyer,** Wilhelm: Das Vaterunser für Deutschland. Erschienen in einem Kirchenblatt (?). Keine näheren Angaben.

**Plotzke,** Urban OP: Unsere geistige Not (über die Vorrede zum Vaterunser in der Meßfeier). Erschienen in der „Deutschen Tagespost", Würzburg. Datum des Erscheinens nicht bekannt.

**Reetz,** Abt Benedikt OSB: Abba, Vater! „Vater unser, der Du bist im Himmel". Vermutlich in einem katholischen Kirchenblatt erschienen. Keine näheren Angaben.

**Reubel-Giani,** Theo: Wo das „Vater unser" in Tautsch gebetet wird. Deutsche Sprachinsel in den oberitalienischen Bergen. In: Rottenburger Bistumsblatt, um die Pfingstzeit 1975.

**W.S.:** Das Wunder des Vaterunser! In: Kompaß, Winterthur, 20.1.1949.

**Schips** (?) (Pfarrer, Karsee): Fastenzyklus über das Vaterunser. Maschinengeschriebenes Manuskript mit zus. 64 S. Keine näheren Angaben.

**Schulte,** Josef OMI: Beitragsserie über das Vaterunser. Erschienen Frühjahr 1962, vermutlich in einem katholischen Kirchenblatt.

**Seemann,** Margarete: Vater im Himmel, ich bitte dich... (Gedicht, das sich mit der Brotbitte beschäftigt). Erschienen in Zeitschrift oder Kirchenblatt. Keine näheren Angaben.

**Strickstrock,** Jürgen: „Herr, lehre uns beten!" Zur Gebetswoche um die Einheit aller Christen. In: Regensburger Bistumsblatt, Nr. 2, S. 5, Jan. 1973.

**Vater unser, der du bist im Himmel** – im Osten und im Westen... In: Kirche und Leben, Münster. Erscheinungsdatum unsicher (10.12.1961?).

**Vaterunser der Frauen aus Kanada** aus Anlaß des Weltgebetstags der Frauen am 3. März 1978. Zwei Schreibmaschinenseiten Din-A 4, keine näheren Angaben.

**Das Vaterunser der Motorisierten.** Abgedruckt in einem Blatt (Kirchenblatt?). Keine näheren Angaben.

**Das Vaterunser des Autofahrers.** In: Kirche und Leben, Münster, 18.8.1974, S. 4.
Anm.: Diesen Text haben die evangelischen und katholischen Kirchengemeinden in Wiesbaden zu Beginn der Ferien an die Autofahrer verteilt.

**Vater unser / Du bist im Himmel.** In: Empor die Herzen. Hrsg. Bischöfl. Jugendseelsorgeamt Speyer als Gebetsaufruf an junge Christen für 1940.

**Das Vaterunser** eine Erinnerung an die Grundwahrheiten der Exerzitien. Gebetszettel. Leutesdorf: Verlag des Johannesbundes (Imprimatur Trier 8. Okt. 1932). 4 S.

**Das „Vaterunser" für die Verstorbenen.** Gebetszettel. Freiburg / Schweiz: Kanisius-Verlag (Imprimatur vom 8.11.1950). 4 S.

**Vaterunser, Das:** gemeinsam für Juden und Christen? Thematik des Oekumenischen Pfingsttreffens Augsburg 1971 (Pressemeldung Nr. 86 des Pressezentrums).

**Vater unser im Himmel.** Das Gebet des Herrn und die christliche Vollkommenheit (Gedanken im Anschluß an die Einführung des neuen Vaterunser-Textes). In: Franziskusblatt, Altötting, Heft 6, 1968. S. 138–140.

**Das Vaterunser:** im Rahmen einer Mariologie. In: Missionskalender (der Benediktiner von St. Ottilien). St. Ottilien 1970. S. 41–80.

**Vaterunser in Altbayerisch.** In: KNA-Mitteilungen Nr. 167 vom 9.8.1958.

**Waldmann,** Georg SJ: Vater Unser. Fastenpredigten, gehalten in der Pfarrei St. Maximilian, München 1950. Vorhandene (maschinengeschriebene u. rotafixierte) Manuskripte: 1. Fastensonntag (zu Matth. VI): 26 2.50; 2. Fastensonntag: (zu Exodus 3,13–15): 5.3.50; 3. Fastensonntag (zu Markus, 1. Kap.): 12. 3.50; Palmsonntag (zu Lk. 18,9–14): 2. 4. 50.

**Weinrich,** Franz Johannes: Vater unser (aus „Die Messe vom Reich Gottes"). In: Begegnung, Köln, Jahrg. 2, Heft 7–8 (unsicher).

**Wieviel ist ein Vaterunser wert?** Eine Erzählung aus dem „Christlichen Pilger", Speyer. Datum nicht mehr feststellbar.

# MUSIKBIBLIOGRAPHIE
# UND DISKOGRAPHIE
# SEIT 1945

2. Teil

# VORWORT

Vorliegende Bibliographie und Diskographie erfaßt alle vokalen und instrumentalen Vertonungen des *Vater unser*, die vorwiegend seit Ende des zweiten Weltkrieges herausgegeben wurden.

Dabei wurden die wichtigsten Choral- und Melodievorlagen, ein- und mehrstimmige Vokalkompositionen in verschiedenen Sprachen und nach unterschiedlichen Textvorlagen, sowie choralgebundene Instrumentalwerke berücksichtigt.

Aus zeitlichen und technischen Gründen konnte der größte Teil der Musikalien nicht eingesehen werden. Daher stützen sich die meisten Angaben auf Kataloge, deren Werkverzeichnisse sehr unterschiedlich und teilweise lückenhaft angelegt sind. Ebenso wird keinerlei Anspruch auf Vollständigkeit erhoben und darauf hingewiesen, daß viele Editionen bereits wieder vergriffen sind.

Sommer 1980                                                    Eleonore Jahnke

# INHALT

## Inhaltsverzeichnis

# Erläuterungen

Fehlt die Angabe der Besetzung bei den einstimmigen Vokalkompositionen, ist im allgemeinen Singstimme + Klavier gemeint.

Lebensdaten sind ebenso wie das Erscheinungsjahr angegeben, soweit bekannt.

Unterbleibt bei den mehrstimmigen Vokalkompositionen ein Zusatzvermerk hinter der Angabe der Stimmenzahl, handelt es sich um vierstimmig gemischten Chor.

## Abkürzungsverzeichnis

| | | | |
|---|---|---|---|
| A | Alt | Harm | Harmonium |
| B | Baß | hrsg | herausgegeben |
| Bar | Bariton | homoph | homophon |
| Bc | Basso continuo | Instr | Instrument(e) |
| Bd | Band | Jak | Jakobus |
| Begl | Begleitung | Kb | Kontrabaß |
| B & H | Breitkopf und Härtel | Kn | Knabenstimme(n) |
| Cemb | Cembalo | M | Männerstimme(n) |
| Ch | Chor | MS | Mezzosopran |
| Cl | Klarinette | Mt | Matthäus |
| Dr | Schlagzeug | Ob | Oboe |
| DDT | Denkmäler deutscher Tonkunst | op | Opus |
| | | Orch | Orchester |
| DTB | Denkmäler deutscher Tonkunst in Bayern | P | Klavier |
| | | Pk | Pauken |
| DTÖ | Denkmäler deutscher Tonkunst in Österreich | Pos | Posaune(n) |
| | | Qufl | Querflöte |
| Fa | Fagott | S | Sopran |
| Fl | Flöte | st, St | stimmig, Stimme(n) |
| Fr | Frauenchor | T | Tenor |
| gem | gemischt(e) | Tr | Trompete(n) |
| gl | gleich(e) | Va | Viola |
| Git | Gitarre | Vc | Violoncello |
| gregor | gregorianisch | Vl | Violine(n) |
| h | hoch | VU | Vaterunser |

166

# 1. Verzeichnis der Grundmelodien

## 1.1. Mit lateinischem Text

**Pater noster** ... Vater unser ... Einfache Singweise an Werktagen und bei Trauergottesdiensten. Pater noster ... Vater unser ... Feierliche Singweise an Sonn- und Feiertagen. Melodie u. Text (nur in lat. Sprache). Luzern, Lörrach: Paulus-Verlag 1965. Wien: Styria 1965.
– In: Der römische Meßkanon (Missale Romanum, Auszug), Ausgabe für den liturg. Gebrauch, S. 38–48. Einsiedeln, Köln: Benziger 1968. Freiburg, Basel, Wien: Herder 1968 (= Nr. 14749).

**Il Pater nostro,** melodia populare. In: Nuovo Canzionere Educativo all' unisono, con accompagnamento di P., Nr. 15. Milano: Ricordi.

**Pater noster.** Ambrosianische Singweise. In: P. Wagner, Einführung in die gregorianischen Melodien Bd. III, S. 60. Wiesbaden: B & H 1962.
– In: Missale Ambrosianum, S. 200/201. Milano: Mediolani Typis Joannis Daverio, Typographi Archiepiscopalis 1946.

**Pater noster.** Mozarabische Singweise. In: P. Wagner, Einführung in die gregorianischen Melodien Bd. III, S. 58. Wiesbaden: B & H 1962.
– In: Libros oficiales de la Capilla Mozárabe en Toledo, abgedruckt in: Estudios sobre la liturgia mozarabe, Bd. I, S. 102/103. Toledo: Diputación Provincial 1965.

**Pater noster.** Span.-franz. Singweise. In: MGG, S. 950, hrsg. v. Fr. Blume. Kassel: Bärenreiter 1962.

**Pater noster,** weitere Singweisen. In: MGG S. 943–950, hrsg. v. Fr. Blume. Kassel: Bärenreiter 1962.
– In: P. Wagner, Einführung in die gregorianischen Melodien Bd. III, S. 58–69. Wiesbaden: B & H 1962.

## 1.2. Mit deutschem Text

### 1.2.1. Lutherisch

**Vater unser im Himmelreich.** Luther. In: Ph. Wackernagel, Das deutsche Kirchenlied, S. 24. Hildesheim: Ohms 1964.
– In: J. Zahn, Die Melodien des deutschen evang. Kirchenlieds, Nr. 2561. Gütersloh: Bertelsmann 1889.
– In: Kirchenlieder nebst ihren Melodien, Nr. 4. Leipzig: Rieter-Biedermann.
– In: Ein Ruf zum Gebet. Hrsg. v. Chr. Rietschel. Berlin: Evangelische Verlangsanstalt 1951.

### 1.2.2. Andere

**Ach unser vatter, der du bist im Himmel, hör, was uns gebrist und was wir jetz begären.** J. Zwick. In: Ph. Wackernagel, Das deutsche Kirchenlied, S. 609. Hildesheim: Ohms 1964. Straßburg Köpphl 1537.
– In: J. Zahn. Die Melodien des deutschen evang. Kirchenlieds, Nr. 8305. Gütersloh. Bertelsmann 1889.

**Ach Vater unser also schon, der du bist in des Himmels Thron.** Schöne und Christl. Creutz- und Kirchengesänger, Straubing 1615. In: Ph. Wackernagel, Das deutsche Kirchenlied, S. 936. Hildesheim: Ohms 1964.

**Ach Vater unser, der du bist im Himmelreich hoch über uns, darumb im Geist.** A. Moibanus. In: Ph. Wackernagel, Das deutsche Kirchenlied, S. 544. Hildesheim: Ohms 1964.

**Ach Vater unser, der du bist im Himmelreich hoch über uns, darum im Geist willst angebetet werden.** König 1738. In: J. Zahn, Die Melodien des deutschen evang. Kirchenlieds, Nr. 8487. Gütersloh: Bertelsmann 1889.

**Ach Vater, der du bist im Himmelreich, dein heilger Nam werd ausgebreit gewaltiglich.** Gesangbüchlein Zwickau 1525. In: J. Zahn, Die Melodien des deutschen evang. Kirchenlieds, Nr. 8484. Kugelmann Augsburg 1540.
– In: J. Zahn, Die Melodien des deutschen evang. Kirchenlieds, Nr. 8485. Amberg 1597.
– In: J. Zahn, Die Melodien des deutschen evang. Kirchenlieds. Nr. 8487. Gütersloh: Bertelsmann 1889.

**O Gott du unser Vater bist.** H. S. Liebenstein 1775. In: J. Zahn, Die Melodien des deutschen evang. Kirchenlieds, Nr. 8488. Gütersloh: Bertelsmann 1889.

**Vater unser, der du bist, Kyrieeleison, gib uns zurkennen Jhesum Christ.** Valentin Babstisches Gesangbuch 1545. In: Ph. Wackernagel, Das deutsche Kirchenlied, S. 229. Hildesheim: Ohms 1964.

**Vater unser, der du bist im Himmel, lehrt uns Jesus Christ.** Gesangbuch Erfurt 1527. In: Ph. Wackernagel, Das deutsche Kirchenlied, S. 545. Hildesheim: Ohms 1964.
– In: J. Zahn, Die Melodien des deutschen evang. Kirchenlieds. Nr. 1975. Gütersloh: Bertelsmann 1889.

**Vater unser, der du in himmlen bist, das ist, du herrschst an aller Orten.** W. Menslin. In: Ph. Wackernagel, Das deutsche Kirchenlied, S. 802/803. Hildesheim: Ohms 1964.

Vater unser, getreuer Gott, groß Jammers Not. Geist. Gesang und Psalmen Augsburg 1529. In: Ph. Wackernagel, Das deutsche Kirchenlied, S. 544. Hildesheim: Ohms 1964. Gesangsbüchlein Augspurg 1562.
– In: J. Zahn, Die Melodien des deutschen evang. Kirchenlieds, Nr. 8555. Gütersloh: Bertelsmann 1889.

Vater unser, wir bitten dich, wie uns hat gelehrt Herr Jesu Christ. S. Pollio. In: Ph. Wackernagel, Das deutsche Kirchenlied, S. 510. Hildesheim: Ohms 1964.
– In: J. Zahn, Die Melodien des deutschen evang. Kirchenlieds, Nr. 7747. Gütersloh: Bertelsmann 1889.

Vater ins Himmels Throne, dein Nam geheiligt werd. A. Lobwasser. In: Ph. Wackernagel, Das deutsche Kirchenlied, S. 870. Hildesheim: Ohms 1964.

Vater unser im Himmelein, zu dir kommen wir Kinderlein. N. Selnekker. In: Ph. Wackernagel, Das deutsche Kirchenlied, S. 234. Hildesheim: Ohms 1964.

Vater unser im Himmelreich, wir dein arm Kinder all zu gleich. J. Leon. In: Ph. Wackernagel, Das deutsche Kirchenlied, S. 495. Hildesheim: Ohms 1964.

Vater unser im Himmelsthron, der du uns rufst durch deinen Sohn. N. Selnecker. In: Ph. Wackernagel, Das deutsche Kirchenlied, S. 254. Hildesheim: Ohms 1964.
– In: J. Zahn, Die Melodien des deutschen evang. Kirchenlieds, Nr. 478. Gütersloh: Bertelsmann 1889.

Vater unser im Himmelreich, Herr Jesu Christ, der du uns lehrest betten gleich, gelobt seist du, Herr Jesu Christ. Havs Kirchenkantorei 1587. In: Ph. Wackernagel, Das deutsche Kirchenlied, S. 1137. Hildesheim: Ohms 1964.

Vater unser im Himmelreich, wir deine Kinder alle gleich. Th. Hartmann. In: Ph. Wackernagel, Das deutsche Kirchenlied, S. 311. Hildesheim: Ohms 1964.

Vater unser ins Himmels Thron, wie hing dein eingeborner Sohn. M. Behm. In: Ph. Wackernagel, Das deutsche Kirchenlied, S. 246. Hildesheim: Ohms 1964.

Vater unser, der du bist im Himmel, geheiligt werd dein Name. M. Valentini Grüseri 1605. In: J. Zahn, Die Melodien des deutschen evang. Kirchenlieds. Gütersloh: Bertelsmann 1889.

Vater unser, der du bist, Kyrie eleison, gieb uns zu'r kennen Jesum Christ! Gesangbuch Babst 1545. In: J. Zahn, Die Melodien des deutschen evang. Kirchenlieds, Nr. 4084. Gütersloh: Bertelsmann 1889.

**Vater unser, der du im Himmel bist, das ist, du herrsch'st an allen Orten.** Straßburg, Köpphl 1537. In: J. Zahn, Die Melodien des deutschen evang. Kirchenlieds, Nr. 8223. Gütersloh: Bertelsmann 1889.

**Vater unser in dem Himmel, dein Nam werd geheiligt, dein Reich komme.** Hannoversches Gesangbuch 1657. In: J. Zahn, Die Melodien des deutschen evang. Kirchenlieds, Nr. 8638b. Gütersloh: Bertelsmann 1889.
– In: Kirchenlieder nebst ihren Melodien, Nr. 4. Leipzig: Rieter-Biedermann.
– In: Ein Ruf zum Gebet. Hrsg. v. Ch. Rietschel. Berlin: Evangelische Verlagsanstalt 1951.

**Vaterunser-Lied.** In: Kinder-Beatmesse: 5 Brote und 2 Fische. Düsseldorf: tvd-Verlag 1978.

**Vater unser, der du bist im Himmel.** Nach einem amerikan. Vater unser (ursprüngl. westind. Calypso). In: Schöne Musika, Nr. 275. Berlin: Burckardthaus-Verl. 1964. Berlin: Evangel. Verlagsanstalt 1964. Vluyn/Kr. Moers: Singende Gemeinde 1964.

## 2. Verzeichnis der Vokalkompositionen

### 2.1. Einstimmig

### 2.1.1. Mit lateinischem Text

**Auerbach,** Otto: m. P. New York: Mills F. A.

**Balthasar,** Florence (geb. 1844): m. Org. o. Orch. ad lib. Mainz: Schott.

**Béon,** Alexandre: m. P. (Harm.), Vc. Leipzig: Cranz.

**Bordese,** L. (1810–1886): S. m. Org. (Harm.). In: Collection Zingarelli Nr. 119. Paris: Lemoine.
– m. P. In: Collection Zingarelli Nr. 123. Paris: Lemoine.
– m. P. Paris: Joubert.

**Bottazzo,** Luigi (1845–1924): op. 300, m. Org. Padova: Zanibon.

**Carretto** del, Cristina: m. P. o. Harm. Torino: Capra.

**Cherubini,** Luigi (1760–1842): m. P. Paris: Leduc.

**Delaporte,** A.: Bar.-Solo, m. P. In: Cantiques Latins, 20 Chants sacrés latins, Nr. 15. Augers: Metzner A.-Leblanc.

**Harcourt d',** Eugène (1881–1918): m. P. (auch franz.). Paris: Lemoine.

**Haynes,** Battison: m. Org. London: Novello.

**Heiller,** Anton (1923–1979): A. m. P. München: Doblinger 1963.

**Höller,** Karl (geb. 1907): S. m. Org. In: Geistliche Gesänge, op. 17, 6. München: Leuckart 1962.

**Hoyte,** W. S.: m. P. London: Novello. Boston: Ditson.

**Jekyll,** C. S.: m. P. London: Weekes & Co.

**Jellief:** m. P. Paris: Durdilly.

**Kersch,** F.: m. P. In: op. 57, Nr. 1. Budapest: Rózsavölgyi.
– m. P. In: op. 57, Nr. 2. Budapest: Rózsavölgyi.

**Lamartine,** Alphonse Marie Prat de (1790–1869): m. P. (Bordèse). Paris: Joubert.

**Lataste:** m. P. Paris: Pérégally A. & Parvy Fils.

**Lorphelin,** S.: m. Org. (P.). Paris: Gallet Emile.

**Marquez,** Ch.: m. Org. Paris: Demets.

**Niedermayer,** Louis (1802–1861): Paris: Heugel.

**Page,** Arthur: m. P. London: Vincent Music Co.

**Peeters,** Flor (geb. 1903): op. 102, m. Org. (P.). (auch engl.); op. 102 f, h. St. (= Ed. Peters 6342a); op. 102g, m. St. (= Ed. Peters 6342b); op. 102h, t. St. (= Ed. Peters 6342c); New York: Peters 1962.

**Pons,** Charles (1870–1957): B. m. Org. (Harm.). Milano: Ricordi.

**Renaud,** E.: m. Org. In: op. 10, Nr. 5. Paris: Costallat.

**Reuchsel,** Amadée (1875–1931): m. P. Lyon: Janin Frères.

**Sancho,** Marraco: m. P. Bilbao: Dotesio.

**Schneider,** Friedrich (1786–1853): m. Org. Berlin: Bornemann J.

**Sunyer:** S. o. T. m. P. Bilbao: Dotesio.

**Vanelli,** G.: Milano: Ricordi.

**Vuidet,** Gast: m. Org. (P.). Nice: Decourcelle P.

**Zeitler,** Josef: op. 12, m. Org. (Harm. o. P.). (auch deutsch). Leipzig: Reinecke.

### 2.1.2. Mit deutschem Text

**Bein,** Wilhelm: Mt 6, 9–13: 1-st. Jugend-Chor (auch 4-st.). Hannover: Hampe 1949.

**Cornelius,** Peter (1824–1874): Singst. m. P.
Aus dem V. u.: op. 2 Nr. 3: Zu uns komme Dein Reich: Das sind goldene Himmelspfade

op. 2 Nr. 8: Führe uns nicht in Versuchung: Als Du auf Erden ...
op. 2 Nr. 9: Erlöse uns von dem Übel: Heilige Liebe, flammendes Herz.
Text: P. Cornelius (u. a.). In: Lieder nach den ersten Drucken rev. u. m. Anmerk. vers. v. M. Friedländer. Leipzig: Peters 1959 (= Peters Nr. 3106).

**Dietrich:** 1-st. Ch. u. Org. In: Choralsingebuch, S. 8, 2 Verse, hrsg. v. O. Brodde. Kassel: Bärenreiter 1949 (= BA 671).

**Dybwad,** E.: m. P. Wien: Rörich & Co.

**Eccard,** Johannes (1553–1611): m. P. In: 17 Choräle, Kahnt: Heft 1, Nr. 4., hrsg. v. C. Riedel. Leipzig: Kahnt C. F.

**Erdmannsdörfer,** Max (1848–1905): op. 33, T. o. S. m. Org. (H). Leipzig: Aibl J.

**Eyken** van, Heinrich (1861–1908): op. 19, m. Org. Berlin: Dreililien.

**Fischer,** Carl August (1828–1892): op. 7, m. Org. (H. P.). Mannheim: Schiele.

**Gantner,** Albert: f. Volkschor u. Org. St. Gallen/Appenzell: Bless W. 1966.

**Gassner,** Ferdinand Simon (1798–1851) B. m. P. (u. VI. ad lib.). Berlin: Simrock.

**Geist,** Christian (um 1640–1711): Mt 6,9–13: Geistl. Konzert f. mittl. St., Str. u. B. C. Frankfurt: Litolff; Peters 1963 (= Kirchenkantaten, Coll. Litolff Nr. 5899).

**Gosswin,** Anton (um 1540–1594): Luther: m. 2 Mel.-Instr. In: Newe teutsche Lieder 1581, Nr. 1, hrsg. v. G. Fellerer. Wolfenbüttel: Möseler 1960 (= Das Chorwerk H. 75).

**Grewelding,** Hansjakob: m. P. Köln: Bieler 1970.

**Hendrik,** B. Mt 6,9–13: m. P. (auch franz.): Leipzig: Rühle.

**Hollaender,** Alexis (1840–1924): op. 55, m. Org. (H. o. P.). (auch engl.). Berlin: Fürstner.

**Knab,** Arnim (1881–1951): Mt 6,9–13: m. Org. Kassel: Bärenreiter 1967 (= Bärenreiter-Ausg. 2085).

**Krebs,** Karl-August (1804–1880): S. (T.) m. P. Berlin: Lienau 1951 (= Hosianna Nr. 88).
– A. (Bar.) m. P. Berlin: Lienau 1951 (= Hosianna Nr. 90).
– S. (T.) m. Org. In: Kirchenarien u. Lieder, hrsg. v. G. Göhler. Frankfurt: Peters 1962 (= Ed. Peters 2451).

172

**Lickl,** C. G. (1769–1843): (1576) … (1567) m. P. In: Klänge d. Andacht, eine Sammlung v. Kirchenliedern u. Chorälen H. X/ Miserere: „Ach, erbarme Schöpfer". Leipzig: Bosworth & Co.

**Mauersberger,** Erhard (geb. 1903): Luther: m. Org. In: Monatssprüche f. d. Jahr 1947 (Oktober). Hildburghausen: Gadow & Sohn 1947 (= Singh. d. Thüringer Kirchenchorwerkes 9).

**Mayer,** Alfons: Mt 6,9–13: m. Org. (H. o. P.). Augsburg: Böhm 1955.

**Janssens,** Peter: V. U. II: Text: Janssens, m. Git.-Beziff. In: Petbiets Gesangbuch. Telgte: Janssens 1970.

**Schaab,** Robert (1817–1887): u. Einsetzungsworte m. Org. Leipzig: Siegel.

**Schneider,** Wilhelm (1783–1843): u. Einsetzungsworte m. Org. Leipzig: Hofmeister.

**Sluničko,** Johann: op. 19,1, S. o. T. m. Org. (P.). Augsburg: Böhm 1950.

**Stimmer,** Kathi: m. Beziff. In: Singt Gott, jubelt ihm, hrsg. v. d. Münchener Provinz d. Redemptoristen. Gars (Inn): Briefe an unsere Freunde 1978.

**Zeitler,** Josef: op. 12, m. Org. (H. o. P.). (auch lat.). Leipzig: Reinecke.

### 2.1.3. Mit fremdsprachigem Text

**Anfossi,** G.: Padre nostro m. P. Milano: Ricordi.

**Harcourt d',** Eugène (1859–1918): Père, qui habites les cieux, m. P. (auch lat.). Paris: Lemoine.

**Hendrik,** B.: Père, qui habites les cieux, m. P. (auch deutsch). Leipzig: Rühle.

**Höller,** Karl (geb. 1907): Our Father which art in Heaven, S. m. Org. (auch lat.). In: op. 17 Nr. 6. München: Leuckart 1962.

**Hollaender,** Alexis (geb. 1840): op. 55, Lord's Prayer, m. Org. (H. o. P.). Berlin: Fürstner.

**Hoyte,** W. S.: Lord's Prayer (auch lat.). Boston: Ditson.

**Krebs,** Carl (1857–1937): Our Father which art in Heaven, S. o. T. m. P. Berlin: Lienau 1951 (= Hosianna Nr. 88).
– Our Father which art in Heaven, A. o. Bar. m. P. Berlin: Lienau 1951 (= Hosianna Nr. 90).

**Lorphelin,** S.: Notre Père, m. Org. o. P. (auch lat.). Paris: Gallet Emile.

**Peeters,** Flor (geb. 1903): Our Father who art in heaven (auch lat.): op. 102a, h. St. (= Ed. Peters 6342a); op. 102g, m. St. (= Ed. Peters 6342b); op. 102h, t. St. (= Ed. Peters 6342c). Frankfurt: Peters 1962.

**Travaglia,** Silvio: Padre nostro, m. P. Padova: Zanibon.

**Welch,** H. T.: Lord's Prayer m. P. London: Novello.

## 2.2. Mehrstimmig

### 2.2.1. Mit lateinischem Text

#### 2.2.1.1. Allein

**Abbà,** Cornaglia: 2-st., Bar. u. B. m. P. Torino: Blanchi.

**Alig,** Emil: 4-st. Cham/Schweiz: Willi 1965.

**Anonymus:** 5-st. In: Anthologie du motet latin polyphonique en France, S. 35–43, hrsg. v. D. Launay. Paris: Heugel.

**Arcadelt,** Jacobus (um 1500–1568): 8-st. In: Corpus Mensurabilis Musicae 31, X, S. 70–78, hrsg. v. A. Secuy. Roma: American Institute of Music 1970.

**Auvergne d',** Barnard: 3-st., gl. St. m. Begl. Paris: Joubert C.

**Baumann,** Max (geb. 1917): 8-st. Berlin: Merseburger 1964. (= Ed. Merseb. 216).

**Bazin,** François-Emanuel-Joseph (1816–1878): 4-st. Paris: Lemoine.

**Besozzi,** L. D.: Ch. Barcelona: Dotesio.

**Biedermann,** E. J.: 3-st., Fr. o. Kn.-Ch. Boston: Ditson Oliver Company.

**Bordese,** L. (1810–1886): 2-st. (S., B.) m. Org. o. Harm. Paris: Lemoine.
– 4-st., Es-Dur. Paris: Costallat.

**Bortinansky,** Dm. (1751–1825): 5-st. (Berlioz). Paris: Costallat.

**Bruck,** Arnoldus de, (um 1490–1554): 5-st. In: DTÖ 99, S. 81–87, hrsg. v. O. Wesseley. Graz/Wien: Akademische Druck- u. Verlagsanstalt 1961.
– 4-st.: In: DTÖ 99, S. 59–63, hrsg. v. O. Wesseley. Graz/Wien: Akademische Druck- u. Verlagsanstalt 1961.

**Cherubini,** Luigi (1760–1842): 4-st., 2 Vl., 2 Fl., Ob. (Cl.), 2 Fa., Vc., Kb., Org. o. P. Leipzig: Cranz.
– 4-st. Mainz: Schott; Paris: Pérégally (m. Org.); Arras: Procura (m. Org.); Milano: Musica Sacra (m. Org.).

**Commer,** Franz (1813–1887): 4-st., M.-Ch. In: Op. 2, Geistliche Gesänge, Heft 1, Nr. 50. Magdeburg: Heinrichshofen.

**Deslandres,** Adolphe Eduard Marie (1840–1911): 2-st., Bar. u. MS. m. Org. Paris: Deslandres.

**Des Prez,** Josquin (um 1440–1521): 6-st. In: Werken van Josquin Des Prez, Motetten, Bundel XII, S. 47–53, hrsg. v. A. Smijers. Amsterdam: Alsbach G. & Co. 1954.

**Dethier,** Emilie: 4-st., M.-Ch. m. Org. ad lib. Paris: Laudy.

**Dubois,** Theodore (1837–1924): 4-st. m. Org. ad lib. Paris: Heugel & Cie.

**Egaddi:** 4-st. Milano: Ricordi.

**Elton,** Frederick (1808–1877): 3-st., Fr.- o. Kn.-Ch. m. P. Paris: Gallet E.

**Everaerts,** F.: 4-st. m. Org. Mainz: Schott.

**Fauna,** Antonio (1792–1845): T.-Solo u. Tutti: T., 2 B. m. Org. In: op. 81. Paris: Lemoine.

**Faure,** Jean Baptiste (1830–1914): 2-st. Paris: Heugel.

**Gallus,** Jacobus (Jakob Handl) (1550–1591): 8-st. In: DTÖ 12, I. Motettenwerk für das ganze Kirchenjahr, II. Teil, S. 16–19, hrsg. v. G. Adler, Wien: B & H 1919; Heidelberg: Müller W. 1954 (= Heidelb. Chorblätter 35); Wiesbaden: B & H 1979.

**Gevaert,** François-Auguste (1828–1908): 4-st. (auch franz.). Paris: Lemoine.

**Gordigiani,** Giovanni Battista (1795–1871): 4-st., m. Org., A-Dur. Dresden: Hoffmann.

**Gotthard,** Johann Peter (1839–1919): 2-st., Fr.- o. Kn.-Ch. m. Org. Wien: Pazdirek.

**Gounod,** Charles-François (1818–1893): 5-st. Paris: Grus L. & Cie.
– 4-st. London: Weekes & Co.
– 5 Solo-St. u. Ch. Paris: Lemoine.
– 4-st., gl. St. m. Org. (P.). Arras: Procura; Paris: Le Beau A.
– 4-st., (S.S.T.B.) m. Org. (P.). Arras: Procura; Paris: Chondens.

**Gruberus,** Augustanus, Joannes: 4-st. Regensburg: Pustet 1954 (= Die Chorsammlung A 41).

**Hassler,** Hans Leo (1564–1612): 8-st. In: DDT 2, I, Cantiones Sacrae für 4–12 St., S. 105–110, hrsg. v. H. Gehrmann. Leipzig: B & H.

**Henderson,** Ruth-Watson: 4-st. Toronto: Thompson G.

175

**Hiller,** Ferdinand (1811–1885): op. 61, 4-st., m.P. (Org.). Mainz: Schott.

**Jadin,** Hyacinthe (1769–1800): 2-st., MS., Bar.-Solo, m. Begl. Paris: Pérégally.

**Johansson,** Bengt: 3-st., Fr.- o. Kn.-Ch. Helsingfors: Fazer.

**Kedroff,** Nicolas: 4-st. (auch franz.). Wiesbaden: B & H 1954.

**Kent,** James (1700–1776): 4-st. Toronto: Thompson G.

**Kunz,** Konrad Max (1812–1875): 4-st., M.-Ch. m. Blasmusik. Leipzig: Aibl.

**Labinskij,** Aleksander: 4-st., m. P. ad lib. (auch engl. u. tschech.). Wiesbaden: B & H 1954.

**Lambillotte,** Louis (1796–1855): Ch. In: Grands Saluts de Première Collection av. Org. ou Orch. XI. Fête Patronale Nr. 35. Paris: Lemoine.
– Ch. In: Grands Saluts de Deuxième Collection av. Org. ou Orch. V. Pentecôte Nr. 17. Paris: Lemoine.

**Lasso di,** Orlando (um 1532–1594): 6-st. In: Magnum opus musicum, Lat. Gesänge f. 2, 3, 4, 5, 6–10 St., Teil VII, S. 77–81, hrsg. v. F. X. Haberl. Leipzig: B & H.
– 6-st. In: Magnum opus musicum, Lat. Gesänge f. 2, 3, 4, 5, 6–10 St., Teil VII, S. 81–86, hrsg. v. F. X. Haberl. Leipzig: B & H.

**Laurent,** Camille: 3-st., MS., T., Bar. o Contraalto m. Org. o. Harm. In: 12 Morceaux Religieux Nr. 2. Paris: Société nouvelle d'édition musicale.

**Lemacher,** Heinrich (1891–1966): 8-st. m. homoph. Harmoniemusik o. f. Bläser (Org.) m. Ch. Altötting: Coppenrath 1959.

**Lemare,** Edwin H.: 6-st., Es-Dur, Nr. 1. London: Novello.
– 5-st., Finale Amen, G-Dur, Nr. 2. London: Novello.
– 7-st., G-Dur, Nr. 3. London: Novello.

**Lichtenthal,** Pietro (1780–1853): 4-st. m. Org. (P.). In: Album musicale sacro Nr. 1. Milano: Ricordi & Cie.
– 4-st., su i tre suoni, B, C, D. Milano: Ricordi & Cie.

**Liszt,** Franz (1811–1886): 4-st., M.-Ch. m. Org. In: Kirchliche u. Geistliche Gesangswerke Bd. VI, Nr. 2, S. 106–107, hrsg. v. d. Franz-Liszt-Stiftung. Wiesbaden: B & H 1966.
– 4-st. m. Org. In: Kirchliche u. Geistliche Gesangswerke Bd. VI, Nr. 3, S. 108–112, hrsg. v. d. Franz-Liszt-Stiftung. Wiesbaden: B & H 1966.

**Lutgen,** B.: 4-st. m. Org. (H.) o. Orch. Mainz: Schott.

176

**Malotte,** Albert Hay (geb. 1895): 4-st., T.-Solo m. Org. New York: Schirm G.

**Maréchal,** Henri Charles (1842–1924): 4-st., M.-Ch. Paris: Heugel et Cie.

**Marx,** W. B.: 2-st., Kn.-Ch. m. T., B. u. Org. New York: Associated Music Publishers.

**Miné,** A.: B.-Solo u. Ch., nach Verdi. In: Morceaux religieux I, Collection Nr. 71. Paris: Lémoine Henry & Co.

**Nicolai,** Otto (1810–1849): op. 33, 8-st. Köln: Bieler 1964 (= Die Motette 5).

**Nicou – Choron:** 4-st. Paris: Durand A. & Fils.

**Niedermayer,** Louis (1802–1861): MS., Bar., S., T.-Solo m. Org. Paris: Durand A.
– S., A. T. B., Solo m. P. o. Org. Paris: Heugel.

**Nuffel van,** Julius (1883–1953): 4-st. Düsseldorf: Schwann 1955 (= Das Musikblatt B 7257).

**Obrecht,** Jacobus (1450–1505): 4-st. In: Historical Anthology of Music Nr. 76, S. 80–81, hrsg. v. A. T. Davidson u. W. Apel. Cambridge/Massachusetts: Harvard University Press 1947.
– In: Altklassische Polyphonie, S. 131–135, hrsg. v. G. Fellerer. Köln: Volk 1965 (= Das Musikwerk H. 28).

**Ophoven,** Hermann: 4-st., M.-Ch. Mülheim/Ruhr: Haubrich 1966.

**Palestrina da,** Pierluigi Giovanni (um 1525–1594): 5-st. In: Libro Terzo dei Motetti a 5, 6 ed 8 voci, S. 1–5, hrsg. v. R. Casimiri. Roma: Edizione Fratelli Scalera 1940–1943.
– In: Werke v. P. G.da Palestrina Bd. VI, 5-, 6- u. 8-st. Motetten, S. 3–6, hrsg. v. F. Espagne. Leipzig: B & H.
– 8-st. In: Werke v. P. G. da Palestrina Bd. VI, 5-, 6- u. 8-st. Motetten, S. 150–153, hrsg. v. F. Espagne. Leipzig: B & H.

**Papst,** Eugen (1886–1956): 4-st. (auch deutsch). Bonn: Braun-Peretti 1956 (= Papst: Werke für Männerchor).

**Peeters,** Flor (geb. 1903): op. 102i, 2-st., gl. St. m. Org. (P.). (= Ed. Peters 6341); op. 102k, 4-st. m. Org. (P.) (= Ed. Peters 6340); New York: Peters 1962.

**Phinot,** Dominicus (? – zwischen 1557 u. 1560): 5-st. In: Corpus Mensurabilis Musicae 59, II, S. 1–7, hrsg. v. J. Höfler. Roma: American Institute of Musicology 1974.

**Pilot,** A. Le Beau: Solo u. Ch., C-Dur. Paris: Fromont Eugène.

177

**Platania,** Pietro (geb. 1828): 5-st. m. Org. u. Instr. Wiesbaden: Breit-kopf.

**Porta,** Costanzo (um 1529–1601): 6-st. In: Il primo de motetti del Sign. Cl. Merulo da Correggio Bd. I, S. 245–252, hrsg. v. Torchi. Milano: Ricordi (= L'arte Musicale in Italia).

**Portas,** Jacques: 2-st., B. u. Bar. Bilbao: Dotesio.

**Praetorius,** Hieronymus (1560–1629): 8-st. In: DDT 23, Cantiones sacrae, Nr. 3, hrsg. v. H. Leichtentritt. Wiesbaden: B & H 1959; St. Moritz: Laudinella 1972 (= Laudinella-Reihe Bl. 111).

**Praetorius,** Michael (1571–1621): 8-st. In: Musarum Sioniarum Motectae et Psalmi Latini (1607) Bd. X, S. 97–102, hrsg. v. F. Blume. Wolfenbüttel–Berlin: Kallmeyer G. 1931.

**Racine,** C.: 3-st., Fr.-Ch. (auch franz.). Paris: Lemoine.

**Regnart,** Jacobus (um 1540–1599): 4-st. In: Corpus Mensurabilis Musicae 62, V, S. 78–80, hrsg. v. W. Pass. Roma: American Institute of Musicology 1973.

**Roeske,** F. J.: 4-st. Amsterdam: Alsbach & Co.

**Rore** de, Cyprian (1516–1565): 5-st. In: Corpus Mensurabilis Musicae 14, VI, S. 49–53, hrsg. v. B. Meier. Roma: American Institute of Musicology 1975.

**Rousseau,** Samuel (1853–1904): 2-st., gl. St. Paris: Heugel.

**Schaeken,** J. H.: Bar.-Solo u. 4-st. Ch. Bruxelles: Katto.

**Schubert,** Franz (1797–1828): Miniatur-Ch. In: Messe C-Dur. New York: Kalmus E. F. (= Kalmus 453).

**Schütz,** Heinrich (1585–1672): 4-st., SWV 89. In: Cantiones Sacrae 1625, Tischgesänge, IX, op. 4, Nr. 37, S. 136–139, hrsg. v. G. Grote. Kassel: Bärenreiter 1979; Stuttgart: Hänssler 1952 (= Die Motette Nr. 11); Wolfenbüttel: Möseler 1951 (= Lose Blätter 223).

**Schwarz-Schilling,** Reinhard (geb. 1904): 5-st. Augsburg: Böhm 1951.

**Staden,** Johann (1581–1634): 5-st. In: DTB 7, I, Johann Staden I. Teil, S. 24–28, hrsg. v. A. Sandberger. Leipzig: B & H 1906.

**Strawinsky,** Igor (1882–1971): 4-st. m. P. ad lib. Bonn: Boosey & Hawkes 1951 (= Winthrop-Rogers-Church-Series 29).

**Stubbs,** G.: 4-st., M.-Ch. London: Novello.

**Sturm,** Frank: 4-st. Regensburg: Feuchtinger 1950.

**Terrabugio,** Giuseppe (geb. 1842): 4-st. m. Org. Milano: Bertarelli.

**Tivoli da,** Giuliano Buonaugurio (um 1569–1599): 3-st. In Italia Sacra Musica I, S. 124–126, hrsg. v. K. Jeppesen. København: Hansen W. 1962.

**Travaglia,** Silvio: 2-st., gl. St. m. Org. Padova: Zanibon.

**Tschaikowsky,** Peter (1840–1893): 4-st. (auch engl.). New York: Schirmer.

**Verdelot,** Philippe (um 1505–1539): 6-st. In: Corpus Mensurabilis Musicae 28, II, S. 76–82. hrsg. v. A.-M. Bragard. Roma: American Institute of Musicology 1973.

**Verdi,** Giuseppe (1813–1901): 5-st. Stuttgart: Hänssler 1980 (= HE 40.152).

**Willaert,** Adrian (um 1480–1562): 4-st. In: Corpus Mensurabilis Musicae, 3, II, Motetta IV vocum Liber secundus, S. 11–14, hrsg. v. H. Zenck. Roma: American Institute of Musicology 1950.
– 6-st. In: Corpus Mensurabilis Musicae 3, IV, Motetta VI vocum 1542, S. 1–6, hrsg. v. H. Zenck. Roma: American Institute of Musicology 1952.

**Zangius,** Nicolaus (1570–1620): 6-st. In: DTÖ 87, Geistliche und weltliche Gesänge, S. 67–70, hrsg. v. H. Sachs. Wien: Österreichischer Bundesverlag 1951.

### 2.2.1.2. Bestandteil einer größeren Komposition

**Des Prez,** Josquin (um 1450–1521): Motette: „O bone et dulcis Domine Jesu", 4-st. S.: O bone et dulcis Domine Jesu. T.: Pater noster. B.: Ave Maria. In: Werken van Josquin Des Prez, Motetten, Bundel XVIII, S. 85–87, hrsg. v. A. Smijers. Amsterdam: Alsbach G. & Co. 1954.

**Durbec,** L.: Pater noster, Cantate relig. m. P. Reims: Menuesson.

**Gallus,** Jacobus (Jakob Handl) (1550–1591): Missa ad imitationem Pater noster. Für 8-st. Doppelchor, hrsg. v. H. Gillesberger. Wien/ München: Doblinger 1969.

**Palestrina da,** Pierluigi Giovanni (um 1525–1594): Missa: Pater noster, 4-st. In: Il libro decimi delle Messe a 4, 5 e 6 voci, S. 199–225, hrsg. v. L. Bianchi. Roma: Ed. Scalera 1959 (= Istituto Italiano per la Storia della Musica).
– Missa: Panem nostrum, 5-st. In: Il Libro decimi delle Messe a 4, 5 e 6 voci, S. 226–258, hrsg. v. L. Bianchi. Roma: Ed. Scalera 1959 (= Istituto Italiano per la Storia della Musica).

### 2.2.2. Mit deutschem Text

### 2.2.2.1. Allein

**Bach,** Johann Sebastian (1685–1750): Luther: 4-st., 4. Strophe. In: Mehrstimmige Choräle, Fassung aus 1. Teil der Johannes-Passion, hrsg. v. L. Erk. Frankfurt: Peters, (Ed. 10993/10994).
– In: 42 Bach-Choräle. Chorgesänge für den gottesdienstl. Gebrauch m. o. ohne Instr. Nr. 22. Tübingen: Schultheiss 1950.

**Bach,** Wilhelm Friedrich Ernst (1759–1845): T., B., 4-st. Ch. u. Orch. (Vl. I u. II, Va., Vc/Kb, Qufl. I u. II, Ob. I u. II, Fag I u. II, Horn I u. II, Tr I u. II, Pk). In: Geistliche Musik der Bach-Familie. Stuttgart: Hänssler 1979 (= Stuttgarter Bach-Ausgaben; Ser. A: Bach-Archiv, Gruppe 5: Supplement).

**Bein,** Wilhelm: Mt 6, 9–13: 4-st. (auch 1-st. Jugendchor). Hannover: Hampe 1949.

**Blarr,** Oskar Gottlieb (geb. 1934): Mt 6, 9–13: Ch. In: Beliebte Chorsätze neuer geistl. Lieder f. 3-5st. Ch., z. T. m. Instr., Nr. 4 (nach einem südamerik. Spiritual). Regensburg: Bosse 1970 (= BE 804).

**Blummer,** M. (1827–1901): 8-st. Magdeburg: Heinrichshofen.

**Bornefeld,** Helmut (geb. 1906): Luther: I – III, 2–5-st. m. Instr. In: Kantoreisätze Nr. 74–76. Kassel: Bärenreiter 1950 (= Bornefeld: Das Choralwerk; = Bärenreiter-Ausgabe 2221).

**Bruck, Arnoldus de** (um 1490–1554): Luther: 4-st. In: DDT 34, Newe deudsche geistliche Gesenge 1544, S. 74/75, hrsg. v. J. Wolf. Leipzig: B & H 1979, Kassel: Bärenreiter 1979.

**Butz,** Josef: 4-st. u. 3-st. Bonn: Butz 1977 (= Cantus ecclesiae Nr. 751).

**Christoph,** Kurt: Gemeinsames Vaterunser: Mt 6, 9–13: 4-st. M.-Ch. Oberbrombach: Eos-Musikverlag 1969 (= Eos-Chöre).

**Dietrich,** Sixtus (zwischen 1492 u. 1494–1548): Luther: 5-st. In: DDT 34, Newe deudsche geistl. Gesenge, 1544, S. 76–82. Leipzig: B & H 1908.

**Ducis,** Benedictus (um 1490–1544): Luther: 4-st. In: DDT 34, Newe deudsche geistl. Gesenge 1544, S. 70, hrsg. v. J. Wolf. Leipzig: B & H 1908; Stuttgart: Hänssler 1955 (Die Motette Nr. 38b).

**Eccard,** Johannes (1553–1611): Luther: 5-st. In: 29 Chorgesänge im Satz zu 4–8 Stimmen, Nr. 21. Stuttgart: Hänssler 1950; Kassel: Bärenreiter 1979 (= BA 6306).
– Luther: 4-st. In: 29 Chorgesänge im Satz zu 4–8 Stimmen. Kassel: Bärenreiter 1979 (= BA 6306).
– Luther: 4-st. In: Schein, Joh. Herm., Cantional Augsburg. Kassel: Bärenreiter 1979 (BA 6306).

180

**Erythräus,** Gotthard (1560–1617): Luther: 4-st. M.-Ch. Bremen: Eres 1966 (= Eres-Chor-Ausgaben 4986).

**Frank,** Melchior (um 1579/80–1639): Luther: 4-st. In: Contrapuncti compositi 1602, Nr. 1. Stuttgart: Hänssler 1961 (= Geistliche Chormusik. Reihe 1, Die Motette Nr. 287); St. Moritz: Laudinella 1964 (= Laudinella-Reihe Bl. 13).

**Geist,** Christian (um 1640–1711): Mt 6,9–13: f. 2 S. m. 2 Vl, Va da gamba, z.T. auch chorisch bis 5-st. In: Kirchenkonzerte Nr. 4, hrsg. v. B. Lundgren. Frankfurt: Peters 1960 (= Das Erbe deutsch. Musik Bd. 48, ‚Ausgewählte Werke einzelner Meister, Bd. V').

**Gosswin,** Anton (um 1540–zwischen 1597 u. 1598): Luther: 3-st. Fr.-, M.- o. gem. Ch. m. Melodie-Instr. ad lib. (auch f. Ges. m. 2 Melodie-Instr.). In: Newe teutsche Lieder 1581, Nr. 1, hrsg. v. G. Fellerer. Wolfenbüttel: Möseler 1960 (= Das Chorwerk H. 75).

**Gumpelzhaimer,** Adam (1559–1625): 2-st., Kanon in d. Unteroktav. In: Compendium musicae Latino-germanicum 1611, daraus: Vertonungen von Gebetstexten. St. Moritz: Laudinella 1974 (= Laudinella-Reihe Bl. 133).

**Hammerschmidt,** Andreas (1611–1675): Mt 6,9–13: 9-st. In: DDT 40, Nr. 16–18 Musikalische Andachten Nr. 4, hrsg. v. J. Moser. Wiesbaden: B & H 1958; Graz: Akademische Druck u. Verl. Anst. 1958.

**Hassler,** Hans Leo (1564–1612): Luther: 4-st., in 10 Teilen. In: Psalmen u. Christl. Geseng 1607, hrsg. v. C. R. Crosby jr. Wiesbaden: B & H 1965 (= Veröffentlichungen d. Gesellschaft f. Bayer. Musikgesch.); Kassel: Bärenreiter 1950 (= BA 670).

**Hess,** Reimund (geb. 1935): 4-st. m. Org. Wiesbaden: B & H 1979 (= ChB 5106).

**Huber,** Paul: 4-st. Zürich: Hug 1971 (= G. H. 10 953).

**Hufschmidt,** Wolfgang (geb. 1934): (Jak. 1,22), 4-st. (Rogate). Kassel: Bärenreiter 1979 (= BA 3874).
– 30. Juli 1968: 4-st. Ch. u. Lautsprecher (Tonband). Kassel: Bärenreiter 1979 (= BA 6117).

**Jansen, F. Gustav** (1831–1910): op. 21, 4-st. Leipzig: Leuckart.

**Janssens,** Peter: Mt 6,9–13: 4-st. m. Git. u. Org. (P.). In: Der Herr ist mein Sinn, nie werde ich funktionieren. Telgte: Janssens 1977.

**Katt,** Leopold: Mt 6,9–13: 2-st. i. d. Quint. In: Geistl. Kanons. Tübingen: Schultheiß 1947 (= Katt: Jugend singt Nr. 3).

**Kaune,** Karl: Mt 6,9–13: 4-st. In: Das deutsche Lied Nr. 22/23, hrsg. v. K. Kaune. Celle: Moeck 1952.

**Kempkens,** Arnold: 4-st. M.-Ch. Mülheim/Ruhr: Haubrich 1971.

**Kühn,** Rudolf: 4-st. M.-Ch. Darmstadt: Tonos-Musikverlag 1978.

**Kugelmann,** Johannes (? – 1542): Luther: 3-st. gl. St. Kassel: Bärenreiter 1979 (= Bärenreiter-Chorblatt 60).
– Mt 6,9–13: 3-st. gl. St. Göttingen: Vandenhoeck & Ruprecht 1950 (= Das gesungene Bibelwort H. 1).

**Liszt,** Franz (1811–1886): Nr. 1: Mt 6,9–13: 4-st. m. Org. In: Kirchl. u. Geistl. Gesangswerke Bd. VI, S. 98–105, Hrsg. v. d. Franz-Liszt-Stiftung. Wiesbaden: B & H 1966; Leipzig: Kahnt C. F.

**Maistre le,** Mattheus (um 1505–1577): Mt 6,9–13: 4-st. In: Geistl. u. weltl. teutsche Geseng (1566) Nr. 36, hrsg. v. H. Poos. Stuttgart: Hänssler 1972 (= Die Motette Nr. 462, HE 1.462).

**L'Vov,** Aleksěj Fedorovič (1799–1871): 4-st. Stuttgart: Zumsteeg G. A.

**Mauersberger,** Erhard (geb. 1903): Luther: 4-st. In: Monatssprüche für das Jahr 1947 (Oktober). Hildburghausen: Gadow & Sohn 1947 (=Singh. d. Thüringer Kirchenchorwerkes 8).

**Metzger,** Hans-Arnold (geb. 1913): Luther: 4-st. Stuttgart: Hänssler 1956 (= Das EKG 77/241).

**Micheelsen,** Hans-Friedrich (1902–1973): Luther: 3-st. Kassel: Bärenreiter 1960 (= Kleine BA 3246).

**Mittelbach,** Otto: Mt 6,9–13: 4-st., Doppelkanon, auch f. S. u. T. m. 2 Melodieinstr. Augsburg: Böhm & Sohn 1960.

**Müller,** Adolf (1801–1886): 4-st. T T B B o. S A T B. Potschappel: Bellmann & Thümer.

**Nölling,** Willy: M.-Ch. m. Org. (P.) (2 Tr, Horn 2, Pos. ad lib.). Hamm: Hoppe B. 1979.

**Papst,** Eugen: 4-st. M.-Ch. Bonn: Braun-Peretti 1956.

**Poos,** Heinrich (geb. 1928): Mt 6,9–13: 4-st. gl. St. m. Org., Doppelkanon. Stuttgart: Hänssler 1965 (= Geistl. Chormusik Reihe 7, Neue geistl. Chormusik, Nr. 97).

**Praetorius,** Michael (um 1571–1621): Luther: 4-st. In: Musae Sioniae Teil VII (1609), Nr. 19, S. 17/18, hrsg. v. Fr. Blume. Wolfenbüttel: Kallmeyer G. 1939.
– Luther: 4-st. In: Musae Sioniae Teil VII (1609) Nr. 20, S. 18/19, hrsg. v. Fr. Blume. Wolfenbüttel: Kallmeyer G. 1939.

**Rabe,** Emil: 4-st. M.-Ch. m. Bar.-Solo ad lib. Dortmund: Wildt 1953 (= Rabe: Männerchöre).

182

**Radecke,** Rudolf (1829–1893): 4-st., Gedicht m. P./Org. o. H. Gießen: Challier E.

**Reger,** Max (1873–1916): f. drei 4-st. Chöre. (Nachgelassenes unvollendetes Werk, ergänzt von Karl Hasse (1956).) Wiesbaden: B & H 1979 (= B & H's Partiturbibliothek Nr. 3789).

**Resinarius,** Baltasar (um 1485–1544): Mt 6,9–13: 4-st. In: DDT 34, Newe deudsche geistl. Gesenge 1544, S. 66–67. Leipzig: B & H 1908; Heidelberg: Müller W. 1979 (= Die Kantorei Nr. 2).

**Scheel,** Erich Ernst Mt 6,9–13: 4-st. Mülheim/Ruhr: Haubrich 1964.

**Scheidt,** Samuel (1587–1654) Luther: 3-st. m. Gb. In: Geistl. Konzerte I, Nr. 2, S. 5–7. Hamburg: Ugrino 1957.
– Luther: 8-st. In: Cantiones sacrae 1620 Nr. 32. Stuttgart: Hänssler 1960 (= Geistl. Chormusik Reihe 1; Die Motette Nr. 174).

**Schein,** Johann Hermann (1586–1630): Luther: 2 S. u. Instr.-B. ad lib., Bc (Org. o. Cemb.) In: Opella nova, 1. Teil; Geistl. Konzerte 1618, GA Bd. 4, S. 60–64, hrsg. v. S. Helms u. A. Adrio. Kassel: Bärenreiter 1973 (= BA 4494); Stuttgart: Hänssler 1964 (= Geistl. Chormusik Reihe 5; Das geistl. Konzert Nr. 103).
– Mt 6,9–13: A.-, T.-Solo o. T.-, T.-Solo, Ch. (S.S.A.T.B.), VI., Qufl. (VI.), 2 Va., Vc. (u./o. 2 Zinken, 3 Posaunen), Bc. Stuttgart: Hänssler 1980 (= HE 5143/02).
– Luther: 4-st. In: Cantional- o. Gesangb. Augsburg. Konfession 1627/1645 Teil I; Choralsätze zu 4 u. 5 St., GA Bd. 2, S. 86, hrsg. v. A. Adrio. Kassel: Bärenreiter 1965 (= BA 4492a).
– Vater unser, der du bist, Kyrie eleison, 4-st. In: Cantional- o. Gesangbuch Augsb. Konfession 1627/1645 Teil I; Choralsätze zu 4 u. 5 St., GA Bd. 2, S. 87, hrsg. v. A. Adrio. Kassel: Bärenreiter 1965 (= BA 4492a).

**Schieri,** Fritz (geb. 1922): 3-st. gem. o. gl. Ch. In: Altenberger Liedsätze, Nr. 109, hrsg. v. W. Lipphardt. Freiburg: Christophorus-Verlag 1954.

**Schütz,** Heinrich (1685–1672): Mt 6,9–13: 4-st. In: Cantiones Sacrae op. 4, Tischgesänge Nr. 37, SWV 89, S. 136–139, hrsg. v. G. Grote. Kassel: Bärenreiter 1979; Stuttgart: Hänssler 1952 (= Die Motette Nr. 11); Wolfenbüttel: Möseler 1951 (= Lose Blätter 223).

**Schwarz-Schilling,** Reinhard (geb. 1904): 4-st., mehrfach geteilt. Kassel: Bärenreiter 1973 (= musica sacra nova, BA 5429).

**Seitz,** Friedrich: 4-st. In: 4 deutsche Gebete, Nr. 4. Augsburg: Böhm & Sohn 1950.

**Spohr,** Ludwig (1784–1850): f. Soli u. Ch. Berlin: Schlesinger.

**Staden,** Johann (1581–1634): Mt 6,9–13: 3-st. Stuttgart: Hänssler 1973/74 (= Die Motette. Eine Sammlg. geistl. Choralsätze alter Meister Nr. 557). Wolfenbüttel: Möseler 1948/49; Göttingen: Vandenhoeck & Ruprecht 1959 (= Das gesungene Bibelwort, H. 2).

**Stahl,** Johannes: Luther: 4-st. In: DDT 34, Newe deudsche geistl. Gesenge 1544, S. 75–76. Leipzig: B & H 1908.

**Stern,** Hermann: Luther: 2-st. gl. St. Stuttgart: Hänssler 1956 (= Das EKG 77/241).
– Luther: 3-st. In: Unser Monatslied 1947. Stuttgart: Quellverlag 1947.

**Stockmeier,** Wolfgang (geb. 1931): Mt 6,9–13: 8-st., z.T. Sprechstimmen. Wolfenbüttel: Möseler 1970.

**Thelen,** Fritz: M.-Ch. u. Blasorch. (Ruf und Mahnung). Innsbruck: Helbling 1965 (= Helbl. Blasmus. Nr. 3286-B).

**Trexler,** Georg (geb. 1903): 3-st. Berlin: Merseburger 1976 (= EM 242).
– 4-st. Berlin: Merseburger 1976 (= EM 242).
– 8-st. Berlin: Merseburger 1976 (= EM 242).

**Vento de,** Ivo (um 1540–1575): Luther: 3-st. m. Instr. ad lib. In: Newe teutsche Lieder 1572. Stuttgart: Hänssler 1973 (= Das Chorwerk alter Meister HE 4.018).

**Walcha,** Helmut (geb. 1907): Luther: 2-st. In: Monatslied Oktober, hrsg. v. Landesverb. evang. Kirchenchöre Nassau-Hessen. Solingen: Hartkopf 1947.
– Luther: 3-st. In: Monatslied Oktober, hrsg. v. Landesverb. evang. Kirchenchöre Nassau-Hessen. Solingen: Hartkopf 1947.

**Weinmann,** Johann (1477–1542): Luther: 4-st. In: DDT 34, Newe deudsche Geistl. Gesenge 1544, S. 82. Leipzig: B & H 1908.

**Wermann,** Oskar (1840–1906): 3-st. In: 4 Motetten f. 3-st. Ch., op. 73 Nr. 2. Leipzig: Protze H.

**Zangius,** Nikolaus (um 1570–1620): Luther: 5-st. m. Melodie-Instr. ad lib. In: Geistl. u. weltl. Lieder, Köln 1597, hrsg. v. F. Bose. Berlin: Merseburger 1960 (= Veröffentl. d. Instituts f. Musikforsch. Ed. Merseburger 1081).

**Zehetbauer,** Johann Paul: Luther: 4-st. Planegg: Promultis 1977 (= Nr. 2147 a).

**Zeuner,** Martin (1554–1619): Luther: 5-st. In: Geistl. Kirchenlieder zu 5 St., Nürnberg 1616; Publikation älterer prakt. u. theoret. Musikwerke, S. 22/23, hrsg. v. R. Eitner. Leipzig: B & H 1904.

## 2.2.2.2. Bestandteil einer größeren Komposition

**Bieske,** Werner: Vater unser im Himmelreich: Choralkantate für Gemeindegesang, 4-st. Chor u. Bläserchor. Kassel: Bärenreiter 1979 (= Werkreihe f. Bläser u. Sänger BA 3595).

**Heiller,** Anton (1923–1979): Missa super: „Salve regina" et „Vater unser im Himmelreich" Wien: Doblinger 1958 (= Gloria dei).

**Kraus,** Egon (geb. 1912): Vater unser im Himmelreich: Choralkantate für Solo-St. 4-st. Ch. m. Blfl. (Streichquartett o. u. Org. o. Gemeinschaftsmusik. Sätze von Samuel Scheidt, Adam Gumpelzheimer u. a.) (auch engl.) Zürich: Musikverlag zum Pelikan 1954.

**Raphael,** Günter (1903–1960): Vater unser im Himmelreich: Choralkantate op. 58 für 4-st. Chor m. Orch. (Org. ad lib.) o. Streich. u. Org. Heidelberg: Müller W. 1949.

**Rehm,** Otto: Vater unser, der du in dem Himmel bist: S.-, T.-, B.-Solo, 4–7-st. gem. Chor u. 3-st. Knabenchor m. P. (Org.). Augsburg: Böhm 1953.

**Scheidt,** Samuel (1587–1654): Dreierlei Choral in einander componieret: 3-st. m. GB.
In Cantu: Vater unser im Himmelreich.
In Tenore: Christ unser Herr zum Jordan kam.
In Basso: Ich ruf zu dir, Herr Jesu Christ. In: Geistl. Konzerte, Teil I, S. 5–7, hrsg. v. Chr. Mahrenholz. Hamburg: Ugrino-Verlag 1957.

**Schütz,** Heinrich (1585–1672): Vater, Vater, Vater unser: SWV 411; Deutsches Konzert f. S., Mezzo-S., 2 T., B., 2 Vl. ad lib. (4-st.) Ch. m. Orch. u. B.c. (nach Mt 6,9–13). In: Symphoniae sacrae T. 3, Nr. 4, S. 51–61. hrsg. v. W. Bittinger. Kassel: Bärenreiter 1964 (= BA 3426).

## 2.2.2.3. In Sammelwerken ohne Angabe des Komponisten

**Choralkantate:** Vater unser im Himmelreich, 2–4-st. Ch., Streichoder Blockflötenquartett, m. Org. ad lib. Sätze von: J. S. Bach, Adam Gumpelzheimer, H. L. Haßler, Joh. Pachelbel, Michael Praetorius, Samuel Scheidt u. Anonymus (1539), hrsg. v. E. Kraus. Zürich: Pelikan 1979 (= PE 732).

**Frischauf zu hellem Singen:** Jugendliederbuch der landeskirchlichen Gemeinschaften für 1–4 Singstimmen, teilweise beziffert. Berlin: Evang. Verlagsanstalt 1977.

**Geistl. Lieder unserer Zeit** für verschiedene Besetzungen. Gütersloh: Gütersloher Verlagshaus Mohn 1977; Bielefeld: Lutherverlag 1977.

**Hänssler – Chorblatt** Nr. 145: Vater unser im Himmelreich, 3-st. HE 6.145. Nr. 149: Vater unser im Himmelreich, 4-st. HE 6.149. Nr. 150: Vater unser im Himmelreich, 5-st. HE 6.150. Nr. 150: Vater unser im Himmelreich, 3-st. HE 6.150. Nr. 212: Vater unser im Himmelreich, 3-st. HE 6.212. Stuttgart: Hänssler 1963.

**Motetten alter Meister,** hrsg. v. Gottfried Grote. Berlin: Merseburger 1977 (= Ed. Merseburger 325).

**Notenblatt für gem. Chor:** Unser Vater in dem Himmel, 4-st., Nr. 293. Berlin: Evangelische Verlagsanstalt 1969.

**Singheft für Chor:** mit teilweiser Begleitung. Wuppertal: Verlag Singende Gemeinde 1976 (= Nr. 85377).

**Tonsätze zum Kirchenlied** 4-st. Ch., Instr. (Blockfl. oder Str.)-Quartett o. Org. (P.) m. Text. Nr. 90: Vaterunser, Mt. 6,9–13. Nr. 91: O Vater unser, der du in dem Himmel bist. Freiburg: Christoph.-Verl. Herder 1971.

**Vater-Unser-Lieder.** Alte Kirchengesänge in Sätzen für 2 gl. u. 3 gem. St., hrsg. v. H. Beuerle u. P. E. Ruppel. Für 2–3-st. gem., z. T. 1-st. Ch., auch solist.:
Ruppel: Herr, lehre uns beten. (Lukas 11,1) Kanon zu 3 St.
1. Vater unser in dem Himmel, 1-st.
2. Laßt uns schreien, 1-st., Text: Michael Weiße.
3. Vater unser im Himmelreich, 2 Sätze v. Beuerle.
4. Gott, unser Vater, der du bist im Himmel, 2 Sätze v. Beuerle. Text: Justus Gesenius u. David Denicke.
5. Begehren wir mit Innigkeit, 2 Sätze v. Ruppel, Text: M. Weiße.
6. Du hast uns, lieber Herr, 2 Sätze v. Ruppel, Text: Joh. Balthasar König.
7. Gott, Vater, der du bist im Himmel, 2 Sätze v. Beuerle, Text: Jakob Grünwald, nach Melodie v. Peter Schren.
8. Sei Lob und Ehr mit hohem Preis, 2 Sätze v. Beuerle, Text: Paul Speratus.
9. Gott Vater wir bekennen, 2 Sätze v. Ruppel, Text: Philipp d. Jüngere.
10. Ich lob dich, Gott, 2 Sätze v. Beuerle, Text: Philipp d. Jüngere.
11. Vater, dein Name werd von uns gepreiset, 2 Sätze v. Ruppel, Text: Petrus Herbert, nach Melodie v. Petrus Nigidius.
12. Vater aller Ehren, laß, 2 Sätze, Text: Joh. Frank (vielmehr Franck), nach Melodie v. Joh. Crüger.
13. Gott Vater, der du aller Dinge, 2 Sätze v. Ruppel, Text: Angelus Silesius.
14. Vater droben in der Höhe, 2 Sätze v. Ruppel, Text: Heinrich Mühlpfort.
15. Vater unser, der du bist, Kyrie eleison, 2 Sätze v. Ruppel, Text: Ambrosius Moibanus.
Neukirchen-Vluyn: Singende Gemeinde 1962.

**V S G - Blätter:** Nr. 103: Vater unser im Himmelreich. 1–4-st. Fr.-Ch. m. Org. m. Git.-Beziff. Wuppertal: Singende Gemeinde 1969.

## 2.2.2.4. Textabweichungen sowie Textfragmente

**Anonymus:** Ach, Vater unser, der du bist im Himmelreich. 4-st. Text: Ambrosius Moibanus, Pfarrer in Breslau. In: DDT 34, Newe deudsche geistl. Gesänge 1544 S. 72–74. Leipzig: B & H 1908.

**Brassicanus,** Johannes (Johann Kraut): Unser Vater in dem Himmel. 4-st. Wiesbaden: B & H 1954 (= Musik alter Meister H. 2).

**Edelkötter,** Ludger: Unser Vater. 1–3-st. m. Beziff. Text: Wolfgang Poeblau. In: Katakomben: Lieder und Texte für den Gottesdienst. Drensteinfurt: Impulse-Verl. 1974.

**Gallus,** Jacobus (Jakob Handl) (1550–1591): Ach, Vater unser, der du bist im Himmelreich. 4-st. Text: Ambrosius Moibanus. Heidelberg: Müller W. 1957 (= Die Kantorei Nr. 7)

**Homilius,** Gottfried August (1714–1785): Unser Vater in dem Himmel. 4-st. In: Das Chorwerk H. 89, hrsg. v. Fr. Blume. Wolfenbüttel: Möseler 1963.

**Kameke,** Ernst-Ulrich von (geb. 1926): Vaterunser: Manche meinen, du hast dich zur Ruhe gesetzt. 4–8-st. Ch., 4 Solisten u. Sprechchor. Kommentierender Text: Uwe Seidel. Wiesbaden: B & H 1979 (= B & H's Chorbibliothek 3698).

**Keller-Löwy,** Walter: Vater unser, der du bist, das Brot liegt. Alter Kinderreim. In: Güggerüggü. Kinderlieder, 2-st., zum Singen und Spielen auf 2 Sopr.-Fl., m. 3. St. ad lib. (Metalloph./Klingende Stäbe) u. kl. Schlagwerk (Triangel, Schlagstäbe, Schellenrassel). Zürich: Musikverlag zum Pelikan 1965 (= Ed. 757).

**Kronsteiner,** Joseph (geb. 1910): Vater unser, in deine Hände geschehe (1974). 4-st. u. 1-st. Volksgesang m. Org. ad lib. Text: Maria Luise Mumelter. Köln: Styria 1953.

**Oertzen,** Rudolf von (geb. 1910): op. 12, Vater, Vater, Vater. 8-st. Hamburg: Hüllenhagen & Griehl 1953 (ed. 3045).

**Praetorius,** Michael (um 1571–1621): Vater unser im Himmelreich, wir dein arm Kinder allzugleich. 4-st. Text: Johann Leon. In: Musae Sioniae, Teil VII (1609), Nr. 21, S. 19, hrsg. v. Fr. Blume. Wolfenbüttel: Kallmeyer G. 1939.
– Vater unser im Himmelreich, wir armen Kinderlein bitten dich. 4-st. Text: Daniel Rump. In: Musae Sioniae, Teil VII (1609), Nr. 22, S. 20, hrsg. v. Fr. Blume. Wolfenbüttel: Kallmeyer G. 1939.
– Vater unser, der du bist, Kyrie eleison. 4-st. Text: Ambrosius Moibanus. In: Musae Sioniae, Teil VII (1609). Nr. 27, S. 24, hrsg. v. Fr. Blume. Wolfenbüttel: Kallmeyer G. 1939.

187

– Ach, Vater unser, der du bist im Himmel, hör, was uns gebrist. 4-st. Text: Joh. Zwick. In: Musae Sioniae, Teil VII (1609), Nr. 30, S. 27/28, hrsg. v. Fr. Blume. Wolfenbüttel: Kallmeyer G. 1939.
– Ach, Vater unser, der du bist im Himmel, hör, was uns gebrist. 4-st. Text: Joh. Zwick. In: Musae Sioniae, Teil VII (1609), Nr. 31, S. 28/29, hrsg. v. Fr. Blume. Wolfenbüttel: Kallmeyer G. 1939.
– Ach, Vater unser, der du bist im Himmelreich, hoch über uns, darum im Geist. 4-st. Text: Ambrosius Moibanus. In: Musae Sioniae, Teil VII (1609), Nr. 28, S. 25. Wolfenbüttel: Kallmeyer G. 1939.
– Ach, Vater unser, der du bist im Himmelreich, hoch über uns, darum im Geist. 4-st. Text: Ambrosius Moibanus. In: Musae Sioniae, Teil VII (1609), Nr. 29, S. 25, hrsg. v. Fr. Blume. Wolfenbüttel: Kallmeyer G. 1939.
– Unser Vater, der du bist im Himmel. 4-st. in E. Text: Symphorian Pollio. In: Musae Sioniae, Teil VII (1609), Nr. 26, S. 23/24, hrsg. v. Fr. Blume. Wolfenbüttel: Kallmeyer G. 1939.
– Vater unser in dem Himmel. 4-st. Text: Erasmus Alber, In: Musae Sioniae, Teil VII (1609), Nr. 25, S. 22. hrsg. v. Fr. Blume. Wolfenbüttel: Kallmeyer G. 1939.
– O Vater unser, der du bist hoch in des Himmels Reiche. 4-st. In: Musae Sioniae, Teil VII (1609), Nr. 33, S. 30, hrsg. v. Fr. Blume. Wolfenbüttel: Kallmeyer G. 1939.

**Schaab,** Robert (1817–1887): Terzett aus dem Vater unser vom Himmel. In: Geistliches und Weltliches, ausgewählte Stücke, H. IX, Geistliches. Leipzig: Portius.

**Schein,** Johann Hermann (1586–1630): Unser Vater in der Höhe. 1 Strophe Vater Unser nach der Weise: „Freu dich sehr, o meine Seele". Text: Johann Franck. In: Schein, Joh. Herm.: Cantional oder Gesangbuch Augsburg. Konfession 1627, Nr. 312. Kassel: Bärenreiter 1970 (= Kleine Bärenreiterausgabe 6306).

**Schibler,** Arnim (geb. 1920): Ein Vaterunser, zeitgemäß: Vater unser, unser Vater (1965). 3-st. M.-Ch. u. Orch. Zürich: Eulenburg 1972 (= General Music Series 79).

**Vogel,** Heinrich: Vater unser, Du allein. 3-st. In: Erhebet eure Herzen. Neue Geistliche Lieder. Berlin: Merseburger 1952 (= Ed. Merseburger 716).

**Walter,** Johann (1490–1570): O Vater unser, der du bist hoch in des Himmels Reiche. 4-st. In: Geistl. Gesangsbüchlein Wittenberg 1551, 1. Teil: Deutsche Gesänge Nr. 63, S. 118/119. Kassel: Bärenreiter 1943.

**Zimmermann,** Heinz Werner (geb. 1930): Unser Vater in dem Himmel. 7-st. m. Kb. Berlin: Merseburger 1959 (= Ed. Merseburger 451).

**Zoll,** Paul (geb. 1907): Vater unser: Hör uns, Gott! 4-st. M.-Ch., Bar., 1-st. Kn.-Ch. m. Blechmusik u. Org. (Streichinstr.); auch Org. allein. Text: Franz Grillparzer. Heidelberg: Hochstein & Co. 1961.

### 2.2.3. Mit fremdsprachigem Text

**Gevaert,** François-Auguste (1828–1908): L'Oraison Dominicale, 4-st. (auch lat.) Paris: Lemoine.
– L'Oraison Dominicale, 3-st. (auch lat.) Paris: Lemoine.
– Lord's Prayer, 3-st. Boston: Schirmer D. C.

**Jackson,** Samuel: Lord's Prayer, 4-st. Boston: Ditson.

**Janáček,** Leoš (1854–1928): Otče, náš, jenž jsi na nebesich, 4-st. m. Harfe u. Org. (auch deutsch). Praha: Státní hudebni vydavatství 1963.

**Kedroff,** Nicolas: Notre Père, 4-st. (auch lat.). Paris: Bessel & Cie. 1954.

**Křenek,** Ernst (geb. 1900): Five Prayers. Fünf Gebete über das P.N. als C.f. 4-st. Fr.-Ch. London: Universaledition 1954 (= UE 12 270).

**Labinskij,** Aleksander: Our Father, 4–5-st. m. P. (auch tschech. u. lat.). Wiesbaden: B & H 1954.
– Otče naš, 4–5-st. m. P. (auch engl. u. lat.): Wiesbaden: B & H 1954.

**Lasso di,** Orlando (um 1532–1594): Père, qui habites les cieux, 5-st. In: Kompositionen mit franz. Text, III. Teil, S. 115–118, hrsg. v. A. Sandberger. Leipzig: B & H.

**Liszt,** Franz (1811–1886): Lord's Prayer, 7-st. m. Org. ad lib. (auch deutsch). Stuttgart: Hänssler, Carus 1979.

**L'Voǯ,** Aleksej Fedorovic (1798–1870): Notre Père, o père, toi qui es, 5–6-st. m. Org. (P.). (auch tschech.). Wiesbaden: B & H 1960 (= Chants religieux russes 2).
– Otče, náš, ize esi, 5–6-st. m. Org. (P.). (auch franz.). Wiesbaden: B & H 1960 (= Chants religieux russes 2).

**Malotte,** Albert Hay (geb. 1895): Lord's Prayer, 4-st. Fr.-Ch. New York: Schirm G.
– Lord's Prayer, 4-st. gem. Ch. New York: Schirm G.
– Lord's Prayer, 4-st. m. Org. New York: Schirm G.
– Lord's Prayer, 4-st., Ch. m. Solo f. h. St. New York: Schirm G.
– Lord's Prayer, 3-st. Fr.-Ch. New York: Schirm G.
– Lord's Prayer, 3-st. Fr.-Ch. u. S.-Solo. New York: Schirm G.
– Lord's Prayer, 2-st. m. Org./P. New York: Schirm G.
– Lord's Prayer, 4-st. gem. Ch. m. Org./P. New York: Schirm G.
– Lord's Prayer, 2-st. Fr.-Ch. New York: Schirm G.
– Lord's Prayer, 3-st. gem. Ch. New York: Schirm G.

189

**Maréchal,** Henry (1842–1924): Notre père, 4-st. M.-Ch. Paris: Heugel et Cie.

**Peeters,** Flor (geb. 1903): op. 102i, Our Father, 2-st. gl.St. m. Org. (auch lat.). New York: Peters 1962 (= Ed. Peters 6340).
– op. 102k, Our Father, 4-st. m. Org. (P.) (auch lat.). New York: Peters 1962 (= Ed. Peters 6340).

**Racine,** C.: L'Oraison Dominicale, 3-st. Fr.-Ch. (auch lat.). Paris: Lemoine.

**Schwarz–Schilling,** Reinhard (geb. 1904): Lord's Prayer, 4-st., mehrfach geteilt. (auch deutsch). Kassel: Bärenreiter (= Musica sacra nova BA 5429).

**Stone,** Robert (1516–1613): Lord's Prayer, 4-st. London: Oxford University Press 1973 (= Oxford Anthems A 305).

**Sweelinck,** Jan Pieterson (1562–1621): Père de nous, qui es là haut és cieux, 3-st. In: Psalmen voor 4, 5, 6, 7 en 8 Stemmen, Derde Boek der Psalmen, hrsg. v. M. Seiffert. Leipzig: B & H.

**Tritant,** G.: Oraison dominicale, 3-st. gl. St. m. Begl. Paris: Pinatel A.

**Tschaikowsky,** Peter (1840–1893): Lord's Prayer, 4-st. (auch lat.). New York: Schirmer.

## 3. Verzeichnis der Instrumentalwerke

### 3.1. Orgel

**Abel,** Otto: Luther: P. (Org. o. Cemb.). In: Choralmusik aus dem 17., 18. u. 19. Jh., Bd. II. hrsg. v. O. Abel. Berlin: Evangelische Verlagsanstalt 1960.

**Ahrens,** Joseph (geb. 1904): gregor.: Org. In: Cantiones Gregorianae, Heft 3. Mainz: Schott 1958.

**Bach,** Johann Sebastian (1685–1750): **Luther: Org. BWV 636.** In: Orgelbüchlein Nr. 37, hrsg. v. d. Bach-Gesellschaft zu Leipzig. Leipzig: B & H 1851–1899.
– In: Bd. VII, S. 58, hrsg. v. H. Lohmann. Wiesbaden: B & H ab 1968 (= EB 6587).
– In: Bd. V, Nr. 48, hrsg. v. C. F. Griepenkerl u. F. Roitzsch. Frankfurt: Peters (= Ed. Peters 244).
– In Orgelschule v. Ernst Kaller, Bd. II, S. 97. Mainz: Schott (= Ed. Schott 2555 b). In: 169 Orgel-Vorspiele zu den Melodien des Choralbuchs für die evangel. Kirche d. Provinzen Rheinland u. Westfalen, Nr. 144. München: Leuckart.
– In: Orgelbüchlein Nr. 37, hrsg. v. H. Keller. Kassel: Bärenreiter 1964 (= BA 145).

**Luther: Org. BWV 682.** In: 3. Teil der „Clavier-Übung", Bd. VIII, S. 49, hrsg. v. H. Lohmann. Wiesbaden: B & H ab 1968 (= DB 6588).
– In: Bd. VII, Nr. 52, hrsg. v. C. F. Griepenkerl u. F. Roitzsch. Frankfurt: Peters (= Ed. Peters 246).
– In: The Church Organist's Golden Treasury, Bd. III, S. 81. Bryn Mawr/Pennsylvania: Ditson 1951.
**Luther: Org. BWV 683.** In: 3. Teil der „Clavier-Übung", Bd. VIII, S. 166, hrsg. v. H. Lohmann. Wiesbaden: B & H ab 1968 (= EB 6588).
– In: Bd. V, Nr. 47, hrsg. v. C. F. Griepenkerl u. F. Roitzsch. Frankfurt: Peters (Ed. Peters 244).
– In: Choralmusik aus dem 17., 18. u. 19. Jh., Bd. II. hrsg. v. O. Abel. Berlin: Evangelische Verlagsanstalt 1960.
**Luther: Org. BWV 737.** In: Bd. V, S. 111, hrsg. v. H. Lohmann. Wiesbaden: B & H ab 1968 (= EB 6589).
– In: Bd. III, S. 90, hrsg. v. J. S. Bach-Institut Göttingen. Kassel: Bärenreiter 1962.
– In: Bd. VII, Nr. 53, hrsg. v. C. F. Griepenkerl u. F. Roitzsch. Frankfurt: Peters (= Ed. Peters 246).
– In: Orgelspiel im Kirchenjahr, Nr. 52, hrsg. v. H. Rohr. Mainz: Schott 1951 (= Ed. Schott 4336).

**Bach,** Johann Christoph (1642–1703): Vater unser: Org. In: 11 Chorale Preludes, Nr. 6. New York: Liturgical Press.
– In: 44 Choräle zum Präambulieren (Choralfughetten), hrsg. v. M. Fischer. Kassel: Bärenreiter 1961 (= BA 285).

**Baldamus,** Fr.: Vater unser: Org. In: Easy Chorale Preludes, Bd. II. Magdeburg: Rubach.

**Bausznern** Waldemar von, (1866–1931): Vater unser: Org. In: Chorale Preludes, Bd. II. Lohr: Schauenburg M.

**Beck,** Albert: Vater unser: Org. In: 76 Choral Preludes. River Forest/Illinois: Beck A.

**Bender,** Erich Alfred (geb. 1913): Vater unser: Org. In: Orgelbuch zum EKG, Bd. III. Kassel: Bärenreiter 1955 (= BA 2823).

**Berg,** Gottfrid: Vater unser: Org. In: Atta (= 8) Koralförspel, Nr. 6. Stockholm: AB Nordiska Musikförlaget 1955 (= Nord. 4466).

**Böhm,** Georg (1661–1733): **Luther: Org.** In: Sämtliche Werke, Bd. II, S. 132, hrsg. v. G. Wolgast. Wiesbaden: B & H 1952.
– In: Masterpieces of Organ Music, fol. 56, Nr. 2, hrsg. v. N. Hennefield. New York: Liturgical Music Press 1944 (= Liturg. MP 124).
**Luther: Org.** In: Sämtliche Werke, Bd. II, S. 149, hrsg. v. G. Wolgast. Wiesbaden: B & H 1952.

**Luther: Org.** In: Sämtliche Werke, Bd. II, S. 138, hrsg. v. G. Wolgast. Wiesbaden: B & H 1952.
– In: Masterpieces of Organ Music, fol. 6, Nr. 3, hrsg. v. N. Hennefield. New York: Liturgical Music Press 1944 (= Liturg. MP 124).

**Bornefeld,** Helmut (geb. 1906): Vater unser: Org. In: Das Choralwerk, Heft 3, Nr. 57/58. Kassel: Bärenreiter 1952 (= BA 2214).

**Bossler,** Kurt (1911–1976): Luther: Org. In: 8 Choralvorspiele, Bd. II. Berlin: Merseburger 1969 (= Ed. Merseb. 892).

**Brieger,** Otto (1835–1904): Vater unser: Org. In: op. 7: 73 Organ Preludes on Well Known Chorales of Evangelical Hymnal. München: Leuckart.

**Brunner,** Adolf (geb. 1901): Luther: Org. In: Choralvariationen für Orgel. Stuttgart: Hänssler 1969 (= Collegium instrumentale 16022).

**Bubali,** Eugenio: gregor.: H. (Org.). Roma: Van Eerenbeemt.

**Busch,** Adolf Georg Wilhelm (1891–1952): Vater unser: Org. In: 8 Choral Preludes. New York: Schirmer G.

**Buxtehude,** Dietrich (1637–1707): **Luther: Org.** In: Sämtliche Orgelwerke, Bd. III, S. 32, hrsg. v. J. Hedar. København: Hansen W. 1952.
– In: Orgelwerke, Bd. III, S. 65, hrsg. v. W. Kraft. Wiesbaden: B & H.
– In: 28 Orgelchoräle d. 17. u. 18. Jh. anläßlich d. 50-jährigen Bestehens d. Bernischen Organistenverbandes, Nr. 17. Kassel: Bärenreiter 1939 (= BA 2207).
– In: Ausgewählte Orgelwerke, Bd. II, Nr. 22, hrsg. v. H. Keller. Frankfurt: Peters 1939 (= Ed. Peters 4457).
– In: Manuals only, S. 14, hrsg. v. Power Biggs. New York: Associated Music Publishers 1963.
– In: Schule des Klassischen Triospiels, Nr. 3, hrsg. v. H. Keller. Kassel: Bärenreiter 1928 (= BA 243).
– In: Choralmusik aus dem 17., 18. u. 19. Jh., Bd. II, hrsg. v. O. Abel. Berlin: Evangelische Verlagsanstalt 1960.
– In: Orgelspiel im Kirchenjahr: 62 leichte Choralvorspiele alter Meister, Nr. 50, hrsg. v. H. Rohr. Mainz: Schott 1951 (= Ed. Schott 4336).
– In: Masterpieces of Organ Music, Fol. II, S. 9, hrsg. v. N. Hennefield. New York: Liturgical Music Press 1947 (= Liturg. M. P 107).
**Luther: Org.** In: Sämtliche Orgelwerke, Bd. III, S. 50, hrsg. v. J. Hedar. København: Hansen W. 1952.
– In: Orgelwerke, Bd. III, S. 71, hrsg. v. W. Kraft. Wiesbaden: B & H.
– In: Masterpieces of Organ Music, Fol. 71, hrsg. v. N. Hennefield. New York: Liturgical Music Press 1953 (= Liturg. MP 335).

**David,** Johann Nepomuk (1895–1977): **Vater unser: Org.** In: Choralwerk für Orgel, Heft 13, Nr. 4, 5, 6. Wiesbaden: B & H 1959 (= EB 5571).
**Vater unser: Org.** Kleine Partita m. 3 Variationen. In: Choralwerk für Orgel, Heft 2, Nr. 13. Wiesbaden: B & H 1932 (= EB 5571).
**Vater unser: Org.** In: Choralwerk für Orgel, Heft 17, Nr. 46. Wiesbaden: B & H 1970 (= EB 5571).

**Diebold,** Johannes (1842–1929): gregor.: Org. In: op. 109: 20 Preludes, Interludes & Postludes, Nr. 8. Regensburg: Feuchtinger – Gleichauf.
– In: Organ Preludes, Vol. I, S. 121, hrsg. v. J. S. Edson. Metuchen/N.J.: The Scarecrow Press 1970.

**Doppelbauer,** Josef Friedrich (geb. 1918): Luther: Org. Partita (1965). München: Doblinger 1966.

**Dragt,** Jaap (geb. 1930): Vater unser: Org. In: 4 Chorale Preludes. Goes/Netherlands: Ars Nova.

**Dupré,** Marcel J. J. (1886–1971): Vater unser: Org. In: op. 28: 79 Chorales. New York: Gray H. W.

**Edmundson,** Garth (geb. 1900): **Vater unser: Org.** In: 4 Modern Preludes on Old Chorales. New York: Galaxy Music Press 1950.
**Vater unser: Org.** In: 7 Polyphonic Preludes in Christian Liturgy. Glen Rock/N.J.: Fischer J.

**Ehrlinger:** Vater unser: Org. In: Einfache Choralvorspiele zum Evangelischen Kirchengesangbuch mit dem Bayerischen Anhang, S. 160. München: Kaiser 1959.

**Enckhausen,** Heinrich Friedrich (1799–1885): Vater unser: Org. In: 73 Chorale Preludes for Organ. Kassel: Nagel's Musikarchiv 1931.

**Grabner,** Hermann (1886–1969): **Vater unser: Org.** In: Orgelbuch zum EKG, Bd. III, hrsg. v. O. Brodde. Kassel: Bärenreiter 1955 (= BA 2823).
**gregor.: Org.,** op. 27: Fantasie on the Liturgical „Paternoster". Lindau: Kahnt C.F. 1927.

**Grande,** Dieter: Vater unser im Himmel: Melodie Peter Janssens. In: Instrumentalsätze für jugendgemäße Gesänge im Gottesdienst, hrsg. v. d. Berliner Ordinarienkonferenz. Leipzig: Benno-Verlag 1972.

**Grote,** Hermann: Vater unser: Org. In: op. 25: 28 Chorale Preludes in Trio Form, Vol. II. St. Louis, Mo.: Grote H.

**Haase,** Karl (geb. 1871): Luther: Org. In: Preludes on Hymns of the Lutheran Hymnal, Nr. 379. St. Louis, Mo.: Concordia Publishing House (= Aurelia – K. Haase).

193

**Hasse,** Karl (1883–1960): Vater unser: Org. In: op. 7: 17 Chorale Preludes. Leipzig: Rieter-Biedermann.

**Hassler,** Hans Leo (1564–1612). Luther: Org., Fugue, Baroque Suite. Brooklyn, N.Y.: Musicus (Bedell).

**Hellenberg,** Kurt: Vater unser: Org. In: Orgelbuch zum EKG, Bd. 3, hrsg. v. O. Brodde. Kassel: Bärenreiter 1955 (= BA 2823).

**Hennig:** Vater unser: Org. In: Orgelvorspiele zum Evangelischen Kirchengesangbuch, Nr. 314, hrsg. v. H. M. Poppen. Berlin: Merseburger 1953 (= Merseb. 814).

**Hesse,** Adolf Friedrich (1809–1863): **Vater unser: Org.** op. 39. In: 285 Vorspiele zu 170 Chorälen der evangelischen Kirche, Nr. 238, hrsg. v. G. Merk. München: Leuckart.
**Vater unser: Org.:** op. 57: Variationen über das Vaterunser. Hofheim: Hofmeister.

**Hessenberg,** Kurt (geb. 1908): Vater unser: Org. In: Orgelbuch zum EKG, Bd. III, hrsg. v. O. Brodde. Kassel: Bärenreiter 1955 (= BA 2823).

**Heussenstamm,** George: Vater unser: Org., op. 6: Partita. St. Louis, Mo.: Concordia Publishing House.

**Heiller,** Anton (1923–1979): Luther: Org. Partita. Mainz: Ars viva 1967 (= Ed. AV 15).

**Hiss,** Franz: gregor.: Org., op. 10: Pater noster nach dem Kirchenjahr (festlich u. bei Trauerämtern). Zürich: Hug.

**Hovland,** Egil (geb. 1924): Vater unser: Org. (H.). In: 100 Salmeforspill til praktisk bruk ved gudstjenesten for Orgel eller harmonium, Nr. 75. Drammen/Norwegen: Lyche 1957 (= Lyche 333).

**Huber,** Klaus (geb. 1924): Luther: Org.: Adagietto super „Vater unser im Himmelreich". In: In memorian Willy Burkhard, Nr. 2. Kassel: Bärenreiter 1965 (= BA 4462).

**Johns,** Donald (geb. 1926): Vater unser: Org. In: California Organist, 3 Chorale Preludes, Bd. I. Los Angeles: Avant Music Press.

**Kaminski,** Heinrich (1886–1946): Vater unser: Org. In: 3 Chorale Preludes. Wien: Universal Edition.

**Kammeier,** Hans (geb. 1902): Vater unser: Org. In: Orgelvorspiele zum Evangelischen Kirchengesangbuch, Nr. 241, hrsg. v. H. M. Poppen. Berlin: Merseburger 1953 (Merseb. 814).

**Karges,** Wilhelm (um 1613–1699): Luther: Org. In: Choralbearbeitungen u. freie Orgelstücke d. deutsch. Sweelinck-Schule, 3 Variationen manualiter, hrsg. v. H. J. Moser. Kassel: Bärenreiter 1954 (= BA 2815/2816).

194

**Kauffmann,** Georg Friedrich (1679–1735): Vater unser: Org. In: Masterpieces of Organ Music, Fol. 17, hrsg. v. N. Hennefield. New York: Liturgical Music Press.

**Kickstat,** Paul (1893–1959): **Luther Org.** In: Choralvorspiele, Heft 2. Wolfenbüttel: Möseler 1949.
**Luther: Org.** In: Choralvorspiele, Heft 2. Wolfenbüttel: Möseler 1949.

**Kittel,** Johann Christian (1732–1809): Vater unser: Org. In: Orgelwerke der Bachschule. Bad Godesberg: Forberg 1976.

**Kluge,** Manfred (geb. 1928): Luther: Org. Fantasie in drei Rhythmen, 9 Strophen. Wiesbaden: B & H 1964 (= EB 6444).

**Krause,** Paul (1880–1946): Vater unser: Org. In: op. 25: 20 Choral Impressions. München: Leuckart.

**Krebs,** Johann Ludwig (1713–1780): Luther: Org. (P.). In: Klavierübung, Nr. 7. Leipzig: Peters 1959 (= Ed. Peters 4178).

**Krieger,** Johann (1652–1735): Luther: Org.: Fughette. In: DTB XVIII, S. 213, hrsg. v. M. Seiffert. Leipzig: B & H 1917.
– In: Sammlung: Alte Orgelmusik I, Nr. 17. Berlin: Merseburger 1952 (= Ed. Merseb. 811).
– In: Choralvorspiele für den gottesdienstlichen Gebrauch, S. 63. Kassel: Bärenreiter (= BA 1223).
– In: 80 Choralvorspiele deutscher Meister, Nr. 67. Frankfurt: Peters 1951 (= Ed. Peters 4448).
– In: Orgelspiel im Kirchenjahr, Nr. 51, hrsg. v. H. Rohr. Mainz: Schott 1951 (= Ed. Schott 4336).
– In: Seasonal Chorale Preludes IV, S. 15. London: Oxford Music Press 1962.
– In: Ricercare, Canzonen und Fugen d. 17. u. 18. Jh., S. 32, hrsg. v. W. Hillemann. Kassel: Nagel 1956 (= Nagel's Musikarchiv 87).

**Kuhne,** Fr.: Vater unser: Org. In: Anthology of Sacred Music. St. Louis, Mo.: Concordia Publishing House.

**Leupold,** Anton Wilhelm (1868–1940): **Luther: Org.** In: Orgelbuch zum EKG, Bd. 1, hrsg. v. O. Brodde. Kassel: Bärenreiter 1954 (= BA 2821).
**Vater unser: Org.** In: Orgelbuch, 35 Choralvorspiele. Berlin: Merseburger 1980 (= Ed. Merseb. 828).

**Linke,** Norbert (geb. 1933): Luther: Org. In: Organ Pops. Choralvorspiele für Orgel, Nr. 10. Heidelberg: Müller W. 1972.

**Lorentz,** Johann: Luther: Org. In: Choralbearbeitungen u. freie Orgelstücke d. deutsch. Sweelinck-Schule, 2 Variationen, hrsg. v. J. Moser. Kassel: Bärenreiter 1954 (= BA 2815/2816).

**Lüdders,** Paul: Vater unser: Org. In: Orgelchoräle I, Nr. 51. Hamburg: Hüllenhagen 1954 (= Ed. 3056).

**Manz,** Paul: Vater unser: Org. In: 10 Chorale Improvisations, Bd. 2. St. Louis, Mo.: Concordia Publishing House.

**Mendelssohn Bartholdy,** Felix (1809–1847): Luther: Org.: op. 65, 6: Organ Sonata in d minor. Frankfurt: Peters 1966 (Ed. Peters 1744f).

**Micheelsen,** Hans Friedrich (1902–1973): Luther: Org. In: Organisten-Praxis. Hamburg: Huellenhagen & Griehl.

**Middelschulte,** Wilhelm (1863–1943): Vater unser: Org. Canon and Fugue on „Vater unser". München: Leuckart.

**Moore,** Margery: Vater unser: Org. 2 Chorale Preludes. London: Novello 1934.

**Moser,** Rudolf (1892–1960): Luther: Org. op. 82. In: 25 Choralvorspiele, Nr. 23, hrsg. v. Organistenverband Basel-Land aus Anlaß des 25jährigen Bestehens. Lausanne: Foetisch 1947 (= Ed. 1915).

**Müller-Zürich,** Paul (geb. 1898): Vater unser: Org. In: 25 Orgelchoräle, op. 63, Nr. 22. Bern: Krompholz 1961, (= Ed. 538).

**Pach,** Walter (geb. 1904): Luther: Org. Partita canonica super „Vater unser im Himmelreich". München: Doblinger 1967.

**Pachelbel,** Johann (1653–1706): **Luther: Org.** In: DTB IV, 1, Nr. 55, hrsg. v. A. Sandberger. Leipzig: B & H 1903.
– In: Ausgewählte Orgelwerke, Bd. III, Nr. 2, hrsg. v. K. Matthäi. Kassel: Bärenreiter 1950 (= BA 287).
– In: Alte Meister des Orgelspiels, Nr. 10, hrsg. v. K. Straube. Frankfurt: Peters 1929 (= Ed. Peters 4301).
– In: Choralmusik aus dem 17., 18. u. 19. Jh., Bd. II, hrsg. v. O. Abel. Berlin: Evangelische Verlagsanstalt 1960.
– In: Anthology of Sacred Music, Vol. I, Nr. 19. St. Louis, Mo.: Concordia Publishing House 1948.
– In: The Church Organist's Golden Treasury, Bd. III, S. 76. Bryn Mawr/Pennsylvania: Ditson 1951.
**Luther: Org.** In: DTB IV, 1, Nr. 56, hrsg. v. A. Sandberger. Leipzig: B & H 1903.
– In: Orgelschule Merkel op. 177, S. 68. Frankfurt: Peters 1929 (= Ed. Peters 3558).

**Papperitz,** Benjamin Robert (1826–1903): Vater unser: Org. In: op. 15: 34 Chorale Preludes, Bd. II. Bad Godesberg: Forberg R.

**Pasquet,** Jean: Vater unser: Org. Meditation. New York: Morris H.

**Peeters,** Flor (geb. 1903): **Luther: Org.** In: op. 69: Ten Chorale-Preludes, Nr. 3. Frankfurt: Peters 1960 (= Ed. Peters 6024).

196

**Vater unser: Org.** In: op. 100: Hymn Preludes for the Liturgical Year, Vol. 19. Frankfurt: Peters.

**Pepping,** Ernst (geb. 1901): Luther: Org. In: Praeludia, Postludia zu 18 Chorälen. Mainz: Schott 1969 (= Ed. Schott 6040/6041).

**Pisk,** Paul Amadeus (geb. 1893): Vater unser: Org. Chorale Prelude on Our Heavenly Father. In: California Organist, Bd. 49. Los Angeles: Avant Music Press.

**Piutti,** Karl (1846–1902): **Vater unser: Org.** In: Anthology of Sacred Music. St. Louis, Mo.: Concordia Publishing House.
**Vater unser: Org.** In: op. 34: 200 Choralvorspiele. Leipzig: Rieter-Biedermann.

**Poppen,** Hermann (1885–1956): Vater unser: Org. In: Orgelbuch zum neuen Gesangbuch-Anhang „Singende Gemeinde". Heidelberg: Hochstein 1949.

**Post,** Piet (geb. 1919): Vater unser: Org. Partita. Goes/Niederlande: Ars Nova.

**Praetorius,** Jacob (1586–1651): Luther: Org. In: Choralbearbeitungen für Org., Nr. 6, hrsg. v. W. Breig. Kassel: Bärenreiter 1974 (= BA 5496).

**Praetorius,** Michael (1571–1621): **Luther: Org.** Bicinium, Quodlibet: Vater unser im Himmelreich u. Erhalt uns, Herr, bei deinem Wort. In: Musae Sioniae IX, Nr. 60. Wolfenbüttel: Kallmeyer 1929 (= GA M. Praetorius).
**Luther: Org.:** 2 Bicinien. In: Musae Sioniae IX, Nr. 61 u. 62. Wolfenbüttel: Kallmeyer 1929 (= GA M. Praetorius).
**Luther: Org.:** 5 Tricinien. In: Musae Sioniae IX, Nr. 63–67. Wolfenbüttel: Kallmeyer 1929 (= GA M. Praetorius).

**Reger,** Max (1873–1916): Vater unser: Org. In: op. 67: 52 Leichte Choralvorspiele, Bd. III. Berlin: Bote & Bock.

**Rheinberger,** Joseph (1839–1901): gregor.: Org. In: 5 Hymns. Bad Godesberg: Forberg R.

**Richter,** Ernst Friedrich (1808–1879): Vater unser: Org. In: op. 29: 6 Trio Chorale Preludes. München: Siegel E.F.W.

**Rinck,** Johann Christian Heinrich (1770–1846): Vater unser: Org. In: Anthology of Sacred Music. St. Louis, Mo.: Concordia Publishing House.

**Ritter,** August Gottfried (1811–1885): Vater unser: Org. In: op. 8: 3 Preludes in Old Modes. Mainz: Schott.

**Rohwer,** Jens (geb. 1914): Luther: Org. In: Das jüngste Gericht. 7 Stücke über geistl. Lieder, Nr. 6. München: Doblinger 1971.

197

**Rumpf,** Wilhelm (1900–1964): Vater unser: Org. In: 165 Choralvorspiele zu Melodien evang. Choräle. Bd. II, Nr. 53. Heidelberg: Hochstein 1947 (= Ed. 3875).

**Schaab,** Robert (1817–1887): Luther: Org. In: op. 121, 3: 60 leicht ausführbare Choralvorspiele über die bekanntesten Kirchenmelodien. Dresden: Hoffarth; Bad Godesberg: Forberg R.

**Scheidemann,** Heinrich (1596–1663): **Luther: Org.** In: 46 Choräle für Orgel v. J. P. Sweelinck u. seinen deutsch. Schülern, Nr. 39, S. 209–213, hrsg. v. G. Gerdes. Mainz: Schott 1957.
– In: Choralbearbeitungen, Nr. 28, hrsg. v. G. Fock. Kassel: Bärenreiter 1967 (= BA 5481).
**Luther: Org.** In: 46 Choräle für Orgel v. J. P. Sweelinck u. seinen deutsch. Schülern, Nr. 40, S. 214, hrsg. v. G. Gerdes. Mainz: Schott 1957.
– In: Choralbearbeitungen, Nr. 29, hrsg. v. G. Fock. Kassel: Bärenreiter 1967 (= BA 5481).
**Luther: Org.** In: 46 Choräle für Orgel v. J. P. Sweelinck u. seinen dt. Schülern, Nr. 41, S. 219, hrsg. v. G. Gerdes. Mainz: Schott 1957.
– In: Choralbearbeitungen, Nr. 30, hrsg. v. G. Fock. Kassel: Bärenreiter 1967 (= BA 5481).

**Scheidt,** Samuel (1587–1654): **Luther: Org.** In: DDT I, S. 16. Wiesbaden: B & H.
– In: Bd. VI, Teil I, S. 19–32, hrsg. v. Chr. Mahrenholz. Hamburg: Ugrino 1954.
– In: Ausgewählte Werke für Org. (P.), Nr. 8, V. 1/2, hrsg. v. H. Keller. Frankfurt: Peters (= Ed. Peters 4393 b).
– In: Alte Orgelmusik II, Nr. 10, V. 1. Frankfurt: Wilhelmiana 1959.
– In: Choralvorspiele alter Meister, Nr. 35. Frankfurt: Peters 1952 (= Ed. Peters 3048).
– In: The Church Organist's Golden Treasury, Bd. III, S. 78. Bryn Mawr/Pennsylvania: Ditson 1951.
– In: Masterpieces of Organ Music, fol. 17, Nr. 5, hrsg. v. N. Hennefield. New York: Liturgical Music Press 1944 (= Liturg. MP 171).
– In: Orgelschule v. Ernst Keller, Bd. I, S. 10. Mainz: Schott 1938 (= Ed. Schott 2555 a).
**Luther: Org.** In: DDT I, S. 83. Wiesbaden: B & H
– In: Bd. VI, Teil I, S. 112 ff., Nr. 1, 7 u. 12. Hamburg: Ugrino 1954.
– In: Ausgewählte Werke für Org. (P.), S. 110, hrsg. v. H. Keller. Frankfurt: Peters (= Ed. Peters 4393 b).
**Luther: Org.** In: Choralbearbeitungen u. freie Orgelstücke d. deutsch. Sweelinck-Schule, Bd. I, S. 28, hrsg. v. H. J. Moser. Kassel: Bärenreiter 1954 (= BA 2815).
**Luther: Org.** In: Choralbearbeitungen u. freie Orgelstücke d. deutsch. Sweelinck-Schule, Bd. II, S. 32, hrsg. v. H. J. Moser. Kassel: Bärenreiter 1955 (= BA 2816).

**Schneider,** Johann Christian (1702–1787): **Vater unser: Org.** In: Masterpieces of Organ Music, fol. 17, Nr. 2, hrsg. v. N. Hennefield. New York: Liturgical Music Press 1944 (= Liturg. MP 171).
– In: 51 Orgelchoräle um Joh. Seb. Bach, S. 81, hrsg. v. G. Frotscher. Frankfurt: Peters 1937 (= Das Erbe deutscher Musik, Bd. IX, Ed. Peters 4648).
**Vater unser: Org.** In: 51 Orgelchoräle um Joh. Seb. Bach, S. 82–84, hrsg. v. G. Frotscher. Frankfurt: Peters 1937 (= Das Erbe deutscher Musik, Bd. IX, Ed. Peters 4648).
– In: Wedding Music II, S. 44. St. Louis. Mo.: Concordia Publishing House 1952.
– In: 28 Orgelchoräle d. 17. u. 18. Jh. anläßlich d. 50-jährigen Bestehens d. Bernischen Organistenverbandes, Nr. 28. Kassel: Bärenreiter 1957 (= BA 2207).

**Schreiner,** Alexander (geb. 1901): gregor.: Org. In: Organ Voluntaries, Vol. I. Glen Rock, N.J.: Fischer J.

**Schrenk,** Johannes: Luther: Org. In: Kleine Orgelchoräle. 60 Choralsätze zur Übung u. zum gottesdienstl. Gebrauch, Nr. 52. Ebingen/Württ.: Jehle 1949.

**Schwencke,** Johann Friedrich (1792–1852): **Vater unser: Org.** In: Chorale Preludes. Frankfurt: Peters.
**Vater unser: Org.** In: Chorale Preludes. Frankfurt: Peters.

**Snow,** Francis Williams (1890–1961): Our Father in Heaven: Org. 2 Chorale Preludes. Boston, Mass: Wood B. F.

**Speuy,** Hendrick J. (1575–1625): Vater unser: Org. In: Psalm Preludes, hrsg. v. Noske. Amsterdam: Hewwekemeijer.

**Steigleder,** Johann Ulrich (1580–1653): Vater unser: Org. In: 73 Leichte Choralvorspiele, Bd. II, Nr. 121. München: Leuckart 1952.
– In: Masterpieces of Organ Music, fol. 17, Nr. 7, hrsg. v. N. Hennfield. New York: Liturgical Music Press 1944 (= Liturg. MP 171).
– In: Das Organistenamt, Bd. III, Nr. 108. Wiesbaden: B & H (= EB 6344c).
– In: 28 Orgelchoräle d. 17. u. 18. Jh. anläßlich d. 50-jährigen Bestehens d. Bernischen Organistenverbandes, Nr. 10. Kassel: Bärenreiter 1957 (= BA 2207).
– In: Seasonal Chorale Preludes Bd. IV, S. 14. London: Oxford University Press 1962.
– In: Ritter Collection, 40 Variations on „Vater unser". Berlin: Ries & Erler.

**Stolze,** Heinrich Wilhelm (1801–1868): Vater unser: Org. In: Anthology of Sacred Music. St. Louis, Mo.: Concordia Publishing House.

**Sweelinck,** Jan Pieterson (1562–1621): Luther: Org. 4 Variationen. In: Werken voor Orgel en Clavecimbel, Deel I, S. 195–198, Nr. 54. Amsterdam: Alsbach G. & Co. 1943.

**Telemann,** Georg Philipp (1681–1767): Luther: Org. In: 12 Leichte Choralvorspiele, Nr. 11 u. 12, hrsg. v. H. Keller. Leipzig: Peters 1952 (= Ed. Peters 4239).
– In: Orgelwerke, Bd. I. Kassel: Bärenreiter.

**Vierling,** Johann Gottfried (1750–1813): Vater unser: Org. In: Leichte Choralvorspiele. Wiesbaden: B & H.

**Walcha,** Helmut (geb. 1907): Vater unser: Org. In: Chorale Preludes, Vol. III. Frankfurt: Peters.

**Wedemann,** Wilhelm (1805–1849): Vater unser: Org. In: 76 Leichte Choralvorspiele. Leipzig: Paezschen.

**Weinmann,** Johann (um 1477–1542): Vater unser: Org. In: Seasonal Chorale Preludes, Bd. III, S. 13, hrsg. v. C. H. Trevor. London: Oxford University Press 1963.

**Wettstein,** Heinrich (1868–1934): Vater unser: Org. In: 130 Chorale Preludes. Wilhelmshaven: Heinrichshofen.

**Wiemer,** Wolfgang: Luther: Org. In: 6 Choralvorspiele, S. 7 ff. Wiesbaden: B & H 1962 (= EB 6408).

**Wieruszowski,** Lili (geb. 1899): Luther: Org. In: 25 Choralvorspiele, Nr. 24, hrsg. v. Organistenverband Basel-Land aus Anlaß d. 25-jährigen Bestehens. Lausanne: Foetisch 1947 (= Ed. 1915).

**Wolfrum,** Karl (1857–1934): Vater unser: Org. In: op. 17: Der Cantus Firmus. Gütersloh: Bertelsmann C.

**Zachau,** Friedrich Wilhelm (1663–1712): Vater unser: Org. In: Chorale Preludes. Wiesbaden: B & H.; Kassel: Nagel's Musik Archiv.

**Zipp,** Friedrich (geb. 1914): Luther: Org. In: 10 Choralvorspiele für Orgel. Berlin: Merseburger (= Ed. Merseb. 882).

**Zwart,** Jan (1877–1937): Vater unser: Org. In: Nederlandsche Orgelmuziek, Bd. VII, 5 Orgelchoräle. Koog/Zaan: Zaandam.

### 3.1.1. Orgel mit anderen Instrumenten
**Janssens,** Peter: Mt 6,9–13: Org. (P.) u. 5 Instr. (b- u. c-Stimme/Git., Baß u. Dr.) In: Friedensmesse. Telgte: Janssens 1969.
– In: Wir können nicht schweigen. Telgte: Janssens 1970.

**Krebs,** Karl-August (1804–1880): gregor.: VI. m. Org. (Harm. o. P.). In: Auserlesene Melodien, hrsg. v. A. Piechler. Mainz: Schott 1959 (= Ed. Schott 5059).

**Weyrauch,** Johannes (geb. 1897): Luther: Vc. m. Org. In: Instrumentalmusik zur Trauung, Nr. 9, hrsg. v. H. Gadsch. Berlin: Evangelische Verlagsanstalt 1957.

**Musik für Blechbläser:** Vater unser: Trompete u. Org. In: 9 Choräle alter Meister, hrsg. v. W. Ehmann. Kassel: Bärenreiter 1976 (= BA 5400).

### 3.2. Andere Instrumente

**Hassler,** Hans Leo (1564–1612): Luther: f. Blockflötenquartett (Gamben-, Fiedel-, Streichquartett) o. andere Instrumente. Wolfenbüttel: Möseler 1957 (= Corona Nr. 49, Fugenbuch alter Meister).

**Janssens,** Peter: Mt 6,9–13: m. Git. (Org. o. P.). In: Pietbiets Gesangbuch. Telgte: Janssens 1971.
Mt 6,9–13: m. Git. (P. o. Org.). In: Wir haben einen Traum. Telgte: Janssens 1972.

**Liszt,** Franz (1811–1886): gregor.: P. In: Politische und religiöse Stimmungen, Bd. VII, Nr. 5. hrsg. v. d. Franz Liszt-Stiftung. Wiesbaden: B & H 1966.

**Marsick,** Martin-Pierre-Joseph (1848–1924): gregor.: VI. u. P. (Org.): op. 7: Pater noster. Paris: Durand A. & Fils.

**Rózsa,** Miklós (geb. 1907): gregor.: P. In: Tonfilm: König der Könige. Die Macht, die Größe, der Leidensweg, der Sieg. Eine Geschichte aus der Zeit, als Christus unter den Menschen lebte. Köln: Sidemton (Gerig) 1962 (= A Robbins Publication).

**Tschaikowsky,** Peter (1840–1893): Pater noster: In: Klaviertrio a-moll, op. 58, hrsg. v. M. Farish. New York: Bowker Company 1973.

**Bläserbegleitsätze zu neuen Liedern:** Vater unser: Posaunenchor. Berlin: Evangelische Verlagsanstalt 1976.

**Neue und alte Blasmusik:** Luther: Posaunenchor, 6-st., Nr. 59. Kassel: Eichenkreuzverlag 1962.

### 4. Verzeichnis der Schallplatten

### 4.1. Vokalwerke – Einstimmig

### 4.1.1. Mit lateinischem Text

**Gregorianische Gesänge:** Pater noster: römisch-lateinischer Ritus. Joppich/Benediktinerabtei Münsterschwarzach. Freiburg: Christophorus Verlag (= Chr-SCGIX 73918).

– Das Vaterunser in Liturgie und Meditation. Freiburg: Christophorus Verlag (= Chr-SCGLS 76018).

– Die Mitternachtsmesse: Pater noster. Papst Johannes Paul II., Gesang. Rom: Vox christiana 1978 (= CBS-PP2).

**Christi Geburt in der Liturgie der Äthiopier.** Pater noster: äthiopischer Ritus. Chor des Päpstlichen Äthiopischen Kollegs Vatikanstadt. Freiburg: Christophorus Verlag (= Chr-CLP 73327).

– Das Vaterunser in Liturgie und Meditation. Freiburg: Christophorus Verlag (= Chr-SCGLS 76018).

**Die Weihnachtsliturgie im armenischen Ritus:** Pater noster: armenischer Ritus. Chor des Päpstlichen Armenischen Kollegs, Rom. Freiburg: Christophorus Verlag (=˙ Chr-SCGLX 73705).

– Das Vaterunser in Liturgie und Meditation. Freiburg: Christophorus Verlag (= Chr-SCGLS 76018).

**Die vollständige Liturgie im byzantinisch-slawischen Ritus:**
Pater noster: byzantinisch-slawischer Ritus.
Johannes-Damascenus-Chor, Essen, und Chor des Päpstlichen Russischen Kollegs, Rom.
Freiburg: Christophorus Verlag (= Chr-SCK 70320).

– Das Vaterunser in Liturgie und Meditation.
Freiburg: Christophorus Verlag (= Chr-SCGLS 76018).

**Sonntag der Heiligen Väter:**
Pater noster: byzantinisch-griechischer Ritus
Chor des Päpstlichen Griechischen Kollegs St. Athanasius, Rom.
Freiburg: Christophorus Verlag (= Chr-SCGLX 73704, 2 × 30 cm).

– Das Vaterunser in Liturgie und Meditation.
Freiburg: Christophorus Verlag (= Chr-SCGLS 76018).

### 4.1.2. Mit deutschem Text

**Blarr,** Oskar Gottlieb (geb. 1934) nach einem amerik. Vater unser, Interpr.: Truth. Wesel: Kawohl 1976 (= Young 5105).

**Cornelius,** Peter (1824–1874): Nr. 3: Zu uns komme dein Reich, c-moll. Fischer-Dieskau/Demus. Hamburg: Deutsche Grammophon (= DG 2530219).

**Danke Jesus.** Vater unser im Himmelreich. Martin Mast, Gesang. Wetzlar: Schulte 1976 (= Nr. 33514).

**Das Chorlied.** Männergesangverein Burgsänger/Karl Bürger. Bonn: Hömmerich 1977 (= Nr. Chor-Musik CL 102).

**Du meine Seele singe.** Chor Canta Nova/Rohr u. a. München: Ariola-Eurodisc-Gesellsch. 1974 (= Nr. Music 87839 IU).

**Feldzugschor Nummer 3:** Vater unser. Hildor Janz, Gesang. Lörrach: Janz-Team 1976 (= Nr. 6025).

**Frankenthaler Chöre und Orchester:** Freiwillige Feuerwehr/Spielmanns- u. Fanfarenzug/Volkschor Frank Holzmann, Chor der Versöhnungskirche. Frankenthal: Kulturamt 1978 (= Kerston FK 65056, 2 × 30 cm).

**Janssens,** Peter: Wir haben einen Traum. Gesangsorchester Peter Janssens. Telgte: Janssens 1972 (= Nr. 1003).

– Der Herr ist mein Sinn, nie werde ich funktionieren. Gesangsorchester Peter Janssens. Telgte: Janssens 1978 (= Nr. 1027).

**Lateinamerikanische Beatmesse:** Andariegos/Wild Cats/Oskars Kirchenmäuse. Düsseldorf: Thomas 1977 (= tvd 7703).

**Lieder zum Mitsingen in der Gemeinde für Konfirmandenarbeit, Unterricht und Gottesdienst:** Dionysius-Chor Krefeld/Dionysius-Band Krefeld. Düsseldorf: Schwann 1975 (= Schwann-Studio 0354).

**Musikalische Grüße aus Mutterstadt:** Männergesangverein Liederkranz/Blaskapelle/Roland Hahn. Mutterstadt: Gemeindeverwaltung 1978 (= Kerston 65068).

**Wickendick,** Volker: Worte ins Leben: neue Lieder zum Gottesdienst. Studio Panne und Paulsen. Limburg: Studio Union im Lahn-Verlag 1975 (Nr. SU 460–61).

### 4.1.3. Mit fremdsprachigem Text

**Mahalia Jackson:** The Lord's prayer. Mahalia Jackson, Gesang. Frankfurt: CBS-Schallpl. 1976 (= Embassy EMB 31383); Frankfurt: Bellaphon Records 1976 (= Nr. BMC 114007); Berlin: Deutsche Schallpl. VEB 1979 (= Amiga 855066).

**La Messe en français:** Notre père. Papst Johannes Paul II., Gesang. Paris: Vox christiana 1979 (= RCAZL 37291).

**Lieder des Papstes Johannes Paul II. in Polen:** Vater unser, Segen (Volksweise); Papst Johannes Paul II., Gesang. Pullheim: Crystalschallpl. 1979 (= CRY 45725).

**Gesänge aus altslawischer Liturgie:** Otče naš. Sofijski Mužki Chor Kaval/Dimiter Ruskov. Köln: EMI-Elektrola 1978 (= Deutsche Harmonia Mundi 1 C 065-99733).

203

## 4.2. Vokalwerke – Mehrstimmig

### 4.2.1. Mit lateinischem Text

**Baumann,** Max (geb. 1917): Motetten für 4- bis 8-stimmigen Chor. Windsbacher Knabenchor/Hans Thamm. Haar: Kühl 1977 (= AGK 30107–08, 2 × 30 cm).

**Dubenski,** Arkadi (geb. 1890): Slawische Liturgie. Chor des Bulgarischen Rundfunks. Münster: Fono Schallpl. (= FSM Carus/Audite 53305).

**Gallus** Jacobus (Handl) (1550–1591): Motetten für 4- 12-stimmigen Chor. Windsbacher Knabenchor/Hans Thamm. Haar: Kühl 1975 (= AGK 30105); Zürich: Musikverlag zum Pelikan (= Pel PSR 40623).

**Johnson,** Bengt Emil (geb. 1936): Erkki Pohjola dirigiert. Pohjola/Kinderchor Tapiola. Hamburg: Deutsche Grammophon (= DG 2530812 IMS).

**Liszt,** Franz (1811–1886): Geistliche Chorwerke. Miklós Szabo/Frauenchor des Konservatoriums Györ. Kassel: Disco Center (= DC Hun 11381).

**Nicolai,** Otto (1810–1849): Feierliche Chormusik und Choräle. Anton Lippe/Chor der St.-Hedwigs-Kathedrale Berlin. Hamburg: Teldec (= Tel 641316 AH).

**Perosi,** Lorenzo (1872–1956): Geistliche Chormusik. Karl Norbert Schmidt/Chor der Kirchenmusikschule Regensburg. Freiburg: Christophorus Verlag (= Chr-SCGLX 73784).

**Schütz,** Heinrich (1585–1672): Cantiones sacrae, SWV 89/92. Willi Träder/Niedersächs. Singkreis. Wolfenbüttel: Möseler (= Cam LPT 30008).

**Strawinsky,** Igor (1882–1971): Europäische Chormusik aus alter und neuer Zeit. Kammerchor Leonhard Lechner/Willi Seebacher. Freiburg: Christophorus Verlag 1976 (= Chr-SCGLX 73839).
– Das Vater unser in Liturgie und Meditation. Chor der Staatl. Hochschule für Musik Freiburg. Freiburg: Christophorus Verlag (= Chr-SCGLS 76018).
– Corali del Mondo a Loreto 1977. Giuseppe Rebella/Coro Polifonico Vallegia. Berlin: Mixtur-Schallpl. (= MXT Eco 610).
– Alte Madrigale und moderne Chormusik. Kurt Felgner/Bachchor Frankfurt. Wolfenbüttel: Möseler (= Cam LPM 30042).
– Geistliche Musik I. John-Alldis-Chor London/John Alldis. Düsseldorf: Schwann (= Schw. 0604).

**Tschaikowsky,** Peter Iljitsch (1840–1893): Robev Georgi/Chor Svetoslav Obretenov. Köln: EMI Elektrola (= EMI 157–03557/58, 2 × 30 cm).

204

**Verdi,** Giuseppe (1813–1901: Italian choir music/Monteverdi; Verdi; Scarlatti
Luzerner Vokalsolisten/Franz Xaver Jans. Zürich: Tudor Recording 1978 (= Tud 73029).
– Saltarello Choir
Richard Bradshaw/Saltarello-Chor London. Berlin: Mixtur-Schallpl. (= MXT CRD 1009).
– Corali del Mondo a Loreto 1976
Michaelis-Kammerchor Stockholm. Berlin: Mixtur-Schallpl. (= MXT Eco 601).

**Willaert,** Adrian (1490?–1562): Arti vocali. Hans Kronenburg/Arti Vocali. Berlin: Mixtur-Schallpl. (= MXT Es 46251).

### 4.2.2. Mit deutschem Text

**Bach,** Wilhelm Friedrich Ernst (1759–1845): Geistl. Musik der Bach-Familie. Frankfurter Kantorei. Bach-Collegium Stuttgart. Gächinger Kantorei Stuttgart, Helmuth Rilling (Dir.). Neuhausen: Hänssler 1978 (= Laudate 91511, 5 × 30 cm).

**Fischer,** Gotthilf: Stargala-Fischer-Chöre. Fischer-Chöre/Hans Bertram – Orch. Hamburg: Deutsche Grammophon/Polydor (= Polydor 2664188, 2 × 30 cm oder Polydor 2437517).
– 1000 Stimmen singen für Millionen. Fischer-Chöre/Hans Bertram-Orchester. Stuttgart: Das Beste 1978 (= FCH 540, 6 × 30 cm).
– Großer Gott, wir loben Dich. Fischer-Chöre/Hans Bertram-Orchester. Hamburg: Deutsche Grammophon-Polydor (= Polydor 2371710).
– Fischer-Chöre: Fischer-Chöre/Otto Kraus (Org.-Akk.). Hamburg: Deutsche Grammophon 1974 (= Polydor 2371479).

**Janáček,** Leoš (1854–1928): Janáček: Geistliche Musik. Haupt/Pfaff/Spelz/Ulmer Kantorei/Hug. Münster: Fono Schallpl. (= FSM Carus/Audite 53189).

**Kovalevsky,** Maxime: Blicket auf zu ihm. Jesus-Bruderschaft. Gnadenthal/Limburg: Präsenz-Verlag der Jesus-Bruderschaft 1976 (= Nr. A 2227).

**Fietz,** Siegfried: Womit wir leben können. Siegfried Fietz. Gesang/Botho-Lucas-Chor/Trevor Bastow, P. Joe Moretti, E-Git./Brian Odgers, B.-Git. Limburg: Studio Union im Lahn-Verlag 1978 (= Abakus 90020 oder Studio-Union SU 8802).

**Martin,** Frank, (1890–1975): Motetten und Liedsätze. Berliner Jugendkantorei/Sigurd Bothe. Berlin: Jugendkantorei 1978 (= Nr. Exklusiv-Ton 7621529).

Reger, Max (1873–1916): Meisterwerke der Motettenkunst. Evangel. Jugendkantorei der Pfalz/Göttsche. Zürich: Musikverlag zum Pelikan 1978 (= Pelca PSR 40697). Kantorei Barmen-Gemarke/ Kahlhöfer. Mannheim: Da camera Schallpl. (= Dca 94042).

### 4.2.3. Mit fremdsprachigem Text

Bairstow, Edward (1874–1946): Music for York Minster. Our Father in Heaven. Wilkinson/BBC Northern Singers. Berlin: Mixtur-Schallpl. (= MXT Aby 737).

Festliches Abschiedskonzert der Don Kosaken. Don Kosakenchor/ Serge Jaroff. Hamburg: Deutsche Grammophon/Polydor (= DG Polydor 2634007, 2 × 30 cm).

The Mormon Tabernacle Choir Album: The Lord's prayer. Mormon Tabernacle Choir/Philadelphia Orch. Frankfurt: CBS 1974 (= Nr. 78276, 2 × 30 cm). Frankfurt: CBS 1975 (= Nr. Embassy EMB 31082).

Sifa ya mungu. Lutheran Theological College/Isaak Makanta. Wuppertal: Verein. Evang. Mission 1977. Erlangen: Verl. d. Evang.-Luth. Mission 1977. (= Nr. VM 7)

Steal away to Jesus. Fred-Schecker-Chor. Freiburg: Christophorus Verlag 1978 (= Chr-SCGLU 73880).

### 4.3. Instrumentalwerke

### 4.3.1. Orgel

Asma, Feike (geb. 1912): W. H. Zwart spielt a. d. Bätz-Orgel d. Waalse Kerk, Delft: Vater unser: Variationen und Choral. Willem Hendrik Zwart, Orgel. Berlin: Mixtur-Schallpl. (= MXT 710212).

Bach, Johann Sebastian (1685–1750): Luther: BWV 636.

– Alte schwedische Orgeln. Rune Engsö, Orgel. Kassel: Disco-Center (= DC Bis 027).

– Friedrich Högner spielt Bach. Friedrich Högner, Orgel. Berlin: Mixtur-Schallpl. (= MXT 0815).

– Bach: Das Orgelbüchlein (2) Gertrud Mersiovsky, Orgel. Stuttgart: Intercord Tongesellschaft (= Int 180832).

– Bach: Das Orgelbüchlein (3) Helmuth Rilling, Orgel. Kassel: Bärenreiter-Musicaphon (= BM 1528).

– Hammer-Orgel der St. Martini-Kirche Stadthagen Arno Schönstedt, Orgel. Münster: Fono Schallpl. (= FSM 53711).

– Das Vaterunser in Liturgie und Meditation. Klaus-Jürgen Sachs, Orgel. Freiburg: Christophorus Verlag (= Chr-SCGLS 76018).

**Luther: BWV 682.**
– Bach: Das Orgelwerk (1). Lionel Rogg, Orgel. Köln: FMI-Elektrola ASD (= HMF 521, 6 × 30 cm).

– Bach: Orgelmesse (Clavierübung III). Armin Schoof, Orgel. Wiesbaden: Motette-Ursina Schallpl. (= Mot 1012, 2 × 30 cm).

– Die Dreifaltigkeitsorgel von Ottobeuren. Ton Koopman, Orgel. Hamburg: Teldec Telefunken-Decca-Schallpl. 1977 (= Tel 635375 DX).

– Orgelmesse: dritter Teil der Clavier-Übung. Uwe Karsten Gross, Orgel. Zürich: Musikverlag zum Pelikan 1969 (= Pelca PSR 41001–02, 2 × 30 cm).

**Luther: BWV 683 (683a).**
– Arp-Schnitger-Orgel in der Eosander-Kapelle des Charlottenburger Schlosses. Fritz Heitmann, Orgel. Hamburg: Telefunken Teldec-Schallpl. (= Tel 641977 AJ).

– Orgelmusik alter Meister. Gabor Lehotka, Orgel. Kassel: Disco-Center (= DC Hun 11680).

– Johann Th. Lemckert an den Orgeln der Laurenskerk Rotterdam. Johann Th. Lemckert, Orgel. Berlin: Mixtur-Schallpl. (= MXT VRS 1901).

– Orgelmusik am Dom zu Linz. Kurt Rapf, Orgel. Freiburg: Christophorus Verlag (= Chr-SCGLX 75961).

– Bach: Das Orgelwerk (1). Lionel Rogg, Orgel. Köln: EMI-Elektrola ASD (= HMF 521, 6 × 30 cm).

– Das Vaterunser in Liturgie und Meditation. Klaus-Jürgen Sachs, Orgel. Freiburg: Christophorus Verlag (= Chr-SCGLS 576018).

– Die Dreifaltigkeitsorgel von Ottobeuren. Ton Koopman, Orgel. Hamburg: Teldec Telefunken-Decca-Schallpl. 1977 (= Tel 635375 DX).

**Luther: BWV 737.**
– Die Koenig-Orgel der St. Stevenskerk Nimwegen. Derk Jansen, Orgel. Berlin: Mixtur-Schallpl. (= MXT Es 46282).

– Bach: Orgelwerke. Walter Kraft. Münster: Fono-Schallpl. (= FSM VXDS 101, 18 × 30 cm).

– Bach: Das Orgelwerk (15). Lionel Rogg, Orgel. Köln: EMI Elektrola (= EMI 151–14119/20 Q, 2 × 30 cm). Köln: EMI Elektrola (= HMF 522, 6 × 30 cm).

**Böhm,** Georg (1661–1733): **Luther.**

– Heidrun Decker. Orgel. Buchholz: Musica Viva (= MV 301058).

– Festliches Orgelkonzert. Jörgen Ernst Hansen, Orgel. München: Ariola Eurodisc (= ArXB 89202 K, 2 × 30 cm).

– Die Passion. Jörgen Ernst Jansen, Orgel. München: Ariola Eurodisc (= Ar M 85827 K).

– Die Konrad-Euler-Orgel der Benediktinerinnenabtei Heilig Kreuz, Herstelle/Weser. Käthe van Tricht, Orgel. Bohnhorst: Norddeutsches Tonstudio für Kirchenmusik (= Psal PET 51/161067).

**Buxtehude,** Dietrich (1637–1707): **Luther: H. 3 (I).**

– Das komplette Orgelwerk. Walter Kraft, Orgel. Münster: Fono-Schallpl. (= FSM VXDS 103, 8 × 30 cm).

– Das Orgelwerk (1). Bernard Lagace, Orgel. Berlin: Mixtur-Schallpl. (= MXT C 1731).

**Luther: H. 4, 22.**
– Das komplette Orgelwerk. Walter Kraft, Orgel. Münster: Fono-Schallpl. (= FSM V × DS 103, 8 × 30 cm).
– Das Orgelwerk (1) Bernard Lagace, Orgel. Berlin: Mixtur-Schallpl. (= MXT C 1731).

**Fischer,** Gotthilf: Festliches Konzert: Vater unser. Georg Brausinger, Orgel. Hamburg: Deutsche Grammophon 1976 (= DG Karussell 2430278).

**Janssens,** Peter: Wir können nicht schweigen. Vater unser: Git. (P. o. Org.) Telgte: Janssens 1970 (= Nr. 1001).

**Kluge,** Manfred (1928–1971): **Luther.**

– Die Klais-Orgel der Lutherkirche Wiesbaden: Klaus Uwe Ludwig, Orgel. Wiesbaden: Motette-Ursina-Schallpl. Verl. 1979 (= Nr. 1024–33).

– Manfred Kluge: Uwe Gross, Orgel. Berlin: Uwe Pape 1974 (= LPOD 8) Münster: Fono-Schallpl. (= FSM 53708).

**Mendelssohn,** Bartholdy Felix (1809–1847): **Luther:** Sonate 6.

– Arno Schönstedt spielt Werke der Romantik an der Hammer-Orgel in Stadthagen. Berlin: Pape 1976 (= FSM 63711 POD).

– Oberrheinische Orgeln. Egidius Doll, Orgel. Freiburg: Christophorus Verlag 1976 (= Chr-SCGLX 73856).

**Pachelbel,** Johann (1653–1706): Das Vaterunser in Liturgie und Meditation. **Luther.** Klaus-Jürgen Sachs, Orgel. Freiburg: Christophorus Verlag (= Chr-SCGLS 76018).

**Praetorius,** Michael (1571–1621): **Luther.**

– Norddeutsche Arp-Schnitger-Orgeln. Albert de Klerk, Orgel. Hamburg: Teldec-Schallpl. (= Tel 635054 DX, 2 × 30 cm).

– Deutsche Messe zur Osterzeit. Lothar Stöbel, Orgel. Bohnhorst: Norddeutsches Tonstudio für Kirchenmusik (= Psal PSB32/190266, 2 × 30 cm).

**Reger,** Max (1873–1916): Orgelwerke (1) **Luther:** op. 67, Nr. 39. Heinz Lohmann, Orgel. Mannheim: Da camera Schallpl. (= Dca MRK 19736, 10 × 30 cm). (= Dca 93240).

**Scheidemann,** Heinrich (um 1596–1663): Das Vaterunser in Liturgie und Meditation. **Luther:** 2 Verse mit Satz aus: Görlitzer Tabulaturbuch von S. Scheidt) Klaus-Jürgen Sachs, Orgel. Freiburg: Christophorus Verlag (= Chr-SCGLS 76018).

**Scheidt,** Samuel (1587–1654): Arp-Schnitger (1) **Luther.** Werner Jacob, Orgel. Köln: EMI 187–30214/15, 2 × 30 cm.

**Speuy,** Hendrick (1575–1625): Haite van der Schaaf an den 3 Orgeln der Laurenskerk Rotterdam. **Luther.** Haite van der Schaaf, Orgel. Berlin: Mixtur Schallpl. (= MXT VRS 1912).

**Steigleder,** Johann Ulrich (1593–1635): **Luther.**

– Die Orgel der Dorfkirche zu Lochtum. Gerhart Rohwer, Orgel. Berlin: Mixtur Schallpl. (= MXT Be 30011).

– Musica germanica 1600–1740. Lothar Stöbel, Orgel. Bohnhorst: Norddeutsches Tonstudio für Kirchenmusik (= Psal PET 110/090771)

**Sweelinck,** Jan Pieterszoon (1562–1621): **Luther.**

– Orgelwerke, Vol. 2. Ton Koopman, Orgel. Hamburg: Teldec-Decca-Schallpl. 1977 (= Tel 635374 GK, 5 × 30 cm).

– Arp Schnitger (1) Werner Jacob, Orgel. Köln: EMI Elektrola (= EMI 187–30214/15, 2 × 30 cm).

**Telemann,** Georg Philipp (1681–1767): **Luther.**

– Möllner Komponisten und ihre Lehrer. Franz Haselböck, Orgel. Berlin: Mixtur-Schallpl. (= MXT Be 30009).

– Telemann: Orgelwerke. Franz Lörch, Orgel. Mannheim: Da camera Schallpl. (= Dca 93271/73, 3 × 30 cm).

– Musik für Trompete und Orgel. Johannes Ricken, Orgel. Wiesbaden: Motette-Ursina Schallpl. Verlag (= Mot 2001). (= Mot 1030).

**Zwart,** Jan (1877–1937): Dirk Jansz. Zwart spielt Jan Zwart. **Luther:** Trio und Choral. Dirk Janszoon Zwart, Orgel. Berlin: Mixtur Schallpl. (= MXT CV 0208). (= MXT W 200).

**Zwart,** Dirk Janszoon (geb. 1917): Dirk Janszoon Zwart; 40 Jahre Organist. **Luther.** Dirk Janszoon Zwart, Orgel. Berlin: Mixtur Schallp. (= MXT F 084/85, 2 × 30 cm).

### 4.3.2. Andere Instrumente

**An der Saale hellem Strande. Luther.** Gerhard Buckel, Sprecher/ Evangelischer Posaunenchor/Helmut Lottes. Oberkotzau: Evangelischer Posaunenchor 1978 (= Lorby Bi-929).

**Telemann,** Georg Philipp (1681–1767): **Luther.** Musik für Trompete und Orgel. Johannes Ricken, Orgel. Wiesbaden: Motette-Ursina Schallpl. Verl. (= Mot 2001). (= Mot 1030).

**Tschaikowsky,** Peter Iljitsch (1840–1893): Das Konzert des Jahrhunderts. Pater noster: in: Klaviertrio a-moll, op. 50 Vladimir Horowitz, P.; Isaac Stern, VI.; Mstislav Rostropovič, Vc.; Yehudi Menuhin, VI.; New York Philharmonic. Leonard Bernstein. Frankfurt: CBS 1976 (= CBS 79200, 2 × 30 cm).

# ANHANG

Verzeichnis der Komponisten um 1500–1700

O = unvollständig oder verschollen
+ = Komponisten in den *Libri Quatuor 1619* (siehe S. 13)

| | Name | Stimmenzahl |
|---|---|---|
| | *Name* | *Stimmenzahl* |
| | *Name* | *Stimmenzahl* |
| | *Name* | *Stimmenzahl* |
| | *Name* | *Stimmenzahl* |
| | Anonymus | 3 |
| | Anonymus | 3 |
| | Anonymus | 3 |
| | Anonymus | 5 |
| | Anonymus | 5 |
| | Anonymus | 5 |
| | Anonymus | 7 |
| | Anonymus | 8 |
| | Appiano, Giovanni Maria | 8 |
| | Appiano, Giovanni Maria | 8 |
| | Appiano, Giovanni Maria | 5 |
| | Arcadelt, Jacobus | 8 |
| + | Arnone, Guglielmo | 5 |
| + | Arnone, Guglielmo | 5 |
| + | Arnone, Guglielmo | 6 |
| | Barré, Leonardus | 6 |
| + | Binago, Benedetto | 5 |
| + | Binago, Benedetto | 5 |
| + | Biumi, Giacomo Filippo | 5 |
| + | Borgo, Cesare | 5 |
| + | Borgo, Cesare | 5 |
| + | Borgo, Cesare | 5 |
| | Bruck, Arnoldus de | 4 |
| | Bruck, Arnoldus de | 5 |
| | Celidone, Giovanni Antonio | 8 |
| + | Cima, Giovanni Paolo | 5 |
| O | Clavius, Christophorus | 8 |
| | Coler, Valentin | 4 |

211

| | | |
|---|---|---|
| + | Comanedo, Flaminio | 5 |
| + | Comanedo, Flaminio | 5 |
| + | Corradi, Giovanni Battista | 5 |
| | Daser, Ludwig | 5 *Missa super PN* |
| | Elsbeth, Thomas | 6 |
| | Erbach, Christian | 10 |
| O | Festa, Constanzo | 6 |
| | Formellis, Wilhelm | 6 |
| + | Gabussi, Giulio Cesare | 5 |
| + | Gabussi, Giulio Cesare | 5 |
| + | Gabussi, Giulio Cesare | 5 |
| + | Gabussi, Giulio Cesare | 5 |
| + | Gabussi, Giulio Cesare | 6 |
| + | Gabussi, Giulio Cesare | 8 |
| | Gallus, Anthonius | 3 |
| | Gombert, Nicolas | 5 |
| | Grancini, Michelangelo | 4 |
| | Grancini, Michelangelo | 4 |
| | Grancini, Michelangelo | 4 |
| | Grancini, Michelangelo | 4 |
| | Grancini, Michelangelo | 4 |
| | Grancini, Michelangelo | 4 |
| | Grancini, Michelangelo | 4 |
| | Grancini, Michelangelo | 4 |
| | Grancini, Michelangelo | 8 |
| | Grossi, Giovanni Antonio | 5 |
| | Grossi, Giovanni Antonio | 8 |
| | Grossi, Giovanni Antonio | 8 |
| | Grossi, Giovanni Antonio | 8 |
| | Grossi, Giovanni Antonio | 8 und 16 |
| | Grossi, Giovanni Antonio | 9 |
| | Grossi, Giovanni Antonio | 4-chörig u. Soli |
| | Guerrero, Franciscus | 8 |
| | Handl, Jacob (Gallus) | 8 |
| | Handl, Jacob | 8 *Missa super PN* |
| | Hassler, Hans Leo | 8 |
| | Hellinck, Lupus | 5 |
| O | Jachet da Mantua | 5 |
| | Josquin Desprez | 6 |
| | Josquin Desprez | 4 (3-textig) |
| | Kerle, Jacobus de | 6 (2-textig) |
| | Klein, Salomon | 6 |

213

# Arbeitsbericht der Stiftung „Oratio Dominica" Abteilung „Weltgespräch" und Ökumene von 1965–1984

*Von Walter Strolz, Leiter des Religionskundlichen Instituts der Stiftung, Freiburg i. Br.*

Nach dem Abschluß des Zweiten Vatikanischen Konzils im Jahre 1965 gab der Freiburger Verleger Dr. Dr. h. c. Theophil Herder-Dorneich in seiner Eigenschaft als Vorsitzender der von ihm begründeten Stiftung „Oratio Dominica" den Anstoß zu der Edition „Weltgespräch". Mit seiner wissenschaftlichen Leitung wurde der Verfasser dieses Arbeitsberichts beauftragt. Welche Zielsetzung wurde dieser neuen Initiative gegeben? Es handelte sich darum, den Konzilsanstoß zum *Dialog des christlichen Glaubens mit den Wissenschaften und mit den nicht-christlichen Religionen* aufzunehmen. Schon das Leitwort „Weltgespräch" sollte andeuten, daß es auf dem neu betretenen Feld der interdisziplinären Fragestellung und der Begegnung mit den Religionen von Anfang an darum ging, konfessionelle Grenzen mit dem entschiedenen Willen zu überschreiten, eine weitgespannte *ökumenische* Denk- und Glaubensweise zu fördern. Dies geschah bereits im ersten Planungsstadium der kommenden Kolloquien aus der zentralen biblischen Glaubenserfahrung, daß Schöpfung und Geschichte unauflöslich zusammengehören, daß der Schöpfer der Natur auch der Herr der Geschichte ist, daß dieser Gott der Vater aller Menschen (Mal 2, 10; Apk 17, 26) in der noch unabgeschlossenen, geschichtsoffenen Vielfalt religiöser Überlieferungen ist und bleibt und demzufolge das Ringen um *Katholizität*, um die weltumfassende Durchdringungskraft des Glaubens, eine *urchristliche* Aufgabe ist.

## Weltgespräch

Die *erste Phase* des Dialogs „Weltgespräch" umfaßte die Zeitspanne von 1965 bis 1972. Die interdisziplinären Kolloquien wurden mit zwei Gesprächen über die *Gotteserfahrung* im Griechentum, in der jüdischen und christlichen Überlieferung und in ihrer Widerspiegelung innerhalb der zeitgenössischen Literatur eingeleitet. Der maßgebende Gesichtspunkt dieser fragenden Begegnung war nicht der historische Vergleich, sondern die phänomenologisch behutsame

Vergegenwärtigung verschiedener Gottesbegegnungen in ihrer *existentiellen* Bedeutsamkeit für den heutigen Menschen. Daß dabei der *jüdische* Geschichtsweg als Glaubenserfahrung nach Auschwitz zum Prüfstein für die Sache der Theologie und ihres Wahrheitsanspruches wurde, soll hier ebenso festgehalten werden wie das Faktum, daß die neue Freilegung der *alttestamentlichen* Grundlagen des Christusglaubens zu den wichtigsten Ergebnissen der ersten Kolloquien in den Jahren nach dem Konzilsende gehörten. Das einzigartige Verhältnis, in dem das Christentum *im Unterschied* zu anderen Religionen zum Judentum kraft der *jüdischen Wurzel* seiner Botschaft (Röm 11,18) steht, begann hier schon aufzuleuchten. Was die Gottesfrage betrifft, so wurde sie im Anschluß an die ersten Kolloquien durch die Diskussion naturwissenschaftlicher und biblischer Welterkenntnis und durch die Erläuterung des Atheismus-Problems im Zusammenhang der Begründungsmöglichkeit einer autonomen Moral erweitert. Faßt man das Ergebnis dieser zuletzt erwähnten Besinnung zusammen, so kann folgendes gesagt werden:

Der Atheismus des menschlichen Aufstandes gegen einen Gott, der sich dogmatisch-apologetisch festhalten, beweisen oder rechtfertigen läßt, ist heute vielleicht der Vorläufer für eine Frömmigkeit, in der die Wahrheit nicht mit einer Lehre über etwas, sondern mit ihrer menschlichen Bewährung zusammenfällt. Der Glaube, der sich durch die Fragen des Unglaubens anfechten läßt, auf sie eingeht, sie durchdenkt, der schweigt, wo keine Antwort möglich ist, und antwortet, wo bei aller unaufhebbaren Unsicherheit des menschlichen Daseins dennoch die tragende Gewißheit des Glaubens sprechen und handeln muß, dieser Glaube allein ist glaubwürdig. Eine solche Grundhaltung setzt einen Sprachwandel in den Kirchen voraus, für den es erst wenige Beispiele gibt. Das Buch Hiob und die Klagelieder bleiben, biblisch gesehen, bis zum Ende der Tage die große Schule für eine Gottesbegegnung, die auch in der radikalen Anfechtung des Glaubens, Gegenwart *und* Abwesenheit Gottes *als Zeit Gottes* erfährt.

Mit zwei Kolloquien zur *Welterfahrung in der Sprache* und zum fundamentalen Verhältnis von *Sprache und Wahrheit* wurden philosophische, theologische, psychologische und literaturwissenschaftliche Aspekte dieser Thematik aufgegriffen. Wenn „die Sprache die Mutter der Vernunft und der Offenbarung, ihr Alpha und Omega ist" (Hamann) und der Mensch in der Sprache als dem „Haus des Seins" (Heidegger) wohnt, dann ist die Würde und Auszeichnung des Menschseins an diese wahrhaft grund-legende Existenzerfah-

216

rung gebunden. Die menschliche Begegnung mit der vor-gegebe-
nen Natur und der geschichtlichen Welt als dem Entscheidungs-
und Gestaltungsraum des Menschen wird durch die Benennungs-
und Unterscheidungskraft der Sprache ermöglicht. Wissenschaft
und Glaube, Dichtung und Mythos entspringen ihrem unerschöpfli-
chen Sinnreichtum. Jede mögliche Spielart von Sprachkritik setzt
die Sprache selbst immer schon voraus. Die interdisziplinäre Diskussion dieser Thematik lief in ihrem Ergebnis auf die für die Bewahrung der Menschlichkeit des Menschen entscheidende Einsicht hinaus, daß die *Vielseitigkeit und Vielstimmigkeit der Sprache*
nicht und niemals auf *eine* Sprachmöglichkeit, sei es nun die alltäg-
liche, die wissenschaftliche, die philosophische, die psychologische, die politisch-ideologische oder auf die religiöse und theologische Sprachmöglichkeit, beschränkt werden darf. Nur ein totalitä-
res Herrschaftsstreben und Sicherheitsbedürfnis versucht, eine
einzige Sprachmöglichkeit als allgemeingültige durchzusetzen.
Der Mensch bleibt nur so lange, wie wir aus bitteren geschichtlichen Erfahrungen gelernt haben, ein freies und schöpferisches Wesen, als er auf den *unendlichen* Sinnüberschuß der Sprache vertraut,
aus ihr lebt, spricht, denkt, handelt und schweigt. Oder um das Ergebnis der Sprachbesinnung innerhalb der Edition „Weltgespräch"
anders formuliert zusammenzufassen: der bloß instrumentellen
Bestimmung der Sprache fehlt die Dimension ihres unausschöpf-
baren Sinnes. „Der höchste Begriff vom Menschen kann nur durch
Vielseitigkeit, Liberalität erlangt werden" (Goethe).

Wie der Himmel über der Erde den irdischen Aufenthalt des Menschen durch seine unbegrenzte Offenheit allererst ermöglicht, so
ermöglicht das Sinn- und Bedeutungsgefüge der Sprache das
menschliche Wohnen, das verstehende oder auch mißglückende
Miteinandersein auf dieser Erde. Daß die Sprache Zeichenfunktion
haben kann, daß sie soziales Verhalten begründet, daß sie überhaupt Wirklichkeitserfahrung ermöglicht, daß sie ästhetisch wirk-
sam ist, daß sie nicht auf ihre Aussagefunktion oder auf die Möglichkeit der begrifflichen Bestimmung der Dinge eingeengt werden
darf, daß sie geschichtliche Wandlungsvorgänge nicht nur begleitet, sondern initiiert, daß die wachsende Vielfalt menschlicher
„Sprachspiele" nicht ins Zusammenhanglose auseinanderfällt, daß
die Sprache im dichterischen Wort, als Prophetie, in der Sprache
philosophischer Besinnung mächtig ist, daß sie Sprache des Gebetes und der Empörung sein kann, daß sie noch im Schweigen Sinn
stiftet und über dem Todesgeschick des Menschen waltet – dies alles weist auf den *universalen*, Welt und Sinn erschließenden Cha-

217

rakter der Sprache hin. Und nur weil die Sprache allem instrumentellen Gebrauch *zuvor* die genannten und noch andere Möglichkeiten schon enthält, kann sie *auch* funktionell betrachtet werden.

Die Auseinandersetzung mit *Grundpositionen heutiger Naturwissenschaft* wurde nach den bisher genannten Veranstaltungen in zwei Kolloquien aufgenommen. Im ersten Gespräch über die Naturwissenschaft als geschichtliches Phänomen wurden wichtige Wegstrecken innerhalb der historischen Entfaltung der Naturwissenschaft dargestellt und wirkungsgeschichtlich gedeutet. Innerhalb dieser Erläuterung wurde die Maßgeblichkeit der Anfänge naturwissenschaftlichen Denkens bei den Griechen besonders herausgestellt. Am Beispiel von Kybernetik und Molekularbiologie wurde im Hinblick auf das 20. Jahrhundert die Entwicklung eines neuen Denkstils in den Naturwissenschaften verfolgt. Es wurde das umstrittene Verhältnis zwischen der morphologisch-ästhetischen Betrachtungsweise der Natur, wie sie die Gestaltungsforschung prägt, und der rational-kausal vorgehenden Biologie offenkundig. Allerdings, von welchem methodischen Ansatz aus der Naturwissenschaftler auch immer an sein „Objekt" herangeht, er setzt in jedem Fall einen Vertrauensakt. Er erwartet, daß die Natur von bestimmten Gesetzmäßigkeiten erfüllt ist, die mathematisch formuliert werden können. Obwohl diese Hoffnung, wie die Entfaltung der neuzeitlichen Naturwissenschaft und die Atomphysik seit 1945 zeigen, nicht enttäuscht worden ist, gilt es doch festzuhalten, daß die naturwissenschaftliche Berechnung der Natur immer mit einem Abstraktionsvorgang verbunden ist. Sie steht unter dem Zwang, verallgemeinern zu müssen, wenn sie zu einem „Naturgesetz" kommen oder sogar zu einer einheitlichen „Weltformel" gelangen will, nach der das Universum aufgebaut ist. Heisenberg wies in den letzten Jahren seines Lebens öfters auf die Begrenztheit dieses in der mathematischen Abstraktion begründeten Naturverständnisses hin. Zur Eigenart ihrer Sprache sagte er u. a.:

„Die Sprache der Naturwissenschaften muß, da es sich hier um die sorgfältige Darstellung einer unermeßlichen Fülle von Einzelheiten handeln soll, zu einer Art von Präzisionsinstrument ausgebildet werden. Dies kann durch Axiomatisierung ihrer begrifflichen und logischen Strukturen erreicht werden. Durch diese Idealisierung zum Präzisionsinstrument löst sich die Sprache aber wieder vom gemeinten Gegenstand ab. Man kann nur noch am Erfolg erkennen, wieweit man die Natur mit einer solchen Sprache ergreifen kann."

218

Das zweite Kolloquium mit dem Schwerpunkt auf der naturwissenschaftlichen Fragestellung handelte vom *Sinn der Evolution*. An diesem Gespräch beteiligten sich Vertreter der Physik, der Paläontologie, der Biologie und des Alten Testaments. Zur Diskussion stand vor allem die Frage, welche Faktoren aus den genannten Forschungsgebieten Evolution hervorbringen und steuern und welche Sinnzusammenhänge innerhalb der Natur als eines offenen Kosmos sich darin zeigen. Der biblische Beitrag richtete sich auf die Entfaltung der Frage nach der *Vertrauenswürdigkeit der Natur als Schöpfung*. Diese Glaubenserfahrung gehört, vom *theologischen* Gesichtspunkt aus gesehen, zu den vergessenen oder verdrängten Voraussetzungen naturwissenschaftlicher Erkenntnis. Für das *philosophisch* bestimmte Fragen beruht diese Vorbedingung aller Naturwissenschaft in der Unumgänglichkeit der nicht vom Menschen hervorgebrachten Natur und ihrer rätselvollen Beständigkeit, die allererst das Verhältnis von Natur und Naturwissenschaft ermöglicht. Was der Mensch immer schon unausgesprochen anerkennt, indem er lebt, überspringt er am meisten. „Die für uns wichtigsten Aspekte der Dinge sind durch ihre Einfachheit und Alltäglichkeit verborgen. (Man kann es nicht bemerken – weil man es immer vor Augen hat.) Die eigentlichen Grundlagen seiner Forschung fallen dem Menschen gar nicht auf. Es sei denn, daß ihm *dies* einmal aufgefallen ist. – Und das heißt: das, was, einmal gesehen, das Auffallendste und Stärkste ist, fällt uns nicht auf" (Wittgenstein).

Mit dem Kolloquium über Möglichkeiten und Grenzen der Zukunftsforschung wurde jener Teil des „Weltgesprächs" abgeschlossen, dessen Ergebnis in 10 Einzelbeiträgen (mit Diskussionsberichten) gesammelt vorliegt. Zu den Teilnehmern dieser Kolloquien gehörten u. a.: K. Kerényi †, C. Westermann, G. von Rad †, H. A. Horst †, G. Eder, A. Portmann †, W. Heitler, B. Welte, P. Hünermann, H. Schlier †, J. B. Metz, K. O. Apel, B. Allemann, K. Löwith †, G. Girardi, G. Picht †, E. Ströker, W. Wieser, F. H. Tenbruck, E. Jüngel, E. O. Czempiel, K. Sontheimer, B. Hassenstein, B. S. Frey, R. Gramlich, P. N. Levinson, H. Mohr, K. Lorenz, H. Zoller, J. Blank, H. Tellenbach, A. Rosenberg.

Die aus den interdisziplinären Kolloquien I–X entstandenen Sammlungen wurden durch die *Schriften zum Weltgespräch* ergänzt. Dadurch war es möglich, entweder in den Gesprächen aufgeworfene Fragen zu vertiefen oder an neue Problemstellungen heranzugehen, und zwar gemäß der Grundintention der Edition „Weltgespräch", aus *ökumenischer Weltverantwortung* zu denken. Die Schriften wurden im Jahre 1966 mit einem Sammelband über *Marxisti-*

*sches und christliches Weltverständnis* (mit Beiträgen von B. Bosnjak, W. Dantine, J. Calvez, I. Fetscher) eröffnet. Zwei Jahre später folgte darauf das umfangreiche Werk von O. Loretz und W. Strolz (Hrsg.) über *Die hermeneutische Frage in der Theologie*. Es war der Versuch, mit namhaften jüdischen, evangelischen und katholischen Theologen, mit Philosophen und Psychologen an die Entfaltung der Frage heranzutreten, welche hermeneutischen Grundsätze heute die Begegnung mit der Bibel kennzeichnen. Diese Erörterung vollzog sich auch auf dem Hintergrund der philosophischen Analyse der Sprache durch Wittgenstein und Heidegger. Es kam dabei die tiefe Kluft zwischen einer ursprünglichen Spracherfahrung und der Sprachauslegung der Metaphysik zum Vorschein. Die Theologie ist insofern von dieser philosophischen Sprachkritik betroffen, als sie Leitbegriffe der abendländischen Metaphysik bisher für ihre Selbstbegründung als Wissenschaft immer wieder herangezogen hat. Wie aber, wenn gemäß der biblischen Offenbarung nicht das Sein, der Geist, nicht ein letzter Grund, nicht die Idee des Guten oder die Sprache, sondern das *Wort* Fleisch geworden ist (Joh 1, 14)? Das genannte Werk spiegelt etwas von dem gewaltigen Spannungsverhältnis wider, das durch den Unterschied zwischen der Sprache des Glaubens und der Sache des Denkens gekennzeichnet ist.

Mit dem Werk von P. Duployé *Die Religiöse Botschaft Charles Péguys* wurde die Reihe fortgesetzt. Dieser ärgerniserregende Dichter und Denker der Inkarnation steht hier als der leidenschaftliche Anwalt eines ökumenischen Denkens vor uns, das konsequent seinem Leitspruch folgte: „Man darf Gott nie gegen jemanden lieben!" Durch seine scharfsinnige Kritik der rationalistischen Philosophie und Theologie, durch die Wiedergewinnung der bleibenden Wahrheit des griechischen Mythos, durch seine Solidarität mit Menschen jüdischen Glaubens erscheint Péguy als ein wegweisender Vorläufer einer Glaubensgestalt, in der Geschöpflichkeit und Prophetie zeitkritisch und furchtlos miteinander verbunden sind. Mit dem Buch *Jüdische Hoffnungskraft und christlicher Glaube*, herausgegeben von W. Strolz, wurde die durch einige Kolloquien schon eingeleitete christliche Begegnung mit dem Judentum weitergeführt. Jüdische, evangelische und katholische Autoren stellen sich hier im übereinstimmenden Bewußtsein, daß mit dem Geschehen von Auschwitz jüdischer und christlicher Glaube vor die schärfste Herausforderung und tiefreichendste Erschütterung der Glaubensgewißheit gestellt sind, der Existenzfrage nach der weiterbestehenden Glaubwürdigkeit der biblischen Botschaft. Vergegenwärtigt wird das Geheimnis des geschichtlichen Fortlebens des Judentums, es

220

wird gezeigt, welche Bedeutung die biblischen Landverheißungen für die Erfahrung der ungekündigten Bundestreue Gottes haben. Es wird der unaufhebbaren Auserwählung Israels *gegenüber* der Kirche nachgedacht und darüber hinaus gefragt, wo in den neueren revolutionären Bewegungen jüdisch-prophetisches Erbe durchschlägt. Die Autorenschaft dieses Buches bestätigt die Einsicht Martin Bubers: „Sobald es uns, Christen und Juden, wirklich um Gott selber und nicht bloß um unsere Gottesbilder zu tun ist, sind wir, Juden und Christen, in der Ahnung verbunden, daß das Haus unseres Vaters anders beschaffen ist, als unsere menschlichen Grundrisse meinen."

Mit der Sammlung *Spricht Gott in der Geschichte* wurde vor dem Beginn der internationalen Religionsgespräche der Stiftung OD noch einmal eine aktuelle theologische Fragestellung aufgenommen, die man mit den Leitbegriffen Religion – Glaube – Geschichte – Säkularisierung umschreiben kann. Dieses Werk, mit Beiträgen von F. H. Tenbruck, G. Klein, E. Jüngel, A. Sand, hilft der Erkenntnis zum Durchbruch, daß die unaufhebbare Unsicherheit, welche die conditio humana bestimmt, im Wagnis des Glaubens Freiheit schafft. Es denkend verantworten heißt darauf achten, daß die biblisch vielfach bezeugte Differenz zwischen Heil und Geschichte keiner gesellschaftlichen und politischen Reduktion des Christlichen, aber ebensowenig einer heilsgeschichtlichen Konstruktion geopfert wird.

## Dialog mit den monotheistischen Religionen

Durch die Kolloquien der Edition „Weltgespräch" wurden in der Zeit von 1965 bis 1972 einige fundamentale Voraussetzungen für den Beginn der Bemühungen der Stiftung OD um die Freilegung der künftigen *Konturen einer großen Ökumene* geschaffen. Das christliche Gespräch mit anderen Weltreligionen ist, soll es auch nur ansatzweise gelingen, an die Klärung anthropologischer, philosophischer, moralischer, psychologischer, sprachlicher Vorbedingungen und Sachverhalte gebunden. Durch die Einübung in das interdisziplinäre Gespräch, durch die besondere Berücksichtigung der spannungsvollen Beziehung zwischen Wissenschaft und Glaube, durch den Tiefgang der philosophischen Besinnung und durch die selbstkritische Einstimmung in das christlich-jüdische Gespräch wurden gute Vorbedingungen für die Planung und Durchführung der neuen Aufgabe erarbeitet. Wer nicht in langmütiger Übung gelernt hat, auf den Andern zu hören, auf das von ihm Gesagte einzugehen, es fragend zu würdigen und bisweilen auch kritisch in Frage zu stellen; wer nicht in der Lage ist, das Anderssein des Andersgläubigen unverkürzt zu akzeptieren, wer von seinem Hang nicht lassen kann, andere Grundpositionen des Denkens und des Glaubens mit der eigenen Basis zu verrechnen, der ist für den Dialog nicht geeignet.

Im Herbst 1972 erteilte Theophil Herder-Dorneich, der Vorsitzende der Stiftung, dem Berichterstatter den Auftrag, das Gespräch mit Vertretern der monotheistischen Religionen vorzubereiten. Judentum, Christentum und Islam, deren *gemeinsamer* Glaubensvater *Abraham* ist, sollten nach der Art ihrer Gotteserfahrung hinsichtlich ihrer je eigenen Glaubensüberlieferung und angesichts der heutigen geschichtlichen Situation befragt werden. Diese Grundabsicht erwies sich bald als sehr fruchtbar, denn es kann nicht der Sinn ökumenischer Gespräche sein, in den bloß historischen Vergleich auszuweichen, ohne daß wir uns den Kernfragen des Glaubens stellen, wie sie uns heute aufgegeben sind. „Vergangenes historisch artikulieren heißt nicht", so formulierte Walter Benjamin einmal das Verhältnis zwischen Überlieferung und Gegenwart, „es erkennen, ‚wie es denn eigentlich gewesen ist'. Es heißt, sich einer Erinnerung bemächtigen, wie sie im Augenblick einer Gefahr aufblitzt ... In jeder Epoche muß versucht werden, die Überlieferung von neuem dem Konformismus abzugewinnen, der im Begriff steht, sie zu überwältigen." Der Bischof von Aachen, Klaus Hemmerle – während seiner Freiburger Zeit wiederholt Teilnehmer an Kolloquien –, hat anläßlich seiner Weihe zum Bischof im Dom zu Aachen in sehr eindrucksvoller Weise von dieser (oder: der) ‚großen Ökumene' gesprochen, die Judentum, Christentum und Islam umfaßt, und hat zur Mitarbeit bei ihrer Verwirklichung aufgerufen.

Mit einem jüdisch-christlichen Kolloquium über *Das Vaterunser* – Gemeinsames im Beten von Juden und Christen, hrsg. von M. Brocke, J. J. Petuchowski und W. Strolz (Band 1 in der „*Schriftenreihe zur großen Ökumene"*), wurden die Religionsgespräche der Stiftung OD eröffnet. Es ist in der Wurzel des biblischen Glaubens begründet, daß das *Vatersein Gottes* (Mal 2, 10; Eph 4, 6) für das ganze Menschengeschlecht eine zentrale Offenbarungswahrheit der gnadenhaften Selbsterschließung Gottes ist. Sie ist nicht nur ein besonderer Anknüpfungspunkt für die weltumfassende Ausweitung der Ökumene, sondern Gott *als Vater* erkennen und lieben heißt, die *entscheidende Möglichkeitsbedingung* jeder ökumenischen Bemühung im Glauben wahrzunehmen. Deshalb ist das Gebet Jesu, das Vaterun-

222

ser, *der* ökumenische Grundtext. Die Erläuterung der jüdischen Gebetstexte gemäß der sieben Leitworte des Vaterunsers machen den christlichen Leser mit einer biblisch-nachbiblischen Tradition vertraut, die im Judentum seit vielen Jahrhunderten existenzerhaltend wirkt. Was die „Heiligung des Namens" im jüdischen Beten für das Leben in dieser Welt bedeutet, wird ebenso offenkundig wie die Erfahrung, daß Gott als Vater und König in geschichtlicher Treue von Geschlecht zu Geschlecht und in wirkmächtiger Transzendenz zugleich gegenwärtig ist.

Was das heißt, tritt gerade durch den Unterschied hervor, der zwischen griechisch-kosmologischer Frömmigkeit (Zeus-Hymnus des Kleanthes) und der biblisch-jüdischen Gebetssprache besteht. Die christlichen Autoren dieses Werkes vermitteln durch ihre Beiträge einen wissenschaftlich-exegetisch und existentiell in gleicher Weise perspektivenreichen Einblick in den Geist des Vaterunsers, wie er aus den alt- und neutestamentlichen Quellen zu uns spricht. Die Gebetserfahrung Jesu wird als ein Dokument seines Glaubens und seiner Menschlichkeit erschlossen, ein Dokument, das in seinen tragenden Grundworten in der Kontinuität biblisch-nachbiblisch-jüdischen Glaubens, Betens und Handelns steht.

Das Gespräch zwischen Vertretern der christlichen Theologie, des Islam und der Islamistik aus drei Kontinenten wurde in seinem Ergebnis unter dem Titel *Glauben an den Einen Gott* – Menschliche Gotteserfahrung im Christentum und im Islam, herausgegeben von A. Falaturi und W. Strolz (Band 2), veröffentlicht. Als *gemeinsames* Glaubensbekenntnis konnte beim zweiten Religionsgespräch der Glaube an den Schöpfergott und an ein Letztes Gericht vorausgesetzt werden. Diese Gemeinsamkeit zwischen Christentum und Islam darf allerdings nicht dazu führen, die tiefreichenden Unterschiede zwischen diesen Religionen zu übersehen. In Freiburg brachen sie voll bei der Darstellung des islamischen Jesus-Bildes, in der genaueren Bestimmung der Beziehung zwischen Offenbarung und Tradition und in der Auslegung der islamischen Zeit- und Geschichtserfahrung auf. Von ihr aus ist die Rede von einer „Heilsgeschichte" im jüdisch-christlichen Glaubensverständnis unmöglich. Zu Annäherungen führte hingegen die Analyse der Folgen der Säkularisierung für das Christentum und den Islam, ferner die Wahrnehmung der mystischen Dimension des islamischen Monotheismus und die für beide Religionen bestimmende Einsicht in die Bedeutung poetischer Sprache für die Glaubenserfahrung.

Das *dritte* Freiburger Religionsgespräch versammelte Vertreter des Judentums, des Christentums und des Islam zu einer gemeinsamen Besinnung auf Grundpositionen der monotheistischen Religionen. Das Ergebnis dieser Begegnung, an der Autoren aus europäischen Ländern, aus Israel, West-Afrika, Indien und den USA teilgenommen haben, liegt unter dem Titel *Drei Wege zu dem Einen Gott* – Glaubenserfahrung in den monotheistischen Religionen, herausgegeben von A. Falaturi, J. J. Petuchowski und W. Strolz (Band 3), vor. Als alle Teilnehmer be-wegende Hoffnung erwies sich der in Bibel und Koran ausgesprochene Glaube an die Einzigkeit und Unvergleichbarkeit Gottes im Geheimnis seiner majestätischen Transzendenz. Sie wird durch die Propheten Israels bezeugt, und sie findet ihren Niederschlag in der Erfahrung der Zeitlosigkeit und geschichtlichen Wirksamkeit der Tora in der jüdischen Glaubenserfahrung. In Freiburg wurden aber keineswegs nur grundsätzliche Glaubensfragen der monotheistischen Religionen diskutiert. Mehrere Beiträge richteten sich auf ganz praktische Fragen, wie die Nachahmung Gottes im Judentum oder die Erläuterung der Prinzipien religiöser Erziehung im heutigen Islam. Abschließend wurde freimütig und solidarisch über die Weltverantwortung der Offenbarungsreligionen gesprochen.

Als eine Einübung in den ökumenischen Gebetsgeist des Glaubens an Gott als den Einzigen, den Vater aller Menschen, sind zwei Schriften zu verstehen, die ebenfalls innerhalb der Veröffentlichungen der Stiftung OD erschienen sind, nämlich *Du, unser Vater* (Jüdische Gebete für Christen), ausgewählt und übersetzt von Pnina Navè, und *Denn Dein ist das Reich* (Gebete aus dem Islam), ausgewählt und übersetzt von A. Schimmel mit einem Vorwort von Sergio Kardinal Pignedoli.

Zu den kostbarsten mitmenschlichen Erfahrungen gerade dieser Religionsgespräche rechnet der Berichterstatter die im Dialog gemachte Entdeckung der *Unverfügbarkeit des Andersgläubigen*. Was heißt das näherhin?

Es gilt, hinter allen Worten des jüdischen, des christlichen und des muslimischen Glaubens das ursprüngliche Du des Mitmenschen, des Gesprächspartners, wahrzunehmen. Wir sind leicht geneigt, die ökumenische Bedeutung dieser Erfahrung, die unmittelbar mit der unantastbaren Würde des Menschen als Person gegeben ist, zu unterschätzen. Sie besagt, daß der Mensch über die Verschiedenheit der Glaubensbekenntnisse und Religionen hinaus in das Geheimnis des Unverfügbaren weist. Ja, dieses ist selbst als verborgenes der tragende Ursprung alles dessen, was die Glaubenden einander sagen können und wovor sie vielleicht auch bisweilen in Schweigen verharren. Wer das Geheimnis der Person ehrt und

224

mit dem Propheten darauf hört, daß jeder unaustauschbar bei seinem Namen gerufen ist, dem erschließt sich der Raum der zwischenmenschlichen Begegnung in seiner ontologischen Wesenstiefe. Von ihm her erweist sich dann auch das Glaubensgespräch, fern von jedem Zwang, als ein Akt der menschlichen Freiheit – und vor Gott, dem Einzigen, als freie Huldigung.

Und noch eine andere wesentliche Erfahrung muß festgehalten werden, weil sie unmittelbar mit dem Langmut und der Unterscheidungskraft zusammenhängt, die das Gespräch mit den Weltreligionen von uns fordert, wenn es weitergedeihen und nicht in Resignation oder Synkretismus versanden soll. Wer über die Chancen der großen Ökumene nachdenkt, wird der Frage nicht ausweichen können, inwiefern das monotheistische Glaubensbekenntnis in sich selbst *vorläufig* ist, unabgeschlossen in der Völkerwelt, so lange, bis Gott *dereinst* der Einzige und sein Name einzig auf der ganzen Erde sein *wird* (Sach 14,9; 1 Kor 15,28). Ist dies einmal erkannt, dann wird es eine christliche Theologie der Religionen ohne einen *messianisch* bestimmten Christusglauben nicht geben.

Von der *englischen* Ausgabe der Gespräche mit Vertretern des Judentums und des Islam sind bisher folgende Titel erschienen:
Brocke / Petuchowski (Hrsg.): The Lord's Prayer and Jewish Liturgy;
Falaturi / Schimmel (Hrsg.): We Believe in One God.
Die englische Ausgabe des ersten Trialogs „Drei Wege zu dem Einen Gott" ist vorgesehen.

## Religiöse Grunderfahrungen

Durch den Vergleich, die Zuordnung und Abgrenzung der Glaubenserfahrungen in den monotheistischen Religionen erhob sich eine Frage von grundsätzlicher anthropologischer Bedeutung. Sie läßt sich auf folgende Weise formulieren: Gehen nicht dem möglichen Empfang einer göttlichen Offenbarung in Zeit und Geschichte, ihrem Verständnis und ihrer Bezeugung religiöse Grunderfahrungen voraus, die *allgemeinmenschlich* sind? Ist es zum tieferen Verständnis einer Offenbarungsreligion nicht notwendig, darüber nachzudenken, wie sich diese aus der Geschöpflichkeit des Menschen entspringenden religiösen Urerfahrungen in der Begegnung mit der Natur und den Mächten der geschichtlichen Welt, mit sich selbst und mit dem Tod manifestieren? Könnte eine solche Besinnung nicht die *menschliche* Basis der Glaubwürdigkeit der Religionen erweitern? Bedarf der interreligiöse Dialog, soll er von apologetischen Engpässen und von gesprächslos gesetzten Absolutheitsansprüchen frei bleiben, nicht dieser Auslegung *anthropologisch-religiöser Konstanten* des Menschseins? Und ferner: wie sollen auch zureichende Voraussetzungen für den christlichen Dialog mit den Fernöstlichen Religionen ohne eine Phänomenologie religiöser Grunderfahrungen, die zu den Wesenszügen aller Religionen gehören, geschaffen werden?

Weil die Verantwortlichen der Stiftung OD davon überzeugt waren und sind, daß es sich so verhält, wurde für die Zeit von 1976–1979 ein Dreierzyklus von Kolloquien über religiöse Grunderfahrungen geplant und teilweise auch schon durchgeführt. Das *erste* Kolloquium dieser zweiten Gruppe der Freiburger Religionsgespräche behandelte das Verhältnis von Göttern und Menschen in der Antike, die bleibende Bedeutung mythischer Redeweise im Alten Testament und die weisheitliche Überlieferung in der Predigt Jesu. In mehreren phänomenologisch-historisch ausgerichteten Beiträgen wurden kosmische Grunderfahrungen mittelalterlicher Heilkunde, die Wandlungsvorgänge innerhalb der religiösen Erfahrung im Denken und Dichten des 20. Jahrhunderts und tiefenpsychologische Aspekte des Verhältnisses von Religion und Glaube erläutert. Das *zweite* Kolloquium über religiöse Grunderfahrungen hatte einen Schwerpunkt in der Auslegung *jüdischer* religiöser Anthropologie. So wurde die Gestalt des Melchisedek in einer mutigen Auslegung durch J. J. Petuchowski als eine biblische Leitfigur für die große Ökumene dargestellt. Die Frage der *anthropomorphistischen* Redeweise von Gott in jüdischer Gottesbegegnung wurde dahingehend beantwortet, daß das glaubende Judentum durch deren Bewahrung die immer wieder drohende Gefahr einer Vergeistigung und Entgeschichtlichung der Gotteserfahrung überwinden konnte. Die Analyse psychischer Ursprünge und Strukturen des Religiösen führte auch zur Erkenntnis seiner *kosmischen* Eingebundenheit, während der Beitrag über die Naturbegegnung als religiöses Erlebnis die Kategorien Ehrfurcht und Lobpreis als religiöse Antwort auf den ausbeuterischen Umgang mit der Natur ins Spiel brachte.

Die Ergebnisse dieser beiden Religionsgespräche sind, jeweils herausgegeben von W. Strolz, unter dem Titel *Religiöse Grunderfahrungen* – Quellen und Gestalten (Band 4) und *Kosmische Dimensionen religiöser Erfahrung* (Band 5) 1977 bzw. 1978 erschienen. Als dritte Veranstaltung innerhalb dieses Zyklus wurde im Herbst 1979 ein interdisziplinäres Kolloquium über *Religiöse Bewußtseinsbildung* – Leitfragen und Grundthemen – durchgeführt. An diesem Gespräch

226

waren folgende Wissenschaftsgebiete beteiligt: Religionsphilosophie, Literatur- und Musikwissenschaft, Ökologie, Pastoraltheolo-
gie, Religionspädagogik und Dogmatik. Die Ergebnisse kann man
dahingehend zusammenfassen, daß es gelungen ist, den überlie-
ferten Leitbegriff „religiöse Bewußtseinsbildung" über seine
kirchlich-theologische Bedeutung hinaus in die viel breiter ange-
legte Diskussion über die bleibenden anthropologischen Elemente
der Religion zu stellen. Die Ergebnisse sind – wieder unter der Her-
ausgeberschaft von W. Strolz – unter dem Titel *Religiöse Bewußtseinsbildung* – Leitfragen und Grundthemen als Band 6 erschienen.

Die interdisziplinären Gespräche über religiöse Grunderfahrungen haben vor allem die *unreduzierbare Vielfalt* des Religiösen wieder
ans Licht gebracht. Sie kann weder philosophisch noch theologisch
so systematisiert werden, als ob es möglich wäre, die Phänomene
religiöser Erfahrung auf *einen* Nenner zu bringen. Es kommt im Ge-
genteil alles darauf an, sie in ihrem nicht ersetzbaren Reichtum zu
bewahren, denn an der menschlichen Gottesbegegnung ist die Vielstimmigkeit der sprachlichen und bildnerischen Kräfte der Seele,
der Vernunft und des Gemüts beteiligt. Wo sie nicht ins Auge gefaßt
und mit umsichtiger Entschiedenheit festgehalten wird, ist die ra-
tionalistische Austrocknung der religiösen Anlagen des Menschen
ebenso unaufhaltsam wie die lehrhafte Erstarrung ihrer geschichtlichen Überlieferungen.

Wer vom biblischen Glauben herkommend nach einem Bild für
den Einheit gebenden Ursprung der Vielfalt religiöser Grunderfahrungen über die Zeiten hinweg sucht, kann sich an die biblische Ur-
geschichte halten. Denken, Dichten und Glauben stehen gemäß
mythischer Sprache unter dem Bogen des Einen Bundes, der sich
nach der Verheißung an Noah unwiderruflich über alles Geschaffene spannt (1 Mos 9,8–17).

In das erweiterte Blickfeld der Auslegung religiöser Grunderfahrungen gehören die Kolloquien „Anthropologie des Kults" und
„Schöpfung und Sprache". Inwiefern ist der Mensch kraft seiner
Geschöpflichkeit als ein Wesen anzusehen, zu dessen Seinsverfas-
sung auch die *kultische Dimension* gehört? Diese Frage wurde von so-
ziologischer, religionsphilosophischer, psychopathologischer und
von theologischer Seite aus behandelt. Das Gespräch führte zur
Entdeckung von anthropologisch hochbedeutsamen Konstanten
menschlicher Existenz in der vermittelten Erfahrung des Göttlichen
angesichts seiner kultischen Manifestation. Die zeitkritische Bedeutung gerade dieser interdisziplinären Begegnung liegt darin,

daß sich die kultische Weltauslegung und der ihr angeborene Schöpfungslobpreis – jedenfalls was die monotheistischen Weltreligionen betrifft – heute als lebensbewahrende Alternative zur wissenschaftlich-technischen Weltbeherrschung erweist. Das Ergebnis des Kolloquiums mit Beiträgen von A. Hahn, P. Hünermann, H. Mühlen, R. Schaeffler, H. Tellenbach wurde 1977 unter dem Titel *Anthropologie des Kults* veröffentlicht.

Mit dem Kolloquium über „Schöpfung und Sprache", an dem sich Vertreter der alttestamentlichen Exegese und der Literaturwissenschaft beteiligten, wurde ein erster Schritt zur Entfaltung einer *alle* Bereiche menschlichen Daseins konstituierenden Grunderfahrung gemacht. An die schon vor-gegebene Schöpfung ist menschlicher Weltaufenthalt vielstimmig immer gebunden, und ohne die Sprache käme er in kein verstehendes, erkennendes Verhältnis zur Natur und zu sich selbst. Die Exposition dieser Thematik richtete sich zunächst auf die Vergegenwärtigung der Schöpfung durch das Wort gemäß biblischer Überlieferung. Ergänzt wurde die theologische Fragestellung durch eine feinsinnige Erläuterung der Sprache des Schöpfungslobes in den Psalmen. Darauf folgten vier literaturwissenschaftliche Beiträge zur Sprache als dichterische Schöpfung im Werk Goethes, zum Phänomen des säkularisierten schöpferischen Wortes in Gedichten des 20. Jahrhunderts und eine Interpretation des Hauptwerkes von Hermann Broch „Der Tod des Vergil". Dieses Werk, das man als die umfassendste dichterische Spracherfahrung im Umgang mit dem Unaussprechlichen in unserer Zeit bezeichnen darf, läßt die Möglichkeit der Schöpfungserneuerung aus dem Quell der Sprache erahnen. Das Kolloquium wurde mit literaturwissenschaftlichen Vorüberlegungen zur Analyse und Überwindung der Sprachohnmacht heutiger Verkündigung abgeschlossen. Die Veröffentlichung der genannten Beiträge ist unter dem Titel *Schöpfung und Sprache* (hrsg. von W. Strolz) im Herbst 1979 erschienen.

## Perspektiven künftiger Religionsgespräche

Im Februar 1978 entsandte der Vorsitzende der Stiftung OD den Berichterstatter aufgrund einer Einladung des Weltrats der Kirchen in Genf zu einem *christlich-buddhistischen Dialog* nach Colombo/Sri Lanka. Die Hauptstadt des ehemaligen Ceylon wurde in den letzten Jahren durch zahlreiche ökumenische Konferenzen als Begegnungsort der Weltreligionen ein bevorzugter Platz besonders für

den christlichen Dialog mit Buddhismus und Hinduismus. Die unmittelbar durch die Folgen der Umweltzerstörung hervorgerufene
Hauptfragestellung der hier erwähnten Konsultation richtete sich
auf die Freilegung der religiösen Dimension in den Beziehungen
des Menschen zur Natur. Die Begegnung mit hervorragenden Vertretern des Buddhismus aus Sri Lanka, Hongkong und Thailand,
die, was die Darstellung der christlichen Position betrifft, durch ein
vom Berichterstatter verfaßtes und ins Englische übersetztes Memo-
randum mit vorbereitet wurde, erwies sich für die Fortführung der
ökumenischen Initiative der Stiftung OD als folgenreich. In Colombo wurden diese Bemühungen von einer international breit ge-
streuten Teilnehmerschaft nicht nur respektvoll begrüßt. Es ent-
stand durch die gründliche und geduldige Besinnung auf die christliche und buddhistische Tradition der Naturbegegnung und der
kosmischen Verflochtenheit aller Dinge ein *gemeinsames* Verantwor-
tungsgefühl für die Bewahrung der Natur *aus religiöser Integrations-
kraft.* Das Gespräch von Colombo bestätigte aber auch die anthro-
pologische Bedeutung der Kolloquien über *religiöse Grunderfahrungen* gerade für die christliche Begegnung mit der Spiritualität des
Fernen Ostens.

Durch diese Erfahrungen ermutigt, beauftragte Theophil Herder-Dorneich den Berichterstatter nach seiner Rückkehr aus Colombo Ende Februar 1978 mit der Vorbereitung von Religionsge-
sprächen zwischen Christentum, Buddhismus und Hinduismus.
Weil die *bleibende Pluralität der Weltreligionen* eine Realität der Geschichte ist und die Menschheit von Jahr zu Jahr mehr zu einer glo-
balen Einheit zusammenwächst, ist auch der Dialog zwischen verschiedenen religiösen Überlieferungen ein Gebot der Stunde. Die
Bemühungen um die Vollgestalt einer großen Ökumene verlangen
*in offener Treue zum Christlichen,* daß die Grenzmarken im interreligi-
ösen Dialog weit in bisher unbetretenes Land hinaus versetzt werden. Der Wahrheitsanspruch des christlichen Glaubens ist in eine
neue Phase seiner geschichtlichen Bewährung eingetreten. Ist der
Gott der biblischen Offenbarung, der Gott Jesu Christi, der eine Vater aller Menschen (Eph 4,6), so stellt sich jetzt unabweisbar die
Frage, welche Bedeutung *diese* Glaubenserfahrung für das Verständnis und die partnerschaftliche Anerkennung der nichtchristli-
chen Religionen hat. Dieser epochale Wandel ist mit der Auflösung
der bisherigen Vorherrschaft der Denkweise abendländischer
Theologie und des ihr zugehörigen Missionsverständnisses verbunden. Wenn es auch außerhalb des Christentums seit Jahrtausenden Heilswege gibt, dann ist jetzt die Zeit reif zu fragen, ob nicht die

Religionsgeschichte überhaupt im erweiterten Horizont der nunmehr konkret erfahrenen Einheit der Weltgeschichte *als vielstimmige* und nicht auf *einen* Absolutheitsanspruch reduzierbare Heilserfahrung auszulegen ist. Schon diese Andeutungen lassen auf die Schwierigkeiten schließen, die philosophisch und theologisch zu überwinden sind, wenn es zu einem Dialog in freimütiger Offenheit und ohne ängstliche Absicherungsmaßnahmen kommen soll.

Mit der 4. Phase der ökumenischen Bemühungen der Stiftung Oratio Dominica im Jahre 1980 greift sie zum erstenmal über den Bereich der monotheistischen Religionen hinaus, indem auch das christliche Gespräch mit den Fernöstlichen Religionen auf das Dialogprogramm gesetzt wird. An dieser Stelle ist es besonders wichtig, sich die grund-legende Bedeutung der bisherigen Monotheismus-Gespräche und ihre konsequente Weiterführung gerade für diesen neuen Schritt im Horizont einer *universalen* Ökumene zu vergegenwärtigen. Die Kenntnis der Überlieferung, aus der der eigene Glaube stammt, ist eine unumgängliche Voraussetzung für das Gespräch mit Andersgläubigen. Wenn also die Stiftung Oratio Dominica jetzt in das erst beginnende *Weltgespräch der Religionen* eintritt, zu dem das Zweite Vatikanische Konzil die Christen aufgerufen hat, so tut sie dies vorbereitet durch die vorangegangene Glaubensbesinnung unter den Bekennern des Monotheismus und durch weitere Begegnungen mit Juden und Muslimen.

Für die Zeit von 1980–1984 sind 4 Religionsgespräche geplant, deren thematische Schwerpunkte das *Offenbarungsverständnis* und Fragen der *Eschatologie* in den Weltreligionen sein werden. Im folgenden soll wenigstens andeutungsweise gezeigt werden, in welche Richtung diese kommenden Begegnungen weisen.

Das Religionsgespräch von 1980 galt dem Offenbarungsverständnis im Judentum und im Christentum. Hervorragende Interpreten des jüdischen Glaubens aus Israel und den USA dachten zusammen mit dialogerprobten christlichen Theologen über die Offenbarung – die Gründungs- und Lebensurkunde ihrer Glaubensexistenz – nach. Das Programm verband die historische mit der existentiellen Fragestellung auf eine Weise, daß dadurch das große und fruchtbare Spannungsverhältnis von Offenbarung und Überlieferung, von Zukunftsgewißheit und gegenwärtiger Glaubensbewährung, im Zeitalter nach Auschwitz sichtbar wurde. Maimonides, Spinoza, Rosenzweig und Buber wurden mit ihrem Offenbarungsverständnis ebenso zur Diskussion gestellt wie die Wandlungen des christlichen Offenbarungsverständnisses durch das Konzil und die Frage nach den Perspektiven eines messianischen Chri-

230

stusglaubens im Gespräch mit der jüdischen Messiaserwartung. Die Ergebnisse dieses Symposions wurden im Band 7: *Offenbarung im jüdischen und christlichen Glaubensverständnis* (hrsg. J. J. Petuchowski und W. Strolz) niedergelegt.

Erst nach dieser biblischen Grundlagenbesinnung war es sinnvoll, den Dialog mit Hinduismus und Buddhismus über ihr jeweiliges Offenbarungsverständnis aufzunehmen. Dies geschah im Herbst 1981. Vertreter des Hinduismus aus Indien, des Buddhismus aus Sri Lanka und des Zen-Buddhismus aus Japan erläuterten mit führenden Vertretern der ökumenischen Theologie aus Europa und fernöstlichen Ländern, wie in diesen Religionen Offenbarung erfahren, überliefert und je neu ausgelegt wird. Hauptgesichtspunkte dieser Begegnung waren: Offenbarung im Christentum und Transzendenzerfahrung im Hinduismus als Vollzugshorizont des Heils – biblischer Schöpfungsglaube und kosmische Frömmigkeit in fernöstlichen Überlieferungen – negative Theologie im Christentum und gott-lose Befreiung im Verständnis des Zen-Buddhismus – Endgültigkeit und universale Bedeutung des Christusereignisses angesichts verschiedener Offenbarungsansprüche. In Band 8 der *Schriftenreihe zur großen Ökumene* werden die Beiträge dieses Symposions, herausgegeben von W. Strolz und S. Ueda, unter dem Titel: *Offenbarung als Heilserfahrung im Hinduismus, Buddhismus und im Christentum,* 1982 veröffentlicht werden.

Im Spätherbst 1982 werden Juden, Christen und Muslime zu einem Religionsgespräch mit der Leitthematik „Messianismus und Eschatologie in den monotheistischen Religionen" zusammenkommen.

Die Bekenner des Monotheismus werden zu fragen haben, was ihr Glaube jeweils von den Letzten Dingen verkündet. Sich darauf zu besinnen, ist für die monotheistischen Religionen von lebensentscheidender Bedeutung, weil nicht weniger als die Hoffnung auf die endzeitliche Vollendung aller Dinge in Gericht und Neuschöpfung daran hängt. Zur Aufgabe dieses Religionsgespräches wird es gehören, die Hauptlinien der Eschatologie im Judentum, im Christentum und im Islam herauszustellen. Dazu ist beispielsweise die Antwort auf die Frage zu rechnen, welcher Unterschied im jüdischen Glauben zwischen der Erwartung des Messias und der „kommenden Welt" besteht. Wie versteht das unerlöste Volk der Erlösung gegenüber dem Christentum die gottbestimmte Zukunft des Menschen? Wie ist heute die verborgene Endgültigkeit der Herrschaft Christi auszulegen? Es wird weiter von christlicher Seite zu fragen sein, inwiefern der Glaube an den wiederkommenden Christus zusammen mit der messianischen Hoffnung des Judentums eine Kritik jeder menschlichen Absolutsetzung bedeutet. Eine weitere Fragestellung gilt dem innersten Zusammenhang von Schöpfungsglaube und Eschatologie in den monotheistischen Religionen. Was den Islam angeht, wird speziell die Lehre von der Vorherbestimmung und der Glaubensbereich Auferstehung-Jüngstes Gericht-Paradies zur Diskussion gestellt werden müssen. Außerdem wird zu fragen sein, wie der Islam die fortdauernde Wirksamkeit des Bösen in der Weltgeschichte beurteilt, ohne den Begriff der Heilsgeschichte im jüdisch-christlichen Sinn zu kennen.

Nach dieser Vergegenwärtigung der messianischen Hoffnung und Eschatologie gemäß Bibel und Koran ist für den Herbst 1983 ein abendländisches *Mystik-Kolloquium* geplant. Schon durch das erste fernöstliche Religionsgespräch im September 1981 hat sich nämlich gezeigt, wie unverzichtbar für die christliche Seite im Gegenüber zu Hinduismus und Buddhismus die Vertiefung in die *eigene* Tradition der Nichts-Erfahrung, des Unsagbaren ist. Sie wird im Hinblick auf die Leitgestalten Meister Eckart, Nicolaus von Cusa und Johannes vom Kreuz erläutert. Welche *Sprachwege ins Unsagbare* weisen diese Klassiker? Und welche Fragestellung wird der Kernpunkt des Kolloquiums sein?

Es ist das Existenzproblem der mystischen Erfahrung des Nichts in der abendländisch-christlichen Überlieferung. Es ist jene Weise der Gottesbegegnung, die Gott als mit *nichts* vergleichbar erfährt (Jes 45.5). Von hier aus ist dann zu fragen, ob damit nicht ein Ansatzpunkt gegeben wäre, von dem aus der Dialog mit den Religionen Asiens und ihren spirituellen Heilswegen *ursprünglicher* als bisher geführt werden könnte.

Erst *nach* diesem Schritt, nach der fragenden Durchdringung der eigenen Erfahrungsmöglichkeit des Nichts, des Unsagbaren, der radikalen Unvergleichbarkeit Gottes in allem Sagbaren, ist eine wesentliche Voraussetzung für die Durchführung des *zweiten fernöstlichen Religionsgespräches* der Stiftung Oratio Dominica im Herbst 1984 gegeben. Es wird sich mit der *eschatologischen* Dimension der Heilsbotschaft des Hinduismus und Buddhismus befassen. Das ist um so schwieriger, als diese Religionen weder um einen Schöpfungsglauben, noch um eine Eschatologie im biblischen Verständnis wissen. Wo soll aber dann christlicher Glaube im Dialog mit fernöstlicher Religiosität ansetzen, wenn es sich so verhält? Es wird zunächst einmal darauf ankommen, von den anwesenden Hindus und Buddhisten zu erfahren, welche Zeit- und Geschichtserfahrung jeweils ihrer Religion im Unterschied zur biblischen Überlieferung zugrunde liegt. Tod, Wiedergeburt, kosmische Erneuerung, haben hier mit geschichtlichen Ereignissen, auf die sich jüdisch-christlicher Glaube wie auf einen Felsgrund bezieht, nichts zu tun. Kann und darf aber christliche Theologie angesichts der universalen Bedeutung der Christusbotschaft dies annehmen? So ist denn zurückzufragen, ob sich in der Fernöstlichen Befreiungs- und Erlösungserfahrung nicht trotzdem Letzte Dinge zeigen, und zwar allein schon dadurch, daß alle Menschen solidarisch im Geschick der Sterblichkeit, im Prozeß des Werdens und Vergehens miteinander verbunden sind? Ist in dieser Erfahrung aber nicht die des *Nichts* unüberspringbar eingeschlossen? Muß der gemeinsame jüdisch-christliche Glaube an die *Vaterschaft Gottes für alle Menschen* in seiner *eschatologischen* Bedeutung nicht erst noch entdeckt werden, um zu fruchtbarer Auswirkung in der Großen Ökumene zu gelangen, auf daß daraus eine starke Flügelbildung künftigen Glaubens werde?

Der Berichterstatter und wissenschaftliche Leiter der ökumenischen Abteilung der *Stiftung Oratio Dominica* möchte diesen Rückblick und Ausblick nicht abschließen, ohne wenigstens andeutungsweise zu sagen, wie biblische Glaubensgewißheit, schöpferisches Vertrauen und be-wegende Hoffnung zusammenwirken müssen, um den christlichen Dialog mit den Weltreligionen konsequent weiterzuführen. Die *ontologische* Verbundenheit Gottes mit allen Menschen gründet im Glauben an Gott den Schöpfer und Erlöser in der Einheit seines Wirkens in Schöpfung und Geschichte. Der universale Heilswille Gottes umfaßt nicht nur die ganze Menschheit, sondern alles Geschaffene (1 Mos 9,8–17; Röm 8,18–22). Für den christlichen Glauben ist mit dem auferstandenen Christus die eschatologische Herrlichkeit Gottes bereits erschienen. Aber es bleibt zu bedenken, daß die Lebensspannung *dieser* Botschaft in solidarischer Verbundenheit mit ihrer jüdischen Wurzel (Röm 11,18) ein Zeichen bleibt, dem widersprochen wird (Lk 2,34). Diese Widerspruchserfahrung, vom Kreuz aus bis in das letzte Mysterium der Geschichte hinabreichend, darf im Gespräch mit Andersgläubigen nicht aufgelöst, sondern sie muß durchgehalten werden. Jüdisch-christliche Hoffnung ist kein verfügbarer dogmatischer Besitz. Es gibt sie im Grunde nur als geprüfte und umstrittene. Aber gerade in der bevorstehenden Begegnung dieser Offenbarungsreligionen mit Buddhismus und Hinduismus wird noch etwas Anderes wahrzunehmen sein. Was sich widerspricht, was unvereinbar, ja völlig fremd für den jeweiligen Partner im Gespräch mit Fernöstlichen Religionen bleibt, bedeutet neben der Entdeckung dessen, was ver-

233

wandt oder zumindest vergleichbar ist, nichts Letztes, stellt nicht das unübersteigbare Andere dar.

Das majestätische Geheimnis der Transzendenz Gottes (Jes 40,18) waltet machtvoll über allen Unterschieden und Gegensätzen und ermutigt uns, furchtlos dem größeren Gott entgegenzugehen. Nicht Gott, der schlechthin Unvergleichbare, der als der Ewige alles Geschaffene ins Sein gerufen hat, wird größer, sondern die *menschliche* Gotteserkenntnis wächst und weitet sich stufenweise aus, je intensiver das Weltgespräch der Religionen geführt wird. Ihre partnerschaftliche Begegnung, das geschichtliche Fernziel einer universalen Ökumene bleibt für den jüdisch-christlichen Glauben von der eschatologischen Hoffnung erfüllt, daß der Gott Israels dereinst für *alle* Völker der Einzige und sein Name einzig sein wird (Sach 14,9).

# Schriftenreihe zur großen Ökumene

Bisher sind erschienen:
(Die Bestellnummern sind jeweils in Klammern angefügt.)

## Band 1

**Das Vaterunser**
Gemeinsames im Beten von Juden und Christen.
Hrsg. Michael Brocke, Jakob J. Petuchowski und Walter Strolz.
Mit Beiträgen von Johann Barta, Josef Bommer, Michael Brocke,
Alfons Deissler, Baruch Graubard, Simon Lauer, Pnina Navè, Johannes Oesterreicher, Jakob J. Petuchowski, Cornelius A. Rijk,
Walter Strolz, Anton Vögtle. 2. Aufl. 1980 (17079), 285 S.
Zum ersten Mal versuchen in diesem Buch Juden und Christen gemeinsam, das Vaterunser als ökumenisches Gebet auszulegen.
Durch exegetische, liturgische, historische und pastoraltheologische Beiträge wird dieses Gebet als ein Lebensstrom sichtbar, der
Synagoge und Kirche bis zur Stunde nährt und verbindet.

## Band 2

**Glauben an den einen Gott**
Menschliche Glaubenserfahrung im Christentum und im Islam.
Hrsg. Abdoldjavad Falaturi und Walter Strolz.
Mit Beiträgen von Hamid Algar, Peter Antes, Smail Balić, Josef
Blank, Horst Bürkle, Abdoldjavad Falaturi, Richard Gramlich, Rudi
Paret, Annemarie Schimmel, Raymund Schwager. 1975 (17363),
246 S.
Das Jesus-Bild in der heutigen islamischen und christlichen Theologie – Das Verhältnis von Offenbarung und Tradition – Schöpfung
und Geschichte – ferner das Phänomen der Säkularisierung im Islam und im Christentum – diese Themen werden im Horizont des
beide Religionen bestimmenden Monotheismus interpretiert.

## Band 3

**Drei Wege zu dem einen Gott**
Glaubenserfahrung in den monotheistischen Religionen.
Hrsg. Abdoldjavad Falaturi, Jakob J. Petuchowski und Walter
Strolz.
Mit Beiträgen von Hasan Askari, Michael Brocke, Wilhelm Dantine, Abdoldjavad Falaturi, Albert H. Friedlander, Richard Friedli,
Erwin Gräf, Heinrich Groß, Franz Mußner, Engelbert Mveng, Jakob
J. Petuchowski, Michael Winter. 2. Aufl. 1980 (17693), 247 S.
Vertreter der drei monotheistischen Religionen aus mehreren Kontinenten erläutern hier, ökumenisch engagiert, Glaubenserfahrungen von zentraler Bedeutung (Torah-Glaube, Prophetie, Hoffnung
und Weltverantwortung).

Band 4
**Religiöse Grunderfahrungen**
Quellen und Gestalten.
Hrsg. Walter Strolz
Mit Beiträgen von Gerhart Baumann, Josef Goldbrunner, Simon
Lauer, Ulrich Mann, Hans-Peter Müller, Heinrich Schipperges,
Heinz Robert Schlette, Dieter Zeller. 1977 (17956), 208 S.
Dieser Band faßt das Ergebnis eines interdisziplinären Gespräches
zusammen, an dem sich Religionswissenschaftler, Exegeten, Histo-
riker, Philosophen und Literaturwissenschaftler beteiligt haben –
ein Beitrag zur Phänomenologie religiöser Existenzerfahrungen in
Vergangenheit und Gegenwart.

Band 5
**Kosmische Dimensionen religiöser Erfahrung**
Hrsg. Walter Strolz
Mit Beiträgen von Franz Joseph van der Grinten, Johann Maier,
Karlheinz Müller, Jakob J. Petuchowski, Günter Stemberger, Detlev
von Uslar, Heinrich Zoller. 1978 (18100), 249 S.
Ein perspektivenreiches Buch zur kosmischen Einbindung des
Menschseins: wissenschaftlich breit gefächert, tritt es für ein part-
nerschaftliches Verhältnis zwischen Mensch und Natur, Kosmos
und Geschichte, Kunst und Religion ein.

Band 6
**Religiöse Bewußtseinsbildung**
Leitfragen und Grundthemen.
Hrsg. Walter Strolz
Mit Beiträgen von Günter Allner, Otto Betz, Wilhelm Breuning,
Bernhard Casper, Gisbert Kaufmann, Hildemarie Streich, Paul Mi-
chael Zulehner. 1980 (19143), 199 S.
Dieser Band behandelt sprachkritische, musiktherapeutische, öko-
logische, religionsphilosophische und dogmatische Aspekte religi-
öser Bewußtseinsbildung – ein Beitrag zur Wiederentdeckung der
vielstimmigen Einheit menschlicher Vernunft –, Gemüts- und Glau-
benskräfte.

Band 7
**Offenbarung im jüdischen und** christlichen Glaubensverständnis
Hrsg. Jakob J. Petuchowski und Walter Strolz.
Mit Beiträgen von Peter Eicher, Barry S. Kogan, Hans-Joachim
Kraus, Michael A. Meyer, Jakob J. Petuchowski, Rolf Rendtorff,
Max Seckler, Walter Strolz, Shemaryahu Talmon, Dietrich Wieder-
kehr. 1981 (02092), 263 S. (Gleichzeitig Band 92 der „Quaestiones
disputatae".)
Ein ökumenisch wegweisender Beitrag zum thematisch weitge-

spannten Offenbarungsverständnis in jüdischer und christlicher Auslegungsgeschichte. Offenbarung, interpretiert nicht nur als Lebensgrund vergangener Geschlechter, sondern auch als Zukunft eröffnende Glaubensgewißheit.

Band 8
**Offenbarung als Heilserfahrung im Hinduismus, Buddhismus und im Christentum**
Hrsg. Walter Strolz und Shizuteru Ueda. 1982.
Dieses Werk geht auf das erste Religionsgespräch christlicher Theologen, Indologen und Religionswissenschaftler mit Vertretern asiatischer Religionen zurück. Es behandelt eine Frage von grundlegender Bedeutung für die religiöse Existenz- und Welterfahrung des Menschen. Im Mittelpunkt der Beiträge steht die Erläuterung der hinduistisch-buddhistischen Befreiungserfahrung in Zuordnung zum und Abgrenzung vom christlichen Offenbarungsverständnis.

Weitere Bände folgen.

*In englischer Sprache sind bisher erschienen:*
**The Lord's prayer and jewish liturgy**
Edited by Jakob J. Petuchowski and Michael Brocke.
Editiones Herder in Burns & Oates, London. 1978 (086012-063-5) and Seabury Press, New York, 1978 (77-014-701), 224 p.

**We believe in one God**
The Experience of God in Christianity and Islam.
Edited by Annemarie Schimmel and Abdoldjavad Falaturi.
Editiones Herder in Burns & Oates, London, 1979, and Seabury Press, New York, 1979 (beide Ausgaben mit derselben Bestellnummer: 086012-078-3), 181 p.

In Vorbereitung:
**Three ways to one God**
Edited by Jakob J. Petuchowski and Michael Brocke.

# Veröffentlichungen
## der Stiftung Oratio Dominica

In der „Schriftenreihe zur großen Ökumene" sind bisher die Bände erschienen, die am Schluß des vorstehenden Arbeitsberichts aufgeführt sind.

Vorbemerkung: Die Bestellnummern sind jeweils in Klammern beigefügt. Soweit nicht andere Verlage genannt, sind diese Bücher im Verlag Herder erschienen oder durch seine Vertriebsabteilung erhältlich (soweit nicht vergriffen).

### Bücher der Grundlegung aus der ersten Zeit der Stiftung:

**Das Vaterunser** mit Worten von Reinhold Schneider o.J., 16 S. (vergriffen).

**So sollt ihr beten!** Vater unser ...! Wort des Herrn. Zur Einweihung der Vaterunser-Kapelle im Ibental 25. März 1968 Mariä Verkündigung. 96 S. (vergriffen).

**Ein Zeichen.** Die Vaterunser-Kapelle im Ibental. Illustriert. 2., erw. Aufl. 1976 (17325), 347 S. Als 1. Aufl. ist das Werk unter dem Titel „Die Vaterunser-Kapelle im Ibental" 1969 (281 S.) erschienen.

**Weinrich,** Franz Johannes: Der Psalter des Herrn. Psalmen zu Bildern aus der Vaterunser-Kapelle im Ibental. Illustriert, 1972 (16554), 284 S. (vergriffen).

**Adamas.** Der Mensch in der ewigen Landschaft.
1. Buch: Der erste Mensch – Am Schöpfungsmorgen. 140 Radierungen, davon 85 Farbdrucke, von Theodor Zeller. Text von Johannes Amadeus Lamberti. 1970 (16440), 322 S.
6. Buch: Am Weg des Menschen – Wir in Babel. (angekündigt als: Der Mächtige – In der Späte). Bilder von Agnes Auffinger. Text von Johannes Amadeus Lamberti.
Weitere Bände folgen.
Freiburg, Verlag der Mensch.

**Schallplatte.** Das Vaterunser in Liturgie und Meditation. Privatprägung. 1978.

### Religiöse Grunderfahrungen:

**Petuchowski,** Jakob J.: Melchisedech. Urgestalt der Ökumene. Festschrift für Theophil Herder-Dorneich. Mit einem Nachwort von Franz Mußner und Beiträgen von Walter Zimmerli, Edward Schillebeeckx, Raimondo Panikkar und Walter Strolz. 1979 (18394), 111 S.

**Schöpfung und Sprache.** Hrsg. Walter Strolz. Mit Beiträgen von Gerhart Baumann, Notker Füglister, Werner Kohlschmidt, Werner H. Schmidt, Walter Strolz. 1979 (18698), 159 S.

### Religionswissenschaft:

**Eliade,** Mircea: Geschichte der religiösen Ideen.
Bd. 1: Von der Steinzeit bis zu den Mysterien von Eleusis. Aus dem Französischen von Elisabeth Darlap. 3. Aufl. 1980 (18215), 433 S.
Bd. 2: Von Gautama Buddha bis zu den Anfängen des Christentums. Aus dem Französischen von Adelheid Müller-Lissner und Werner Müller. 1979 (18216), 464 S.
Abschließender Band: Quellentexte. Übersetzt und herausgegeben von Günter Lanczkowski. 1981 (18963), 456 S.

### Religionsphilosophie:

**Kattackal,** Jacob: Religion and ethics in advaita. 1980 (3-451-27 922-3), 260 S. Editiones Herder Freiburg · London · Montreal· · Roma.

### Fundamentaltheologische Fragen:

**Anthropologie des Kults.** Die Bedeutung des Kults für das Überleben des Menschen. Beiträge von Alois Hahn, Peter Hünermann, Heribert Mühlen, Richard Schaeffler, Hubertus Tellenbach. Vorwort von Walter Strolz. 1977 (17909), 157 S.

### Beiträge zur Glaubenspraxis:

**Denn dein ist das Reich.** Gebete aus dem Islam. Ausgewählt und übersetzt von Annemarie Schimmel. Mit einem Vorwort von Sergio Kardinal Pignedoli. 1978 (18081), 125 S.

**Du, unser Vater.** Jüdische Gebete für Christen. Ausgewählt und übersetzt von Pnina Navè. Mit einem Vorwort des Bischofs von Straßburg Léon Arthur Elchinger. 3. Aufl. 1978 (17313), 114 S.
Von diesem Buch erschien 1977 in holländischer Sprache eine Ausgabe unter dem Titel: Gij, Onze Vader. Joodse gebeden voor christenen. Gemeinschaftsverlag Uitgeverij Emmaus, Brugge und Katholieke Bijbelstichting, Boxel. (90-6173 219-0), 124 S.

**Kobbe,** Ursula: Sie brauchen Liebe. Religiöse Erfahrungen mit geistig behinderten Kindern im Licht des Vaterunsers. 1977 (17639), 189 S.

**Lotz,** Johannes B.: Wenn ihr heute Vaterunser betet. Meditationen. 1978 (18163), 125 S.

239

**Sequeira,** A. Ronald: Spielende Liturgie. Bewegung neben Wort und Ton im Gottesdienst am Beispiel des Vaterunsers. 1977 (17759), 223 S.

Als Veröffentlichungen der *Stiftung Oratio Dominica* sind außerdem erschienen:

**Maximos von Sardes,** Metropolit: Das ökumenische Patriarchat in der orthodoxen Kirche. Auftrag zur Einigung. Übertragung aus dem Französischen und Griechischen von Josef Strauss und Friedrich von Halem. Geleitwort zur deutschen Ausgabe von Wilhelm de Vries SJ, Professor am Päpstlichen Orientalischen Institut in Rom. 1980 (17549), 456 S.

**Pesch,** Rudolf: Das Evangelium der Urgemeinde. Wiederhergestellt und erläutert. Erschienen als Band 748 in der Herderbücherei. 1979 (07748), 222 S.

**Zu den Intentionen** der *Stiftung Oratio Dominica* gehören auch die nachstehenden Werke:

**Aus den Psalmen leben.** Das gemeinsame Gebet von Kirche und Synagoge neu erschlossen. Schriftleitung Walter Strolz. Mit Beiträgen von Markus Barth, Edna Brocke, Albert H. Friedlander, Notker Füglister, Roland Gradwohl, Simon Lauer, N. Peter Levinson, Christian Link, Jonathan Magonet, Leo Prijs, Rudolf Schmid, Fridolin Stier, Walter Strolz, Jakob Teichmann, Dieter Zeller, Erich Zenger. 1979 (18219), 223 S.

**Mystische Erfahrung.** Die Grenze menschlichen Erlebens. Mit Beiträgen von Alfons Rosenberg, Alois Haas, Pnina Navè, Richard Gramlich, Alexander Gosztonyi, Franz Hesse, Walter Strolz, einem Vorwort des Verlags und einem Nachwort von Walter Strolz. 1976 (17588), 165 S.

**Sequeira,** A. Ronald: Klassische indische Tanzkunst und christliche Verkündigung. Eine vergleichende religionsgeschichtlich-religionsphilosophische Studie. Erschienen als 109. Band der Freiburger theologischen Studien, mit Illustrationen. 1978 (17948), 328 S.